SHONEN JUMP ADVANCED Manga Edition

クレイモア
Claymore

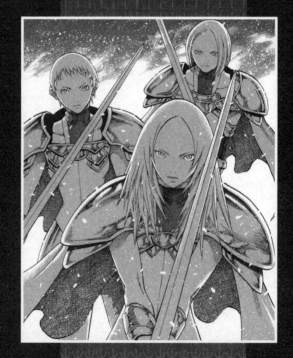

Vol. 11
Kindred of Paradise

Story and Art by Norihiro Yagi

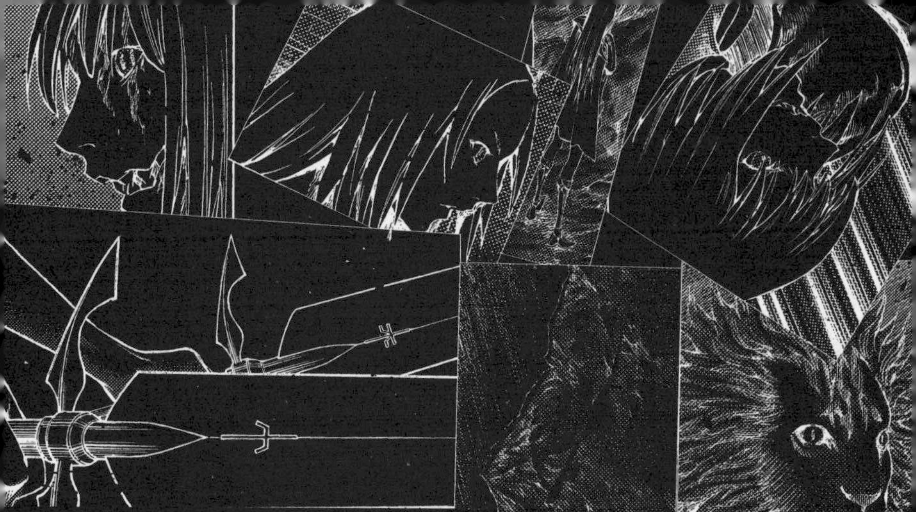

immense broadswords that they carried.

As the battle in Pieta rages on, Clare and the other Claymores prepare to make their final stand. Meanwhile, Isley begins his assault on the forces of the South, and the shadowy Organization decides to deploy its ultimate weapons.

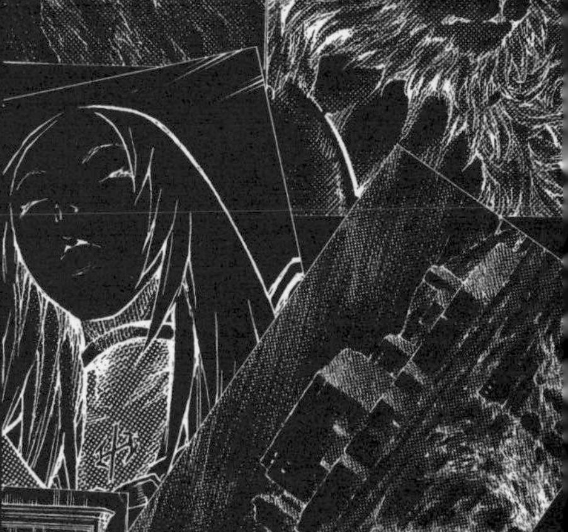

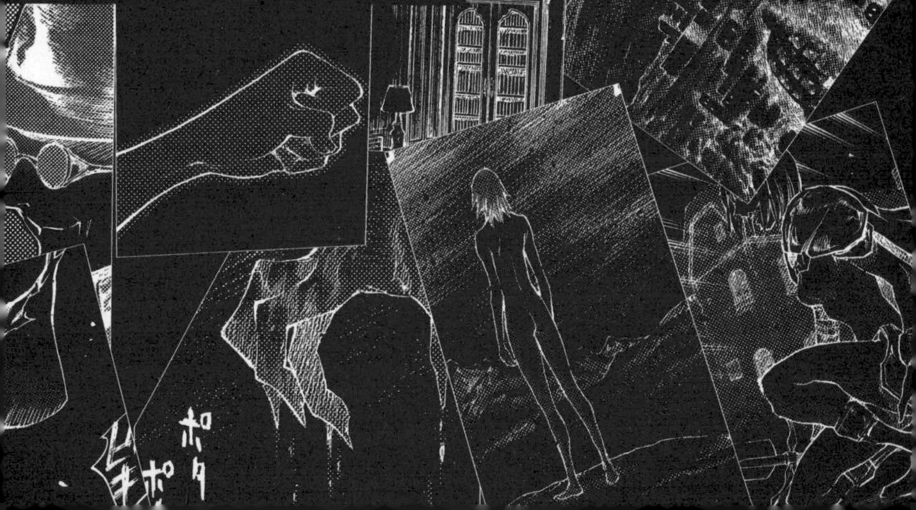
ポタ

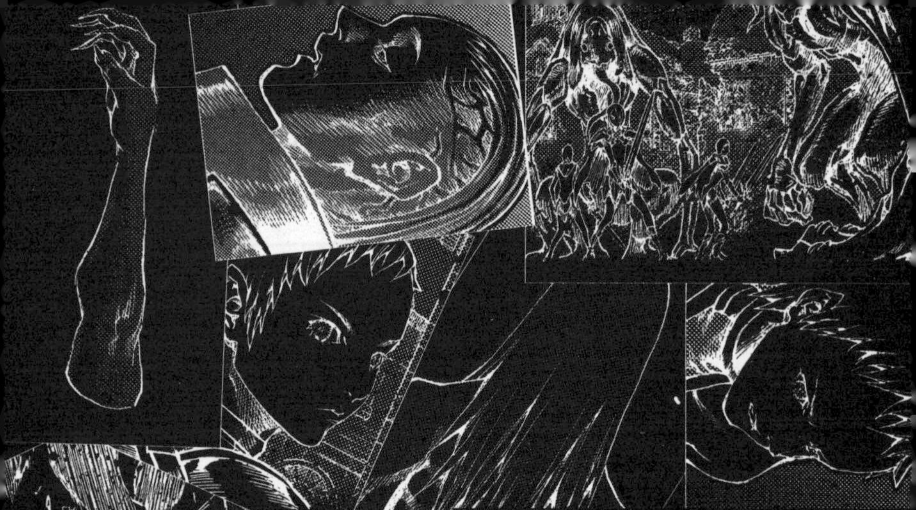

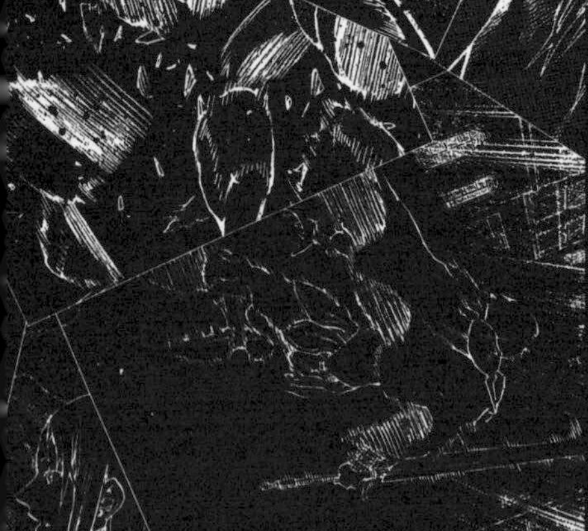

The Story Thus Far

Creatures known as Yoma have long preyed on humans, who were once powerless against their predators. But now mankind has developed female warriors who are half human and half monster, with silver eyes that can see the monsters' true form. These warriors came to be called Claymores after the

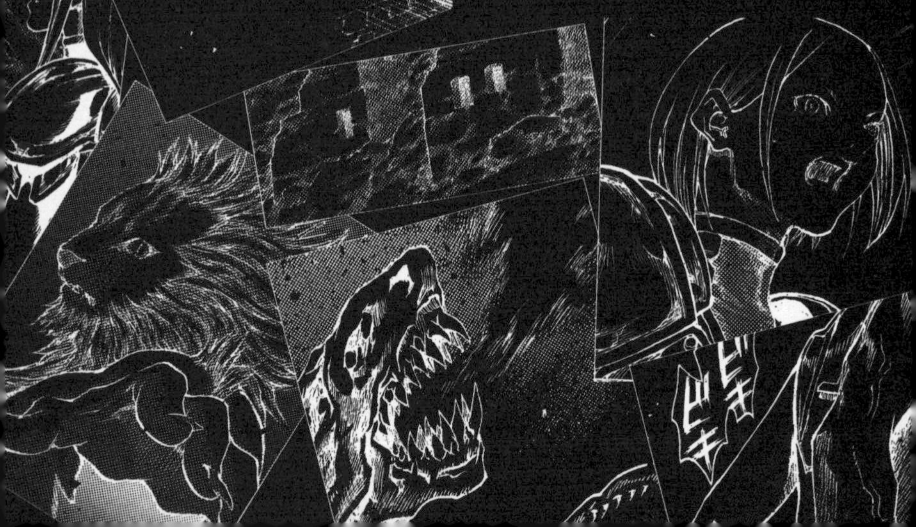
ビキ
ビキ

Claymore

クレイモア

Vol. 11

CONTENTS

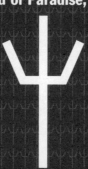

Scene 58: The Assault on Pieta, Part 2

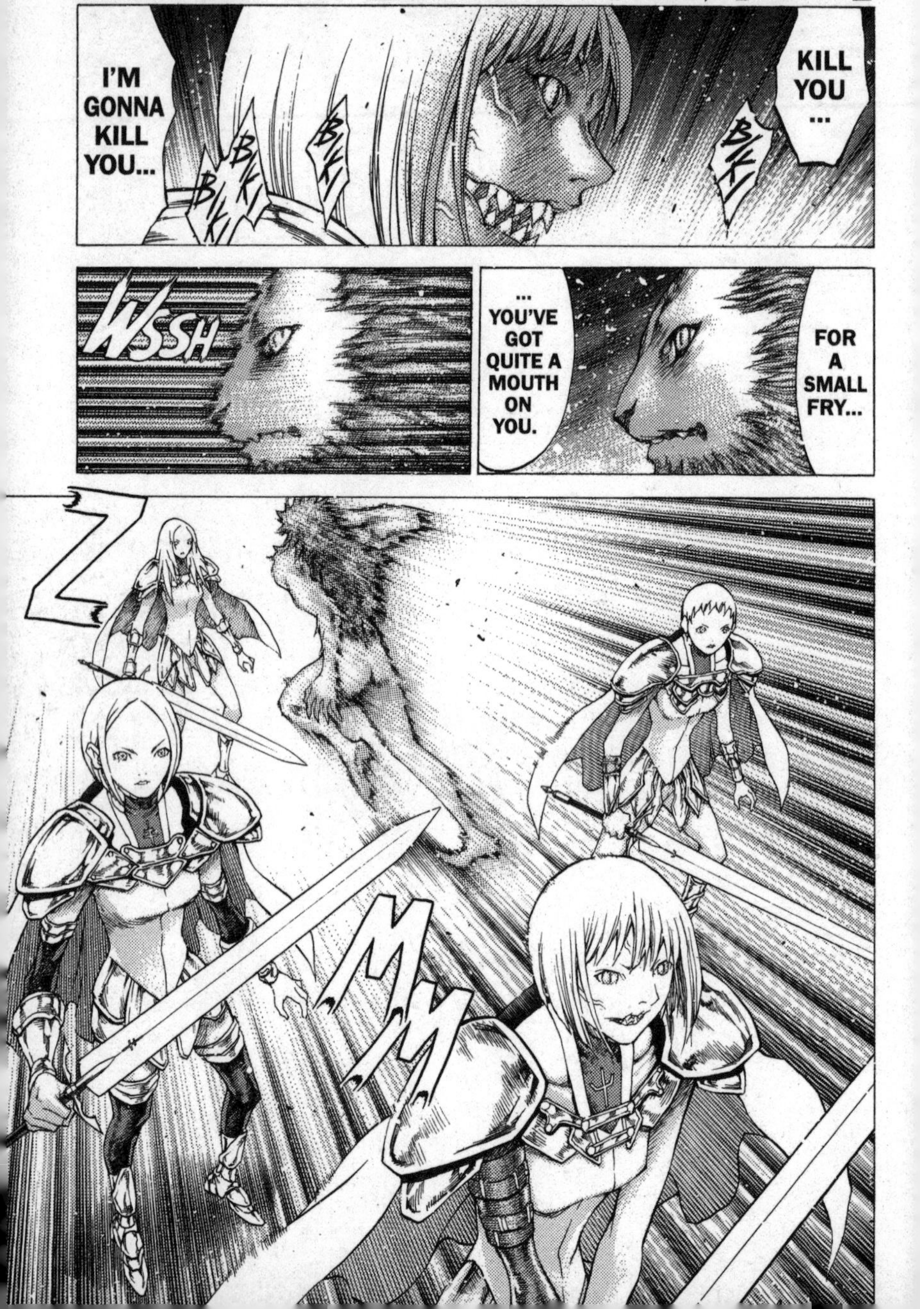
KILL YOU ...
BIKI
BIKI
BIKI
I'M GONNA KILL YOU...
FOR A SMALL FRY...
... YOU'VE GOT QUITE A MOUTH ON YOU.
WSSH
Z
MM

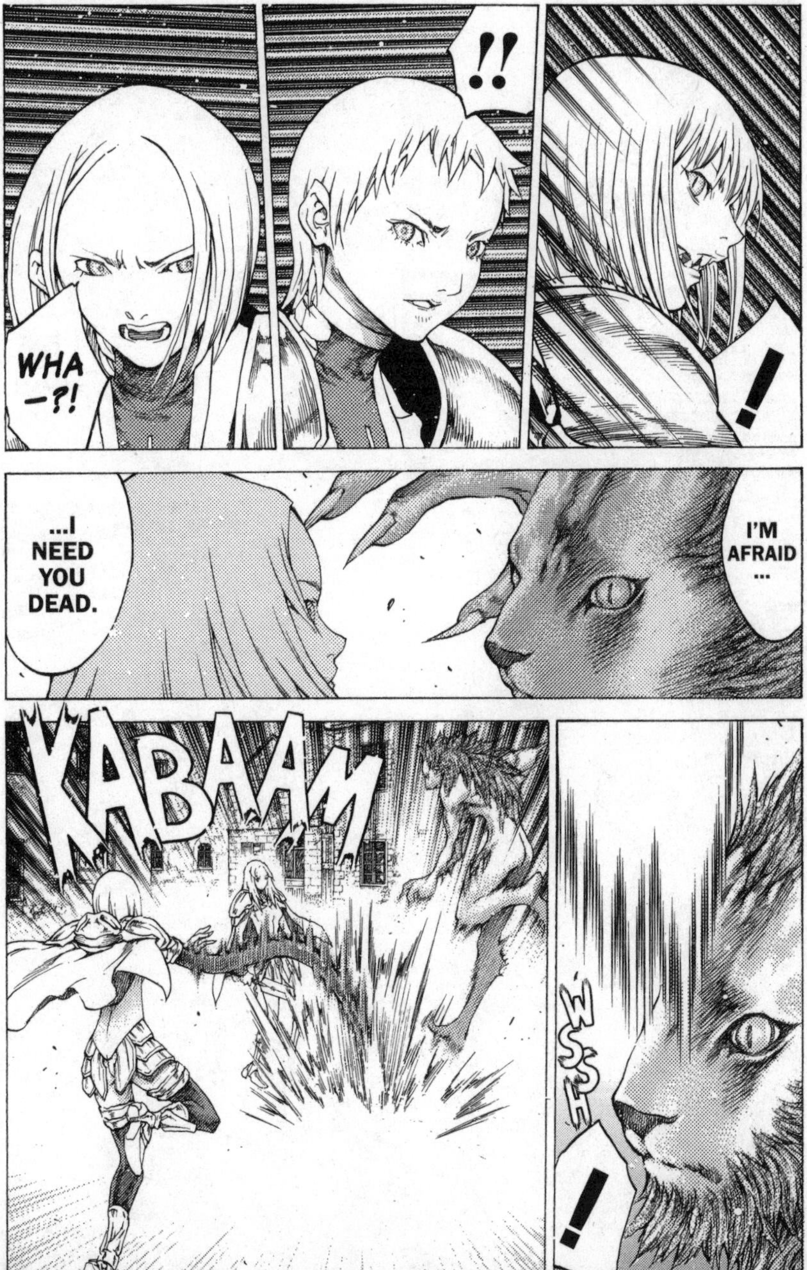
!
!!
WHA—?!
I'M AFRAID...
...I NEED YOU DEAD.
WSSH
!
KABAAM

READ THIS WAY

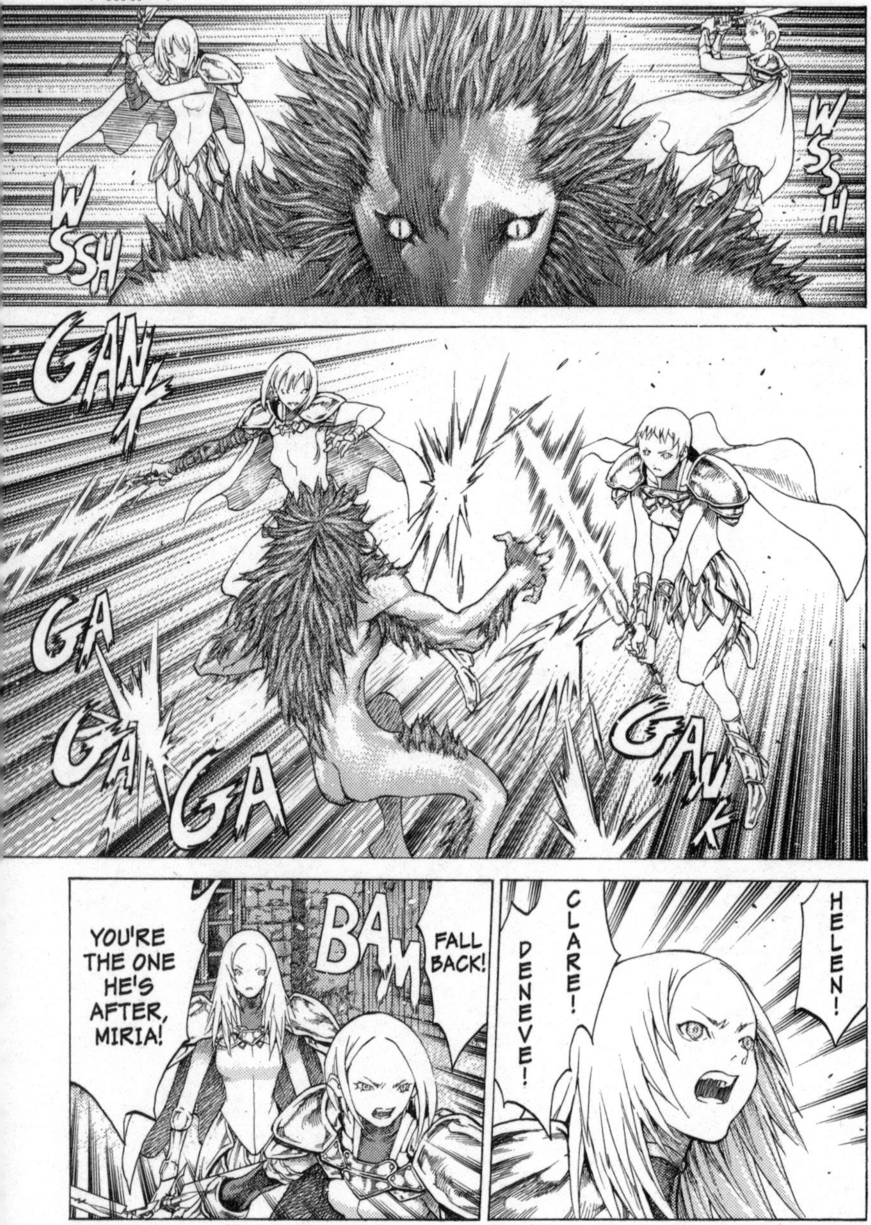
WSSH
WSSH
GANK
GA GA GA
GANK
HELEN!
CLARE!
DENEVE!
FALL BACK!
BAM
YOU'RE THE ONE HE'S AFTER, MIRIA!

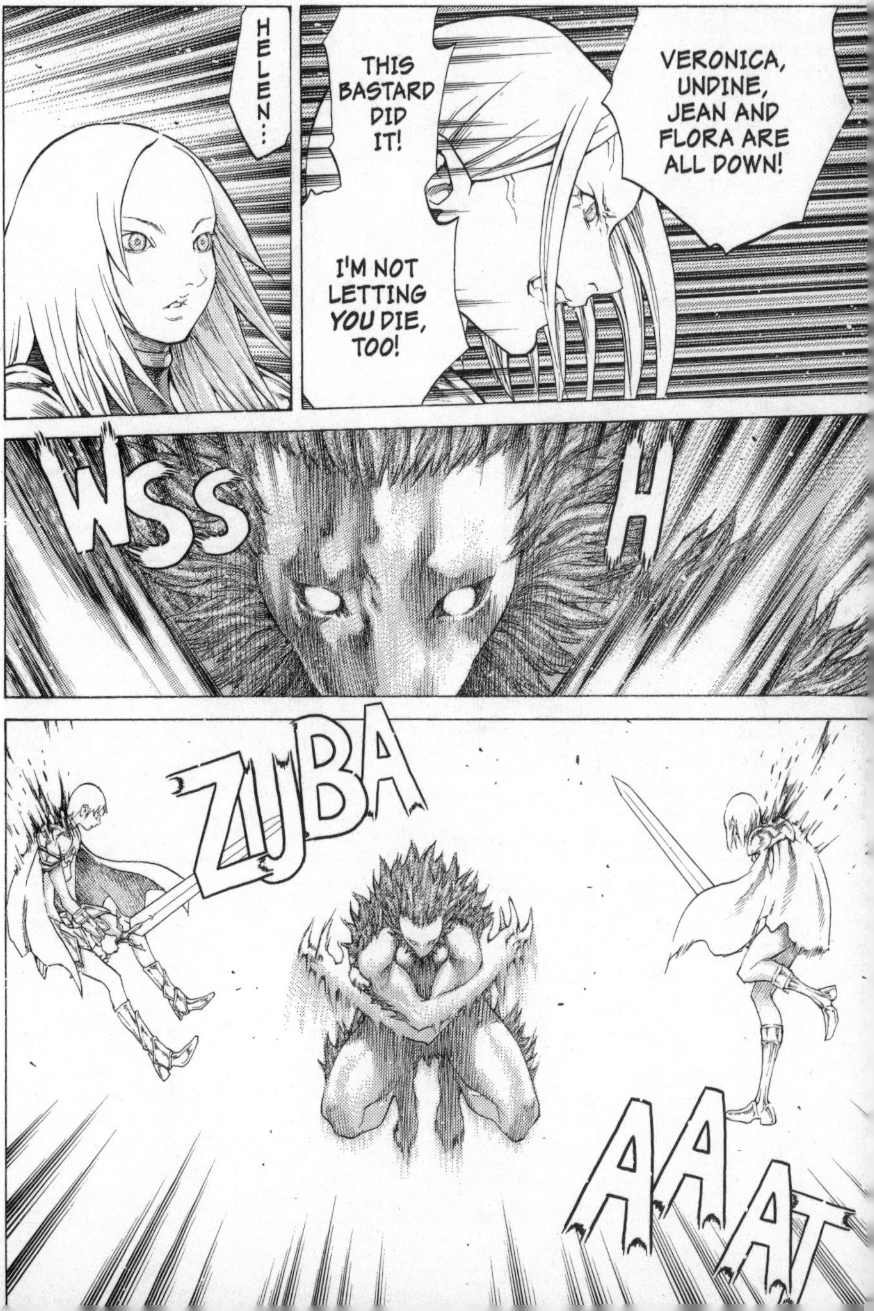
VERONICA, UNDINE, JEAN AND FLORA ARE ALL DOWN!
THIS BASTARD DID IT!
I'M NOT LETTING *YOU* DIE, TOO!
HELEN...
WSSH
ZUBA
AAAT

READ THIS WAY

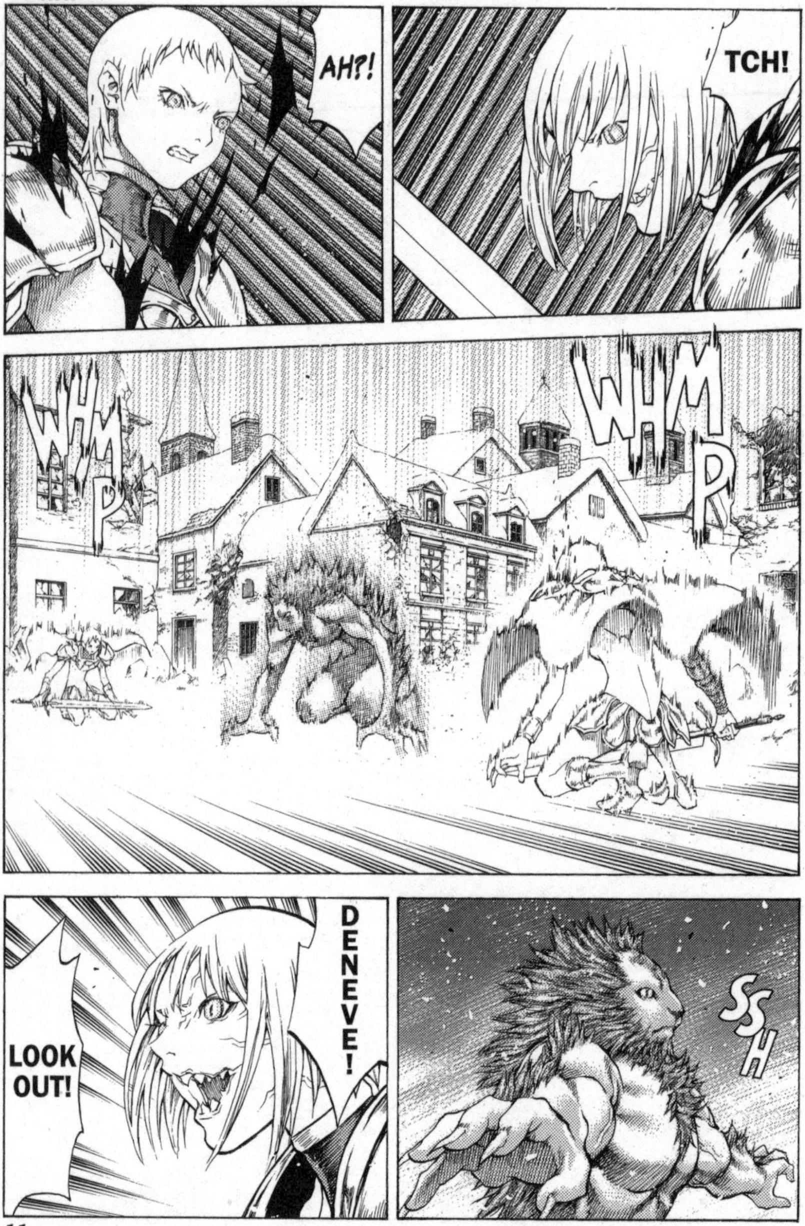
TCH!
AH?!
WHMP
WHMP
SSH
DENEVE!
LOOK OUT!

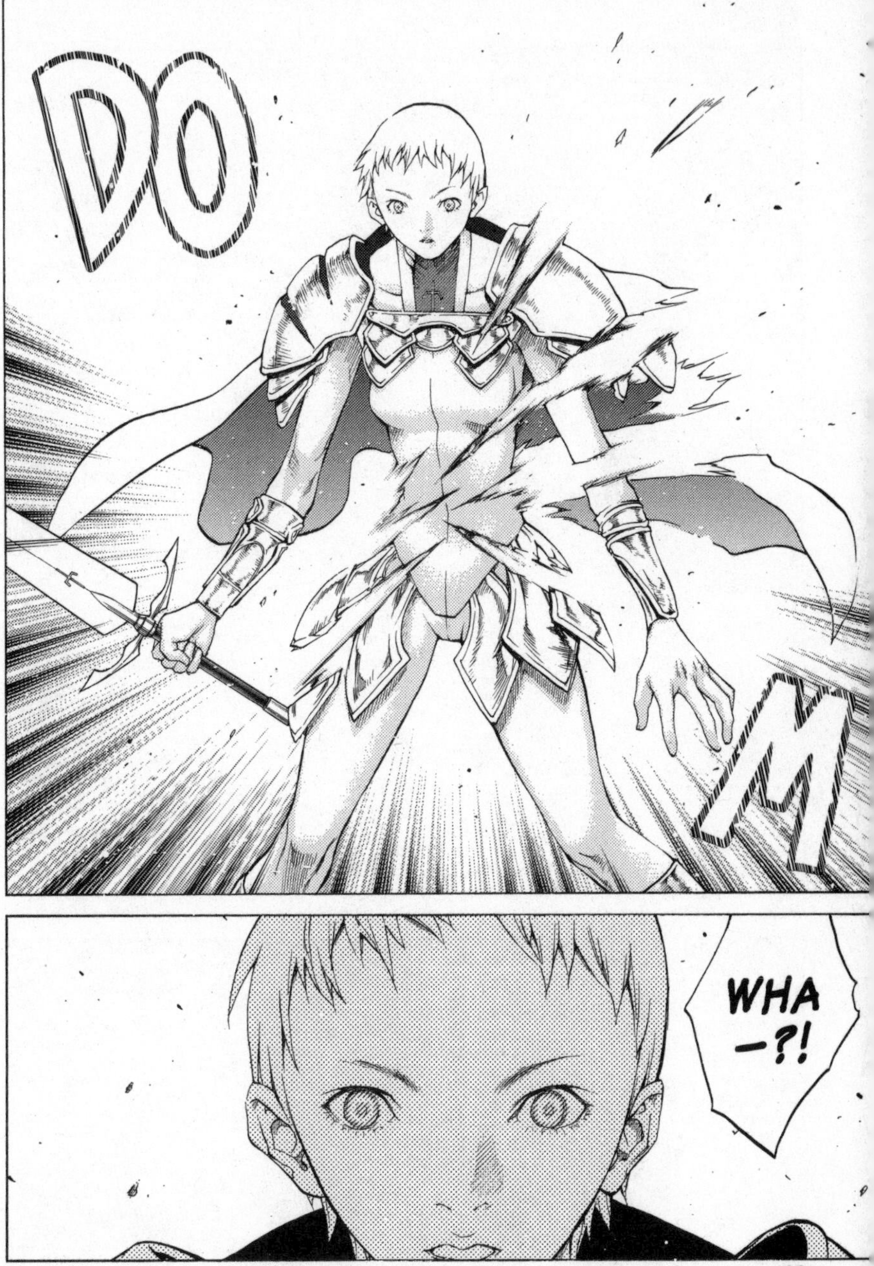
DOM
WHA
-?!

READ THIS WAY

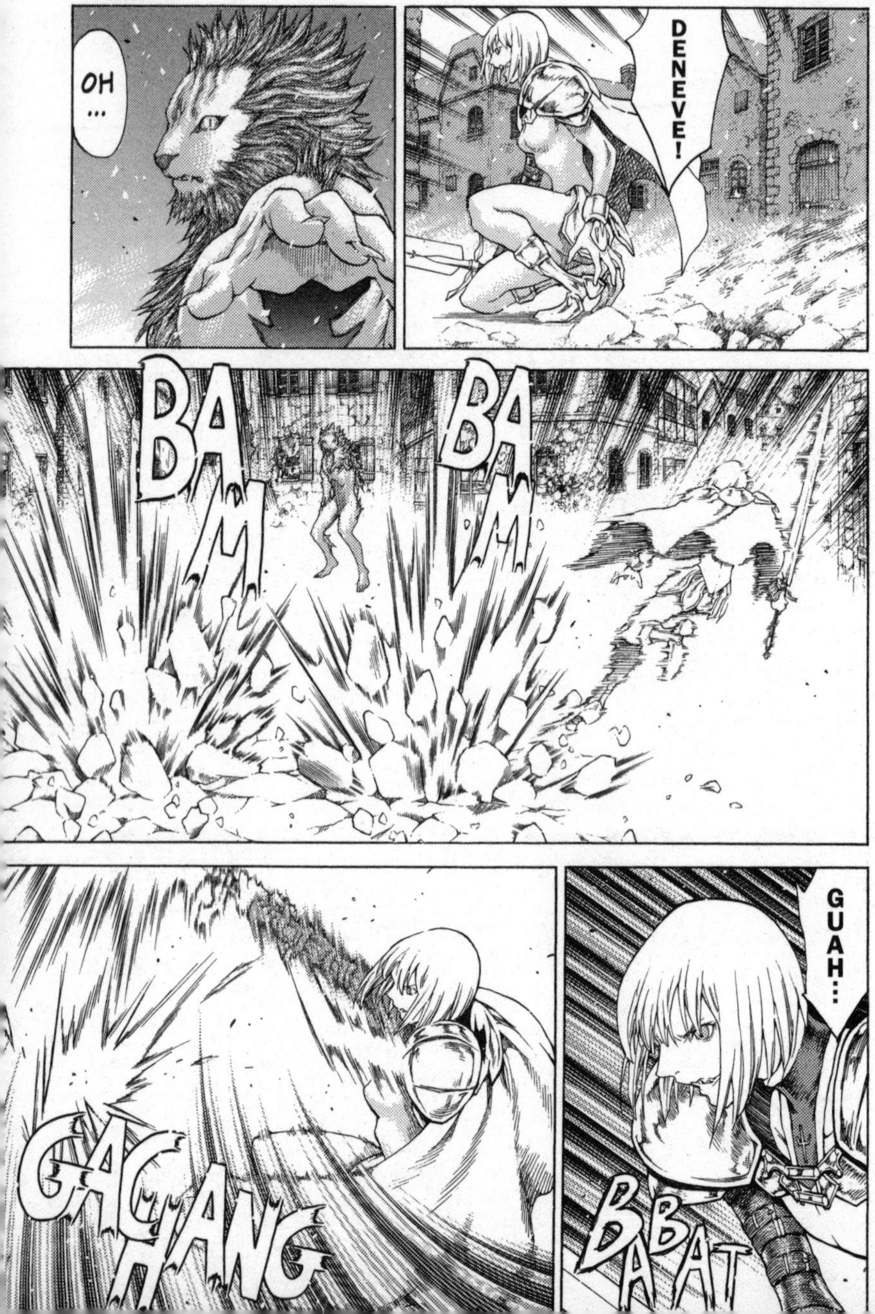
DENEVE!
OH ...
BAM
BAM
GUAH...
BABAT
GACHANG

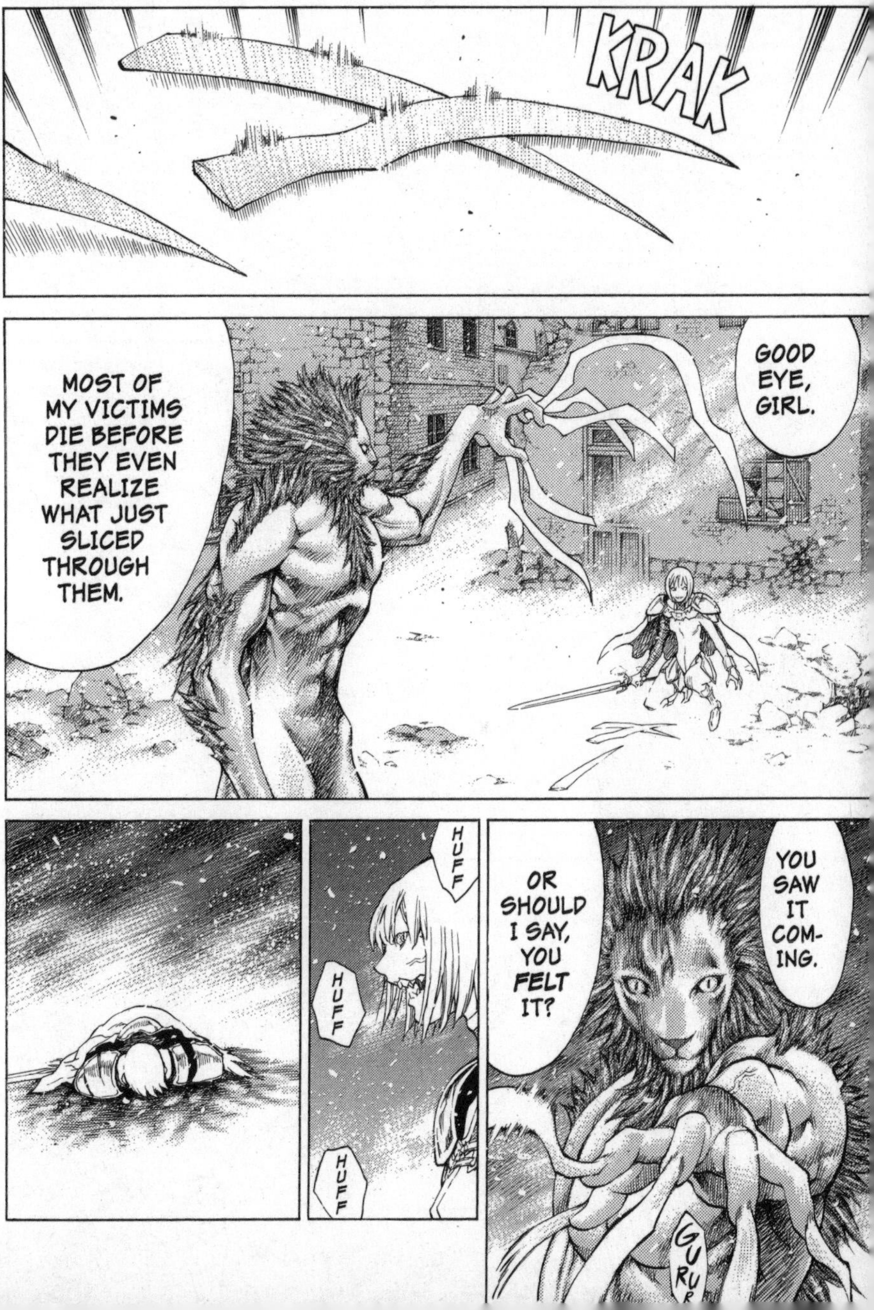
KRAK
GOOD EYE, GIRL.
MOST OF MY VICTIMS DIE BEFORE THEY EVEN REALIZE WHAT JUST SLICED THROUGH THEM.
YOU SAW IT COMING.
OR SHOULD I SAY, YOU FELT IT?
GURU
HUFF
HUFF
HUFF

READ THIS WAY

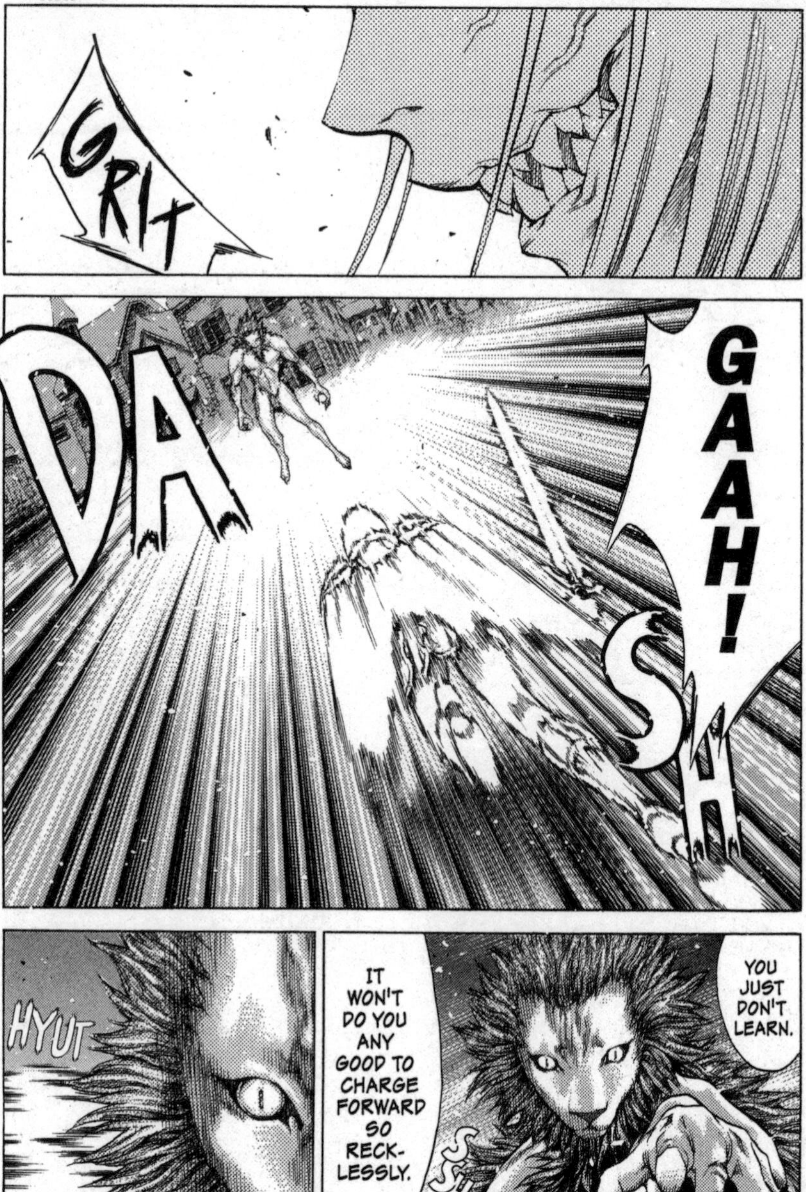
GRIT
GAAH!
DASH
YOU JUST DON'T LEARN.
IT WON'T DO YOU ANY GOOD TO CHARGE FORWARD SO RECKLESSLY.
SSH
HYUT

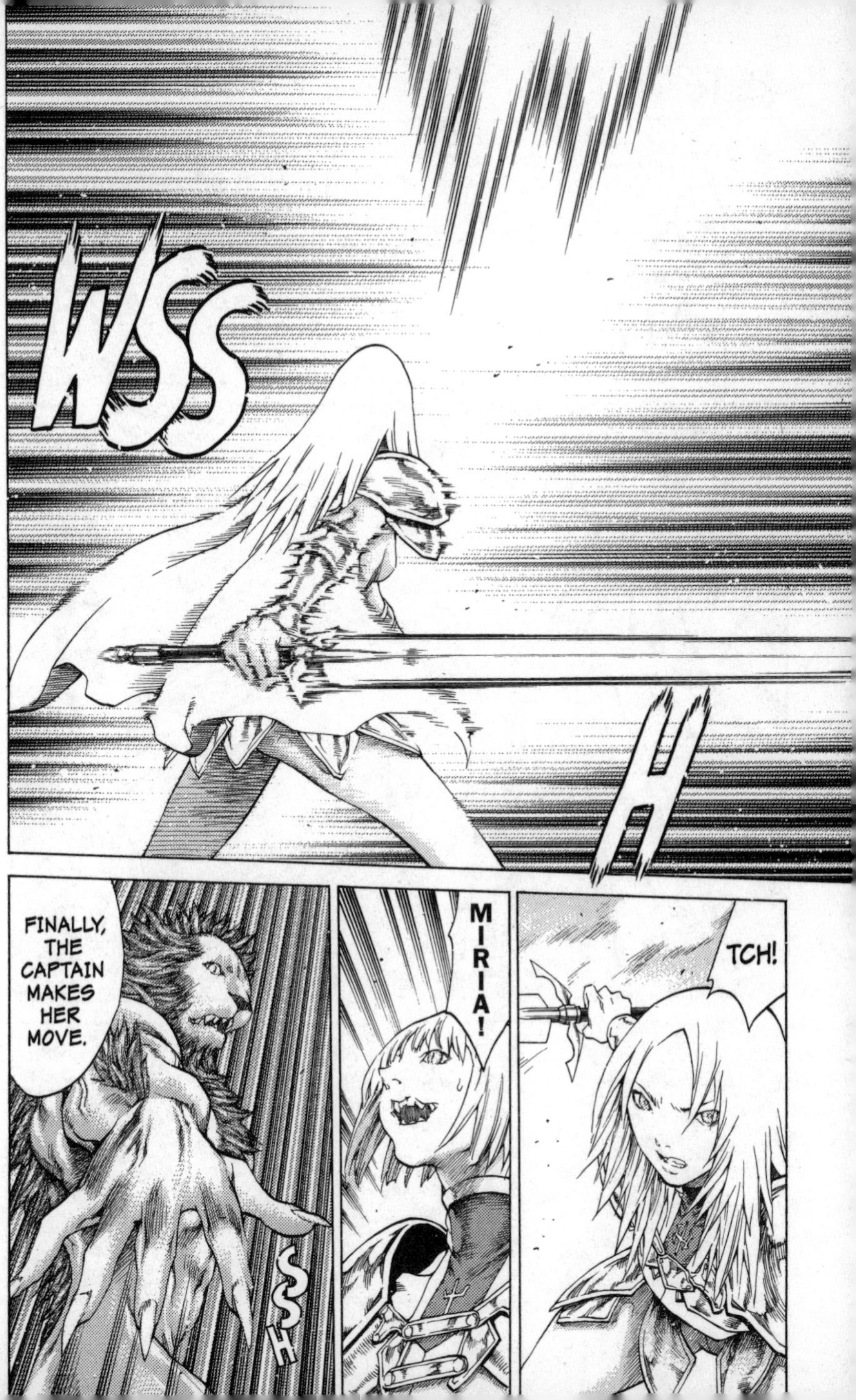
WSS
H
TCH!
MIRIA!
FINALLY, THE CAPTAIN MAKES HER MOVE.
SSH

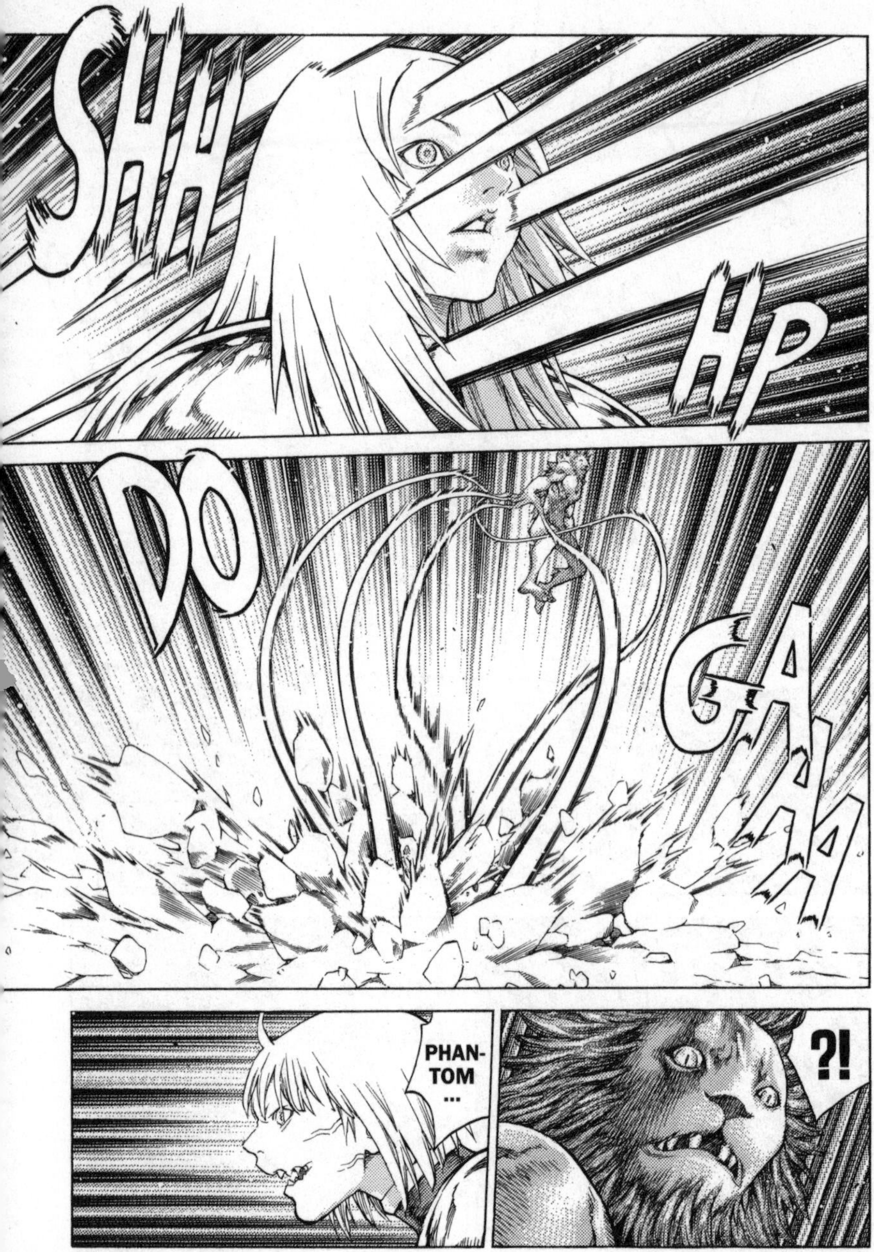
SHH
HP
DO
GAAA
?!
PHAN-
TOM
...

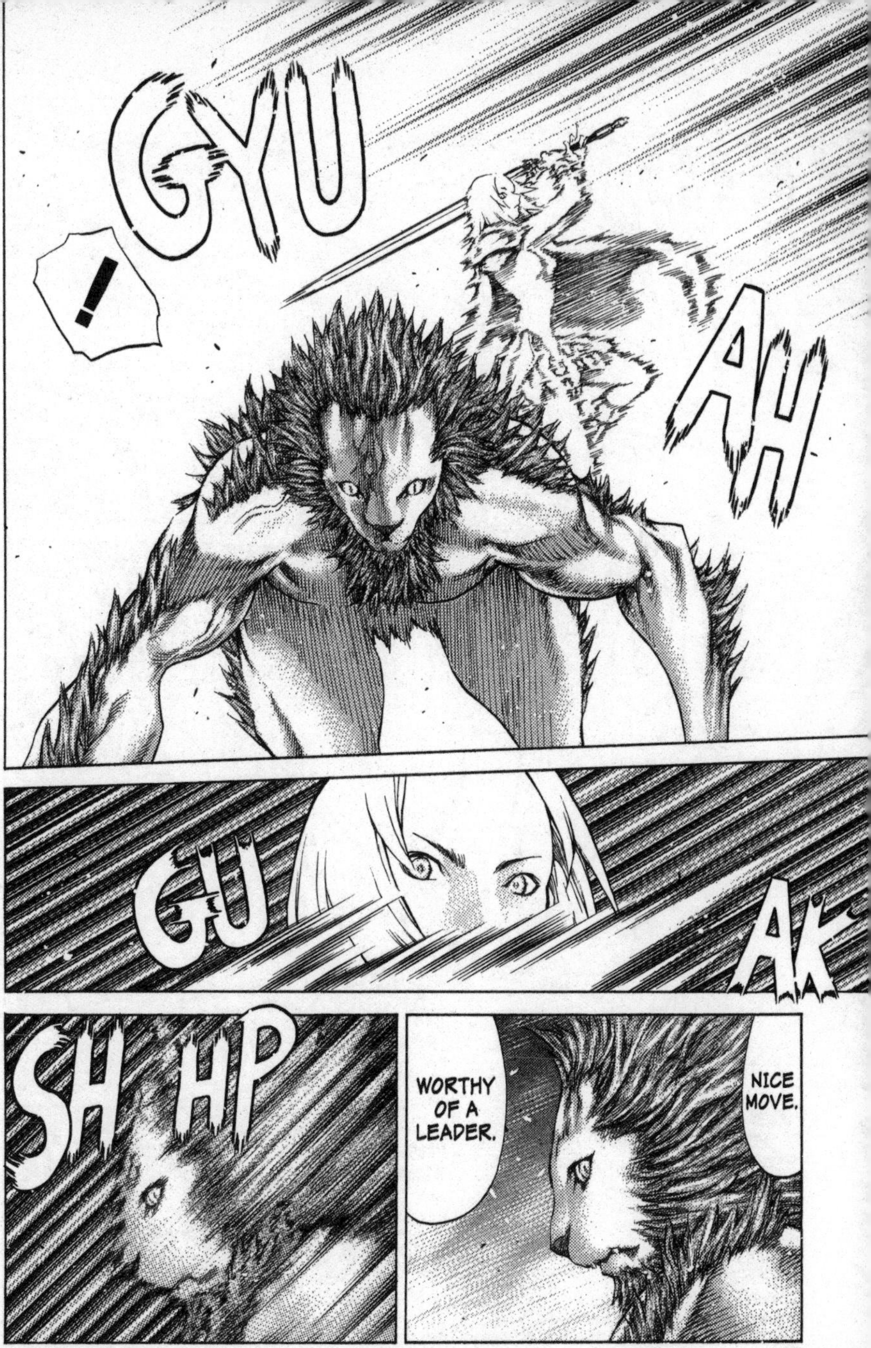

GYU
AH
!
GU
AK
NICE MOVE.
WORTHY OF A LEADER.
SH HP

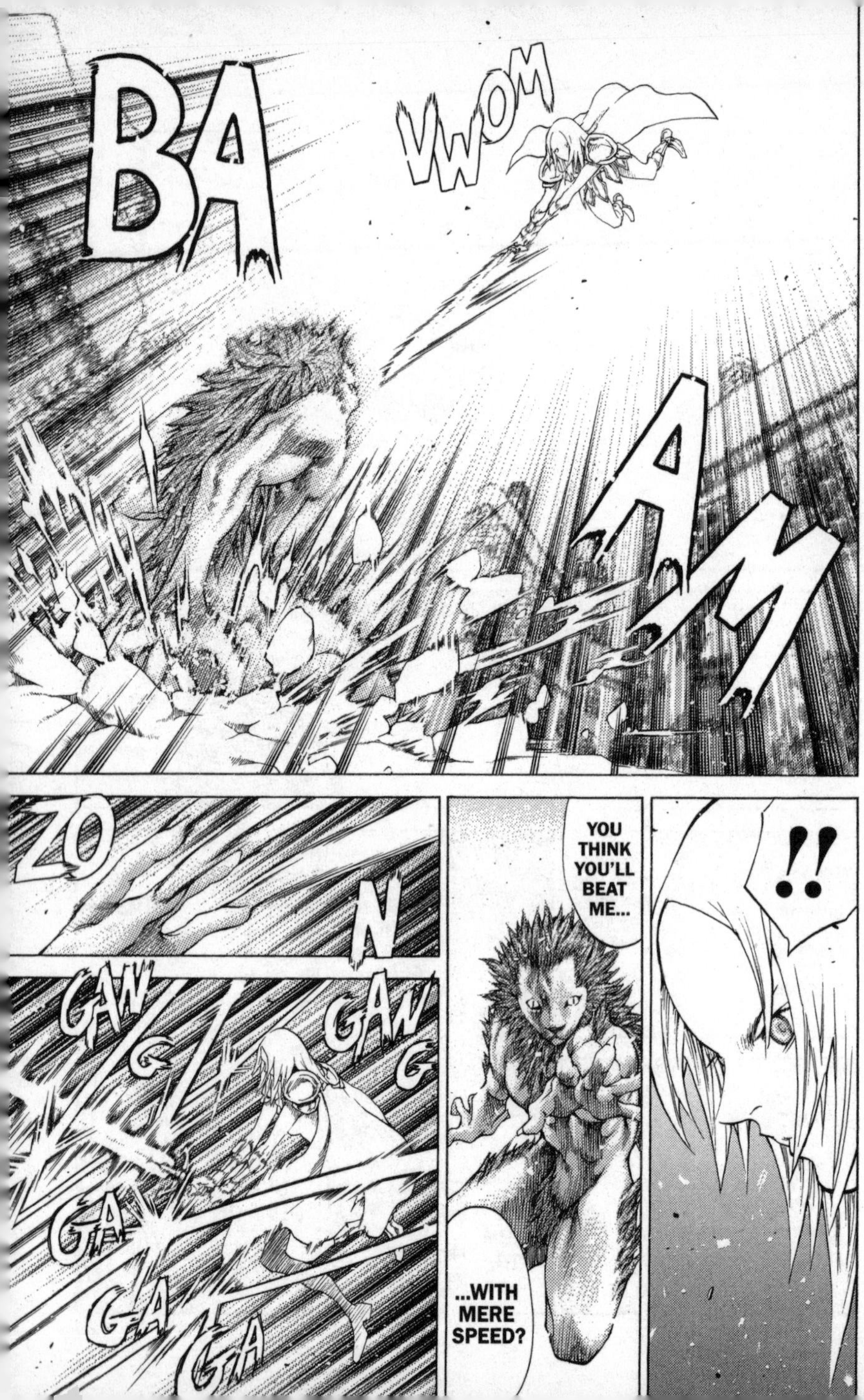
VWOM
BA
AM
!!
YOU THINK YOU'LL BEAT ME...
...WITH MERE SPEED?
ZO
N
GAN
G
GAN
G
GA
GA
GA
GA

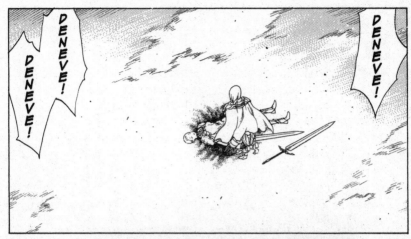

DENEVE!
DENEVE!
DENEVE!
DAMN... HOW PA-THETIC.
IN THE END... I DIDN'T EVEN LAND ONE STRIKE ON HIM.
BE STRONG!
HOLD ON!
YOU CAN'T JUST GIVE UP LIKE THIS!
FORGET ABOUT ME. GO HELP MIRIA AND CLARE.
DON'T LET THEM DIE.
THOSE TWO ARE THE PIVOT OF THIS BATTLE.
WHETHER THEY LIVE OR DIE WILL CONTROL ITS OUTCOME...
RIGHT!
YOU JUST STAY HERE AND HEAL YOUR WOUNDS!
GOT IT?!

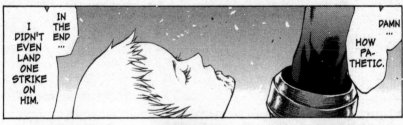

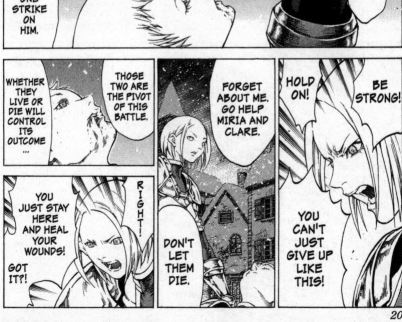

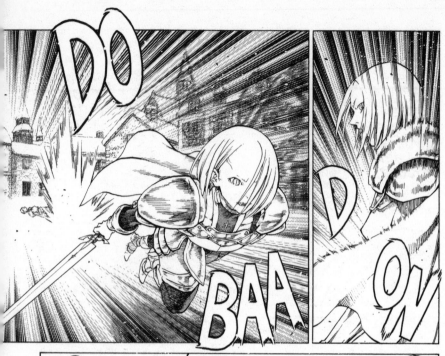

DO

BAA

D ON

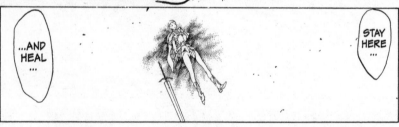

...AND HEAL...

STAY HERE...

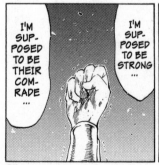

I'M SUP-POSED TO BE THEIR COM-RADE...

I'M SUP-POSED TO BE STRONG...

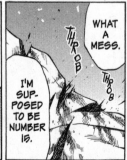

THROB

THROB

WHAT A MESS.

I'M SUP-POSED TO BE NUMBER 15.

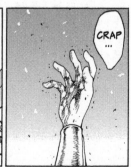

CRAP...

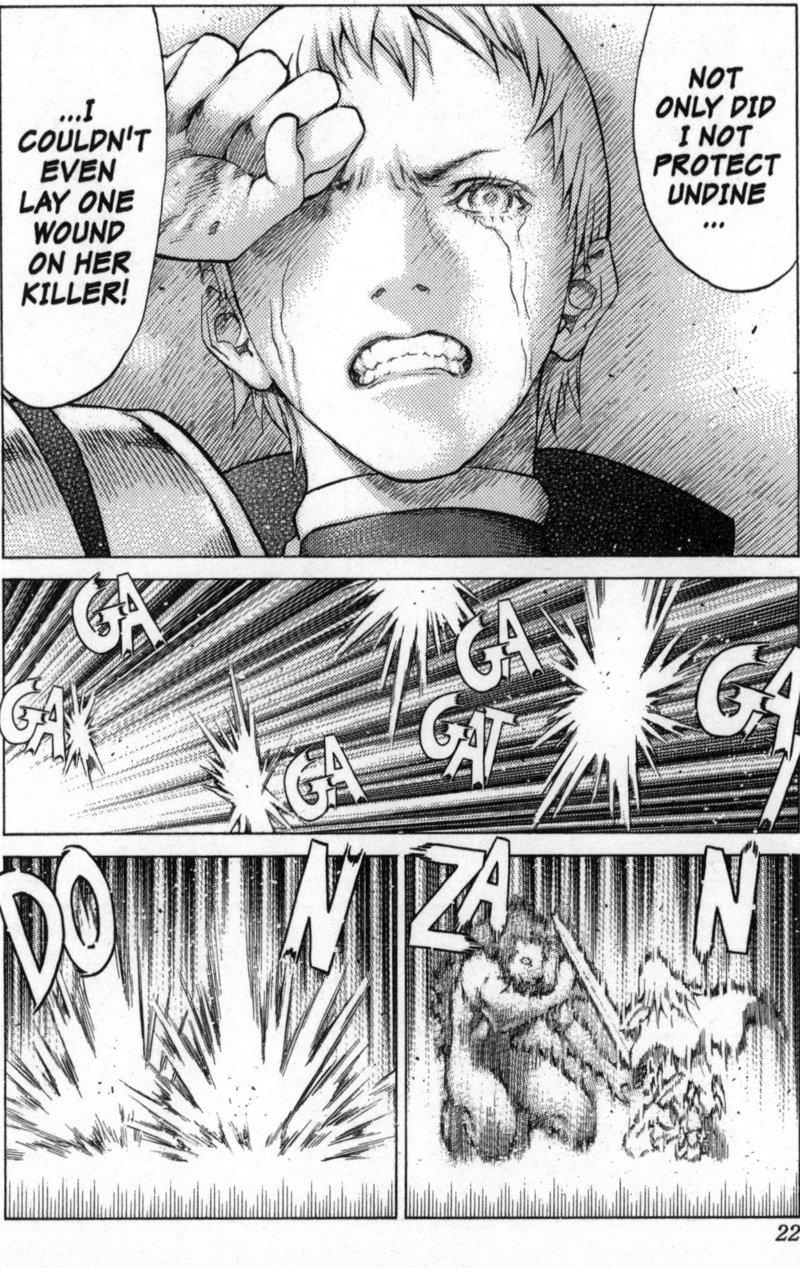
NOT ONLY DID I NOT PROTECT UNDINE ...
...I COULDN'T EVEN LAY ONE WOUND ON HER KILLER!
GAT
GA GAT
GA
GA
GA
ZAN
DON

READ THIS WAY

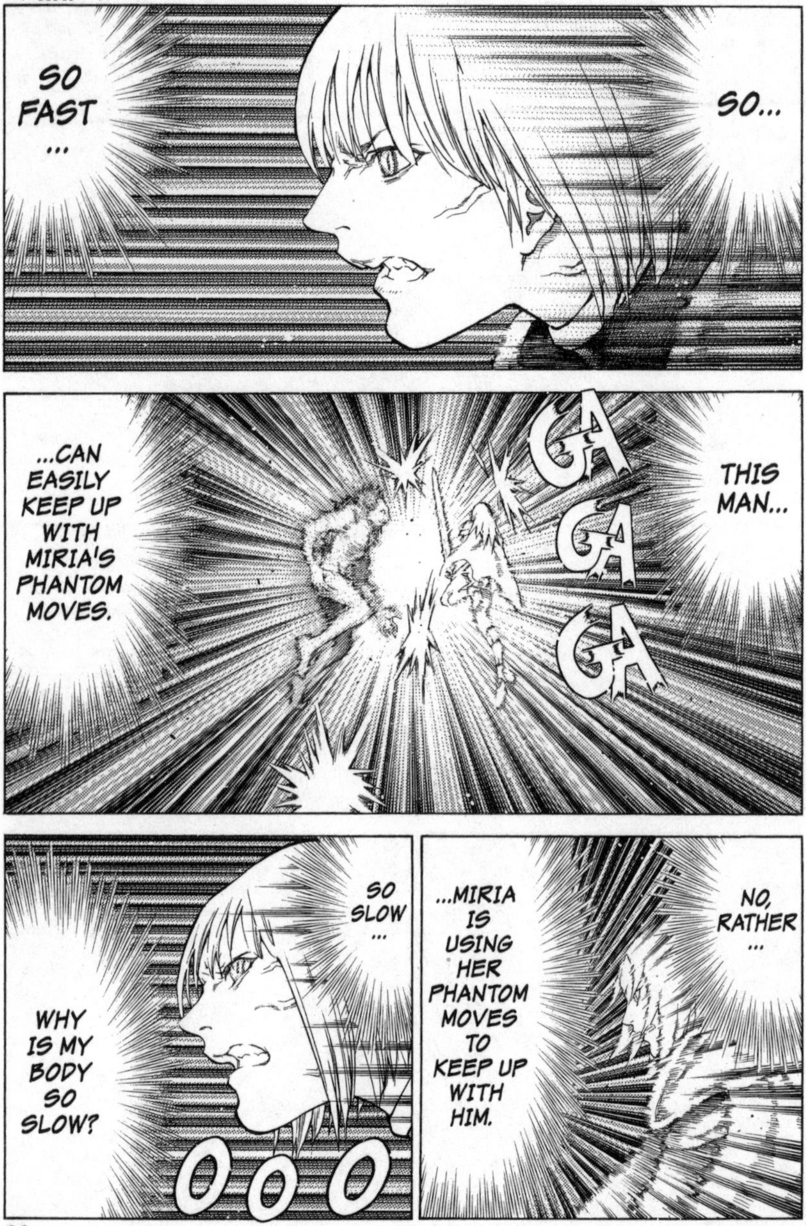
SO...
SO FAST ...
THIS MAN...
GA GA GA
...CAN EASILY KEEP UP WITH MIRIA'S PHANTOM MOVES.
NO, RATHER ...
...MIRIA IS USING HER PHANTOM MOVES TO KEEP UP WITH HIM.
SO SLOW ...
WHY IS MY BODY SO SLOW?
OOO

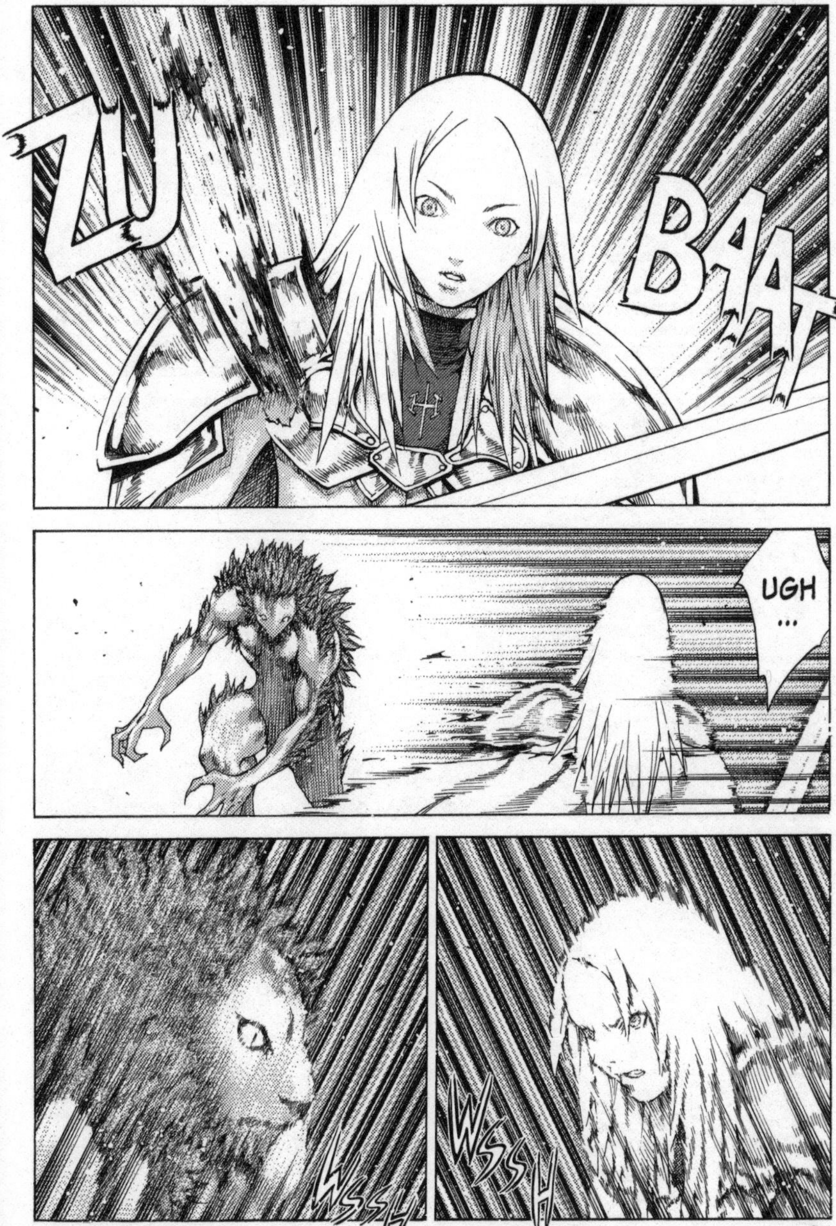
BAAT
ZU
UGH ...
WSSH
WSSH

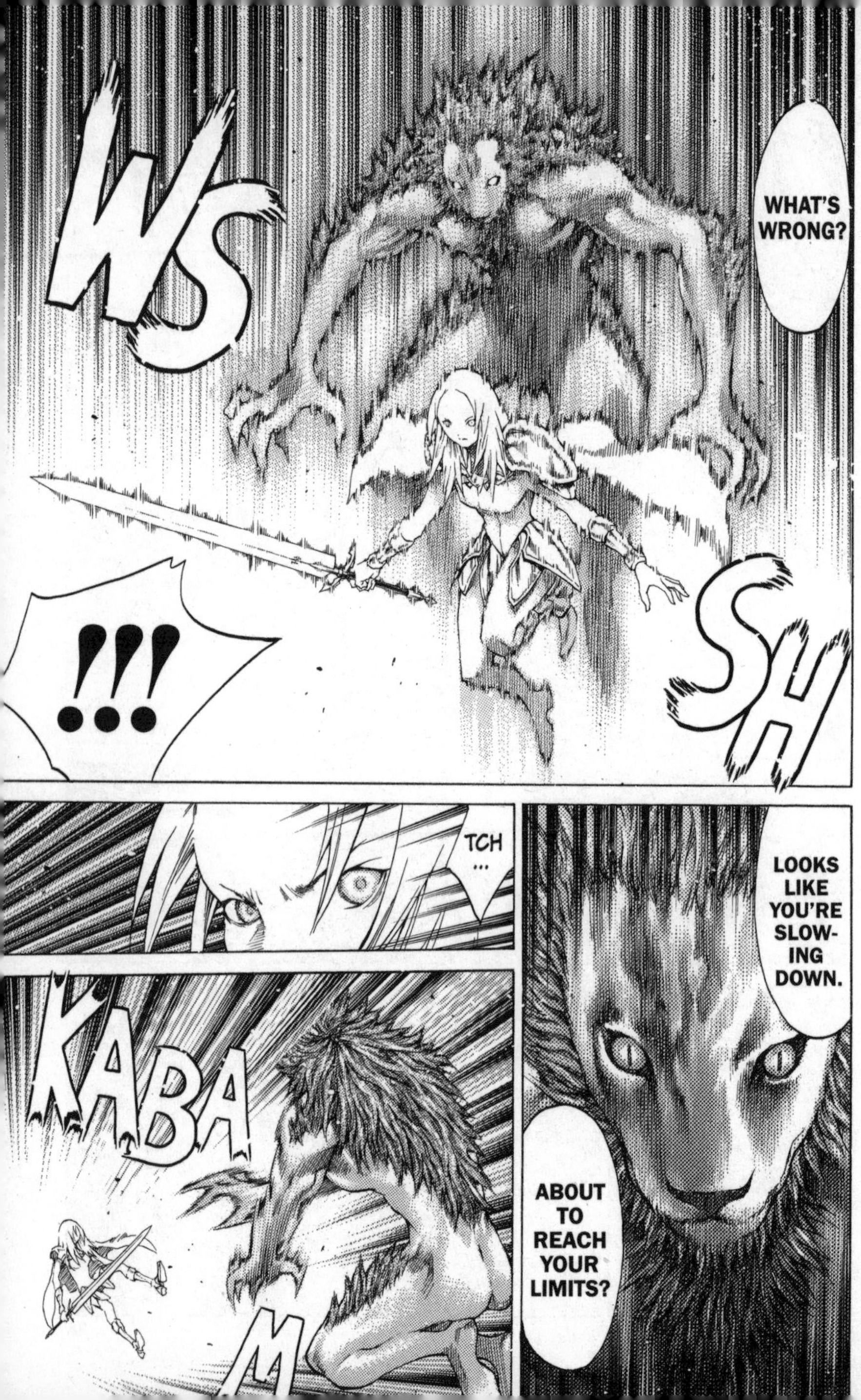
WHAT'S WRONG?
WS
SH
!!!
LOOKS LIKE YOU'RE SLOW-ING DOWN.
ABOUT TO REACH YOUR LIMITS?
TCH ...
KABAM

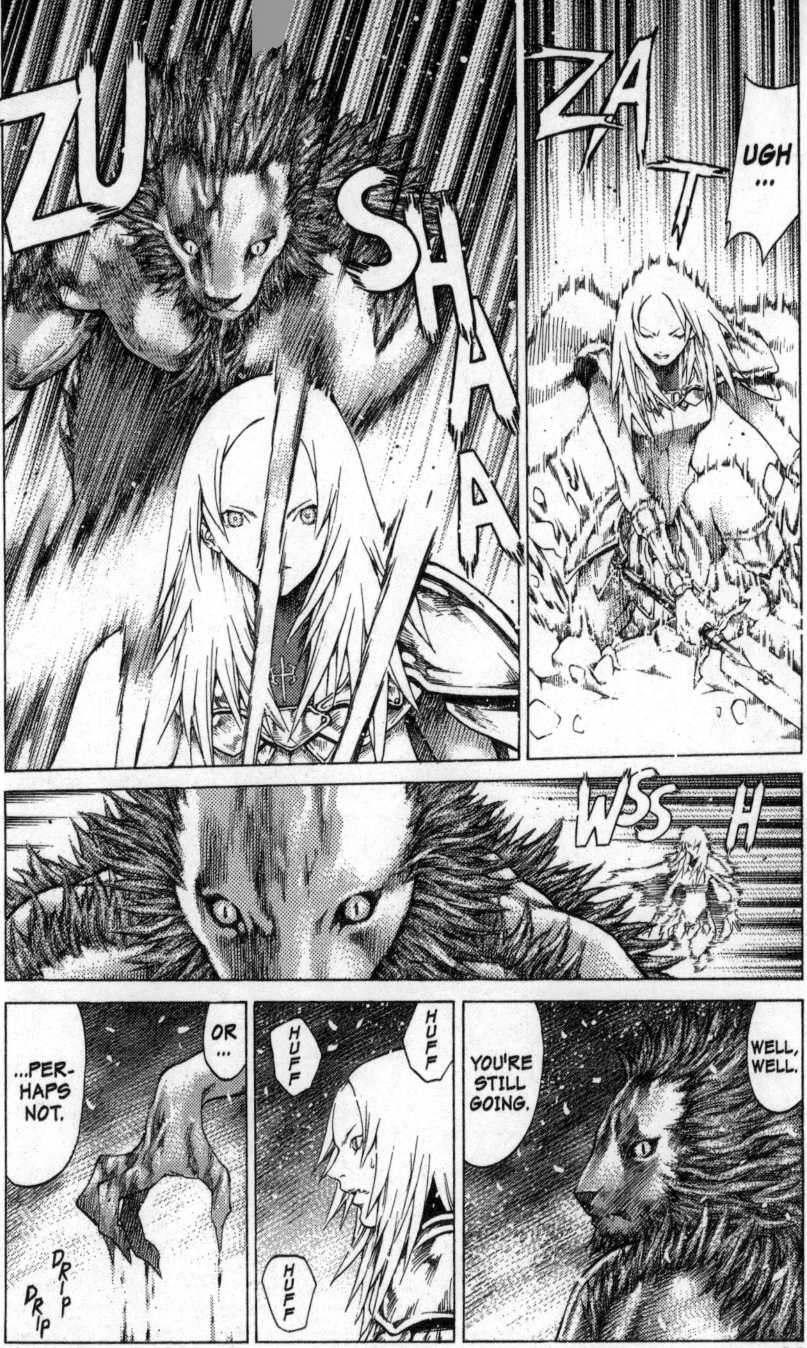
ZAT
UGH ...
ZUSHAAA
WSSH
WELL, WELL.
YOU'RE STILL GOING.
HUFF
HUFF
HUFF
OR ...
...PER-HAPS NOT.
DRIP
DRIP

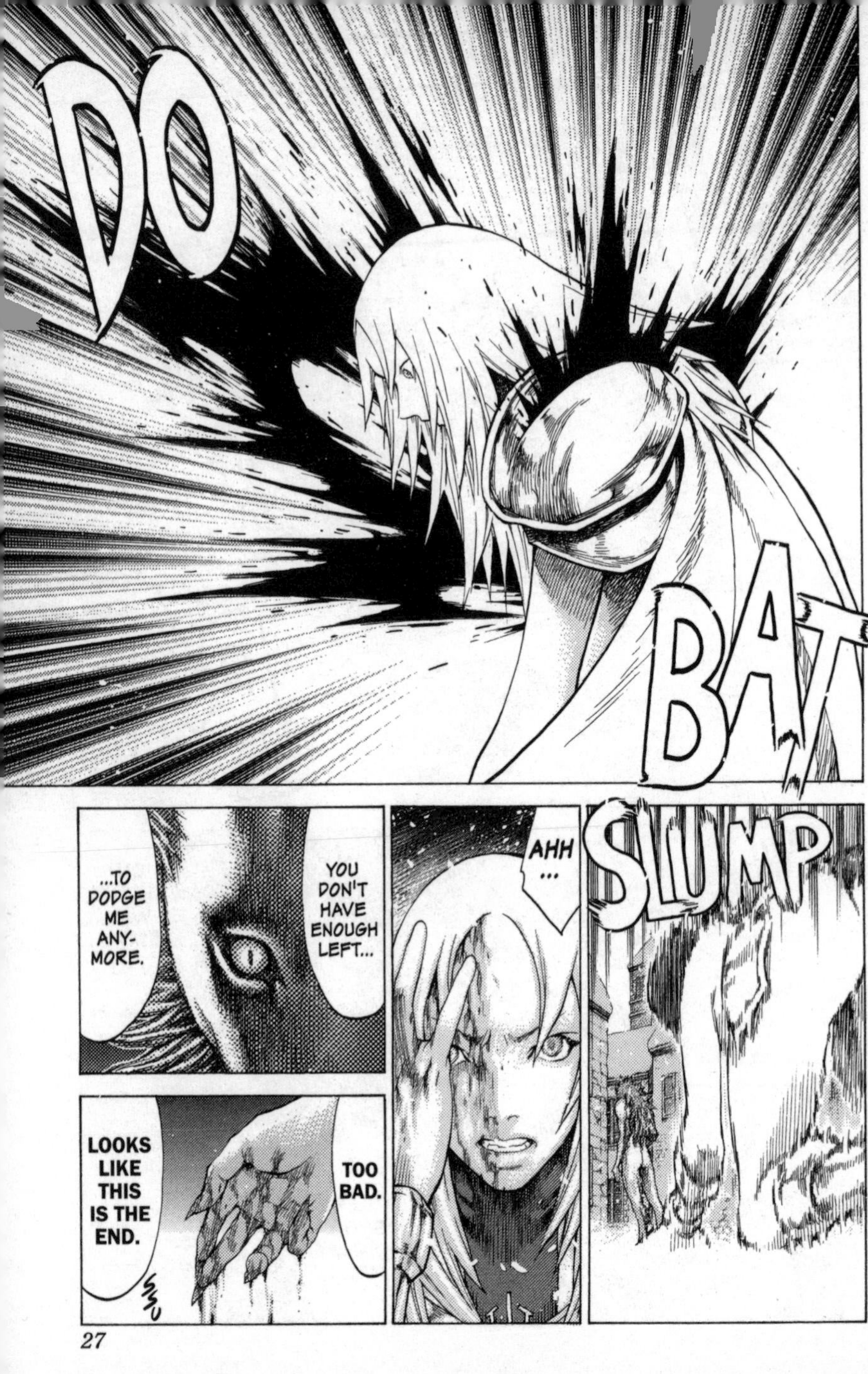
DO
BAT
SLUMP
AHH ...
YOU DON'T HAVE ENOUGH LEFT...
...TO DODGE ME ANY-MORE.
TOO BAD.
LOOKS LIKE THIS IS THE END.
SSU

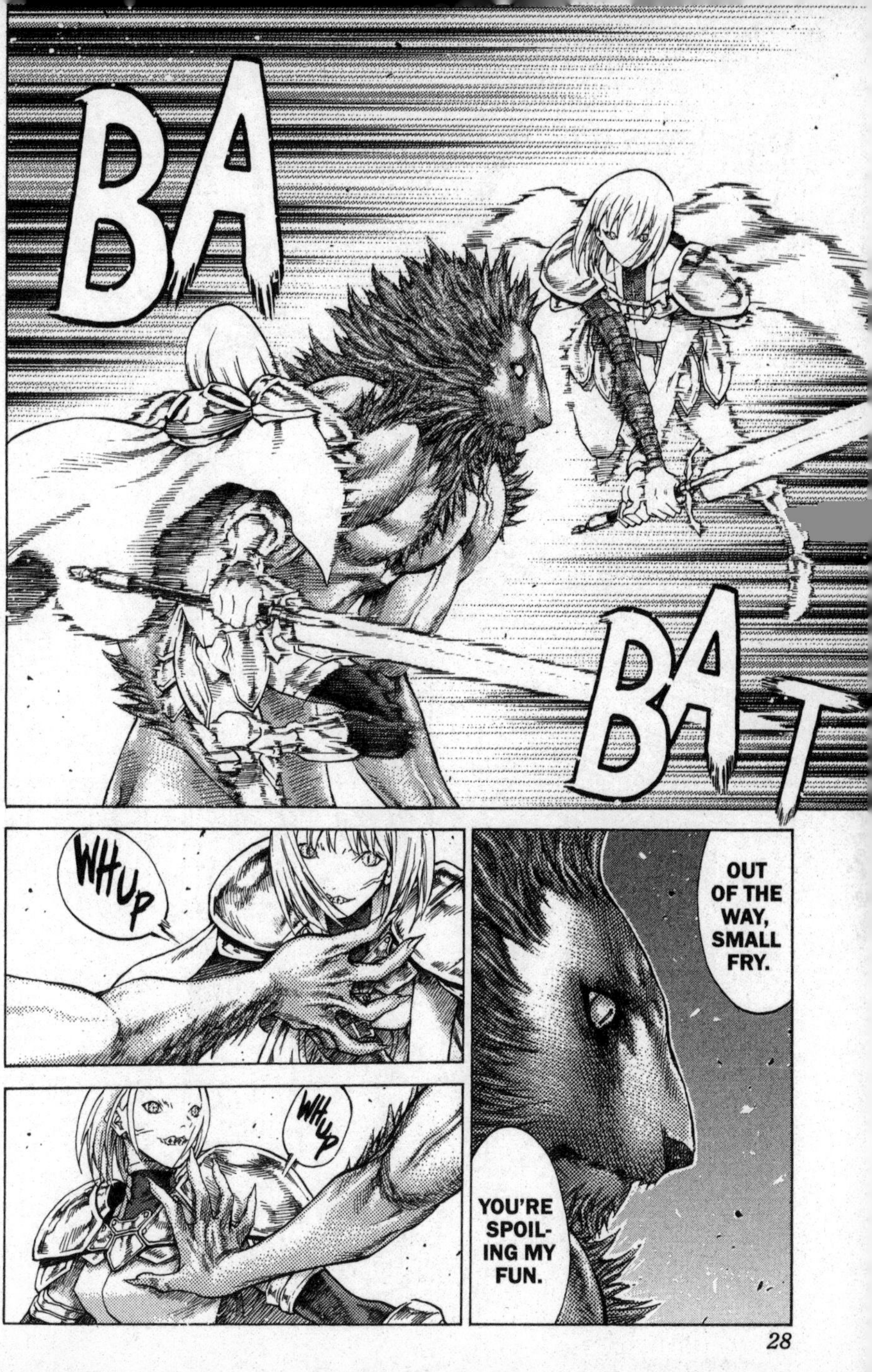
BA
BAT
OUT OF THE WAY, SMALL FRY.
YOU'RE SPOIL-ING MY FUN.
WHUP
WHUP

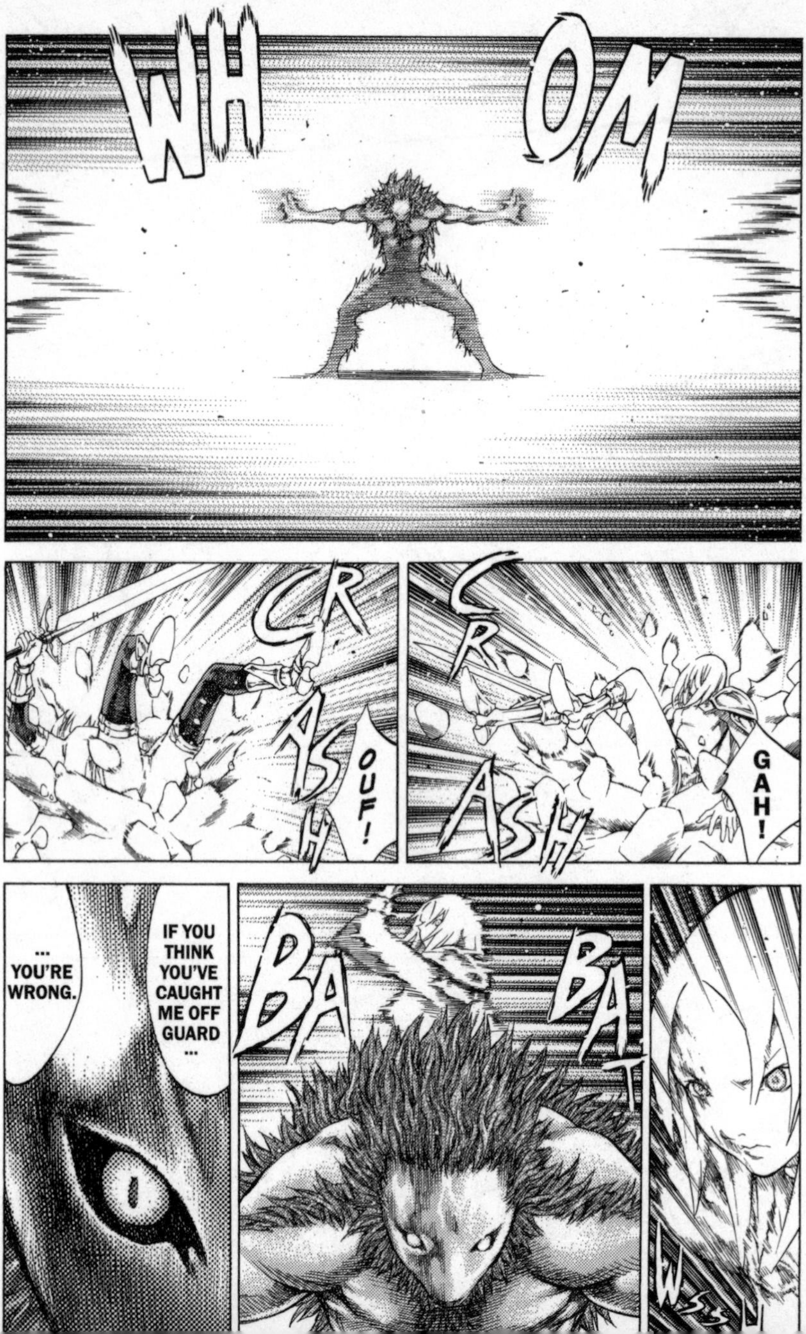
WHOOM
CRASH
GAH!
CRASH
OUF!
BA BAT
IF YOU THINK YOU'VE CAUGHT ME OFF GUARD ...
... YOU'RE WRONG.

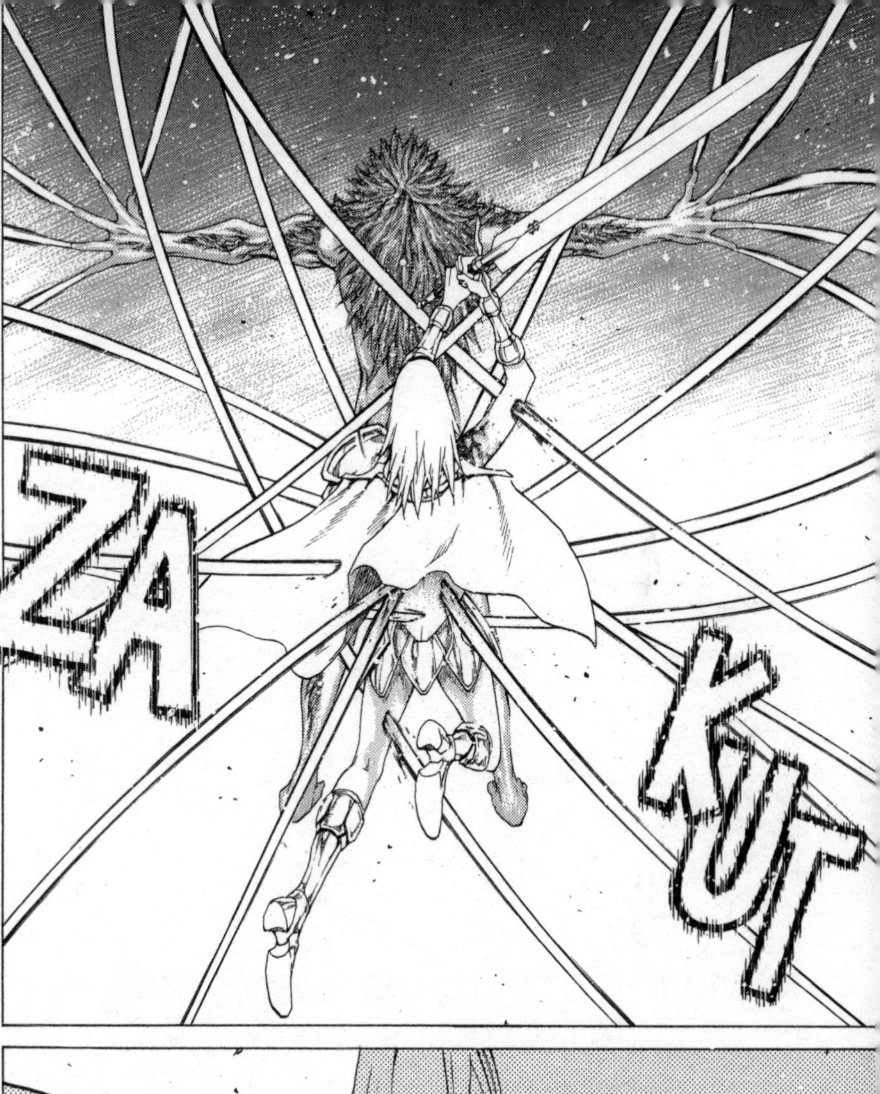
ZA
KUT
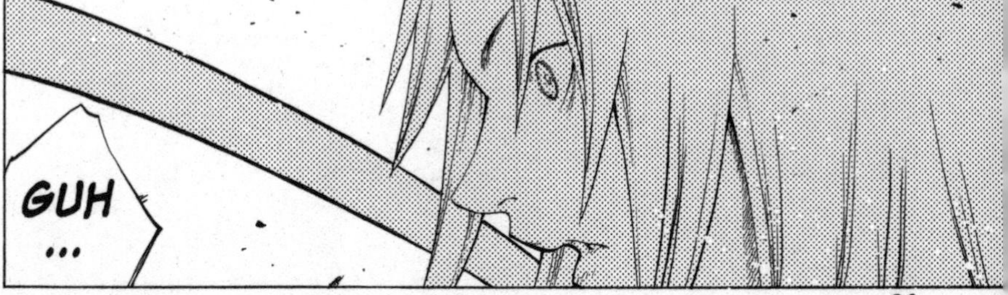
GUH ...

READ THIS WAY

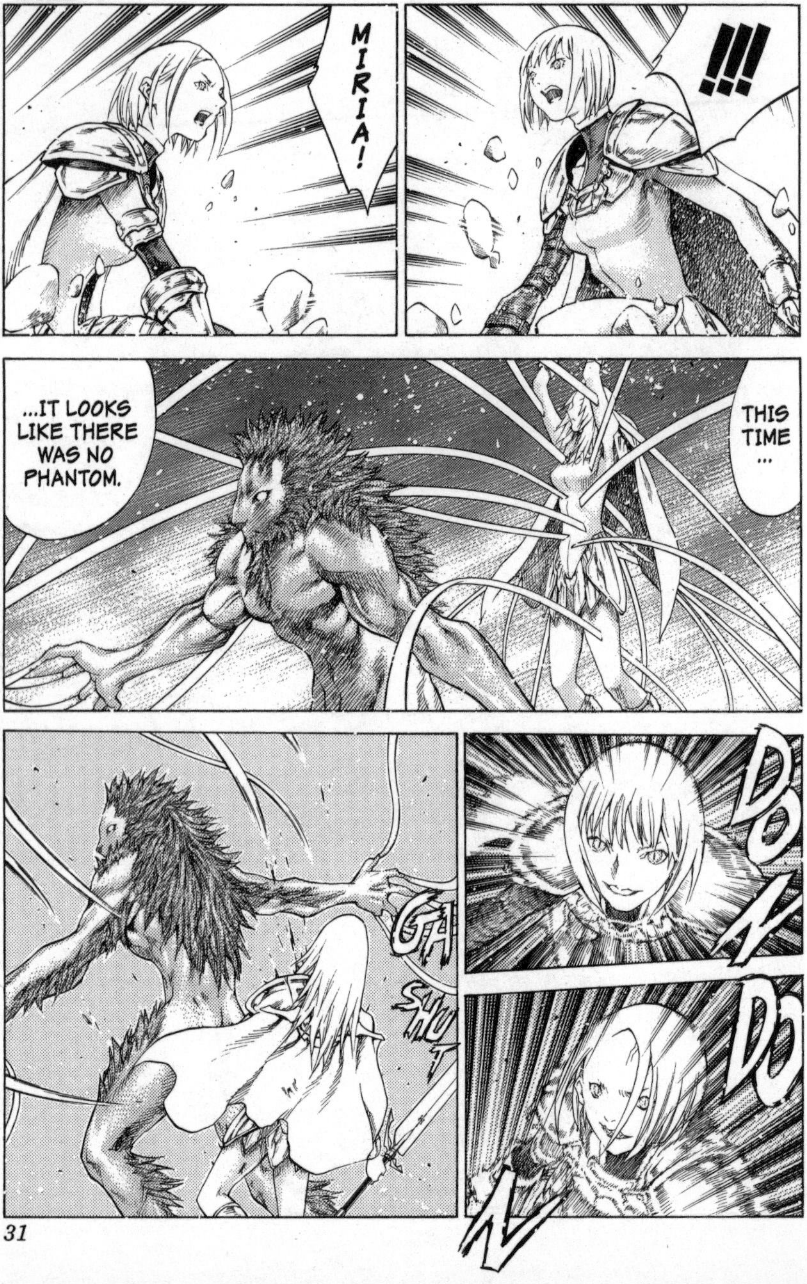
!!!
MIRIA!
THIS TIME ...
...IT LOOKS LIKE THERE WAS NO PHANTOM.
DON
DON
GA
SHUT

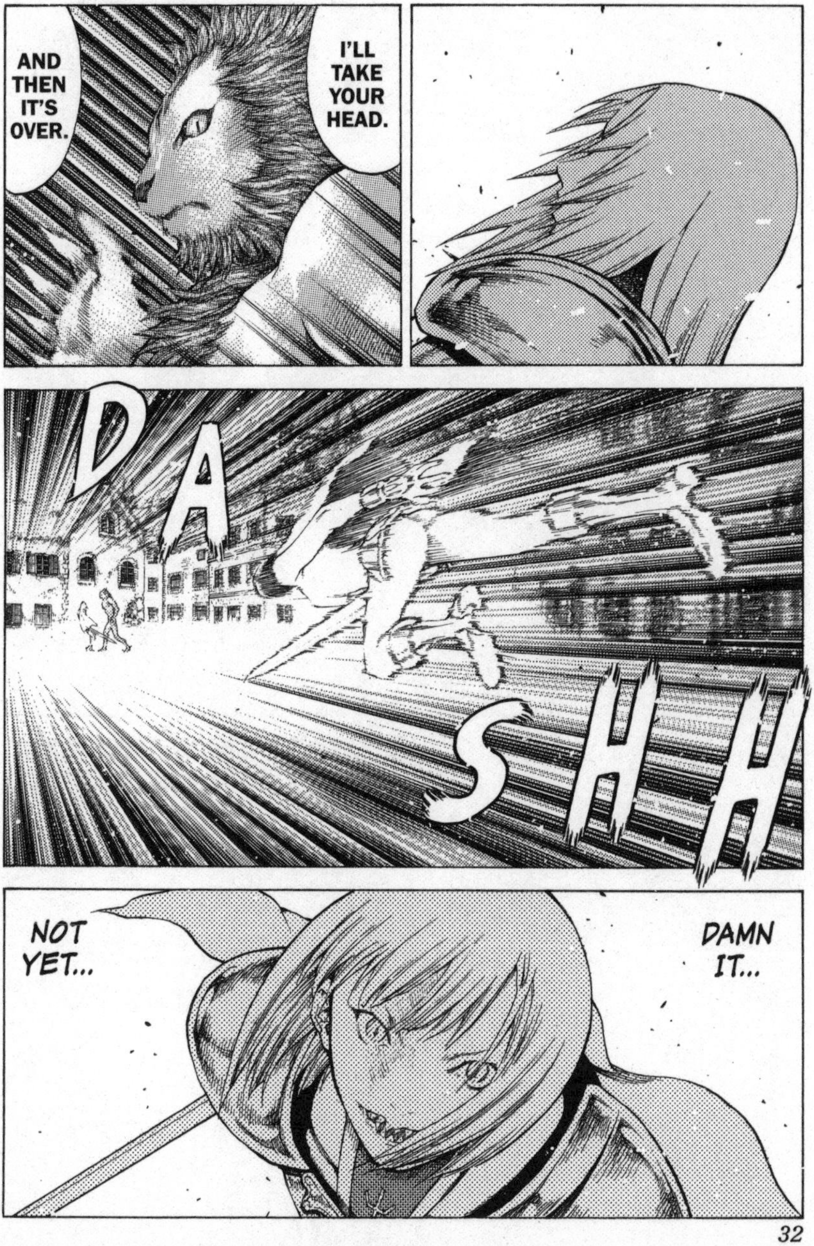
I'LL TAKE YOUR HEAD.
AND THEN IT'S OVER.
DASHH
DAMN IT...
NOT YET...

READ THIS WAY

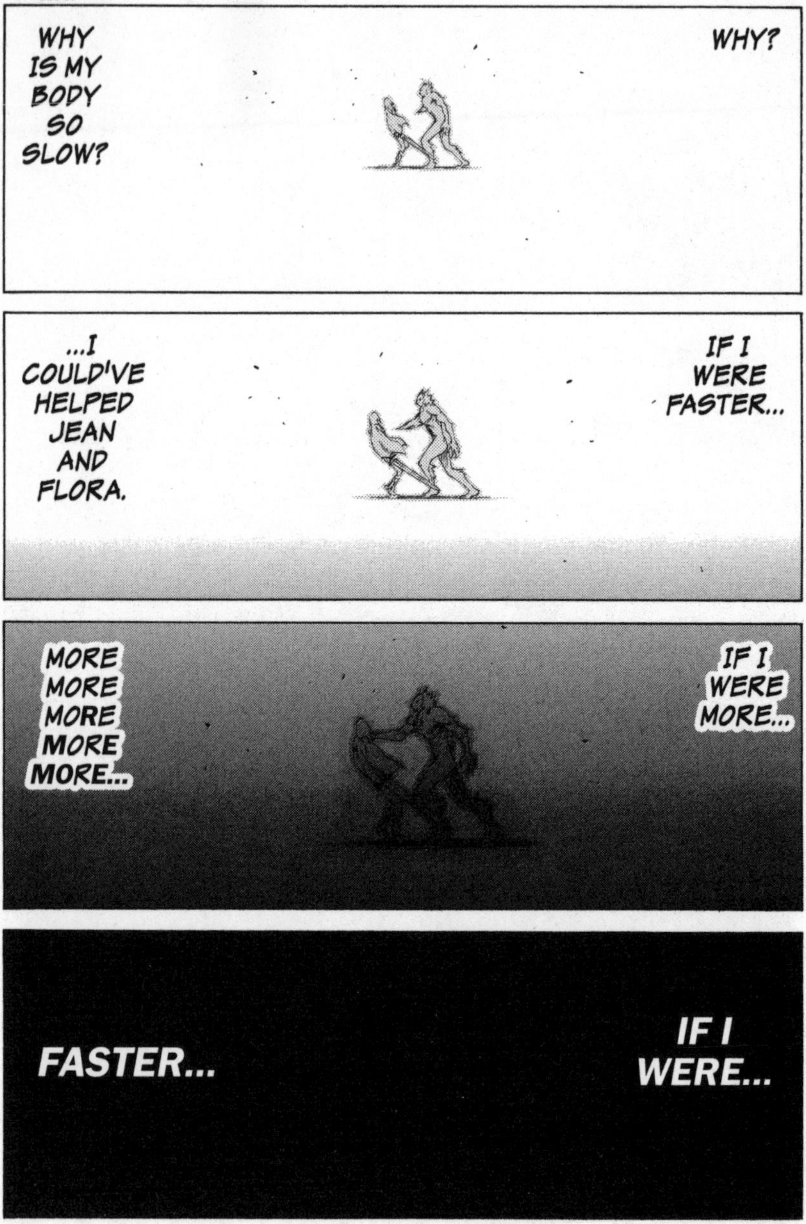

WHY?
WHY IS MY BODY SO SLOW?
IF I WERE FASTER...
...I COULD'VE HELPED JEAN AND FLORA.
IF I WERE MORE...
MORE MORE MORE MORE MORE...
IF I WERE...
FASTER...

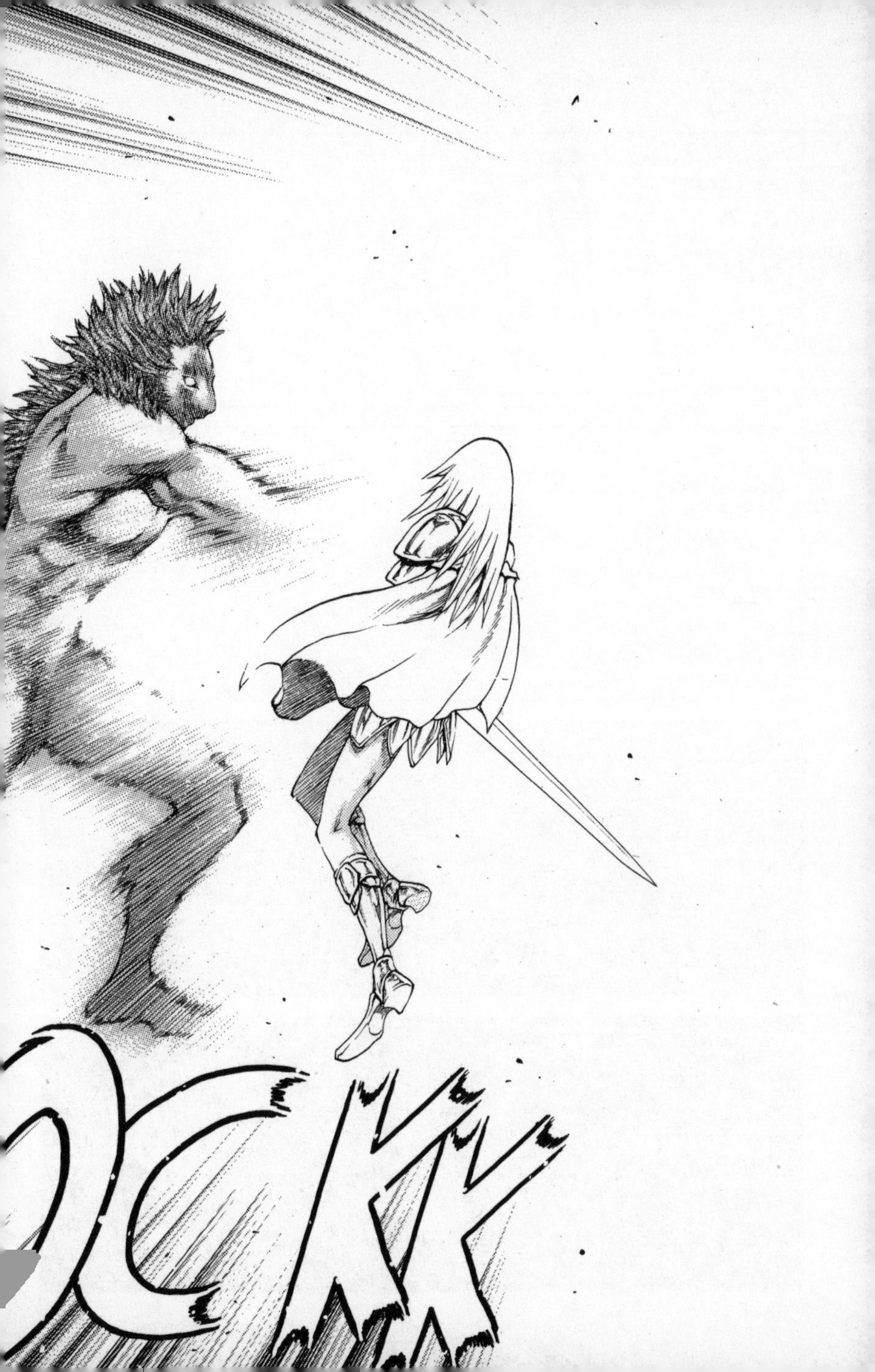

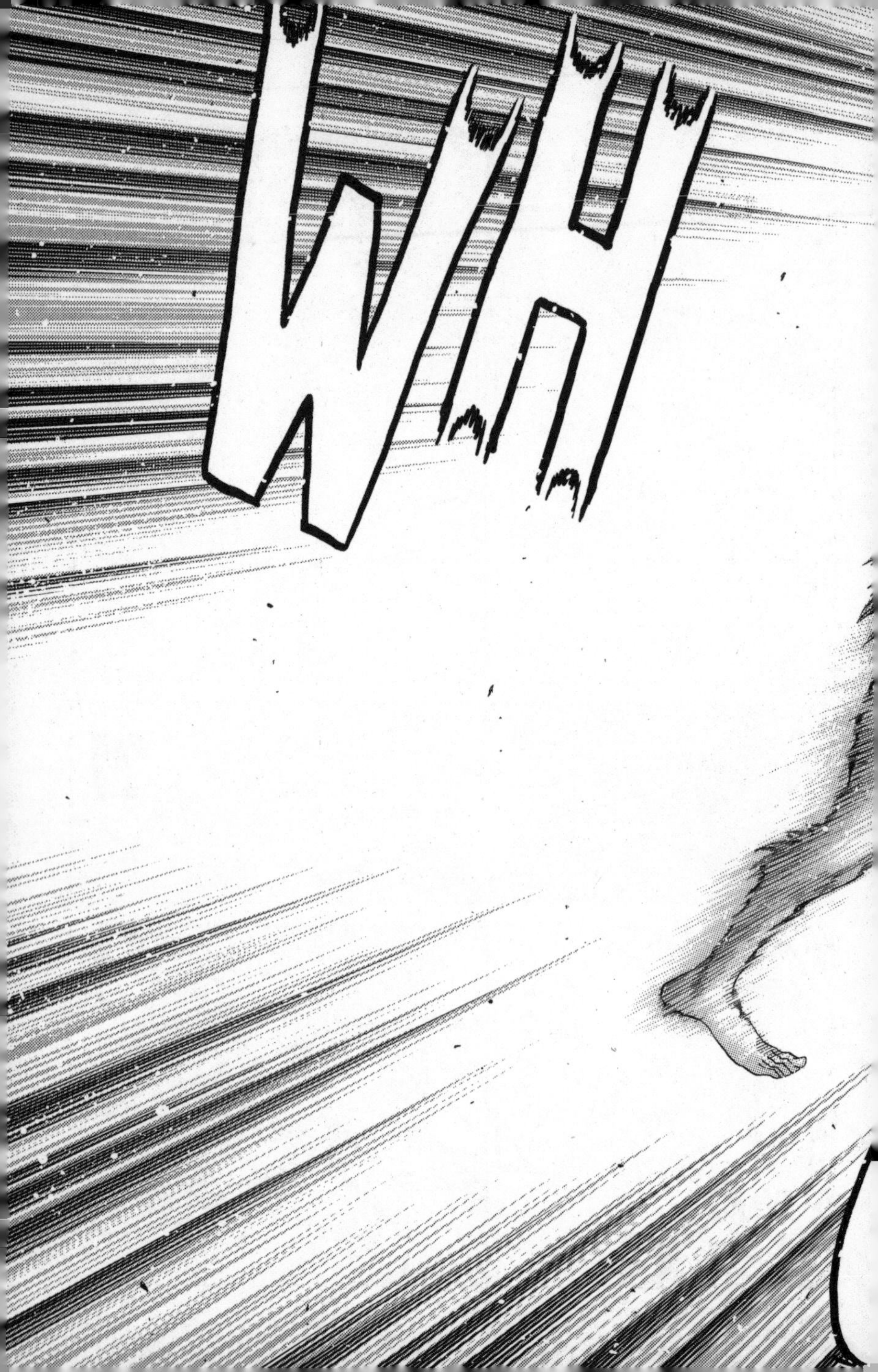
WH

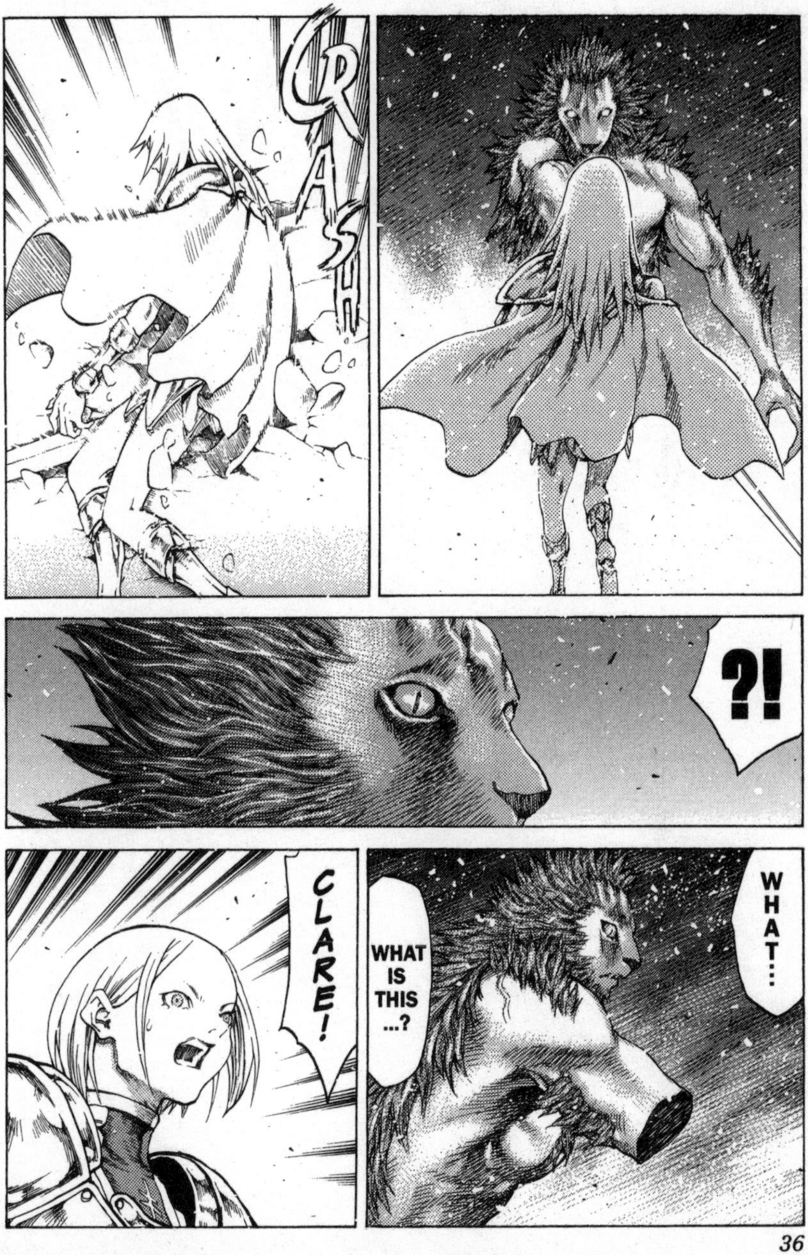
CRASH
?!
WHAT…
WHAT IS THIS …?
CLARE!

READ THIS WAY

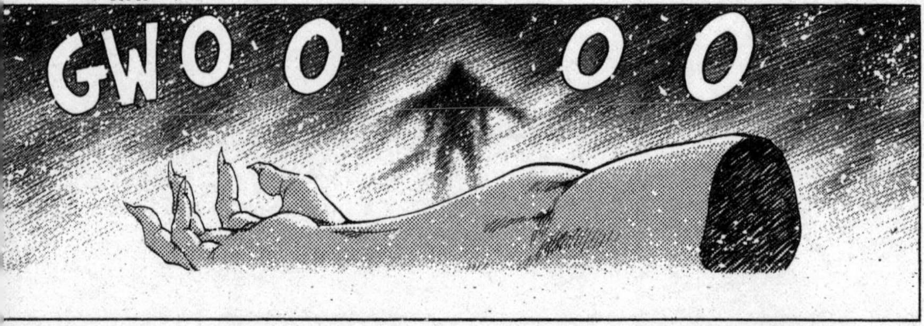
GWOO OO

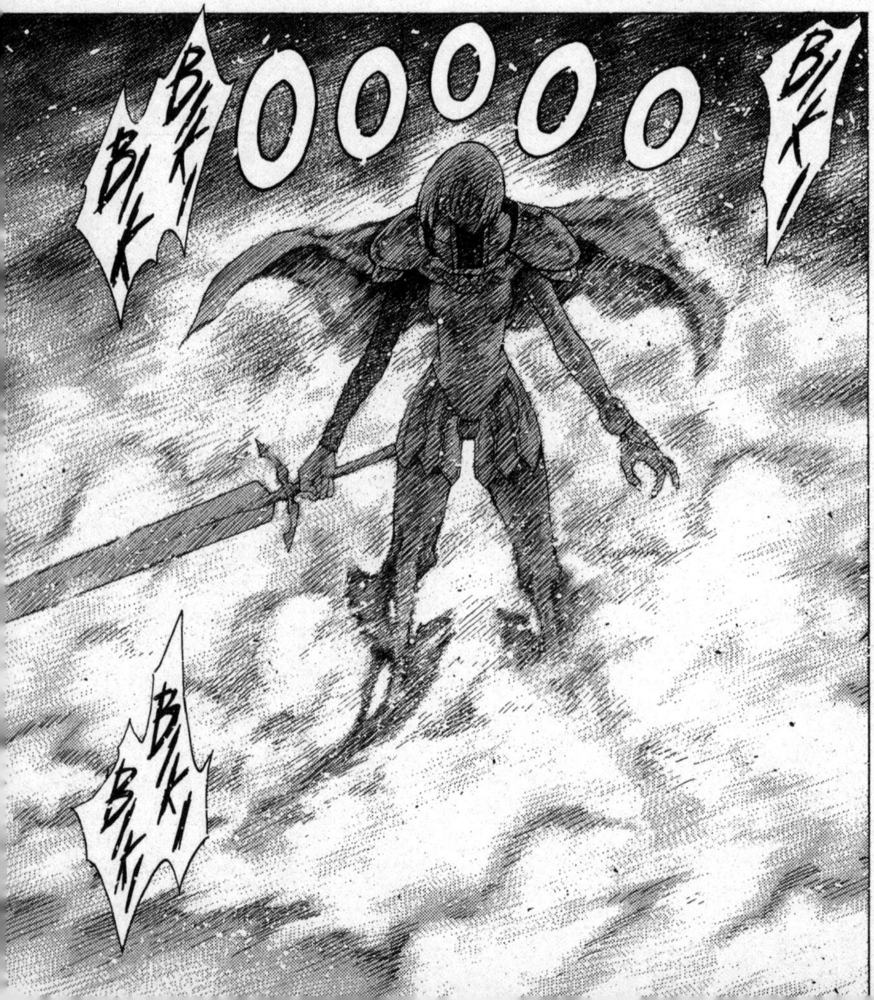
BIKI
OOOOOO
BIKI
BIKI
BIKI
BIKI

クレイモア
Claymore

Scene 59: The Assault on Pieta, Part 3

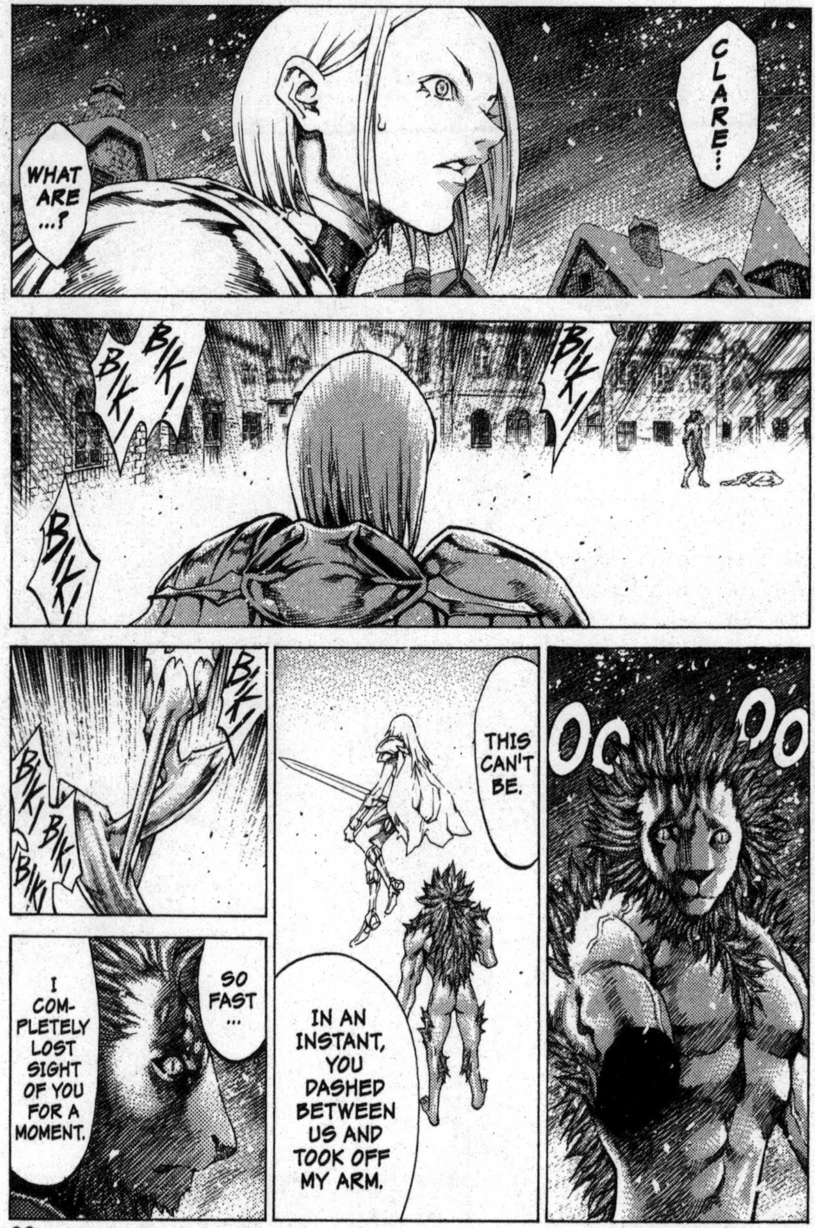
CLARE...
WHAT ARE ...?
BIKI!
BIKI BIKI!
BIKI!
OO
OO
THIS CAN'T BE.
IN AN INSTANT, YOU DASHED BETWEEN US AND TOOK OFF MY ARM.
BIKI!
BIKI BIKI BIKI
SO FAST ...
I COMPLETELY LOST SIGHT OF YOU FOR A MOMENT.

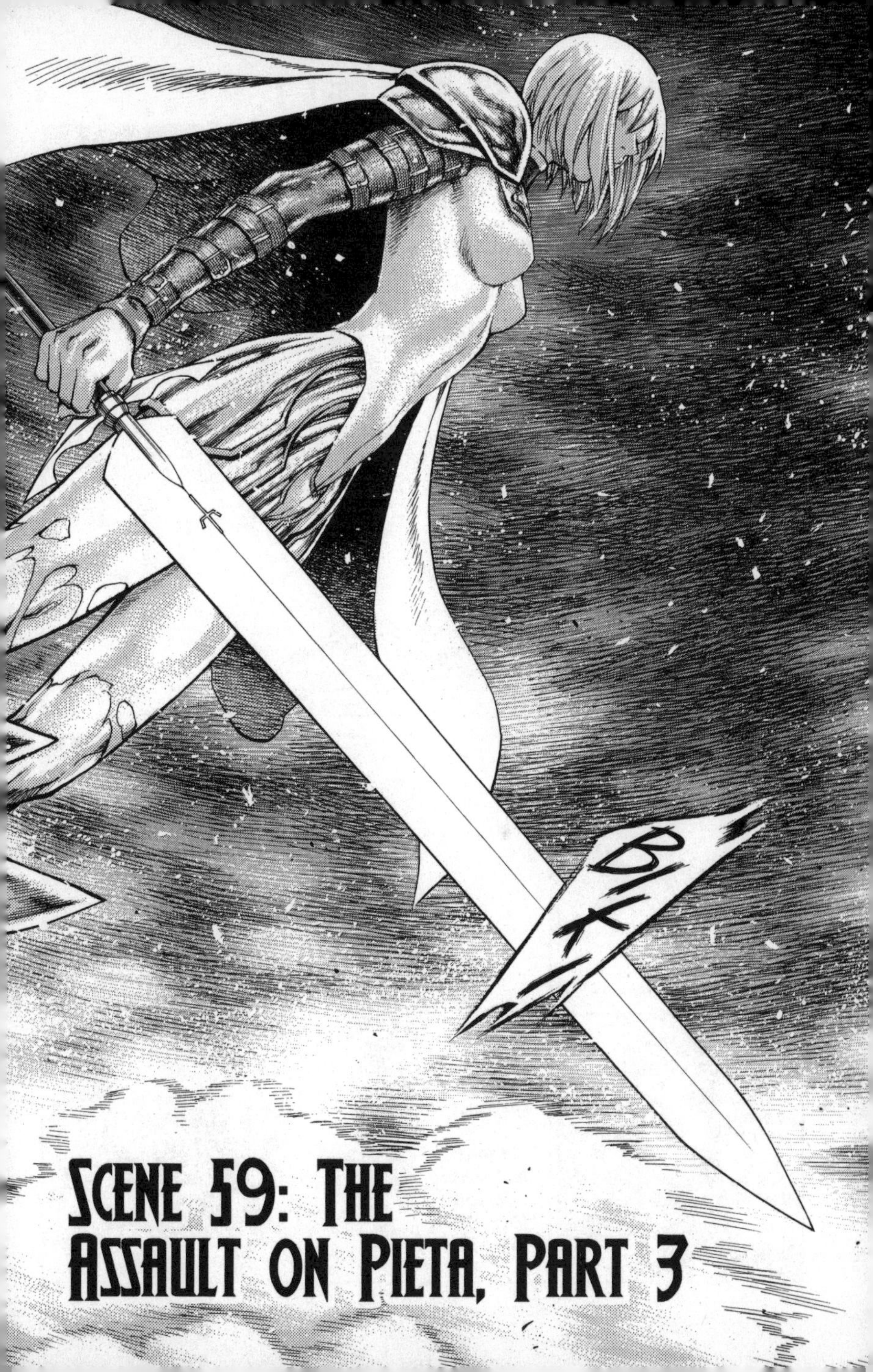
BIK!
Scene 59: The Assault on Pieta, Part 3

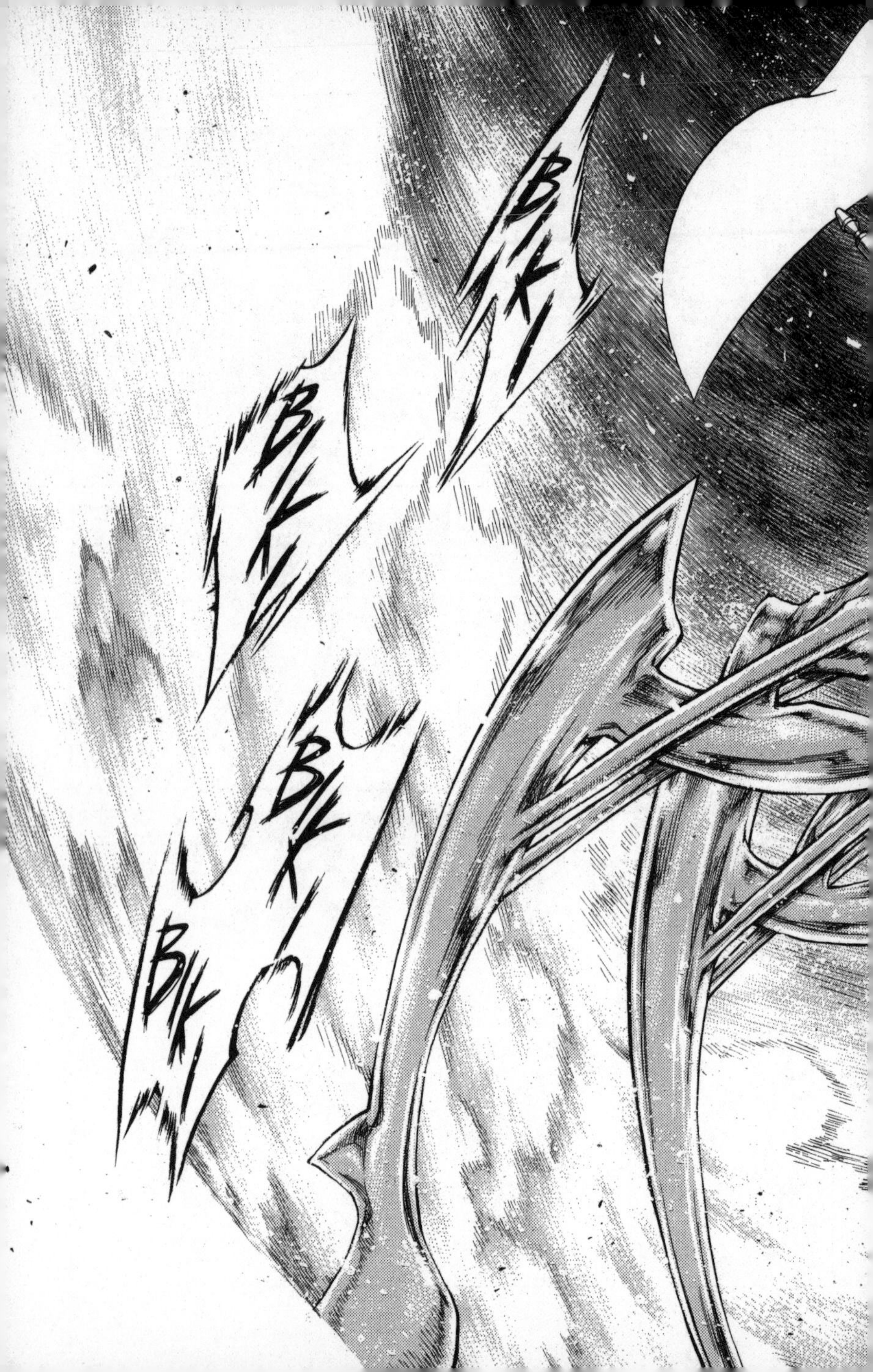
BIKI
BIKI
BIKI
BIKI

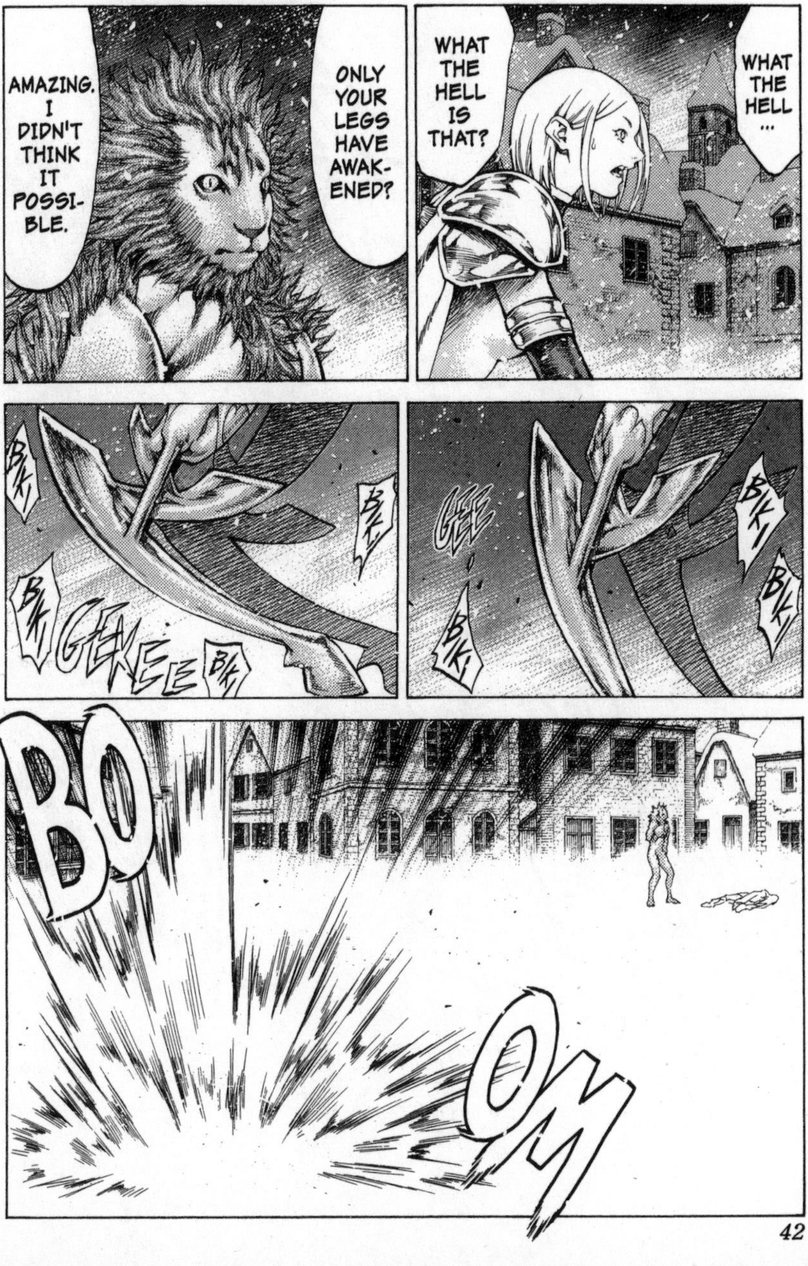
WHAT THE HELL ...
WHAT THE HELL IS THAT?
ONLY YOUR LEGS HAVE AWAKENED?
AMAZING. I DIDN'T THINK IT POSSIBLE.
BIKI
BIKI
GEEE
BIKI
BIKI
BIKI
BIKI
GEKEEE
BIKI
BOOM

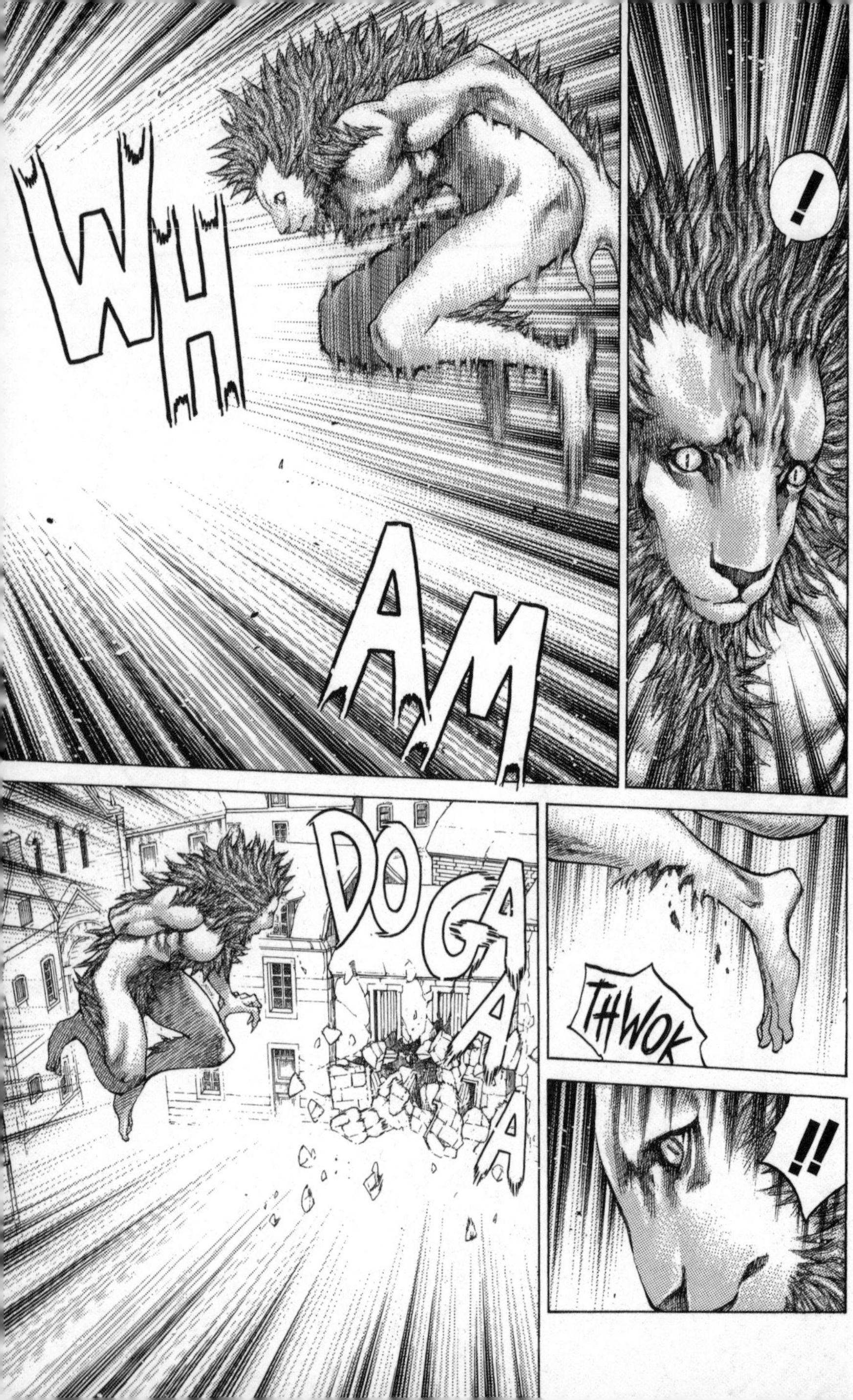
!
WHAM
THWOK
!!
DOGAAA

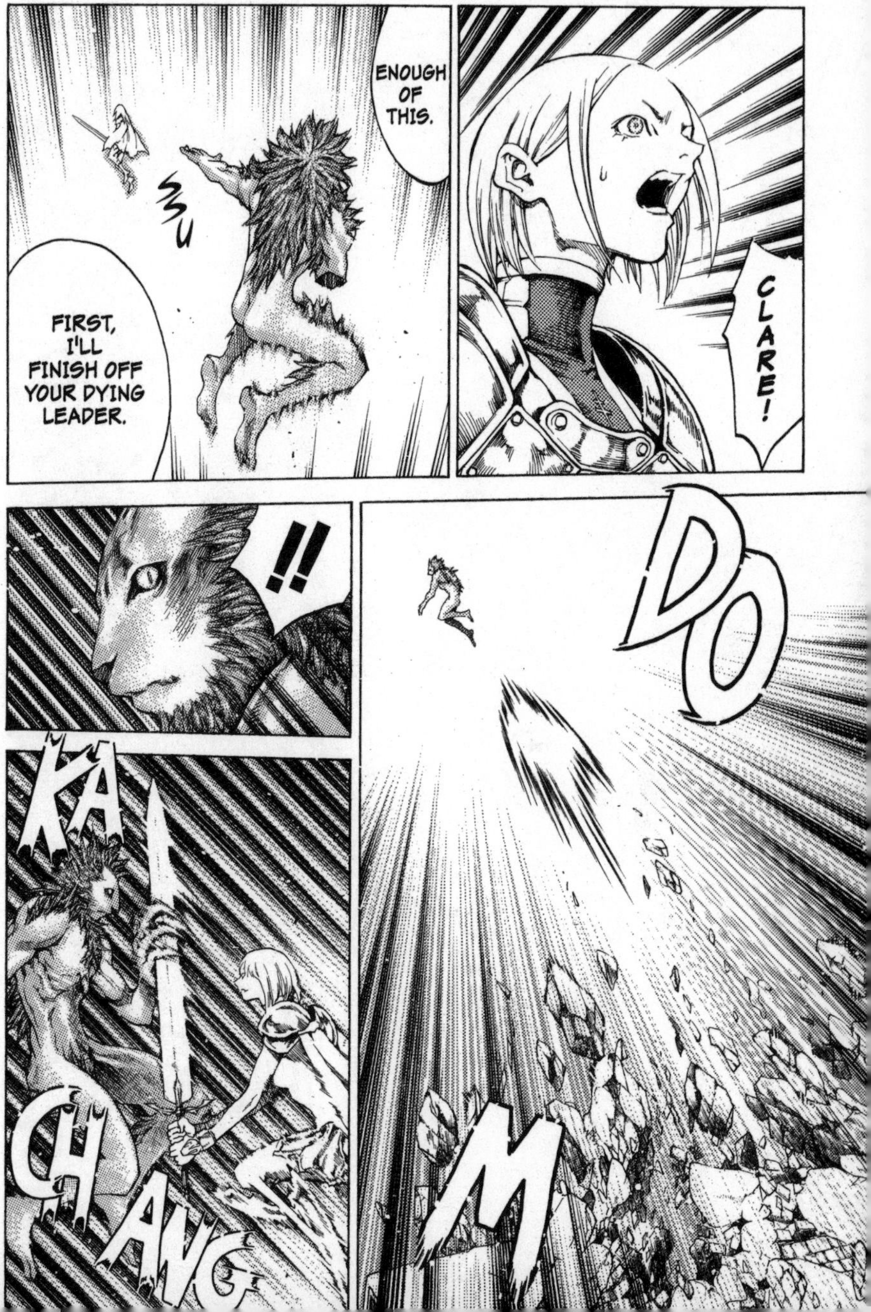
CLARE!
ENOUGH OF THIS.
SWU
FIRST, I'LL FINISH OFF YOUR DYING LEADER.
DO
M
!!
KA
CHANG

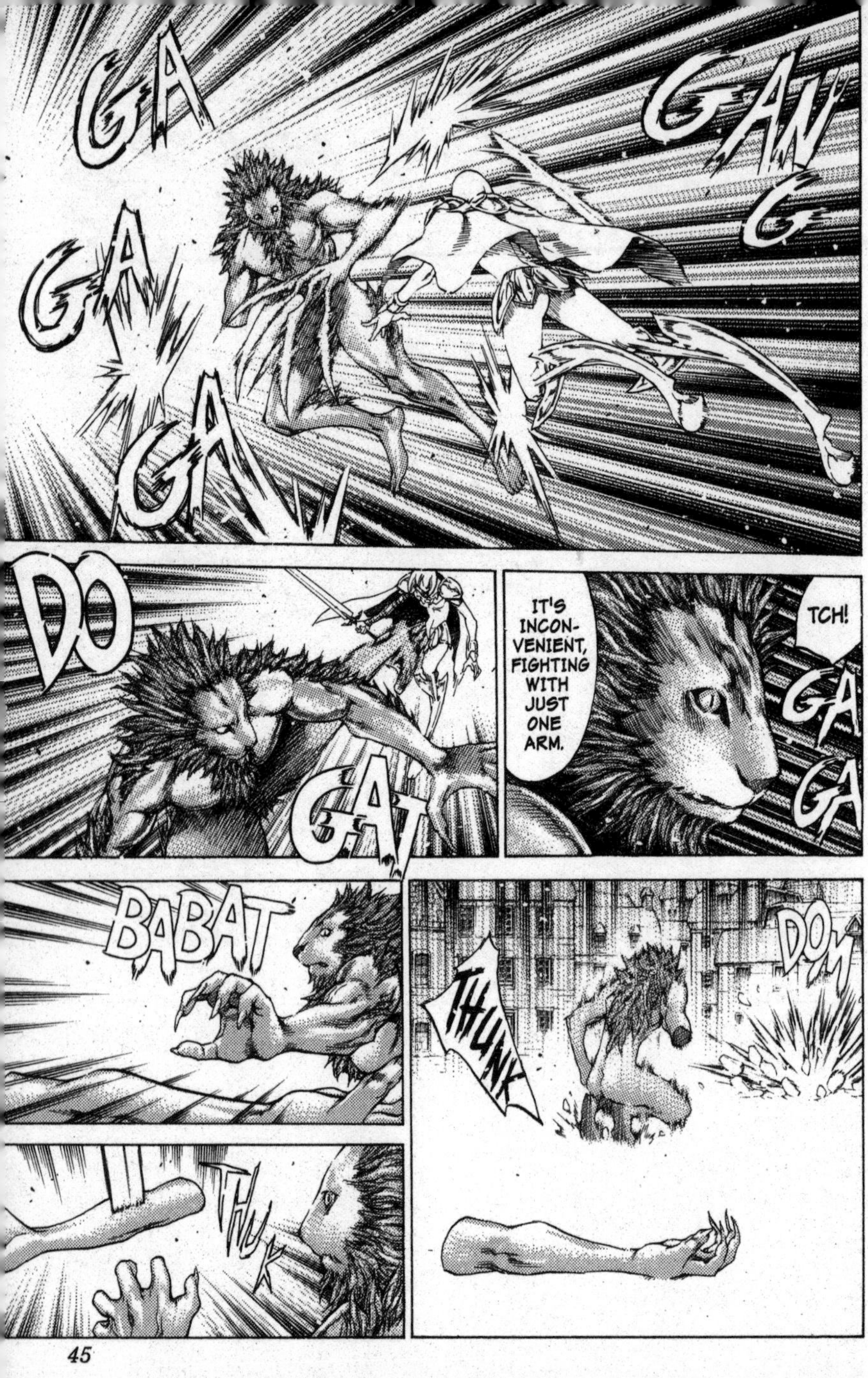
GANG
GA
GA
GA
TCH!
IT'S INCONVENIENT, FIGHTING WITH JUST ONE ARM.
GA GA
DO
GAT
DOM
THUNK
BABAT
THUK

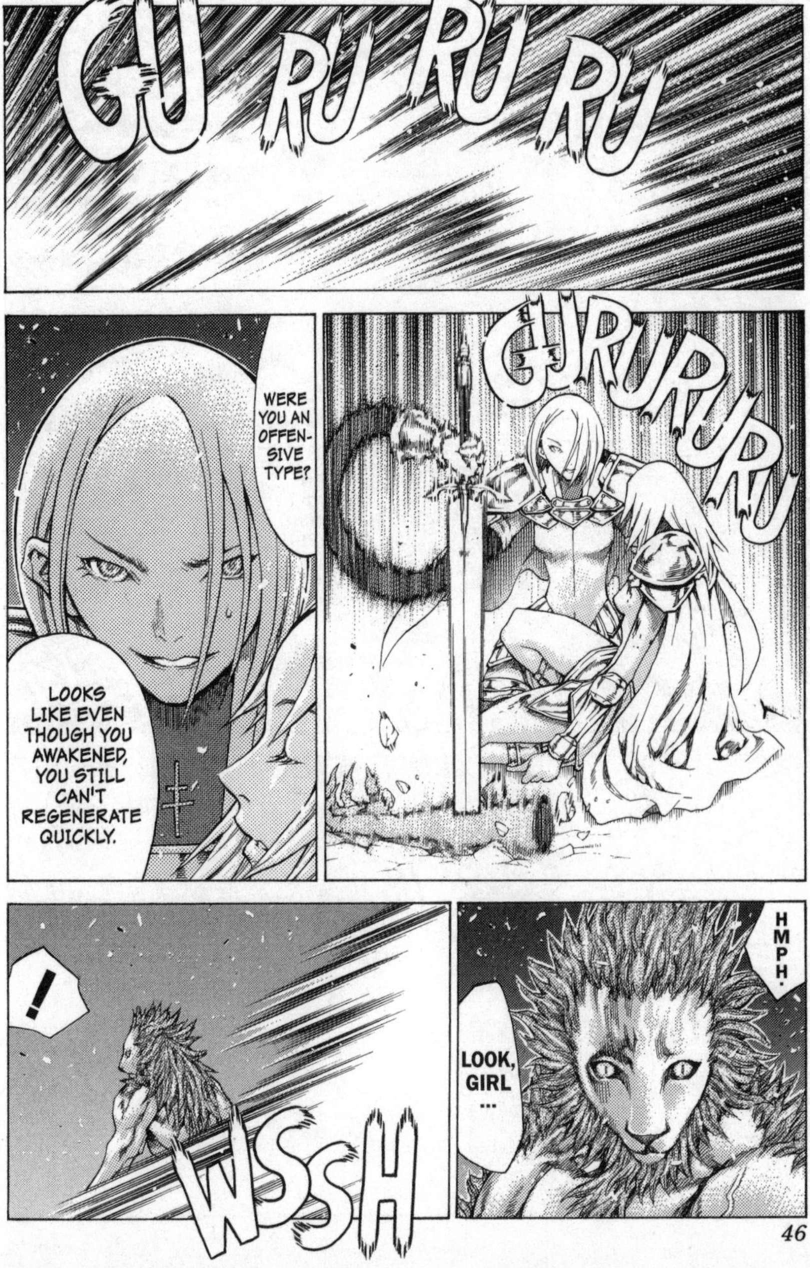
GU RU RU RU RU
GURURURU
WERE YOU AN OFFEN-SIVE TYPE?
LOOKS LIKE EVEN THOUGH YOU AWAKENED, YOU STILL CAN'T REGENERATE QUICKLY.
HMPH.
LOOK, GIRL ...
!
WSSH

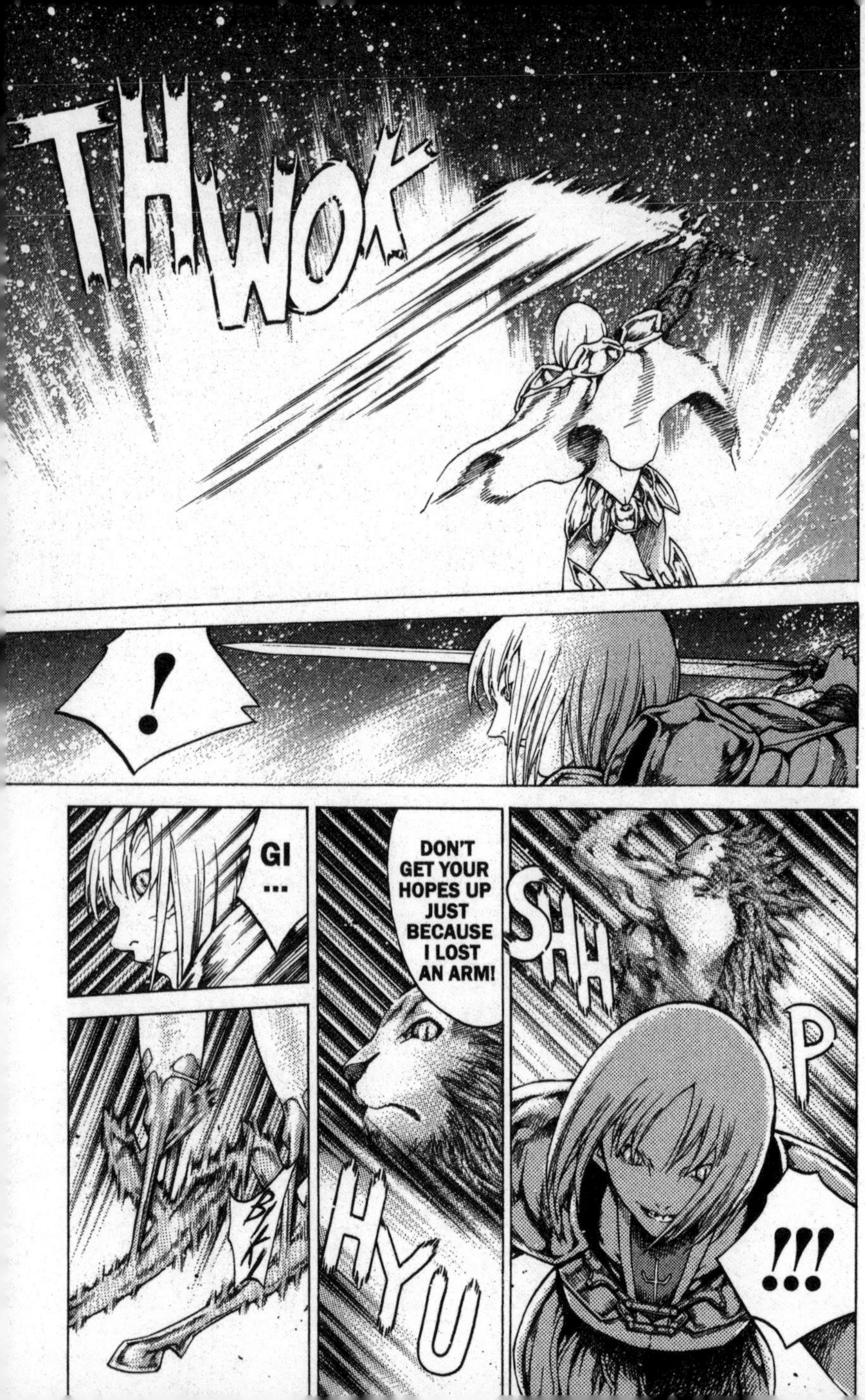
THWOK
!
SHH
P
!!!
DON'T GET YOUR HOPES UP JUST BECAUSE I LOST AN ARM!
HYU
GI ...

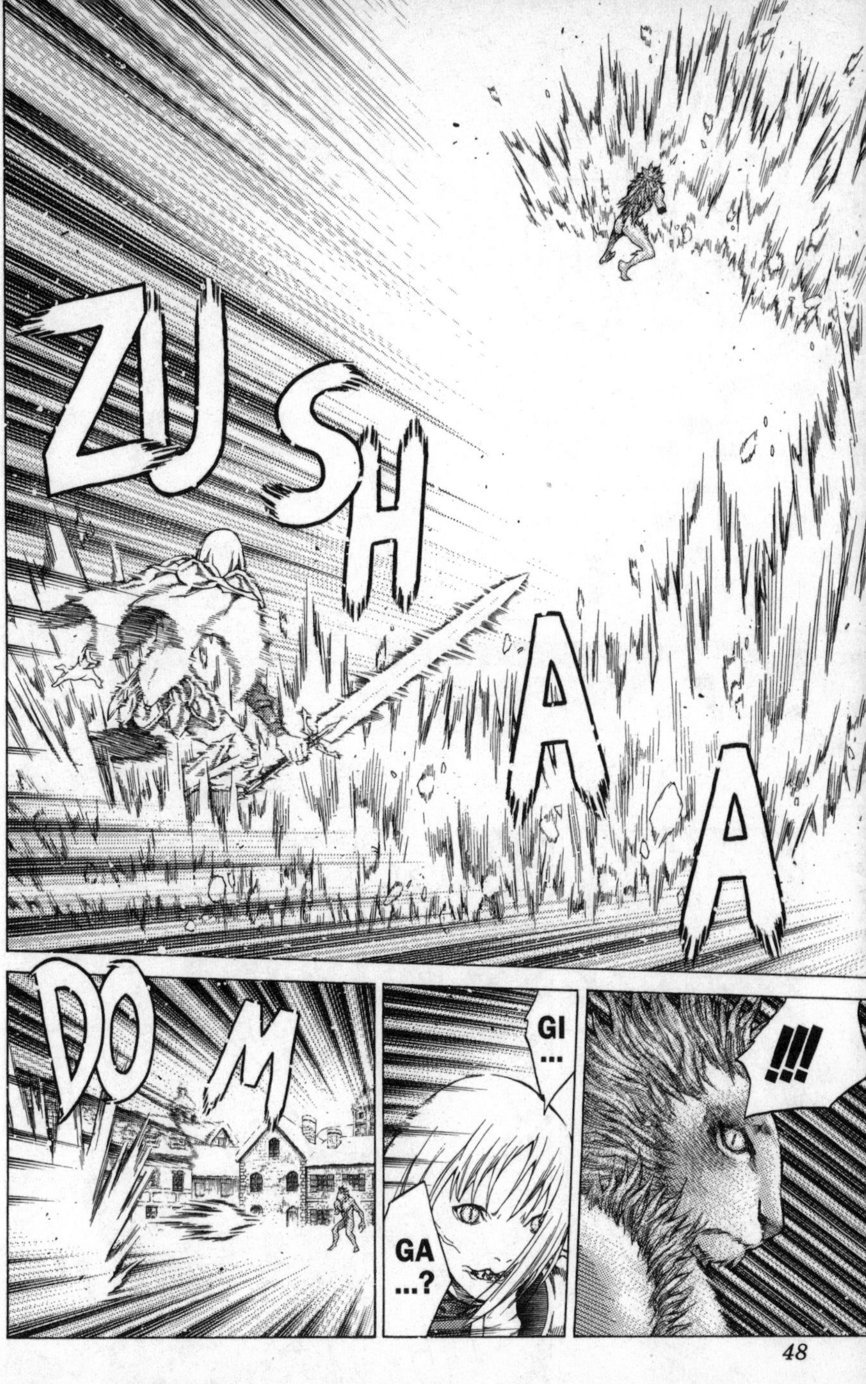
ZUSHAAA
!!!
GI ...
GA ...?
DOM

READ THIS WAY

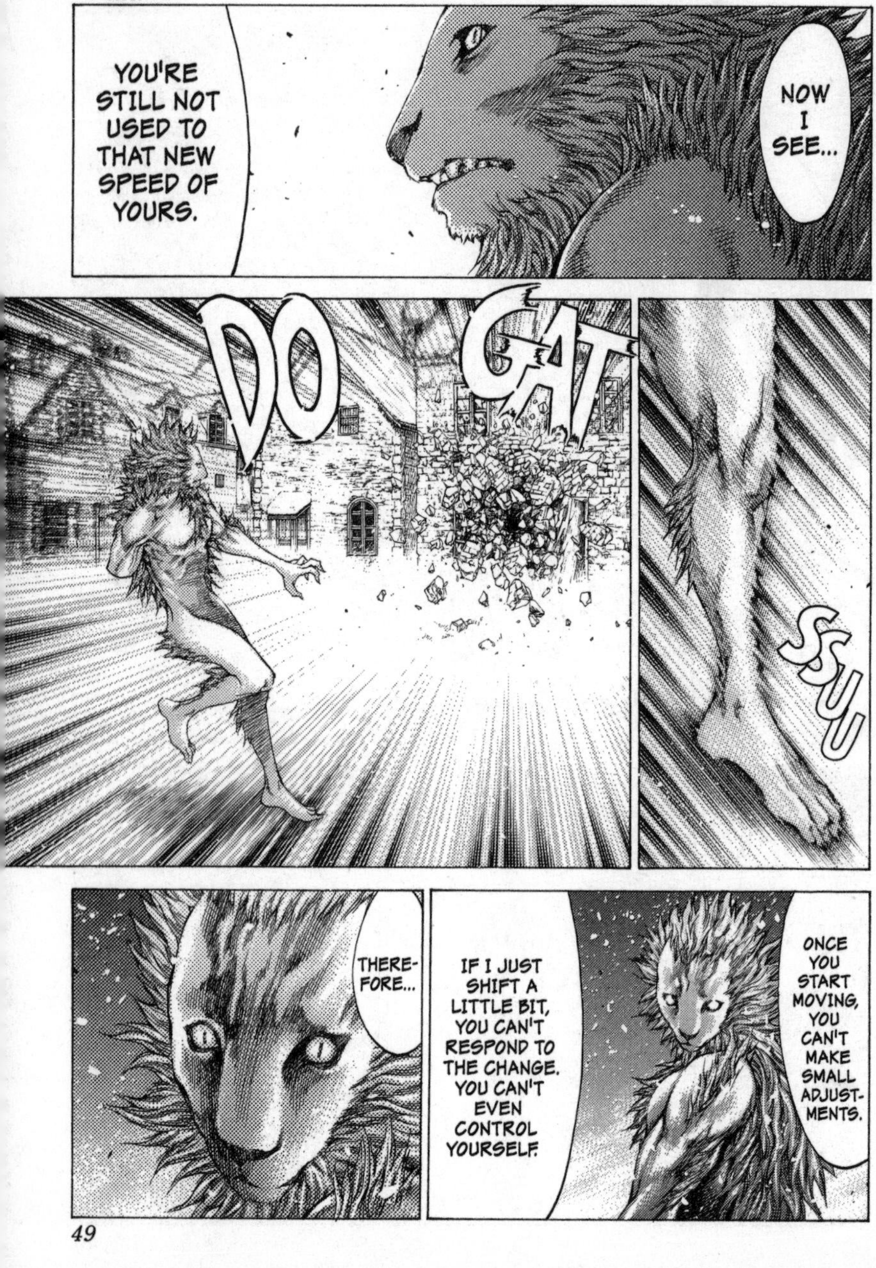
NOW I SEE...
YOU'RE STILL NOT USED TO THAT NEW SPEED OF YOURS.
SSUU
DO
GAT
ONCE YOU START MOVING, YOU CAN'T MAKE SMALL ADJUST-MENTS.
IF I JUST SHIFT A LITTLE BIT, YOU CAN'T RESPOND TO THE CHANGE. YOU CAN'T EVEN CONTROL YOURSELF.
THERE-FORE...

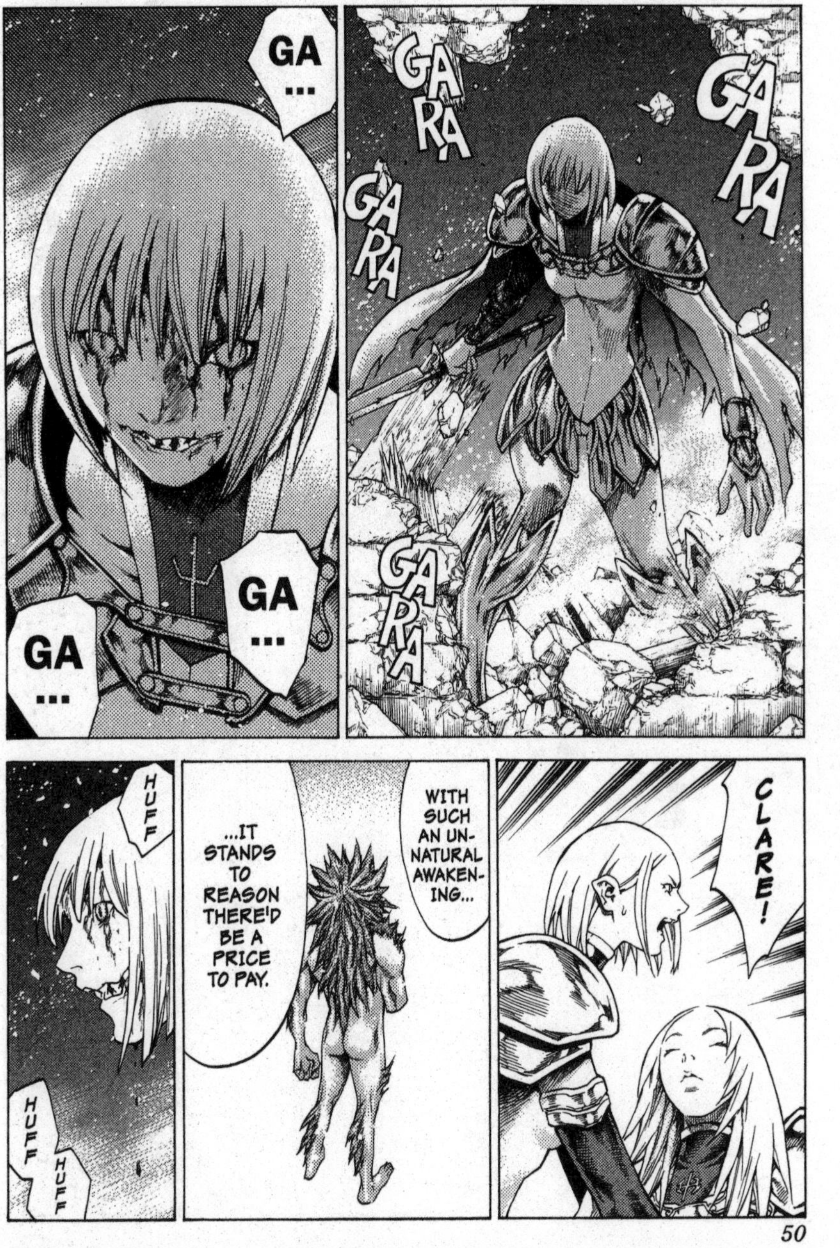

GARA
GARA
GARA
GARA
GA...
GA...
GA...
CLARE!
WITH SUCH AN UN-NATURAL AWAKEN-ING...
...IT STANDS TO REASON THERE'D BE A PRICE TO PAY.
HUFF
HUFF
HUFF

READ THIS WAY

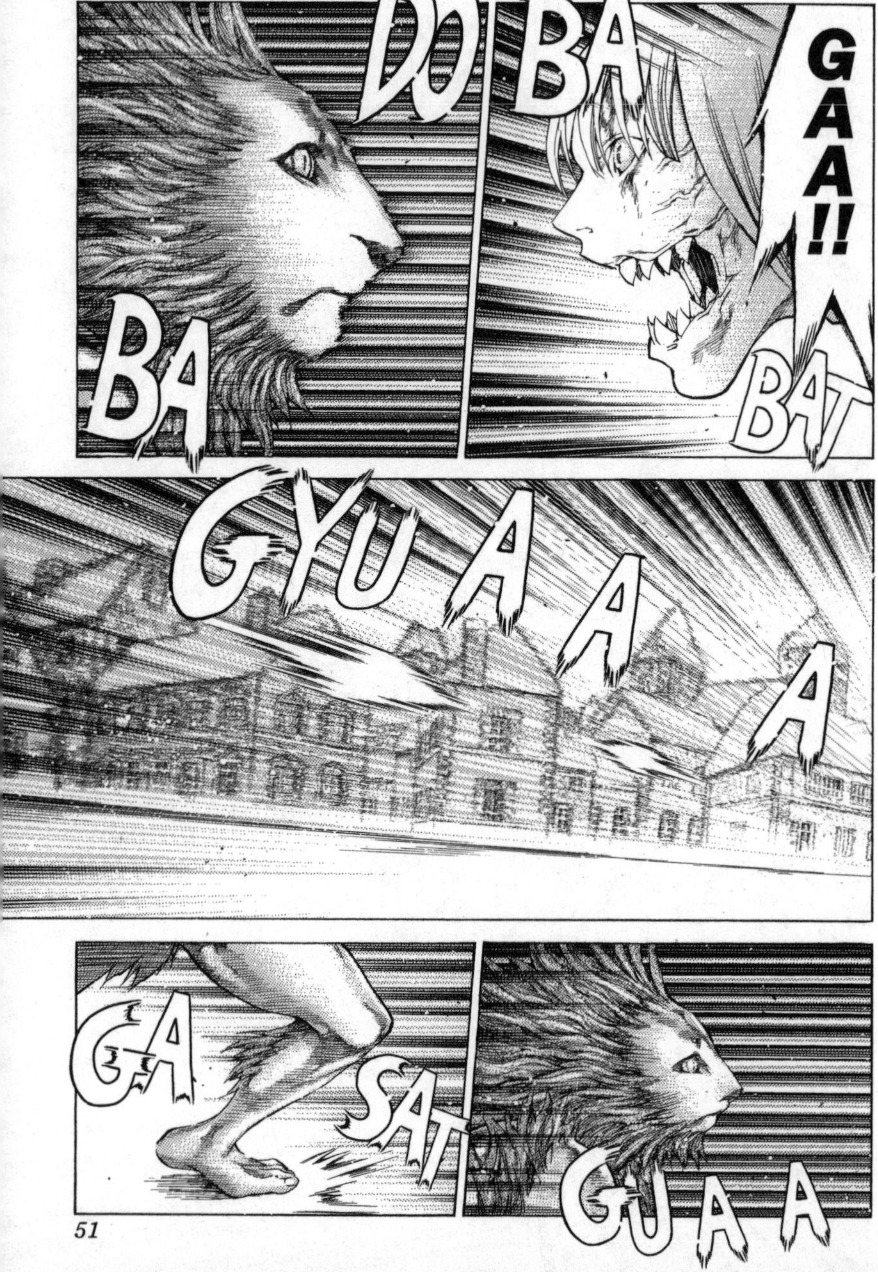

DO BA
GAA!!
BAT
BA
GYU A A A A
GUA A A
GA
SAT

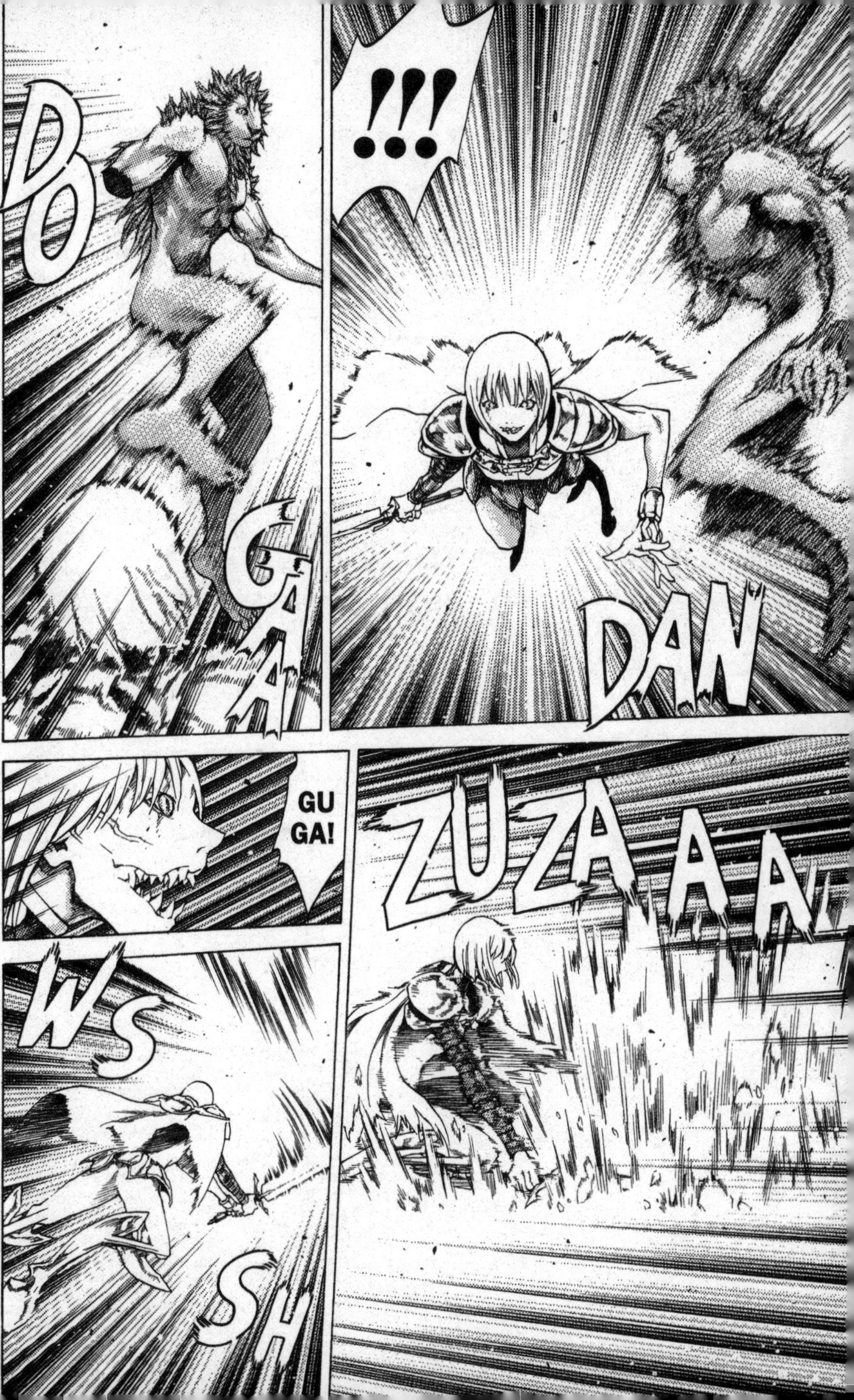
!!!
DAN
DO
GAA
ZUZAAA
GU GA!
WS
SH

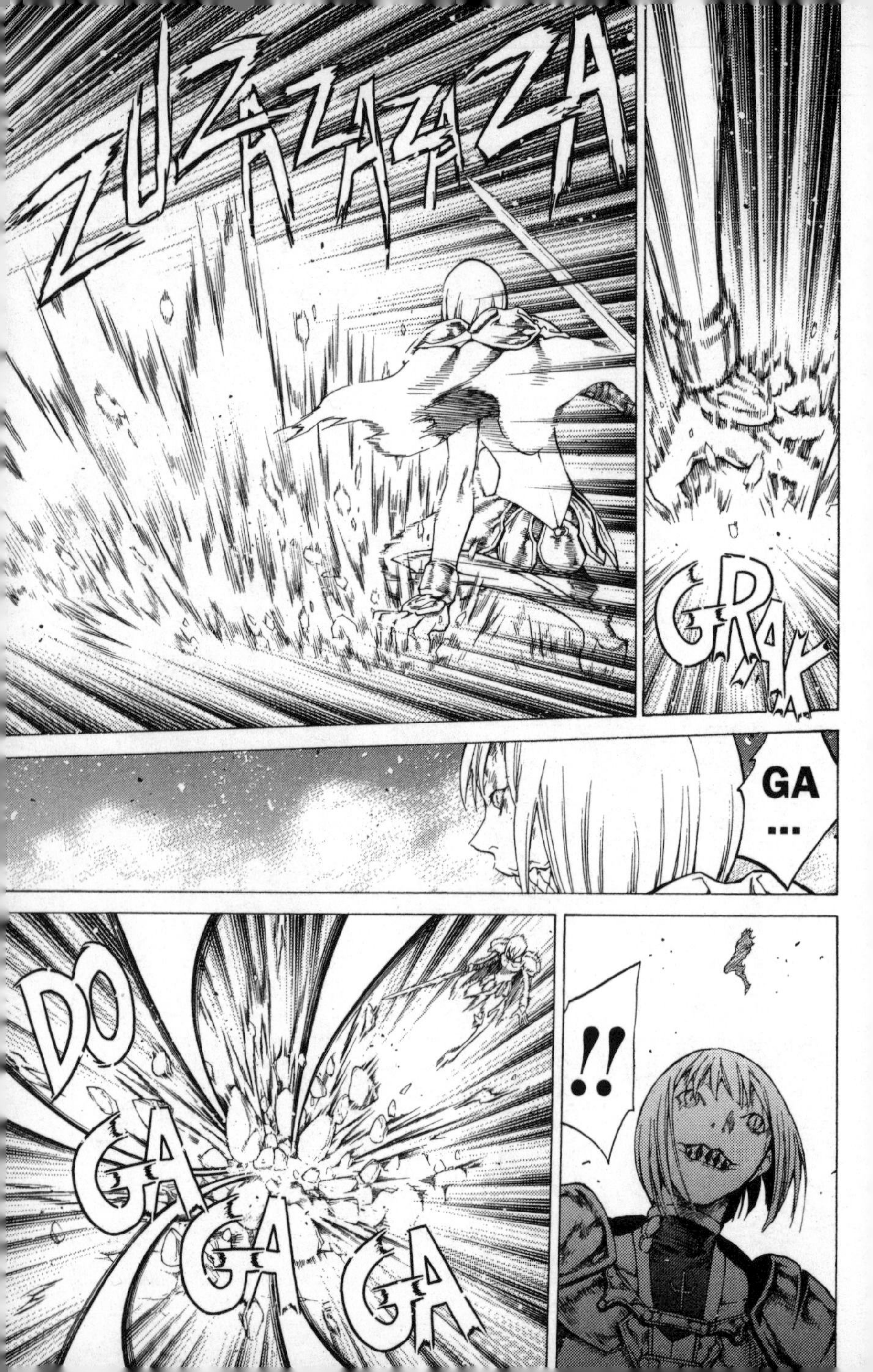
GRAAK
ZUZAZAZAZA
GA...
!!
DOGAGAGA

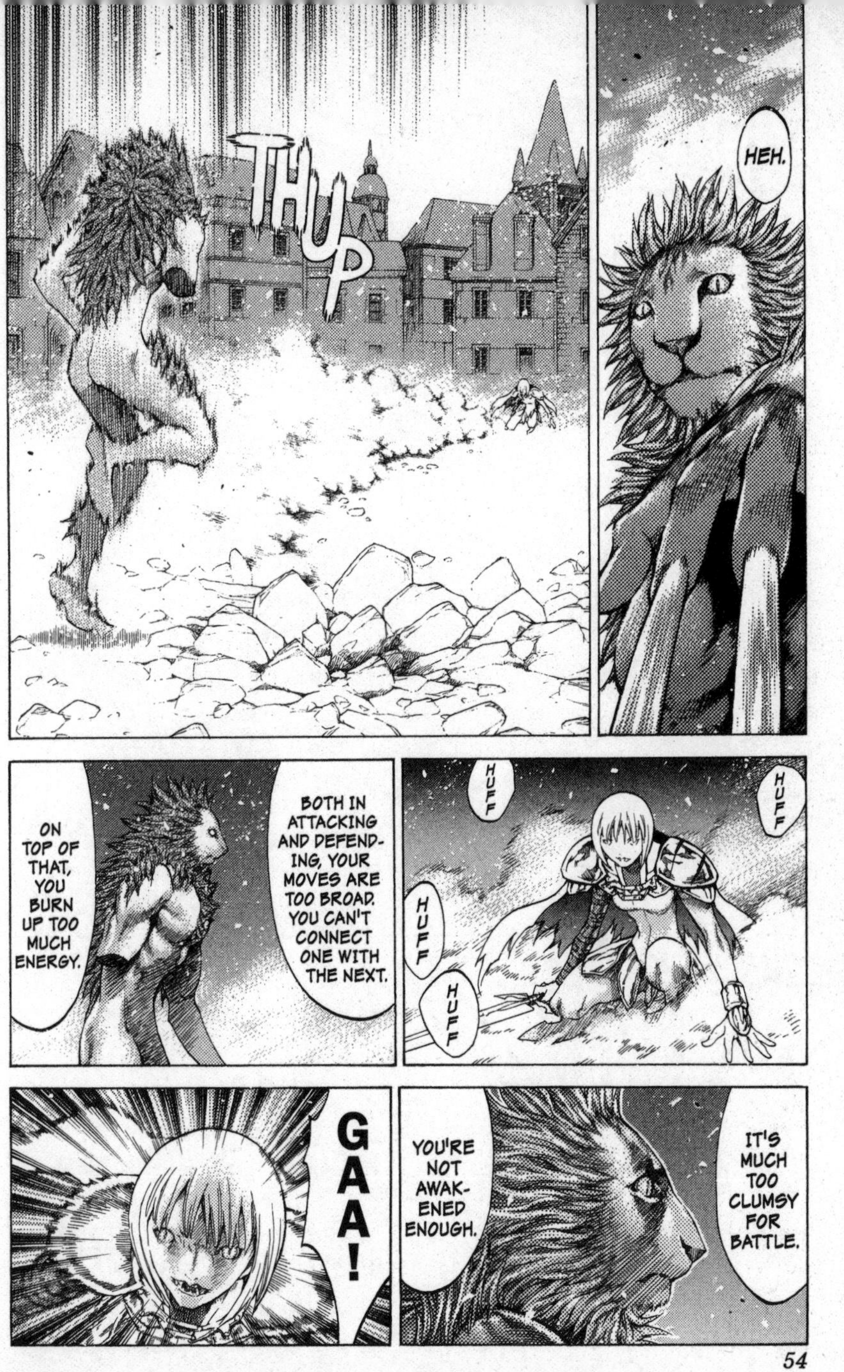
HEH.
THUP
HUFF
HUFF
HUFF
HUFF
BOTH IN ATTACKING AND DEFEND-ING, YOUR MOVES ARE TOO BROAD. YOU CAN'T CONNECT ONE WITH THE NEXT.
ON TOP OF THAT, YOU BURN UP TOO MUCH ENERGY.
IT'S MUCH TOO CLUMSY FOR BATTLE.
YOU'RE NOT AWAK-ENED ENOUGH.
GAA!

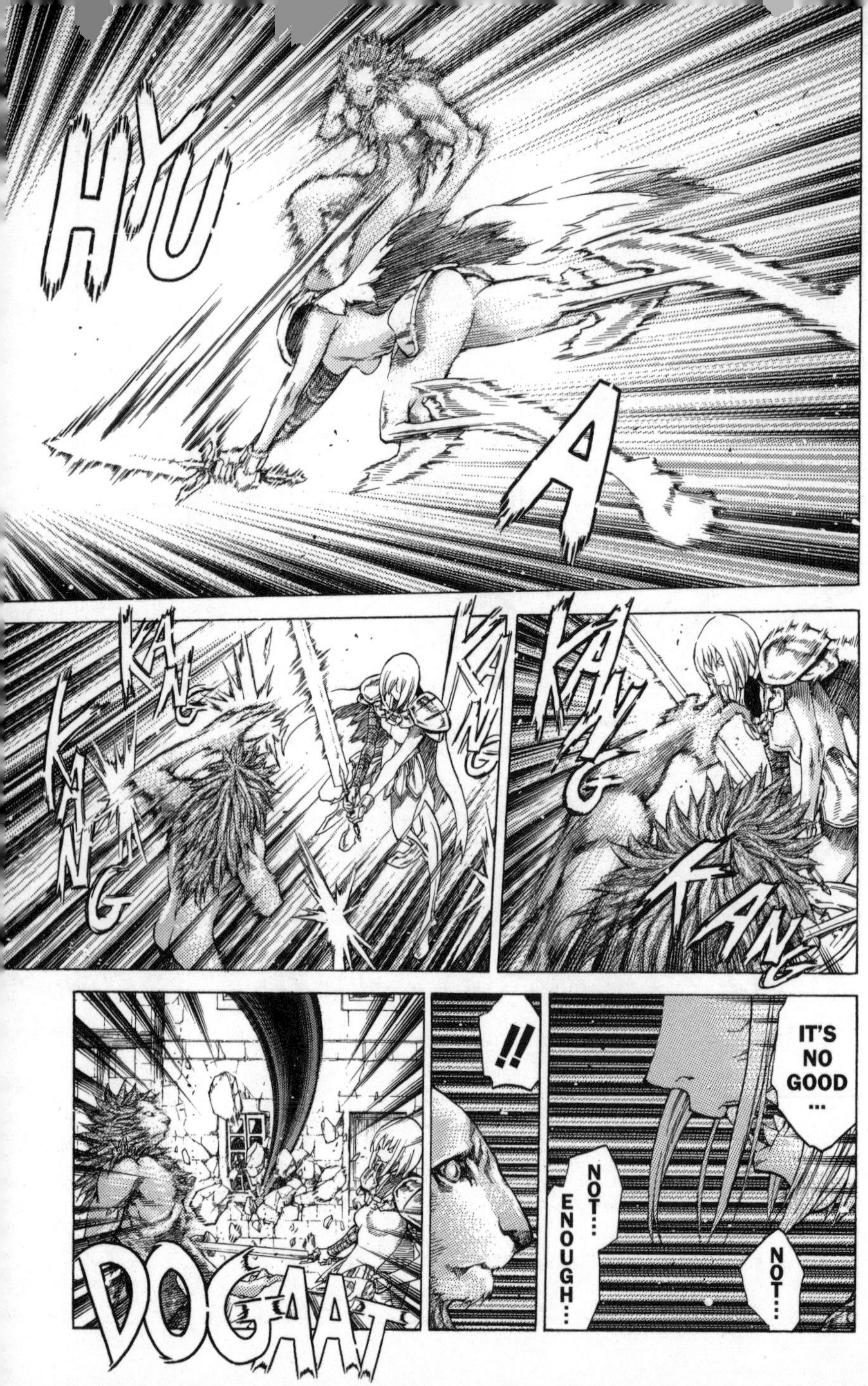
HYU
A
KANG
KANG
KANG
KANG
KANG
IT'S NO GOOD ...
NOT...
NOT... ENOUGH...
!!
DOGAAT

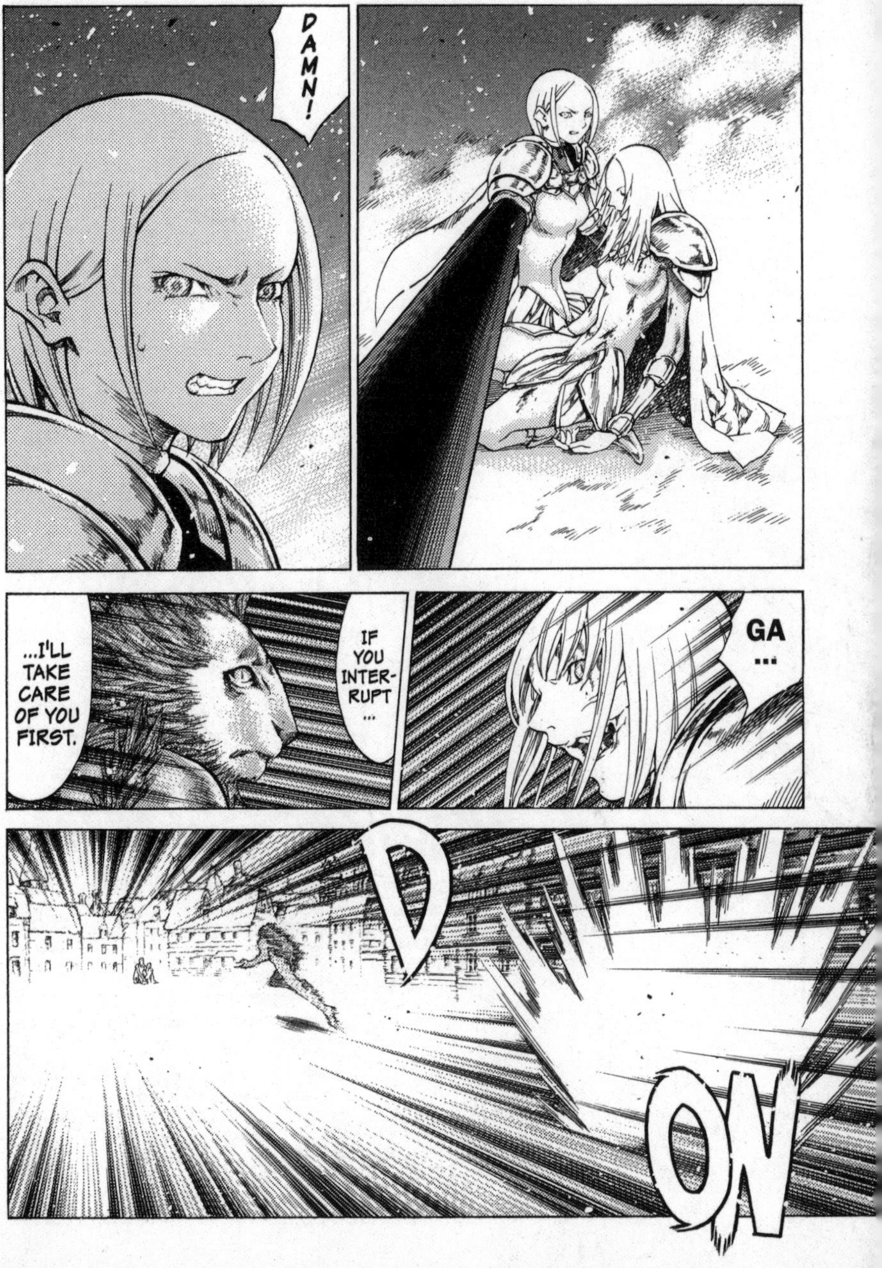
DAMN!
GA ...
IF YOU INTER-RUPT ...
...I'LL TAKE CARE OF YOU FIRST.
DON

READ THIS WAY

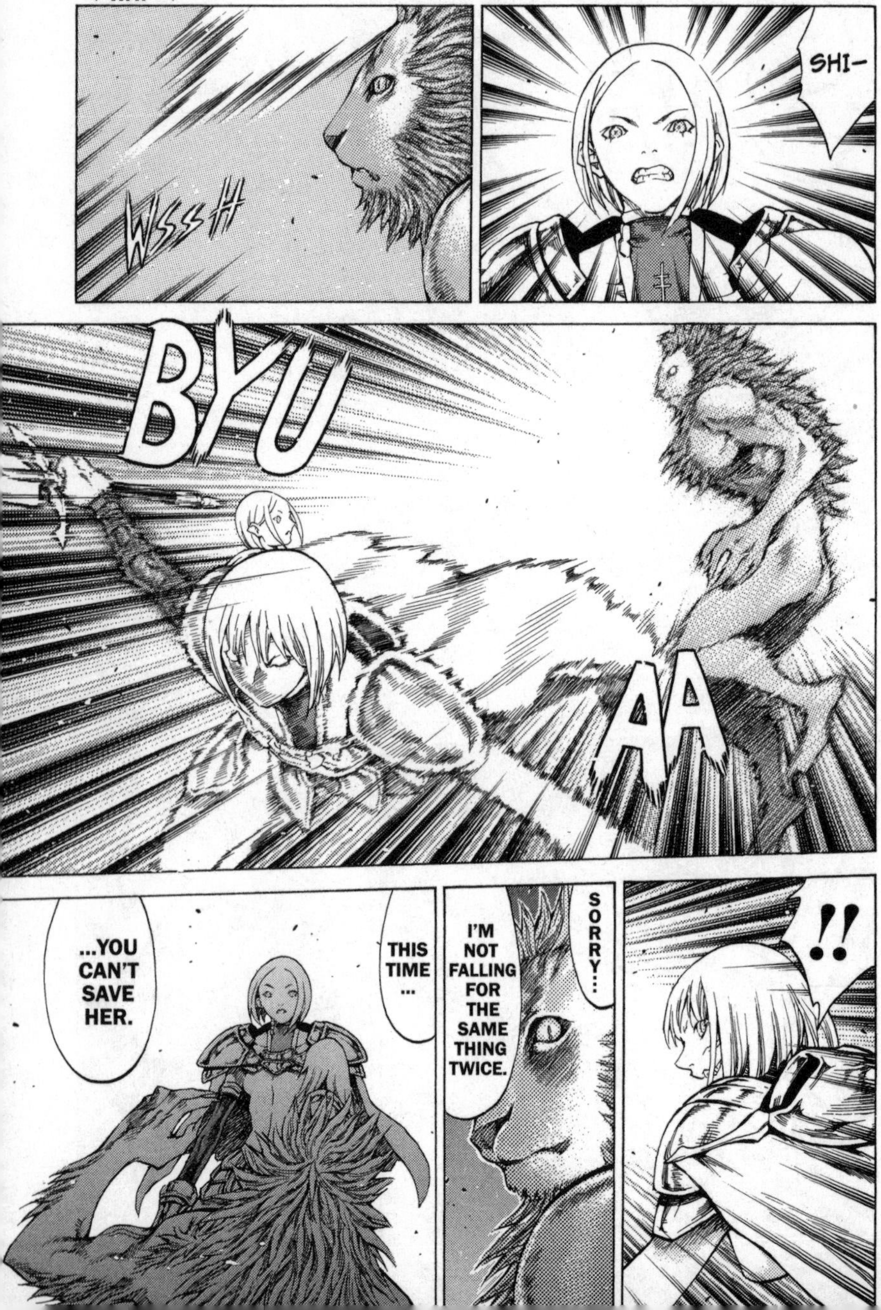
SHI-
WSSSH
BYU
AA
!!
SORRY...
I'M NOT FALLING FOR THE SAME THING TWICE.
THIS TIME ...
...YOU CAN'T SAVE HER.

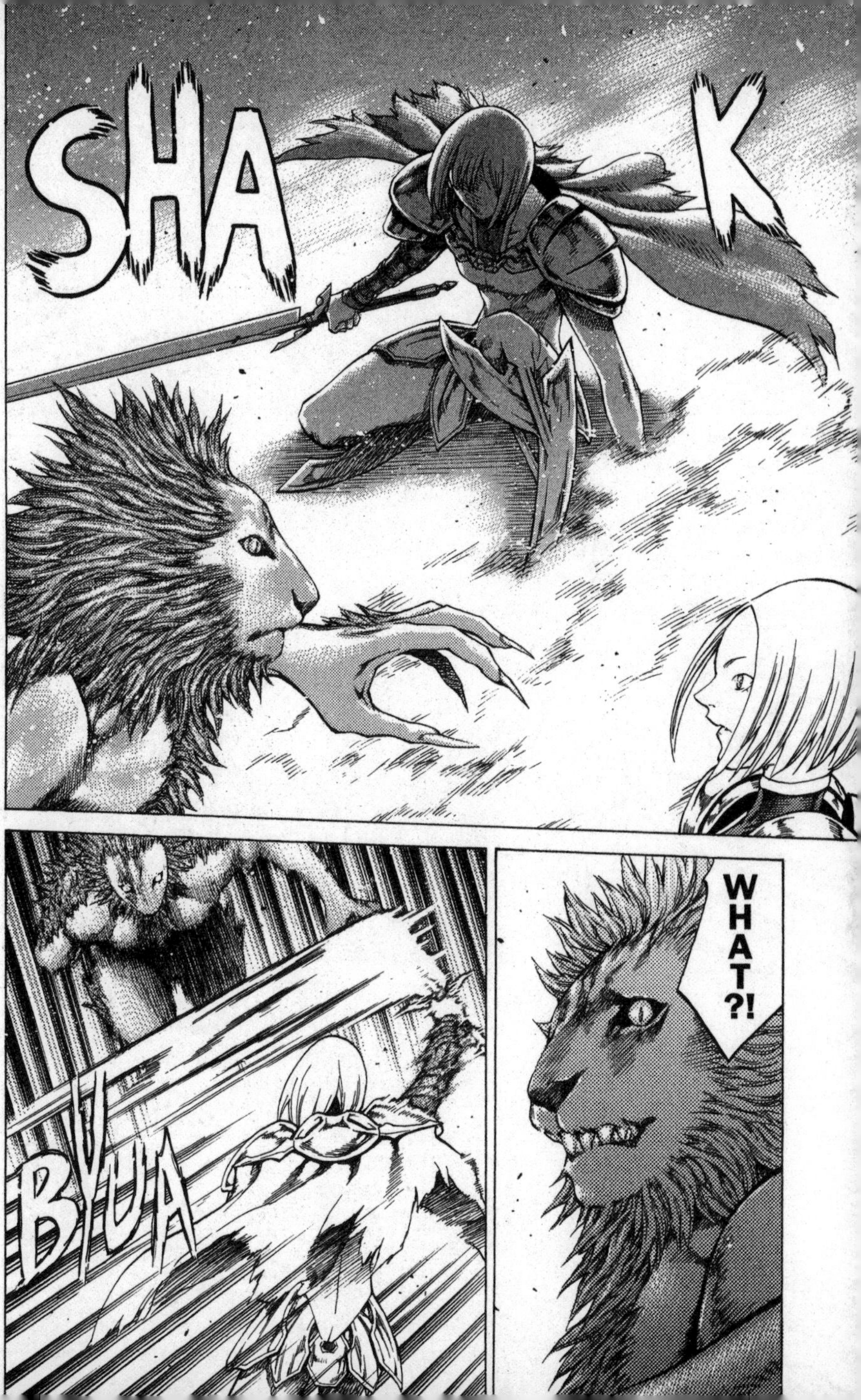
SHAK
WHAT?!
BYUA

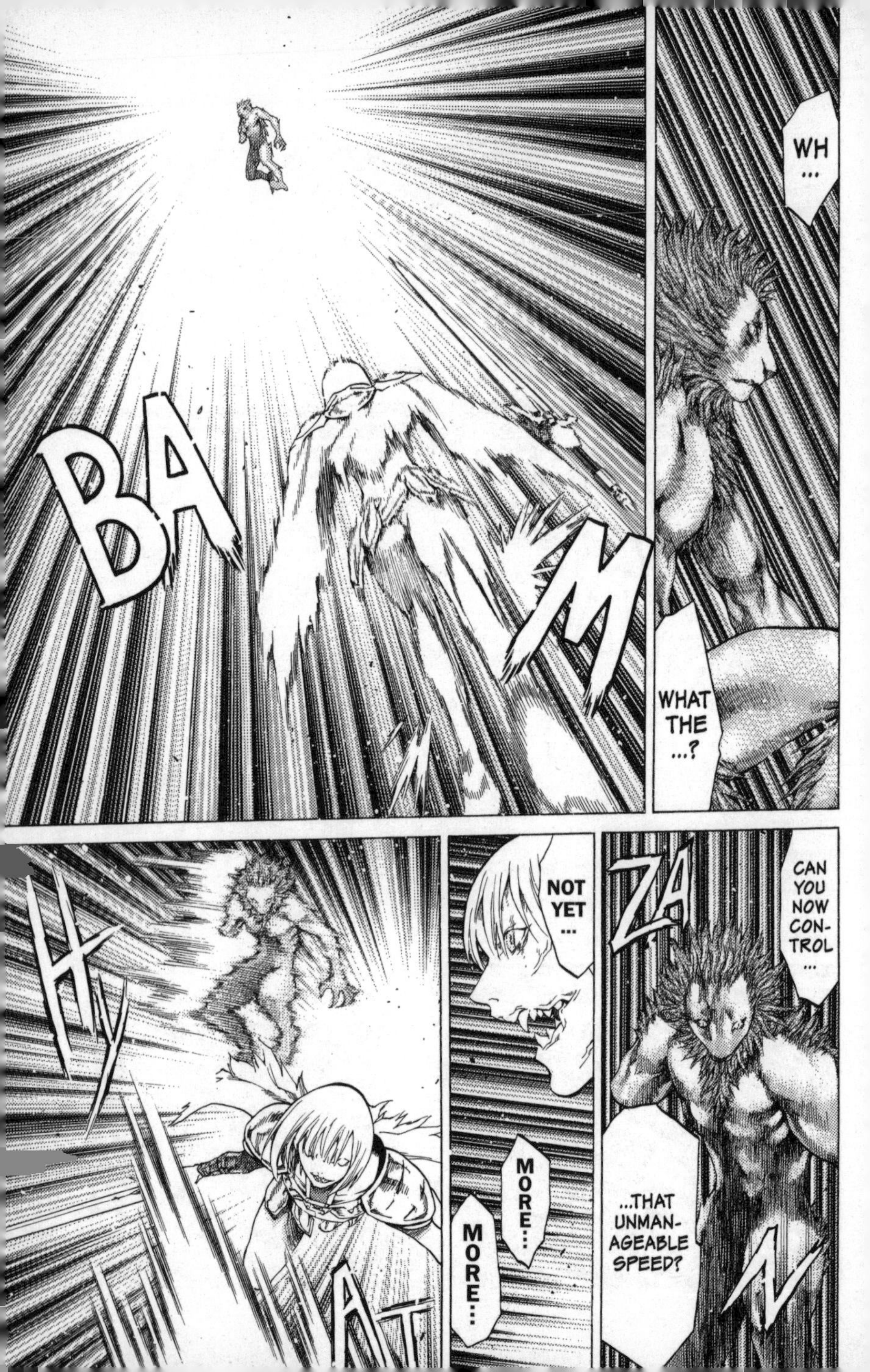
WH...
WHAT THE ...?
BAM
ZAN
CAN YOU NOW CONTROL...
...THAT UNMANAGEABLE SPEED?
NOT YET...
MORE...
MORE...
HYAT

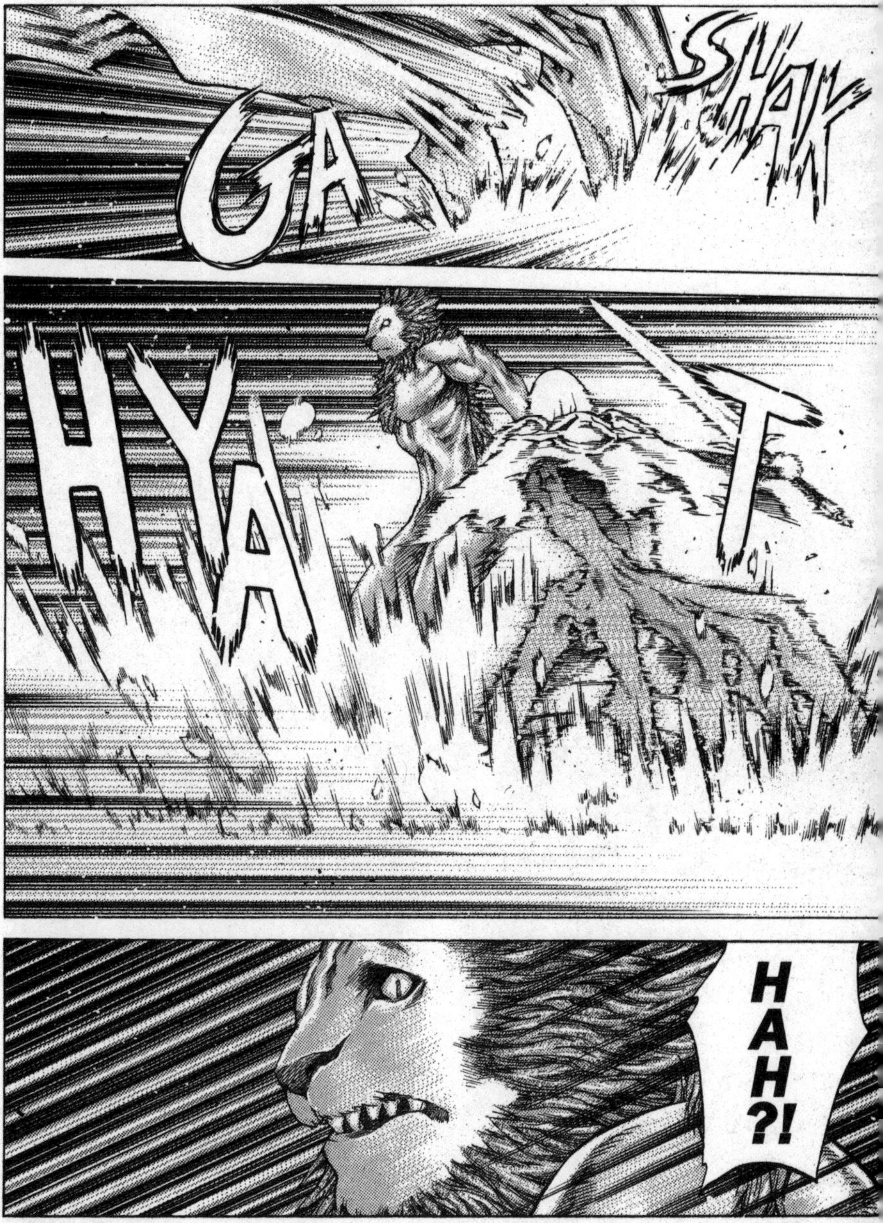
GA
SHAK
HYAAT
HAH?!

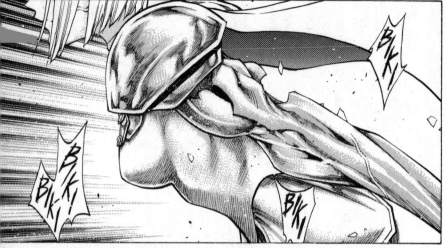

BIKI!

BIKI! BIKI!

BIKI!

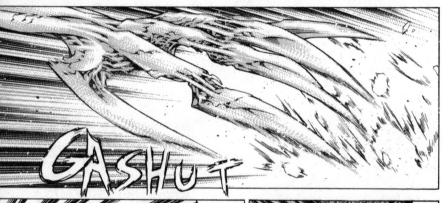

GASHUT

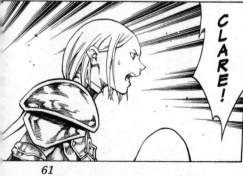

CLARE!

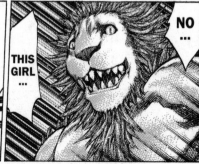

THIS GIRL...

NO...

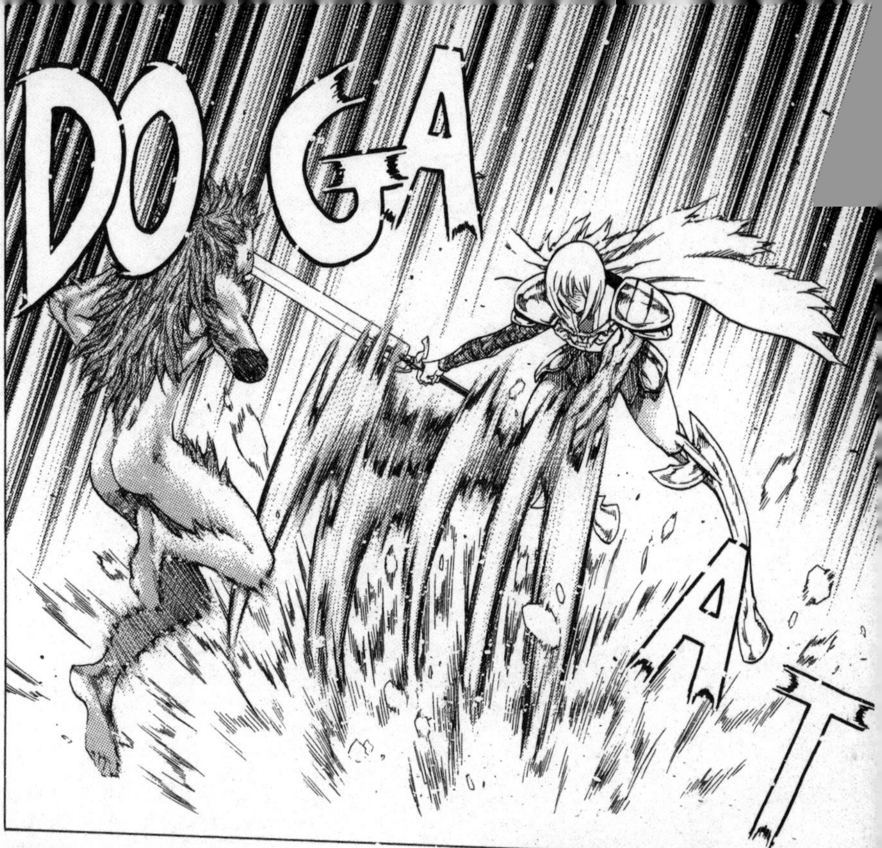
DOGAAT
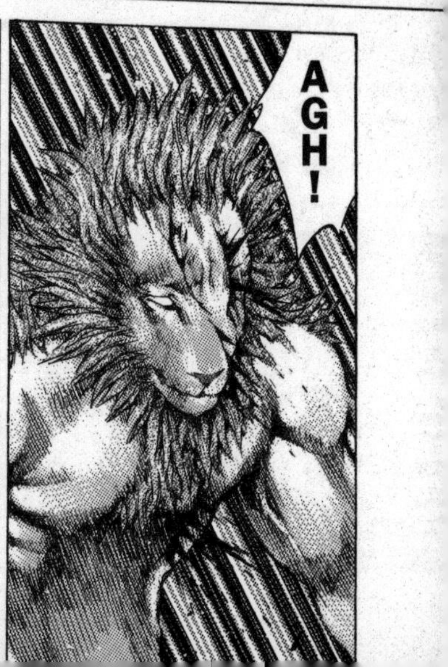
AGH!
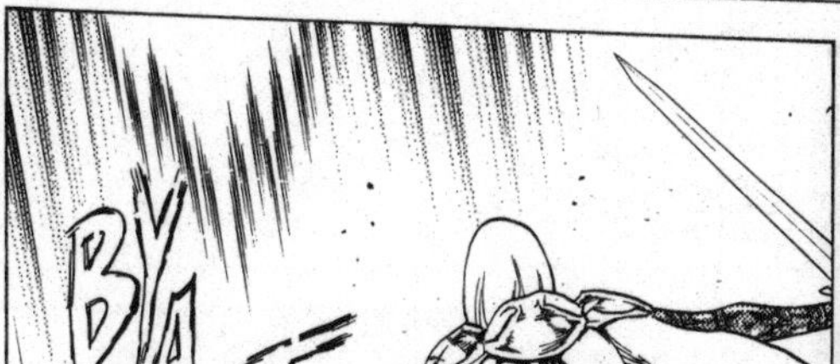
BYAT
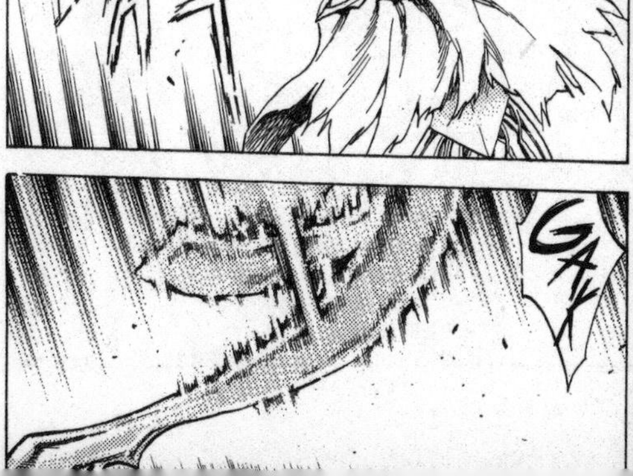
GAK

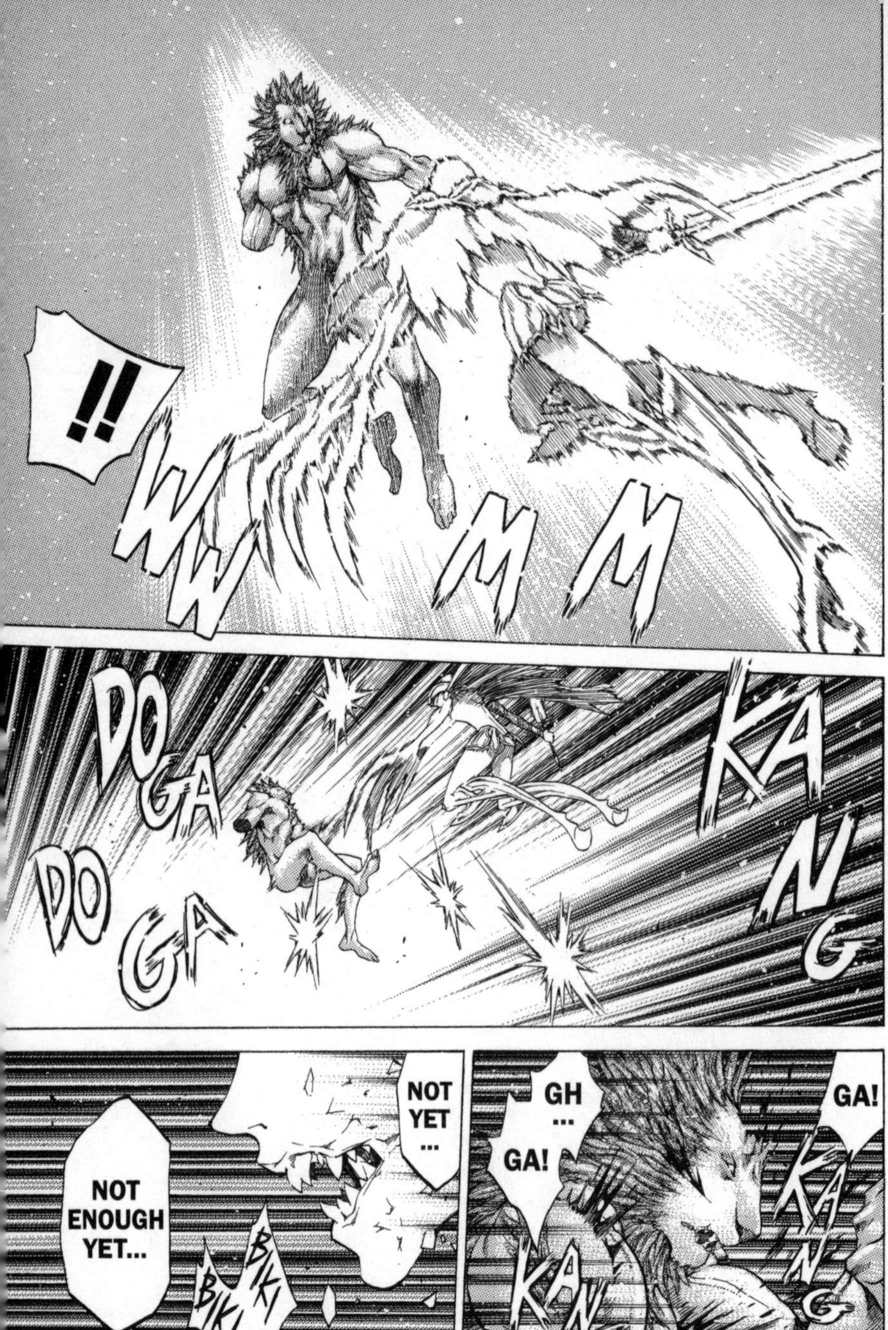
!!
WWWMMM
KANG
DOGA
DOGA
GA!
GH... GA!
KANKANG
KANG
NOT YET...
NOT ENOUGH YET...
BIKI
BIKI

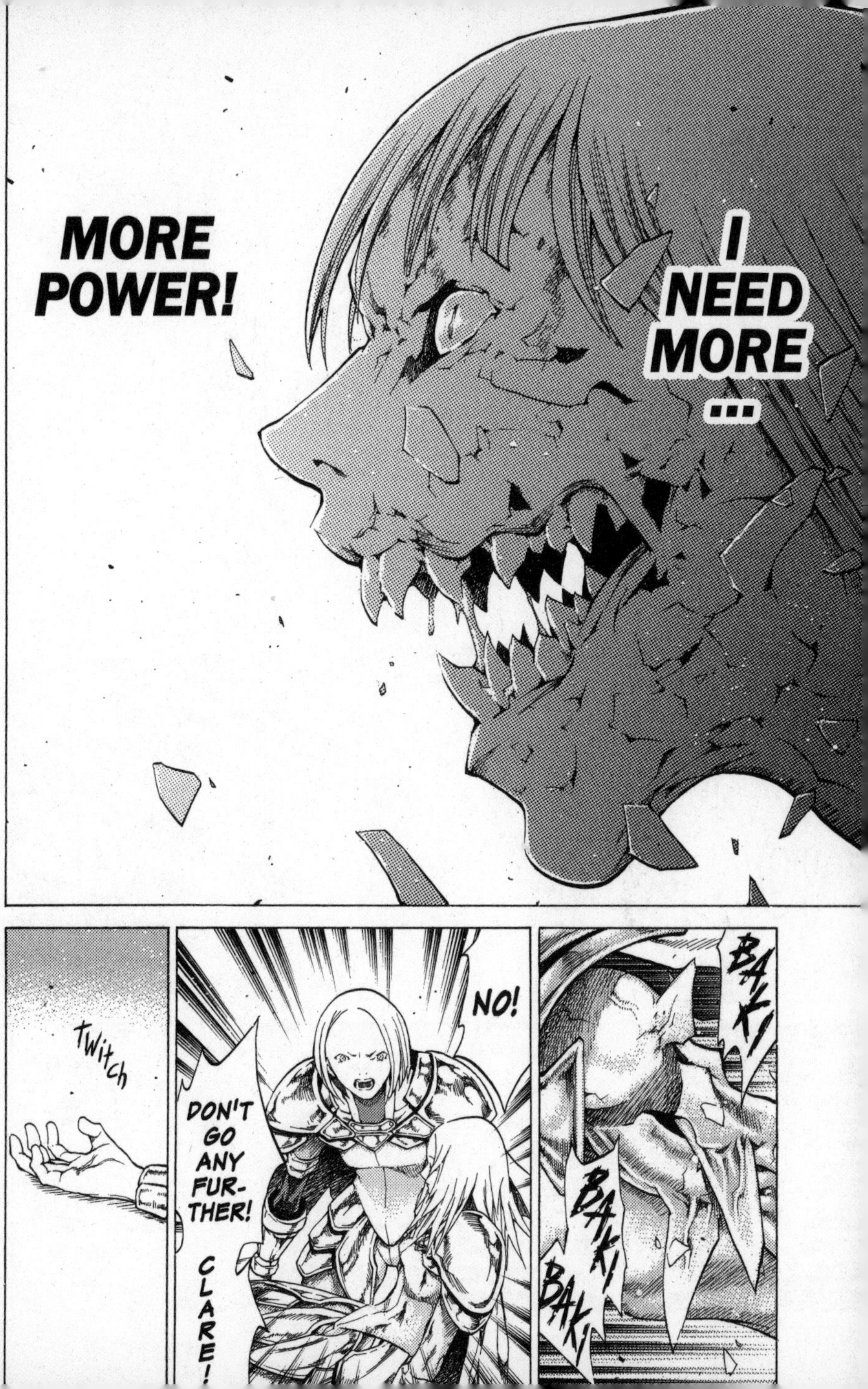
I NEED MORE ...
MORE POWER!
BAKI
BAKI
BAKI
NO!
DON'T GO ANY FUR-THER!
CLARE!
twitch

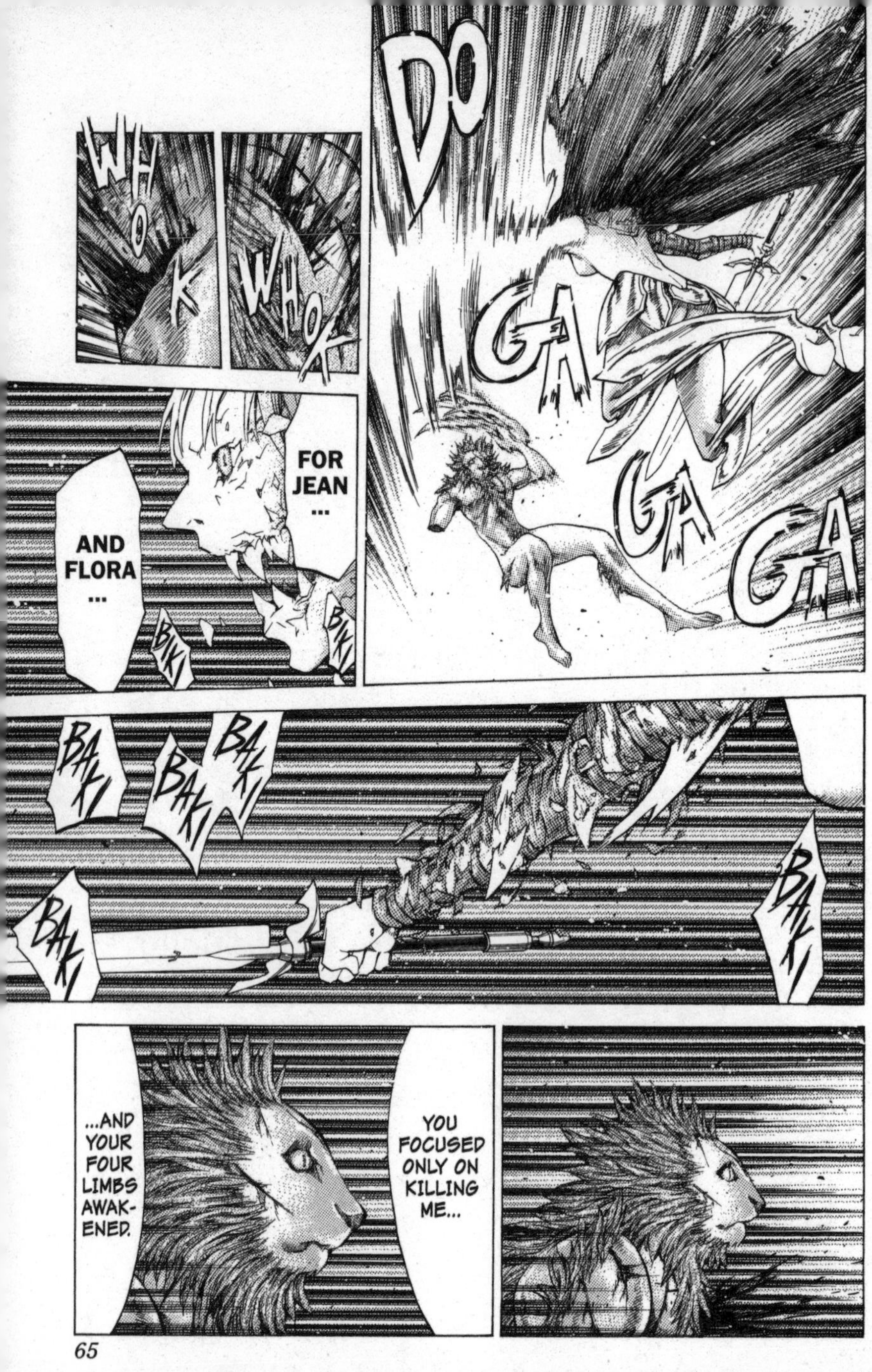
DO
GA
GA
GA
WHOK
WHOK
FOR JEAN ...
AND FLORA ...
BIKI
BIKI
BAKI
BAKI
BAKI
BAKI
BAKI
YOU FOCUSED ONLY ON KILLING ME...
...AND YOUR FOUR LIMBS AWAK-ENED.

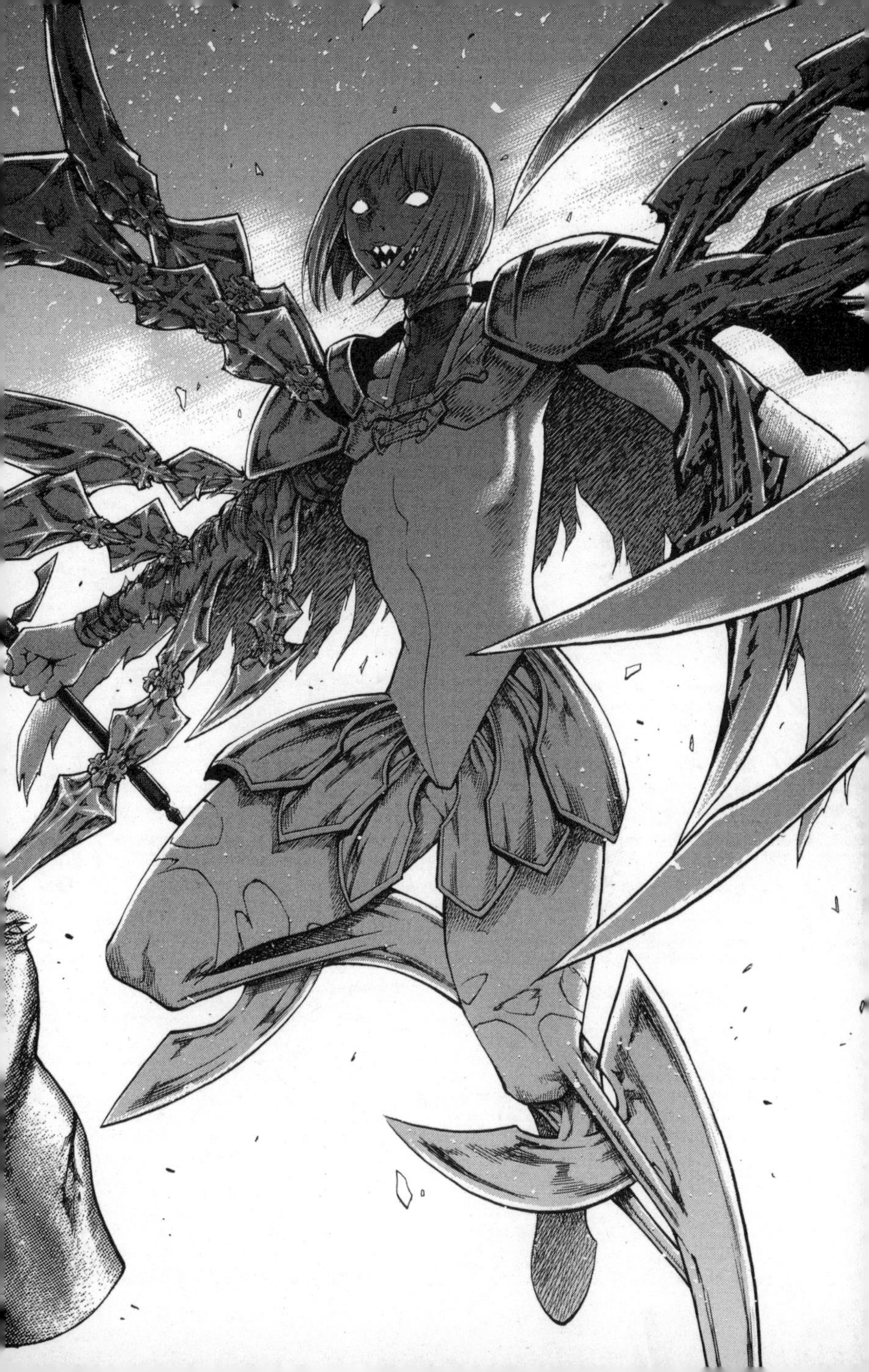

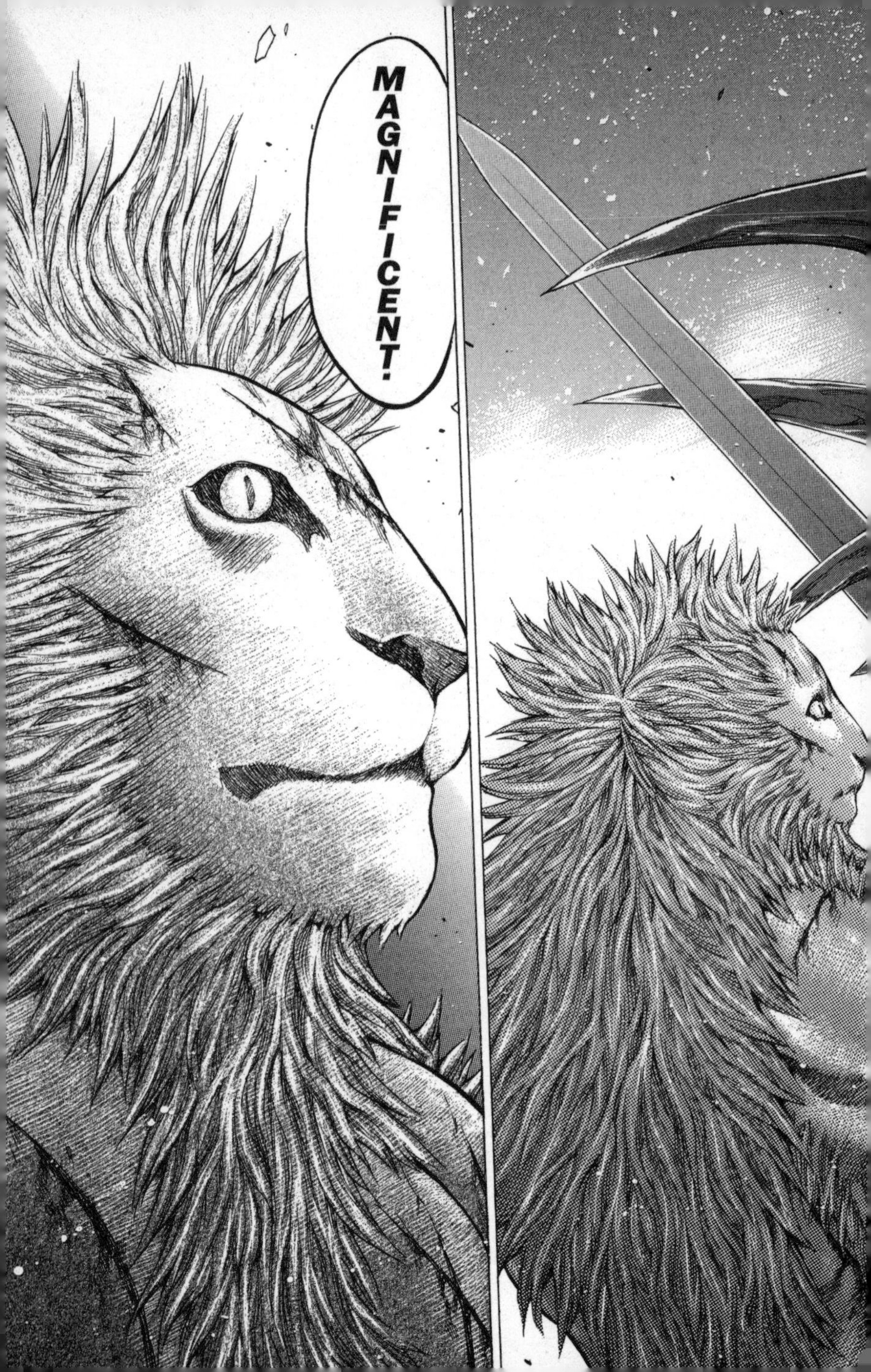
MAGNIFICENT!

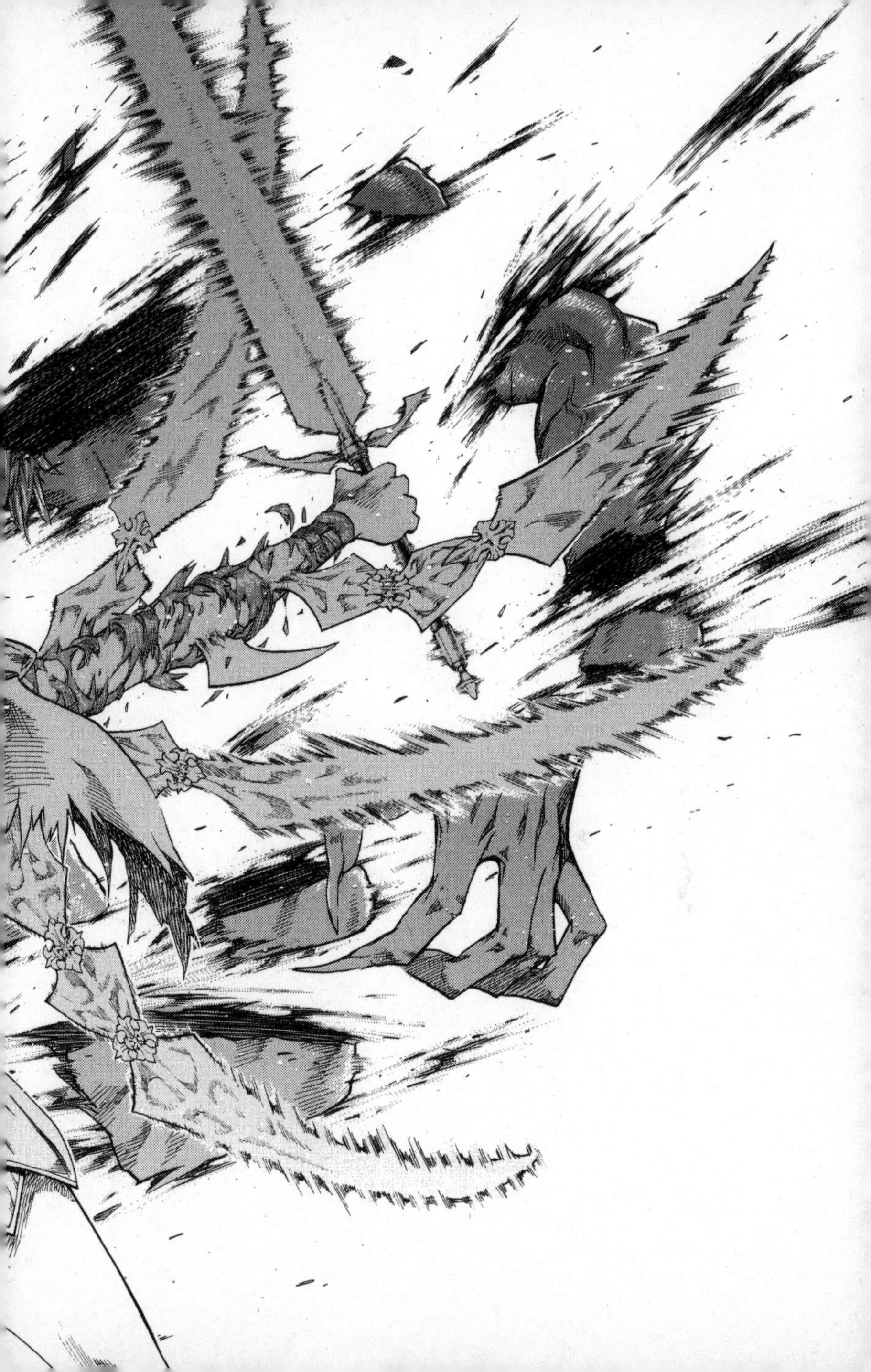

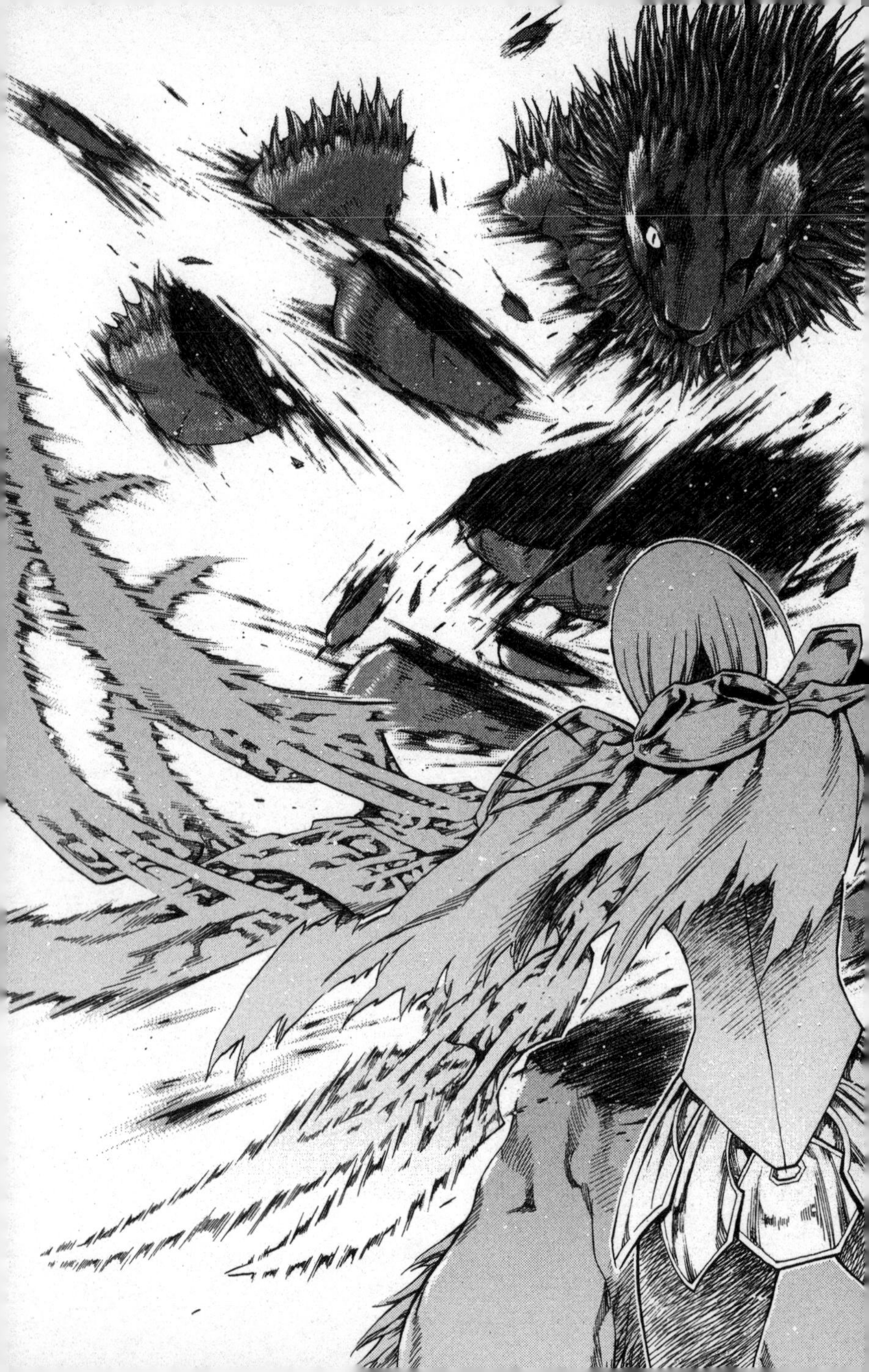

クレイモア
Claymore

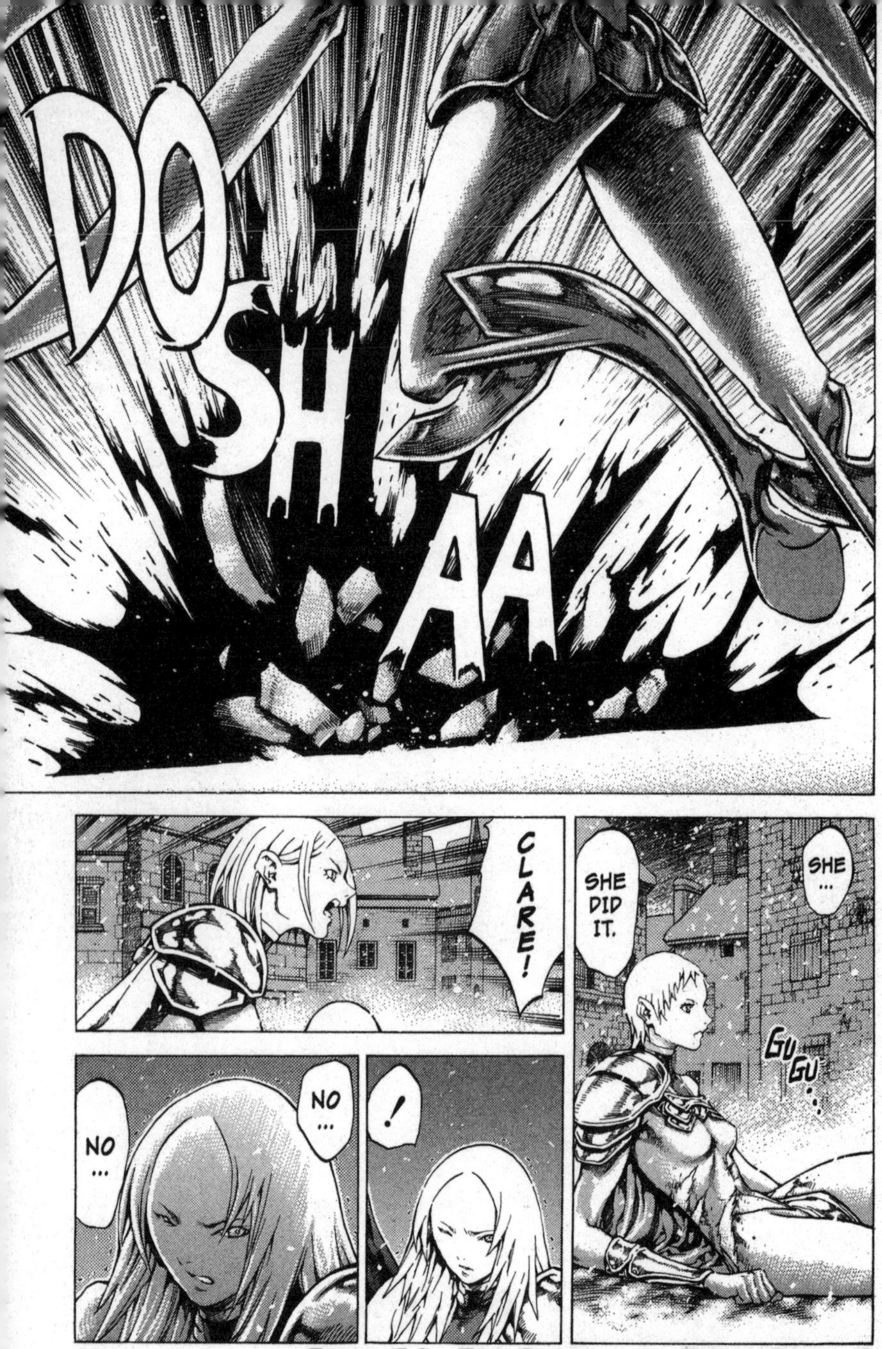
DOSHAA
SHE ...
SHE DID IT.
GUGU ...
CLARE!
!
NO ...
NO ...

Scene 60: The Assault on Pieta, Part 4

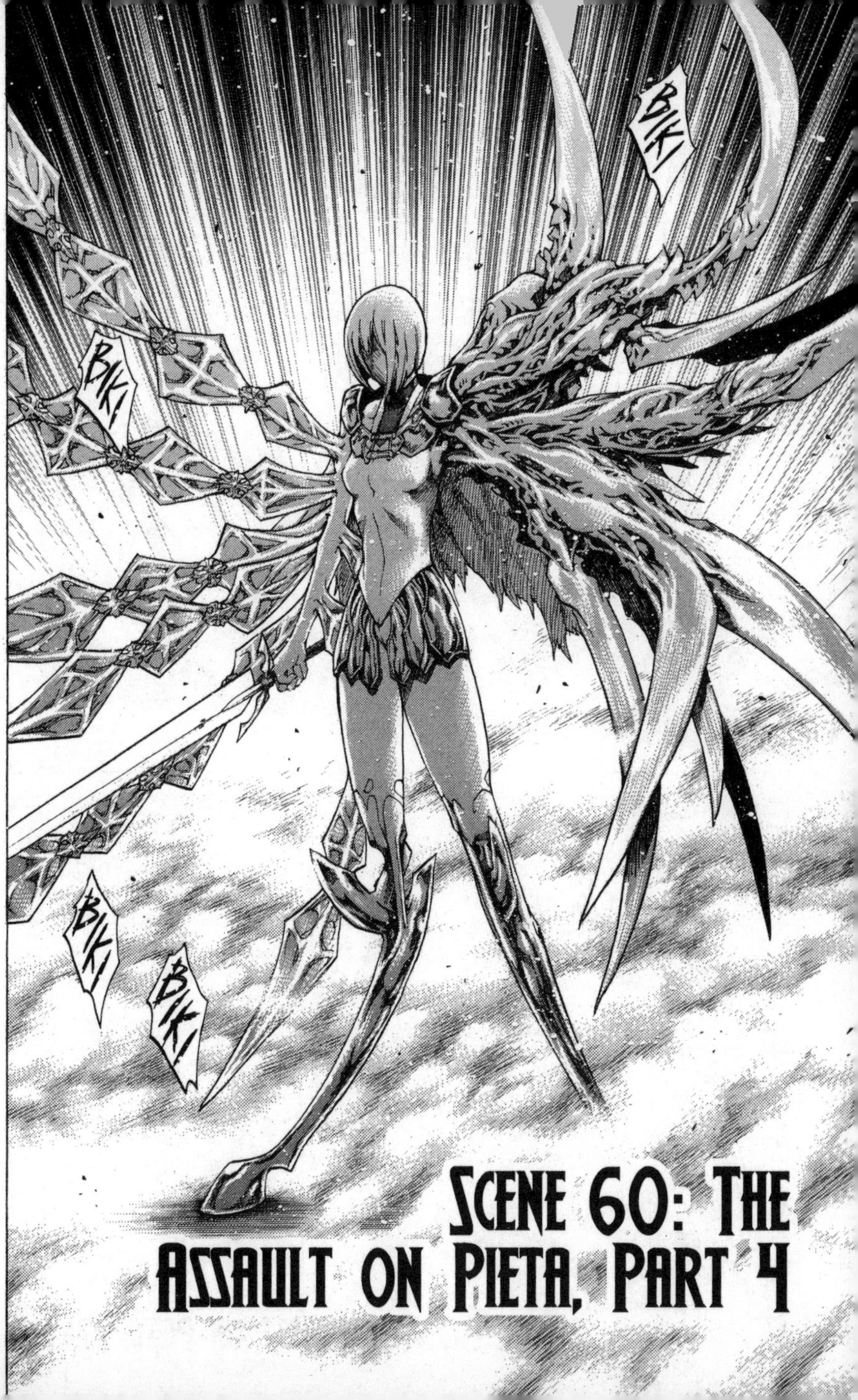
BIKI
BIKI
BIKI
BIKI

Scene 60: The Assault on Pieta, Part 4

READ THIS WAY

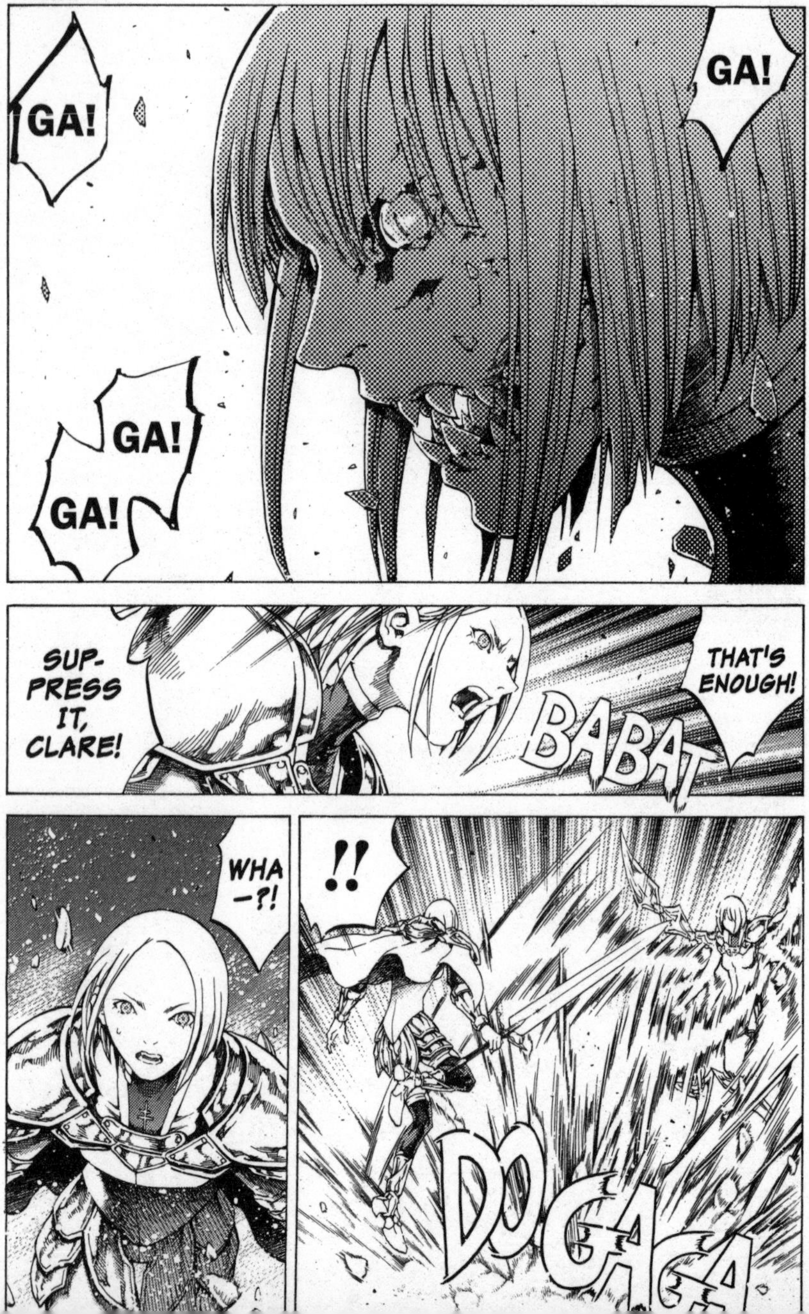
GA!
GA!
GA!
GA!
THAT'S ENOUGH!
BABAT
SUP-PRESS IT, CLARE!
!!
DOGAGA
WHA—?!

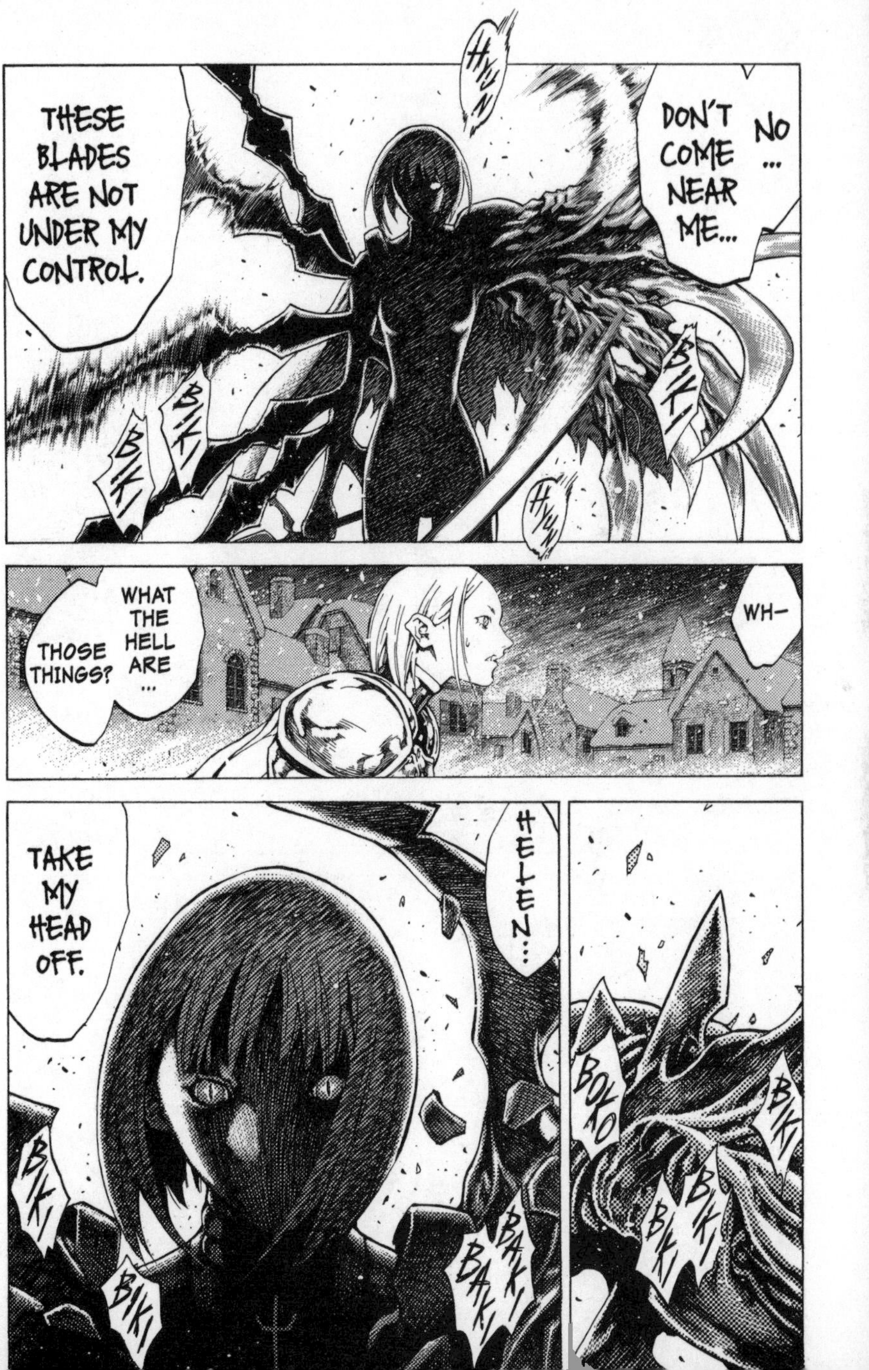
HYUN
NO ...
DON'T COME NEAR ME...
THESE BLADES ARE NOT UNDER MY CONTROL.
BIKI
BIKI
BIKI
HYUN
WH-
WHAT THE HELL ARE ... THOSE THINGS?
BOKO
BIKI
BIKI
BIKI
HELEN...
TAKE MY HEAD OFF.
BAKI
BAKI
BIKI
BIKI

READ THIS WAY

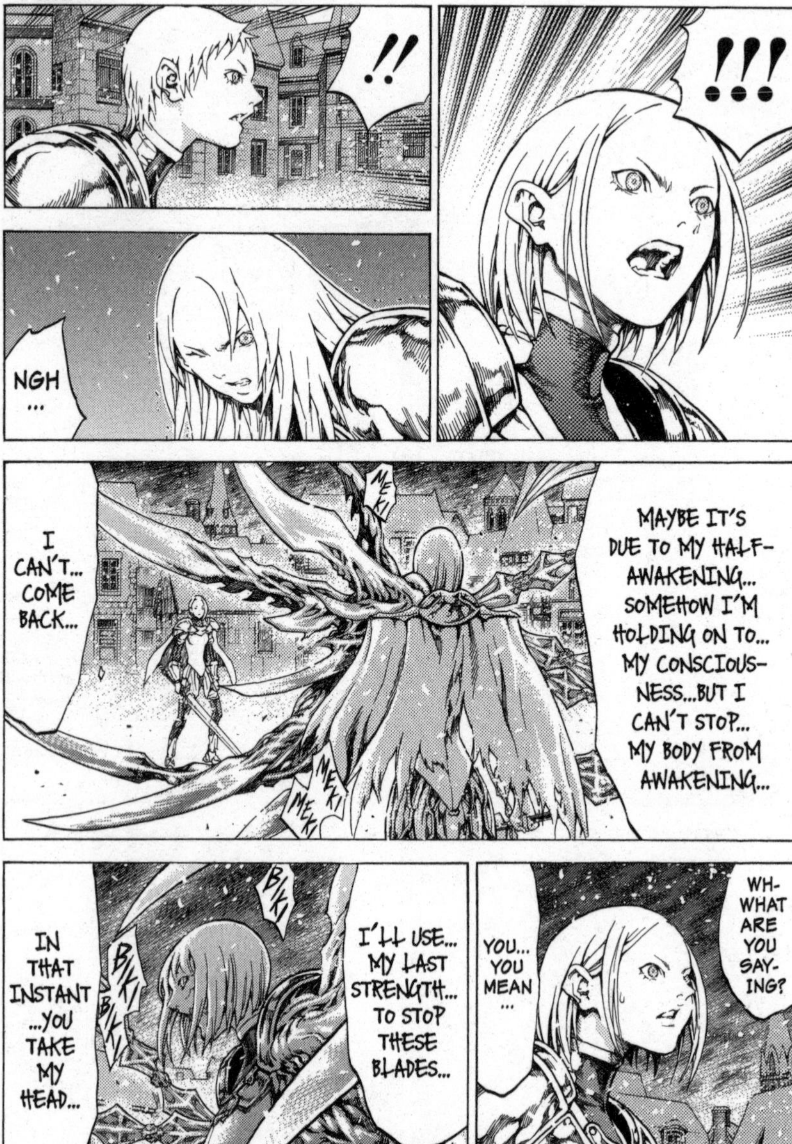
!!!
!!
NGH ...
MAYBE IT'S DUE TO MY HALF-AWAKENING... SOMEHOW I'M HOLDING ON TO... MY CONSCIOUSNESS...BUT I CAN'T STOP... MY BODY FROM AWAKENING...
MEKI
I CAN'T... COME BACK...
MEKI
MEKI
WH-WHAT ARE YOU SAYING?
YOU... YOU MEAN ...
BIKI
I'LL USE... MY LAST STRENGTH... TO STOP THESE BLADES...
BIKI
BIKI
IN THAT INSTANT ...YOU TAKE MY HEAD...
MEKI
MEKI

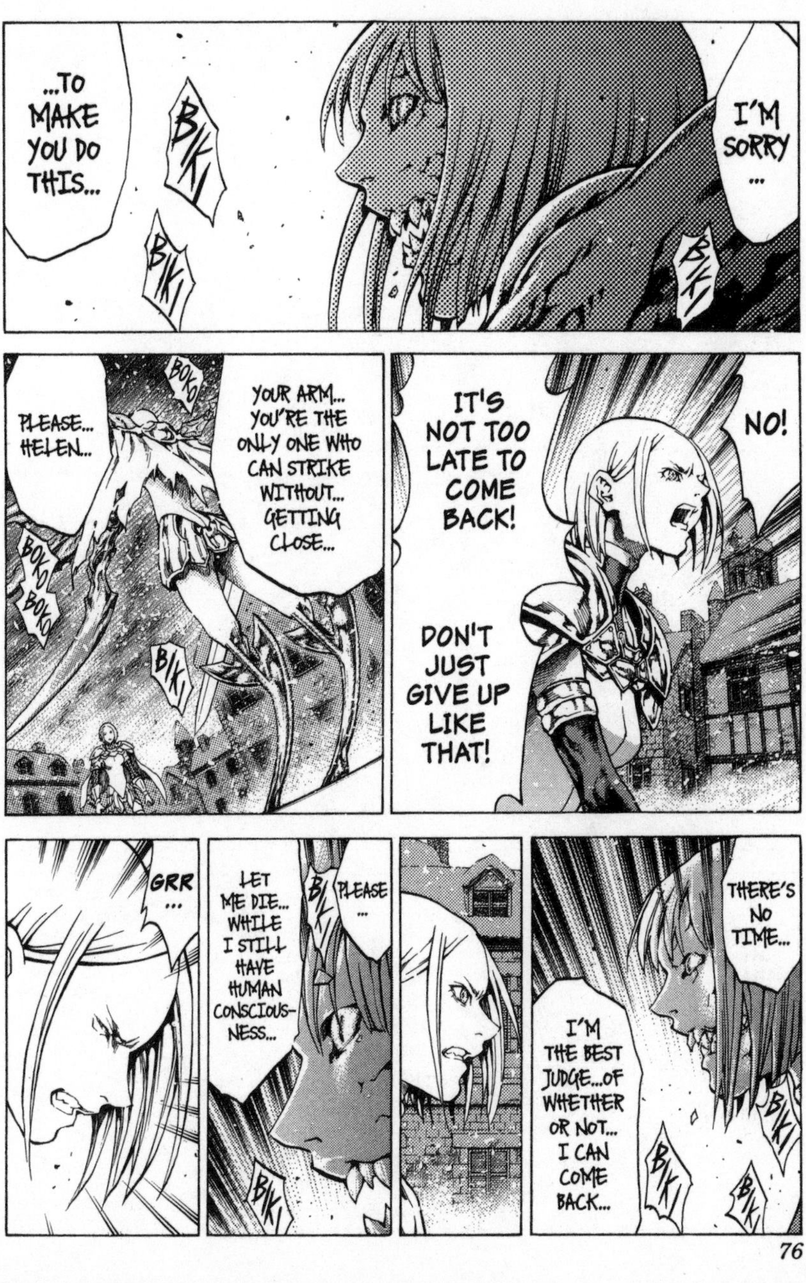
I'M SORRY...
...TO MAKE YOU DO THIS...
BIKI
BIKI
BIKI
NO!
IT'S NOT TOO LATE TO COME BACK!
DON'T JUST GIVE UP LIKE THAT!
BOKO
YOUR ARM... YOU'RE THE ONLY ONE WHO CAN STRIKE WITHOUT... GETTING CLOSE...
PLEASE... HELEN...
BOKO BOKO BOKO
BIKI
THERE'S NO TIME...
I'M THE BEST JUDGE...OF WHETHER OR NOT... I CAN COME BACK...
BIKI
BIKI
BIKI
PLEASE...
BIKI
LET ME DIE... WHILE I STILL HAVE HUMAN CONSCIOUSNESS...
BIKI
GRR...

« READ THIS WAY «

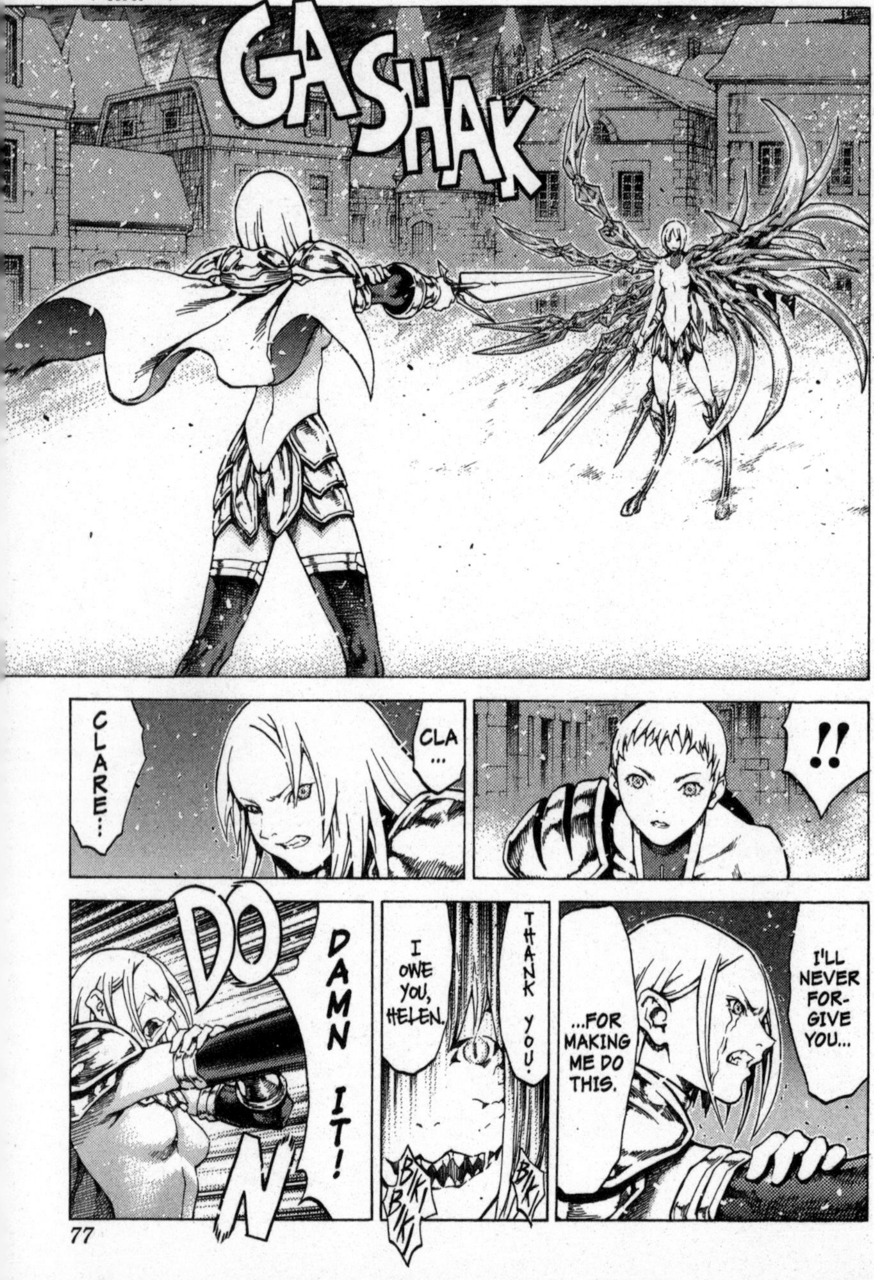

GASHAK
!!
CLA...
CLARE...
I'LL NEVER FOR-GIVE YOU...
...FOR MAKING ME DO THIS.
THANK YOU.
I OWE YOU, HELEN.
BIKI
BIKI BIKI
DAMN IT!
DOON

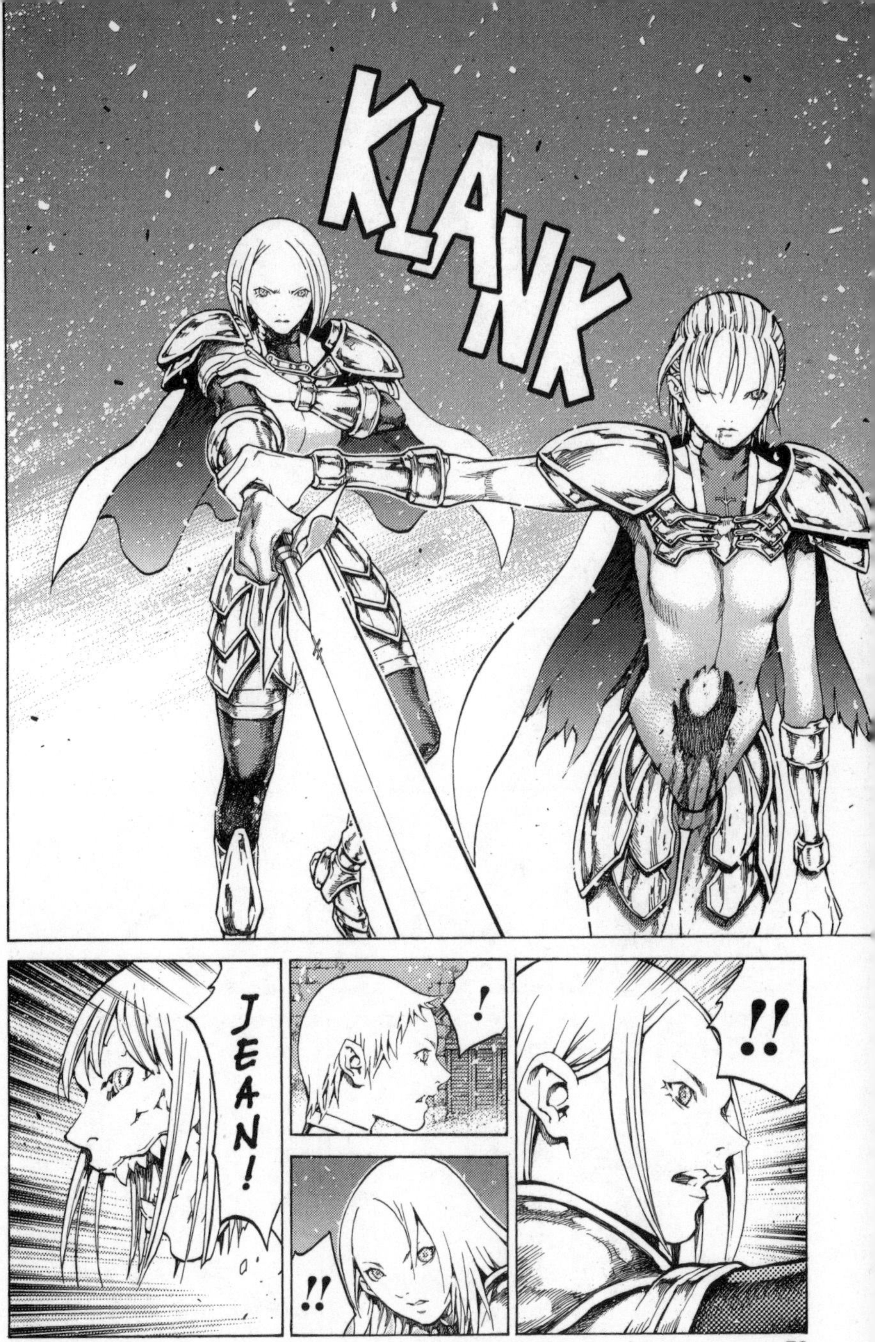
KLANK
!!
!
!!
JEAN!

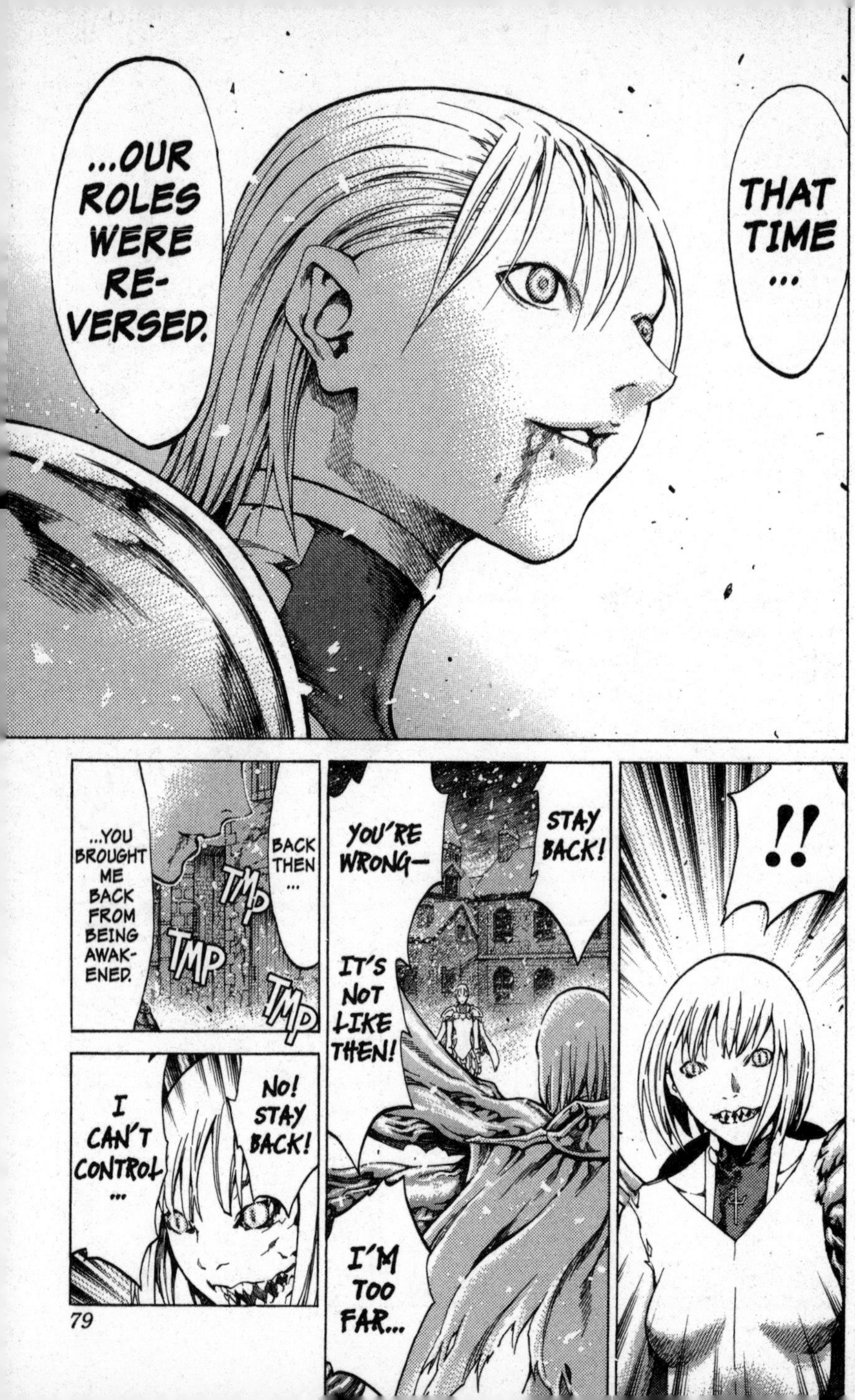
THAT TIME...
...OUR ROLES WERE RE-VERSED.
!!
STAY BACK!
YOU'RE WRONG—
IT'S NOT LIKE THEN!
I'M TOO FAR...
BACK THEN...
...YOU BROUGHT ME BACK FROM BEING AWAK-ENED.
TMP
TMP
TMP
NO! STAY BACK!
I CAN'T CONTROL...

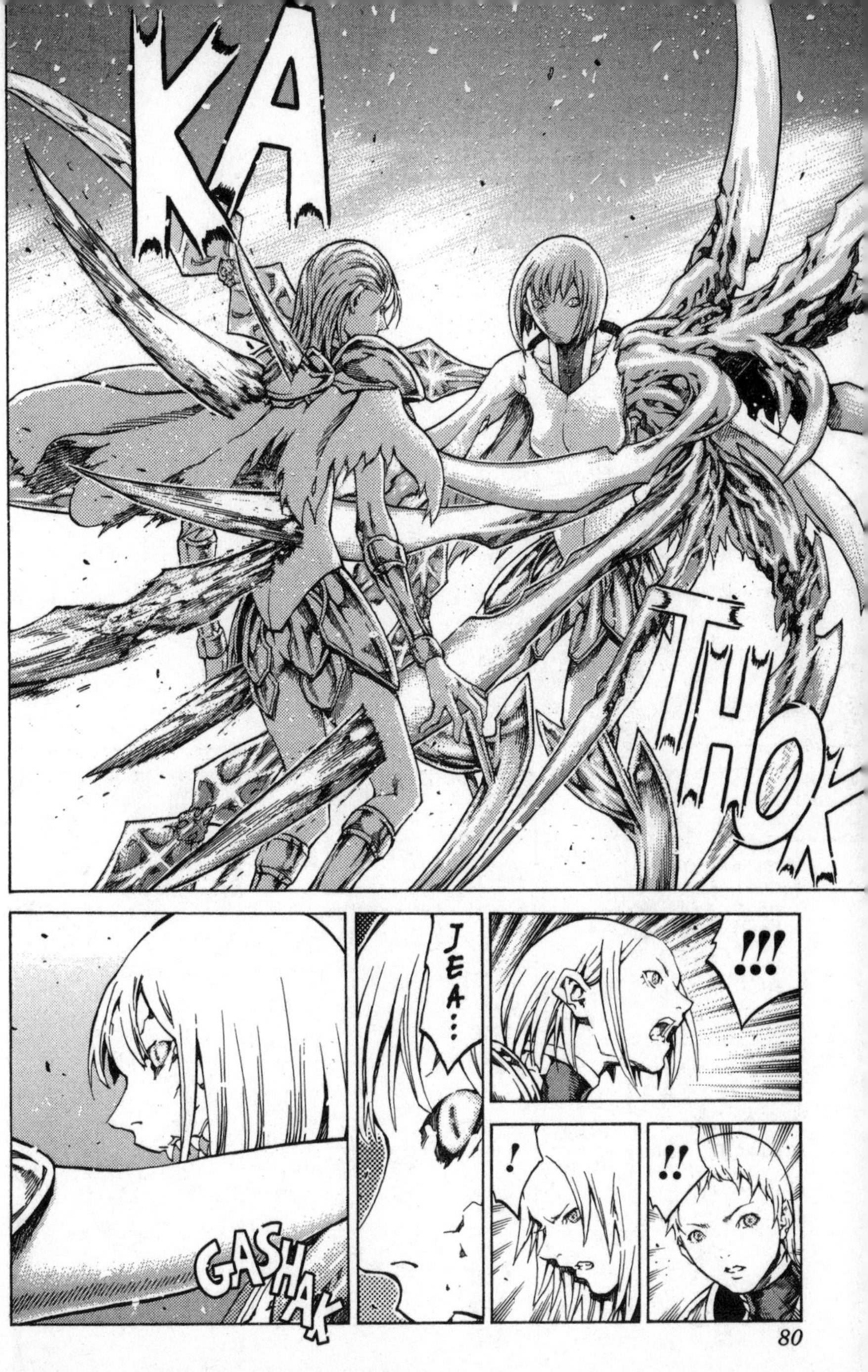
KA
THOK
!!!
!!
!
JEA...
GASHAK

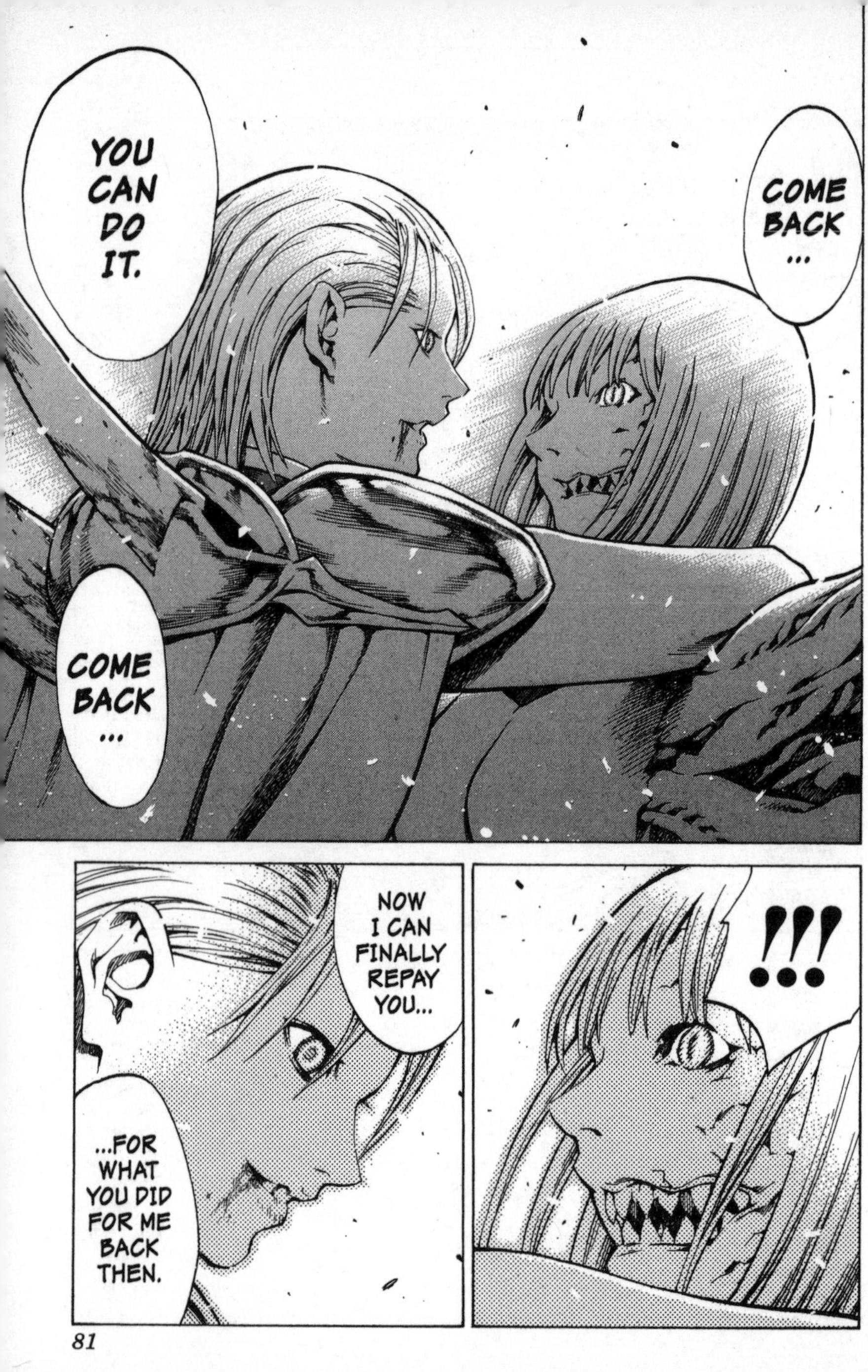
COME BACK ...
YOU CAN DO IT.
COME BACK ...
!!!
NOW I CAN FINALLY REPAY YOU...
...FOR WHAT YOU DID FOR ME BACK THEN.

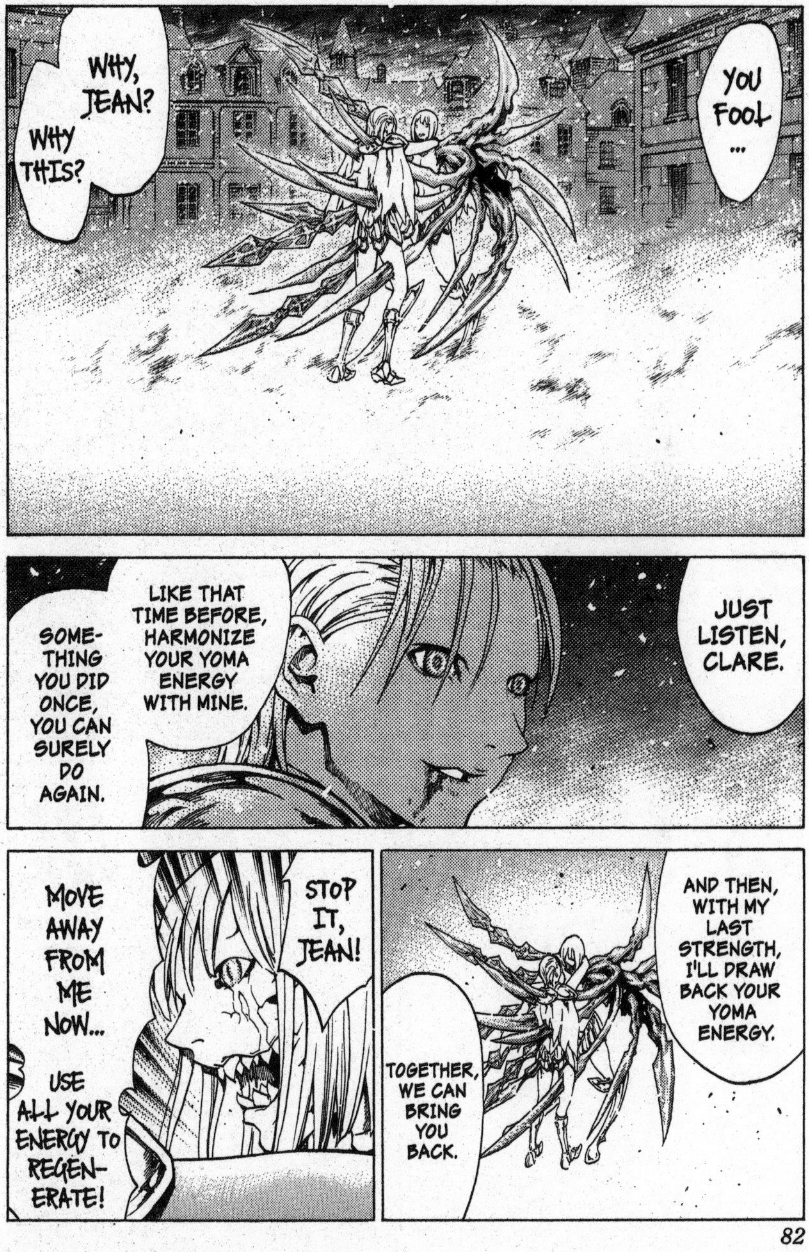
YOU FOOL ...
WHY, JEAN?
WHY THIS?
JUST LISTEN, CLARE.
LIKE THAT TIME BEFORE, HARMONIZE YOUR YOMA ENERGY WITH MINE.
SOME-THING YOU DID ONCE, YOU CAN SURELY DO AGAIN.
AND THEN, WITH MY LAST STRENGTH, I'LL DRAW BACK YOUR YOMA ENERGY.
TOGETHER, WE CAN BRING YOU BACK.
STOP IT, JEAN!
MOVE AWAY FROM ME NOW...
USE ALL YOUR ENERGY TO REGEN-ERATE!

READ THIS WAY

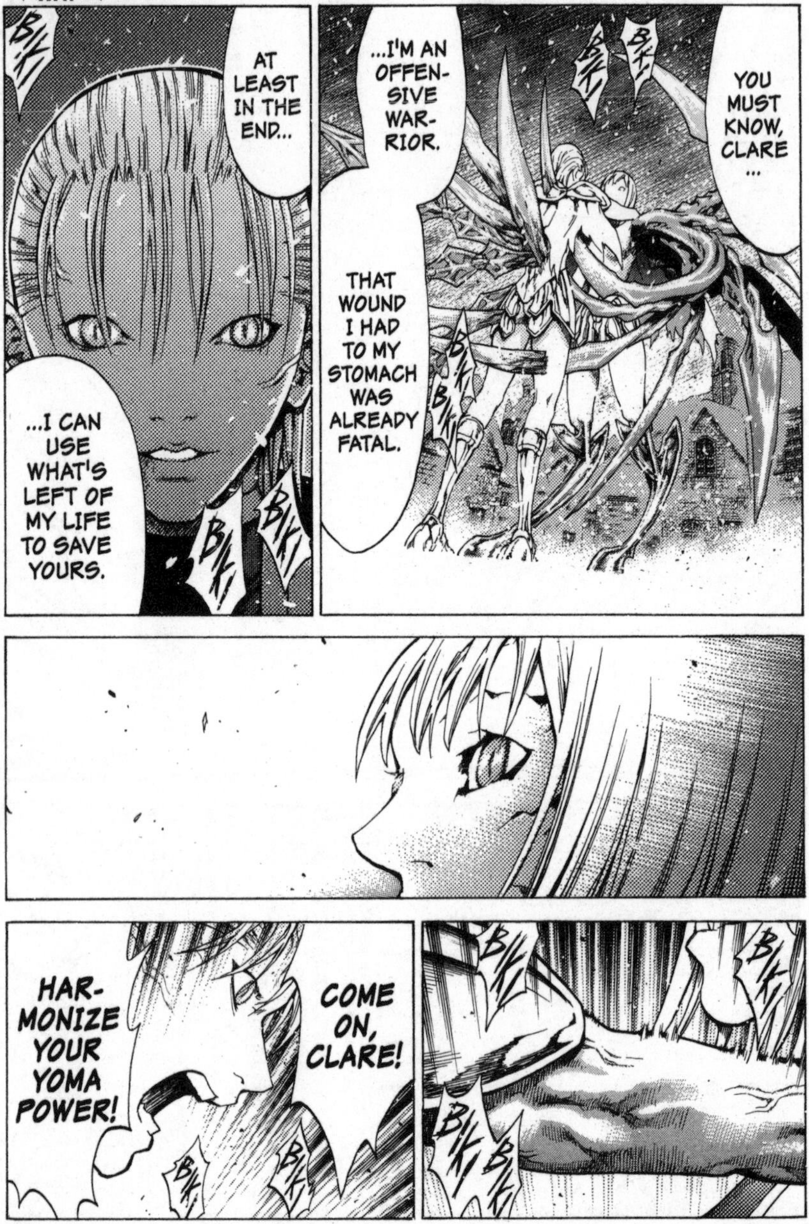
YOU MUST KNOW, CLARE ...
BIKI
BIKI
...I'M AN OFFEN-SIVE WAR-RIOR.
THAT WOUND I HAD TO MY STOMACH WAS ALREADY FATAL.
BIKI
BIKI
AT LEAST IN THE END...
BIKI
...I CAN USE WHAT'S LEFT OF MY LIFE TO SAVE YOURS.
BIKI
BIKI
BIKI
BIKI
BIKI
BIKI
COME ON, CLARE!
HAR-MONIZE YOUR YOMA POWER!
BIKI
BIKI

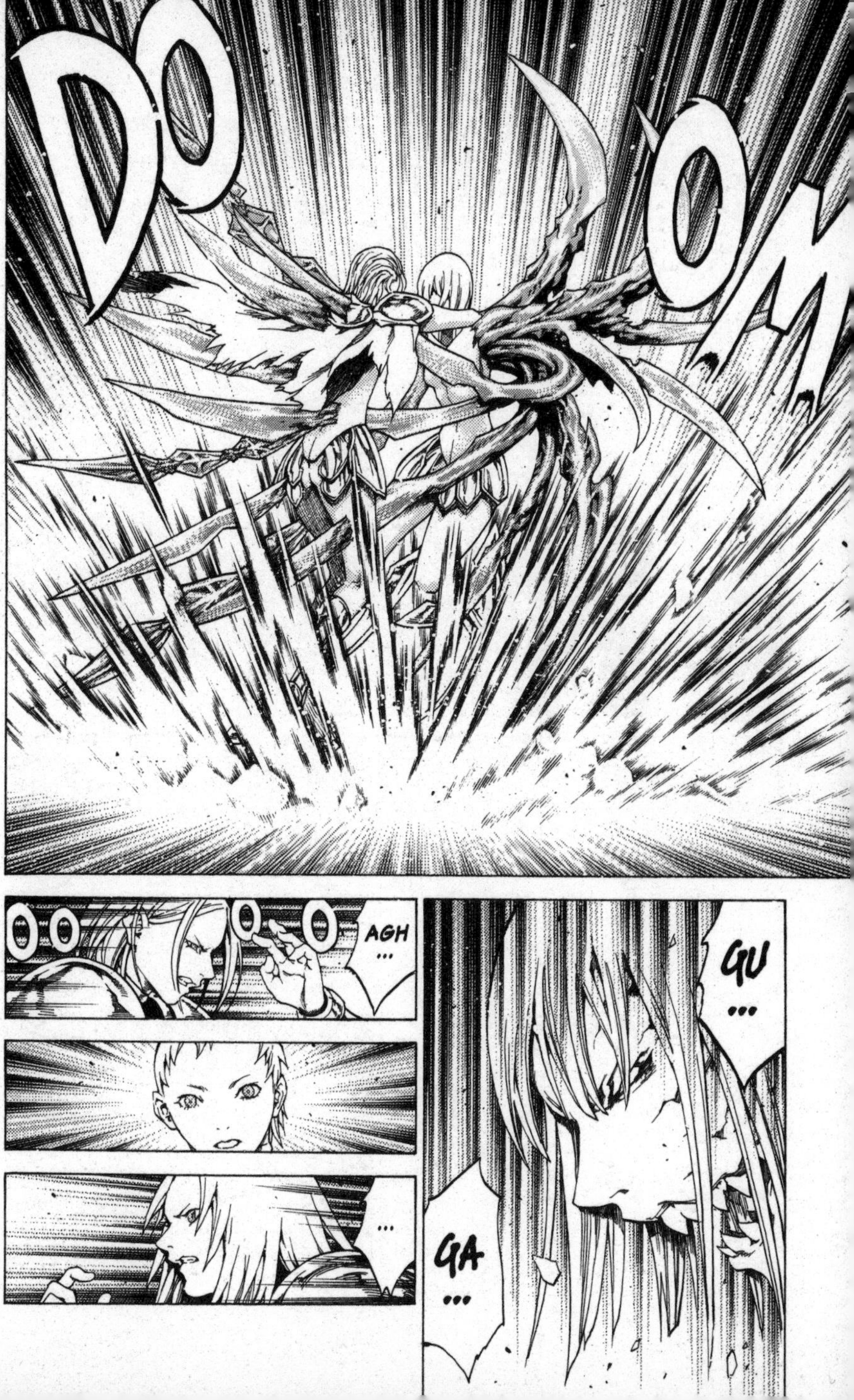
DOOM
GU...
GA...
AGH...
...

READ THIS WAY

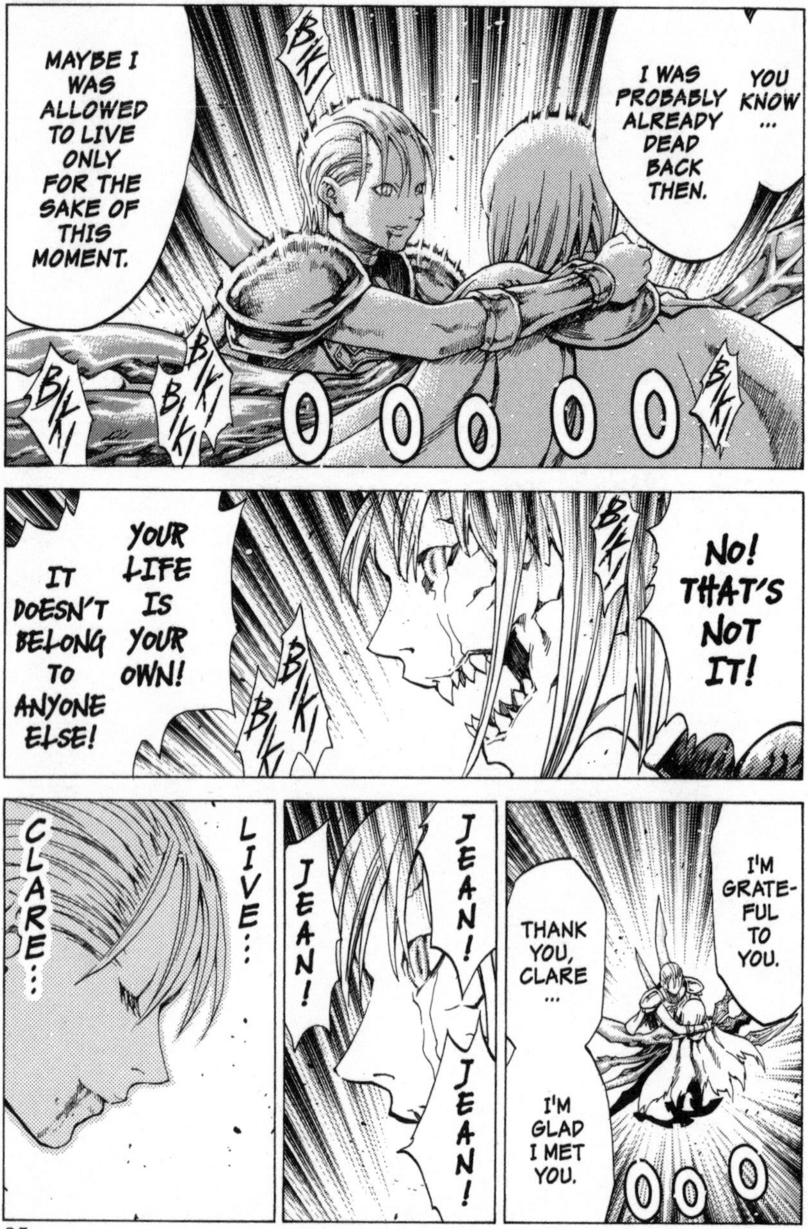

YOU KNOW ...
I WAS PROBABLY ALREADY DEAD BACK THEN.
MAYBE I WAS ALLOWED TO LIVE ONLY FOR THE SAKE OF THIS MOMENT.
BIKI
BIKI
BIKI
BIKI
OOOOO
BIKI
NO! THAT'S NOT IT!
BIKI
BIKI
YOUR LIFE IS YOUR OWN!
IT DOESN'T BELONG TO ANYONE ELSE!
I'M GRATE-FUL TO YOU.
THANK YOU, CLARE ...
I'M GLAD I MET YOU.
OOO
JEAN!
JEAN!
JEAN!
LIVE...
CLARE...

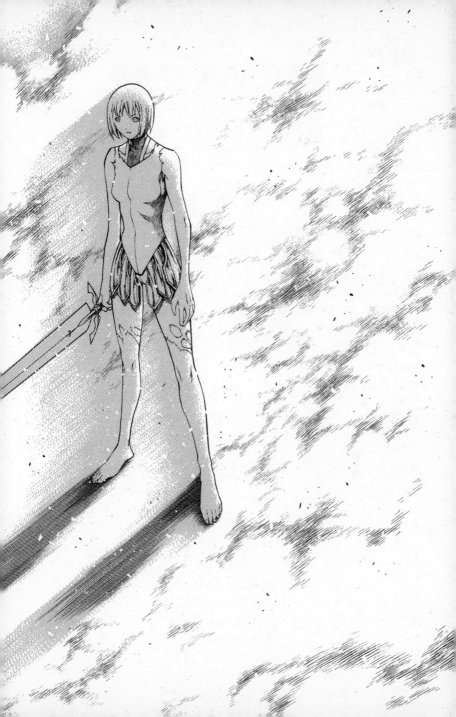

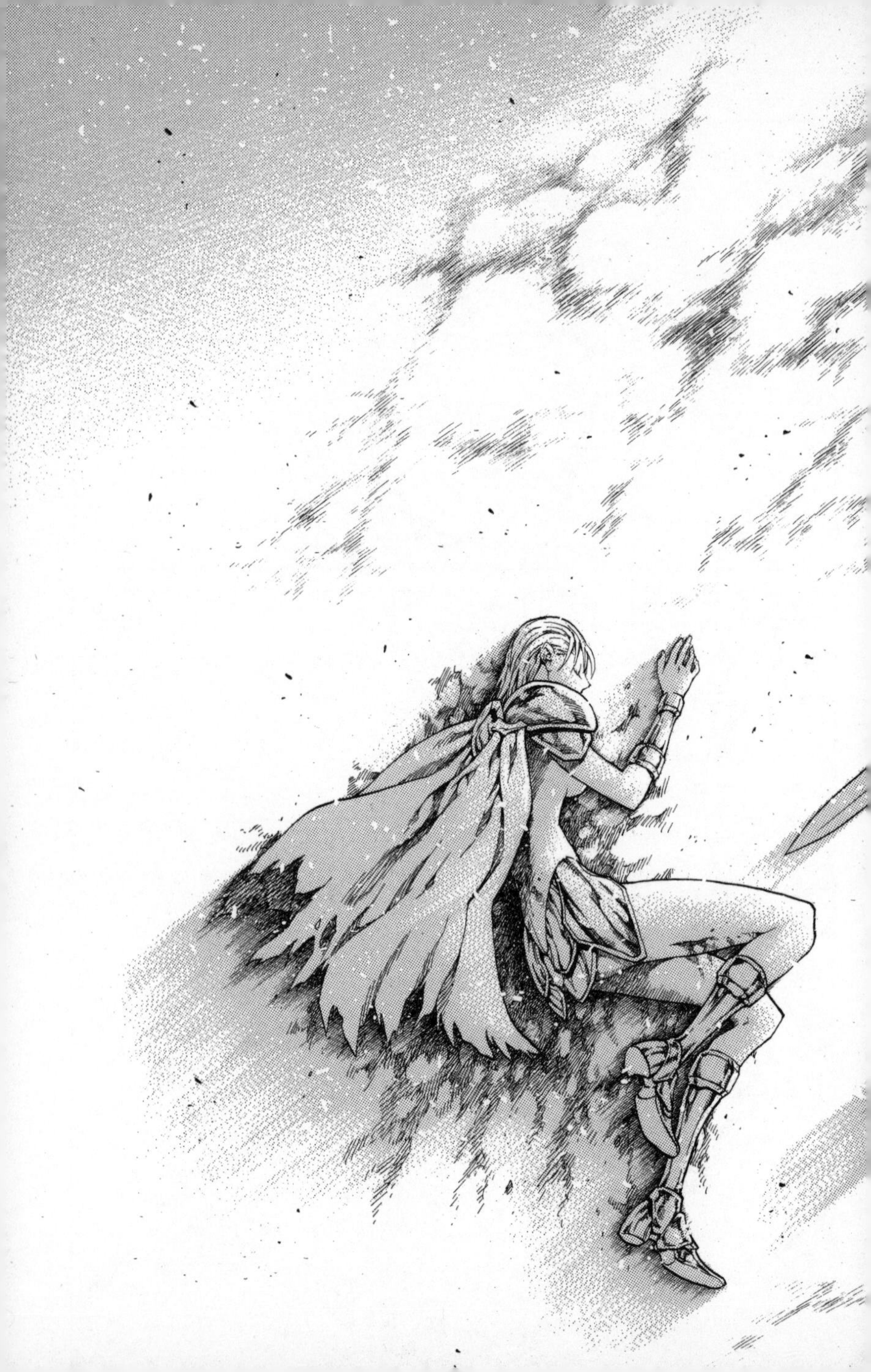

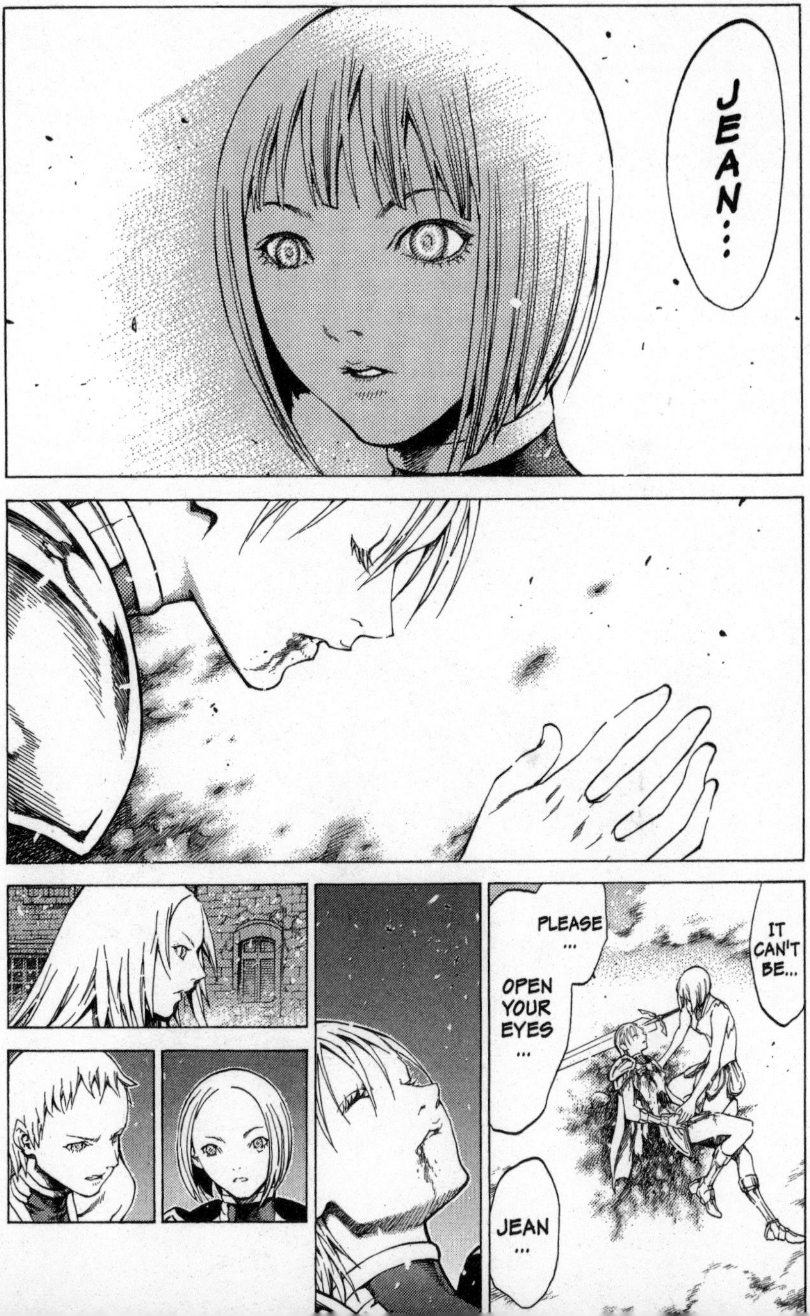
JEAN...
IT CAN'T BE...
PLEASE ...
OPEN YOUR EYES ...
JEAN ...

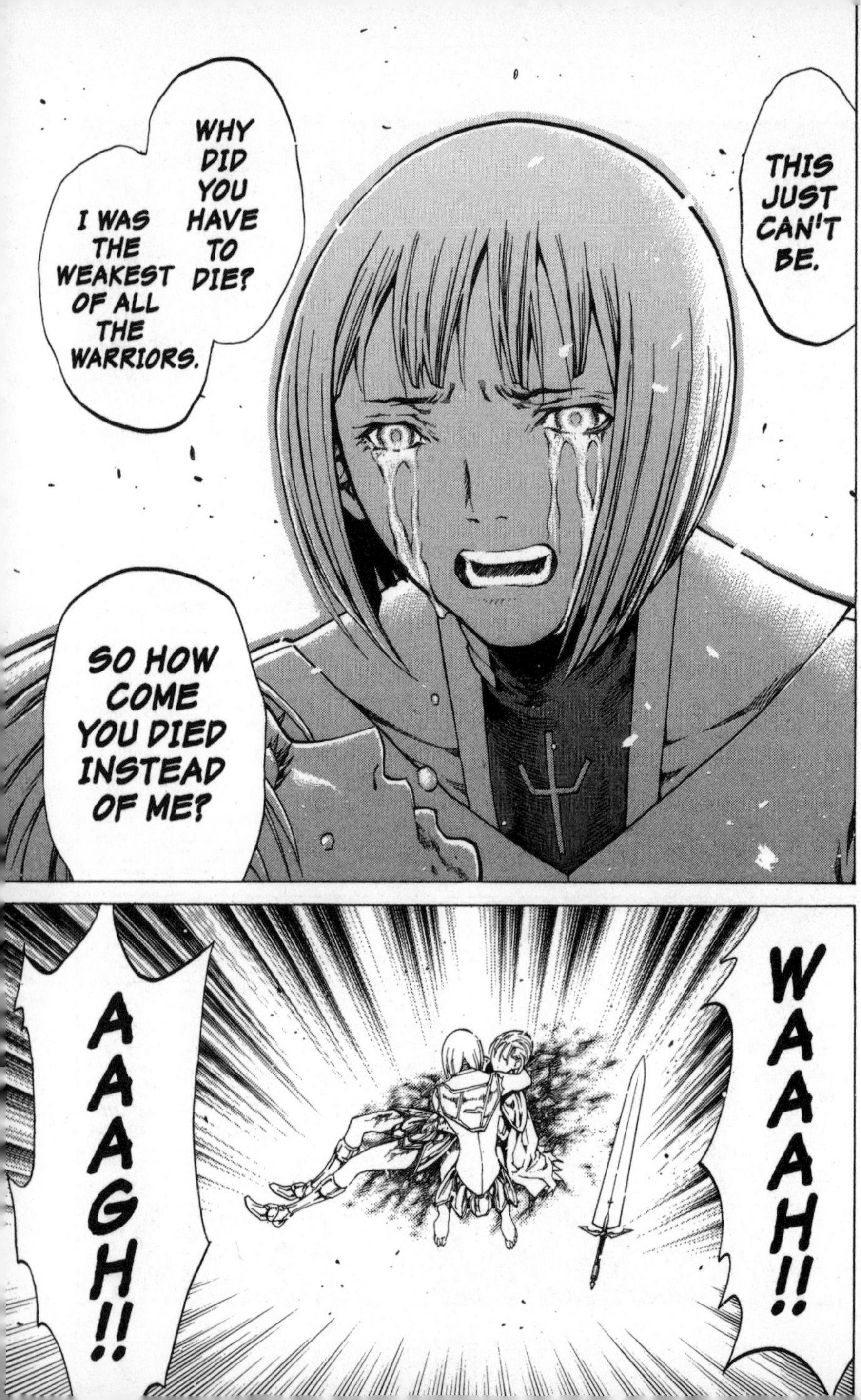
THIS JUST CAN'T BE.
WHY DID YOU HAVE TO DIE?
I WAS THE WEAKEST OF ALL THE WARRIORS.
SO HOW COME YOU DIED INSTEAD OF ME?
WAAAH!!
AAAAGH!!

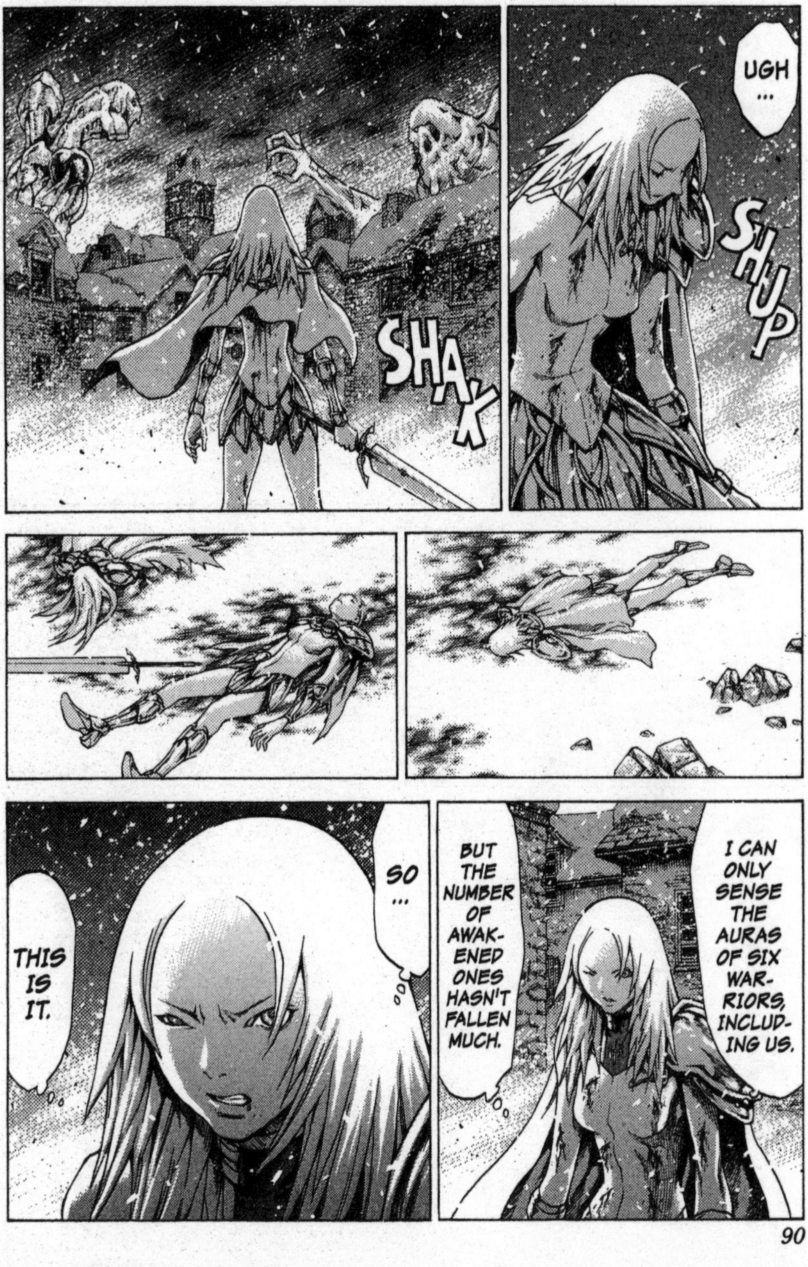
UGH ...
SHUP
SHAK
I CAN ONLY SENSE THE AURAS OF SIX WARRIORS, INCLUDING US.
BUT THE NUMBER OF AWAKENED ONES HASN'T FALLEN MUCH.
SO ...
THIS IS IT.

READ THIS WAY

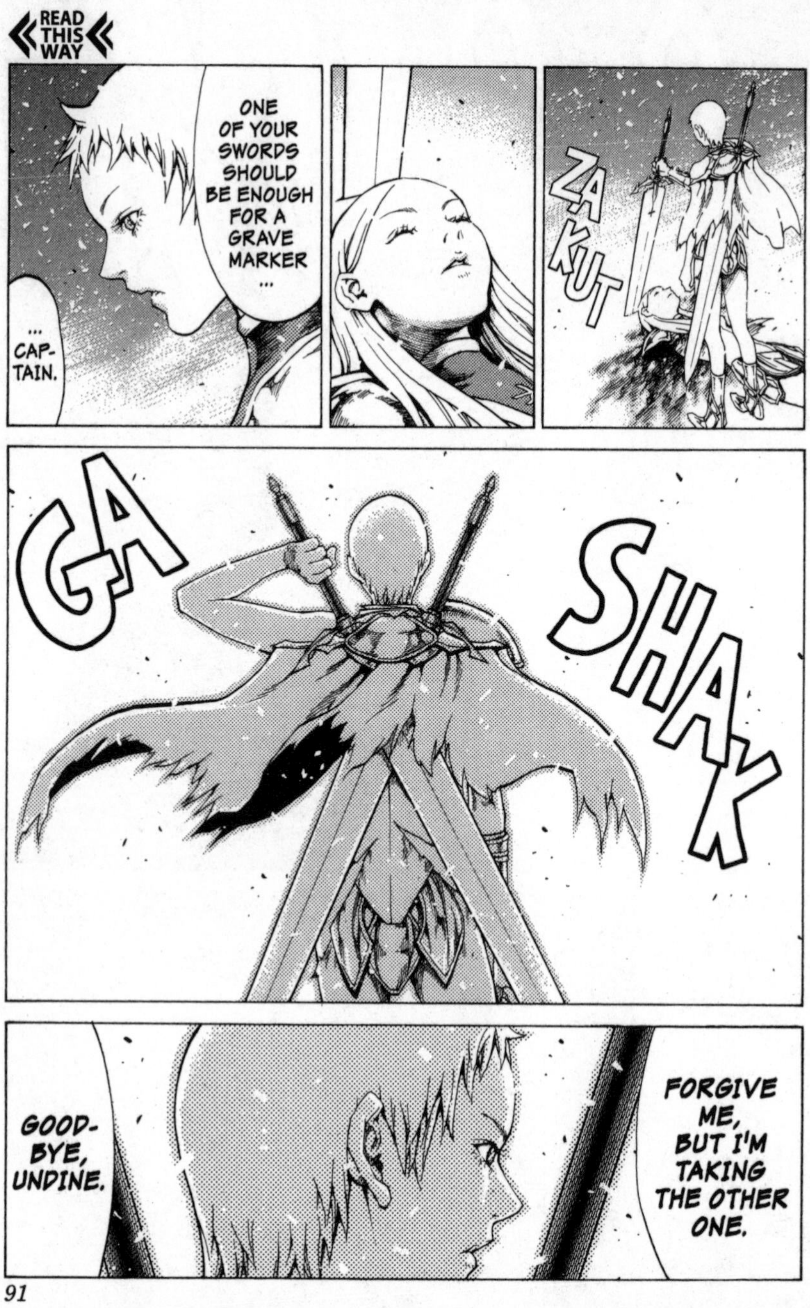

ZAKUT
ONE OF YOUR SWORDS SHOULD BE ENOUGH FOR A GRAVE MARKER ...
... CAPTAIN.
GA SHAK
FORGIVE ME, BUT I'M TAKING THE OTHER ONE.
GOOD-BYE, UNDINE.

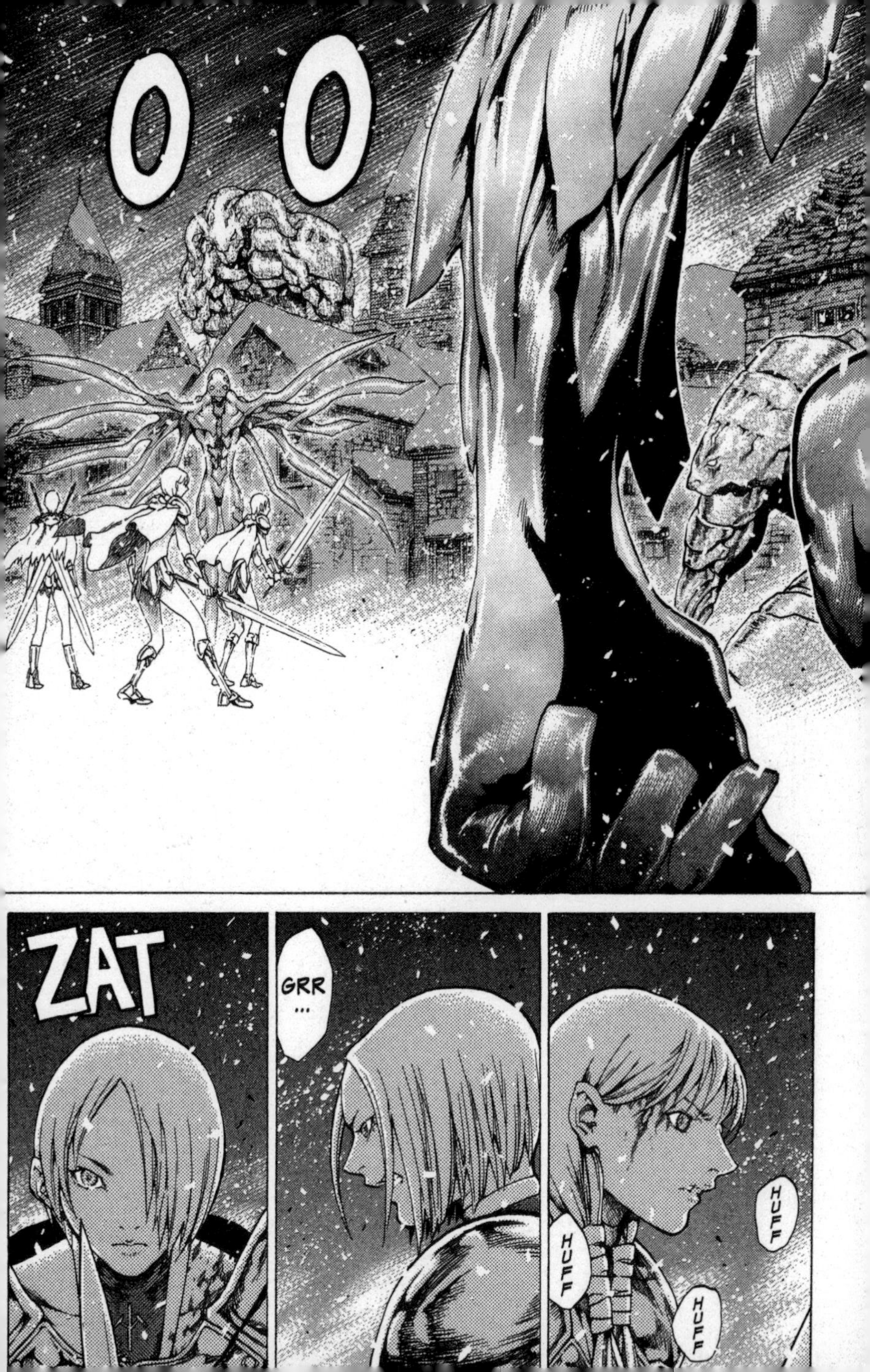
OO
HUFF
HUFF
HUFF
GRR...
ZAT

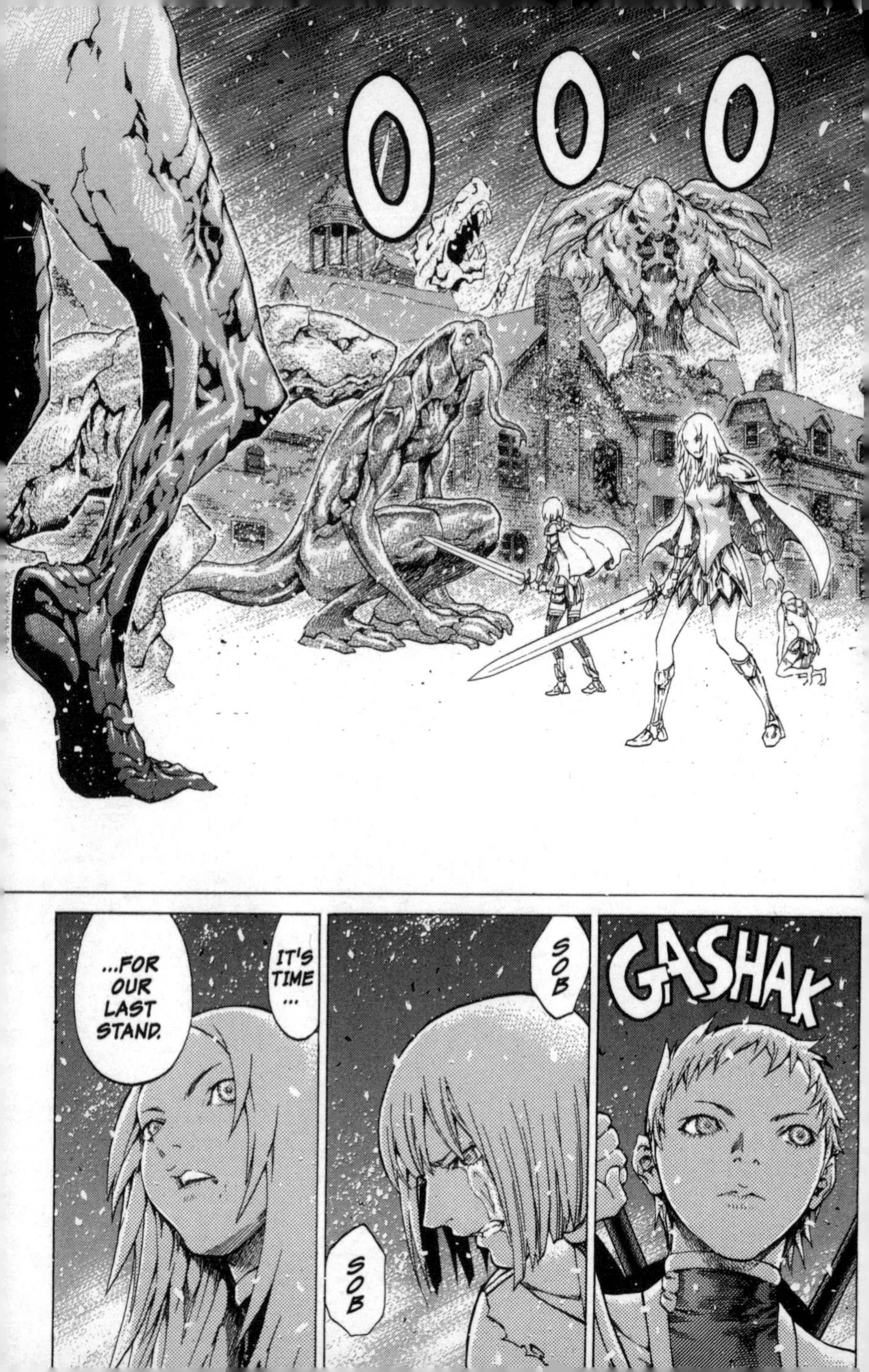
O O O
GASHAK
SOB
SOB
IT'S TIME ...
...FOR OUR LAST STAND.

クレイモア
Claymore

Scene 61: The Assault on Pieta, Part 5

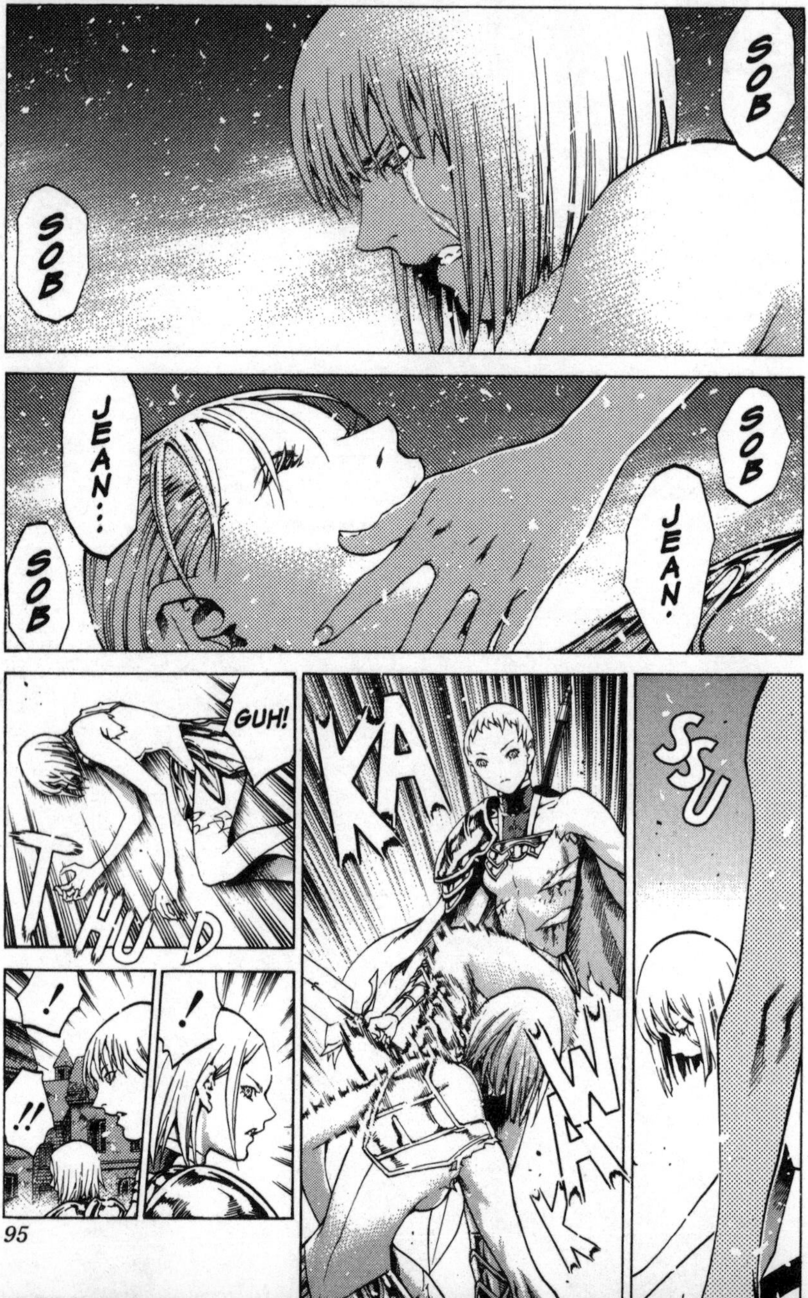
SOB
SOB
SOB
JEAN.
JEAN...
SOB
SSU
KA
WAKA
GUH!
THUD
!
!
!!

Scene 61: The Assault on Pieta, Part 5

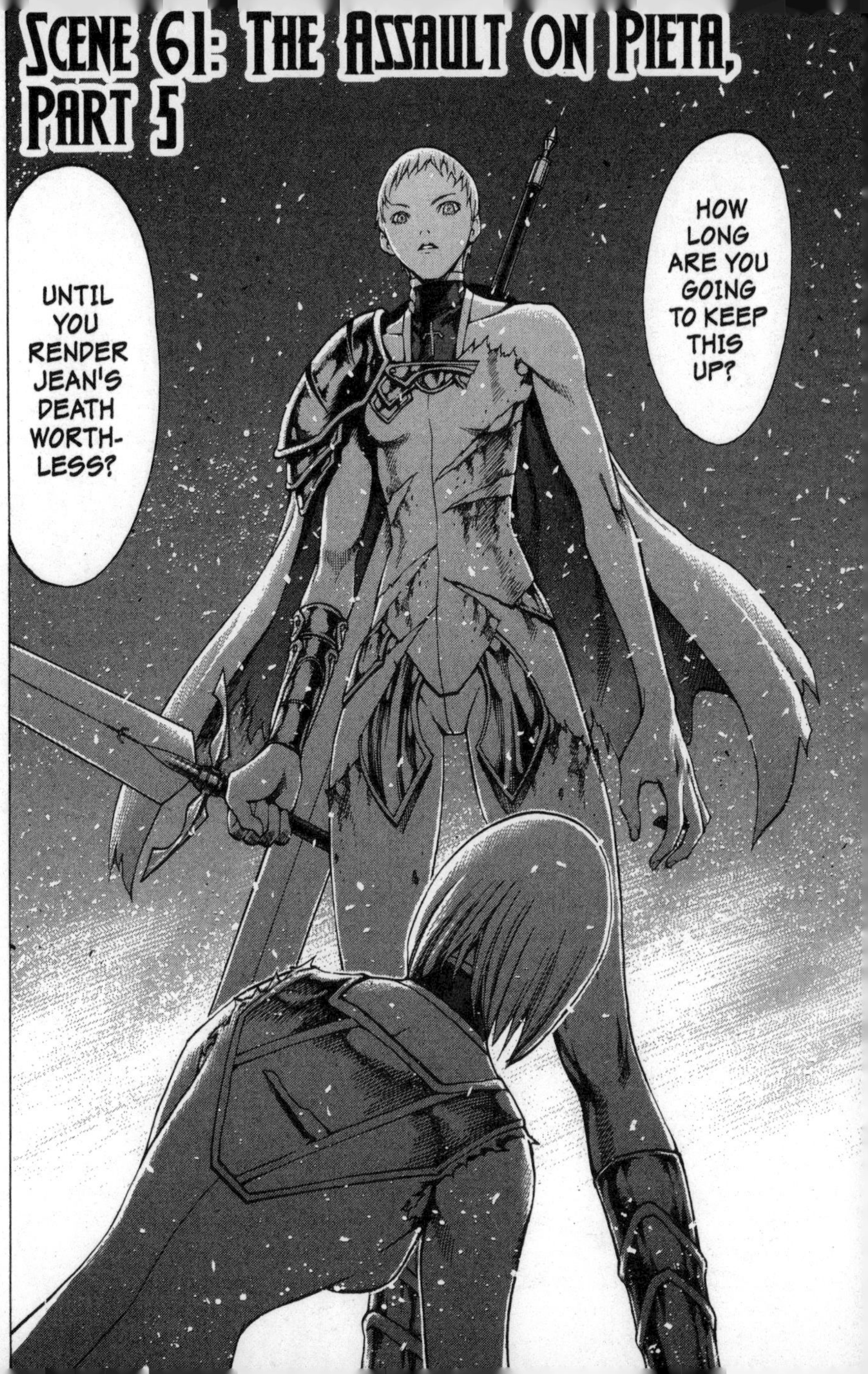
HOW LONG ARE YOU GOING TO KEEP THIS UP?
UNTIL YOU RENDER JEAN'S DEATH WORTH-LESS?

READ THIS WAY

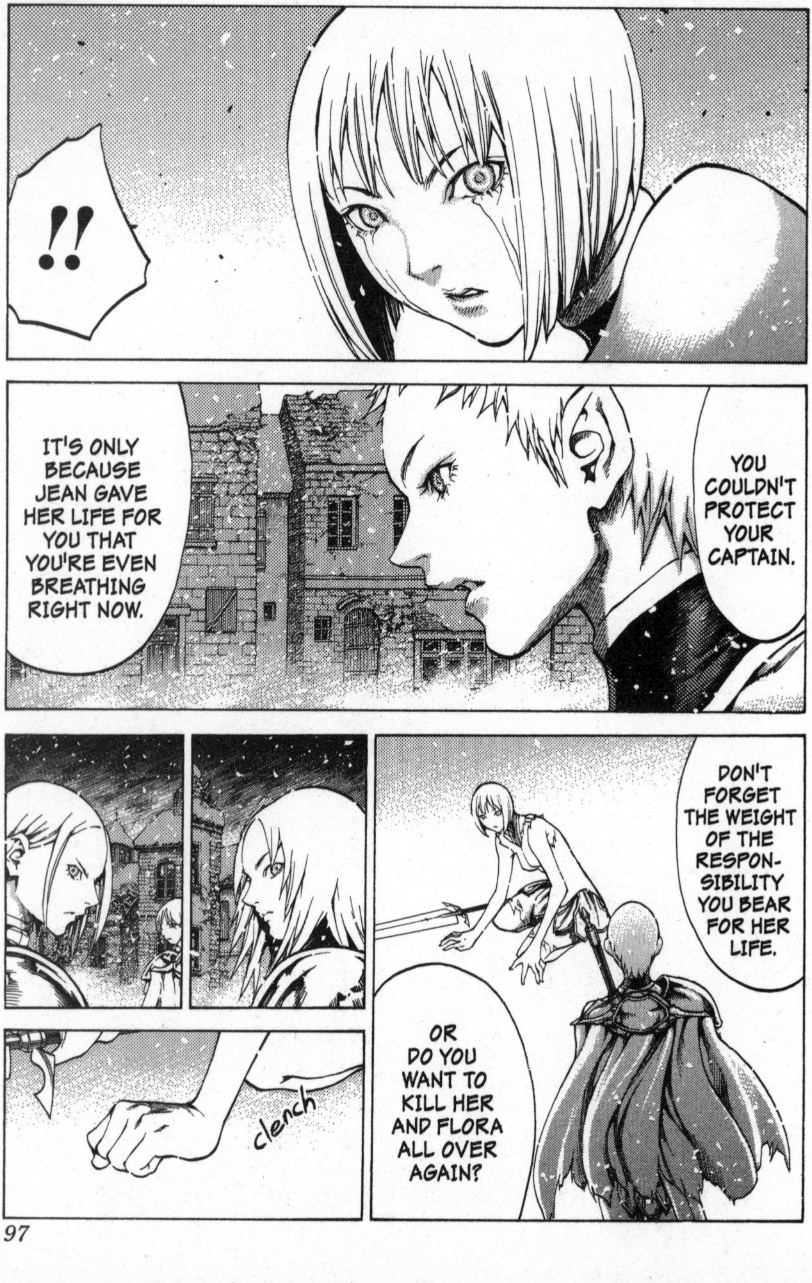
!!
YOU COULDN'T PROTECT YOUR CAPTAIN.
IT'S ONLY BECAUSE JEAN GAVE HER LIFE FOR YOU THAT YOU'RE EVEN BREATHING RIGHT NOW.
DON'T FORGET THE WEIGHT OF THE RESPON-SIBILITY YOU BEAR FOR HER LIFE.
OR DO YOU WANT TO KILL HER AND FLORA ALL OVER AGAIN?
clench

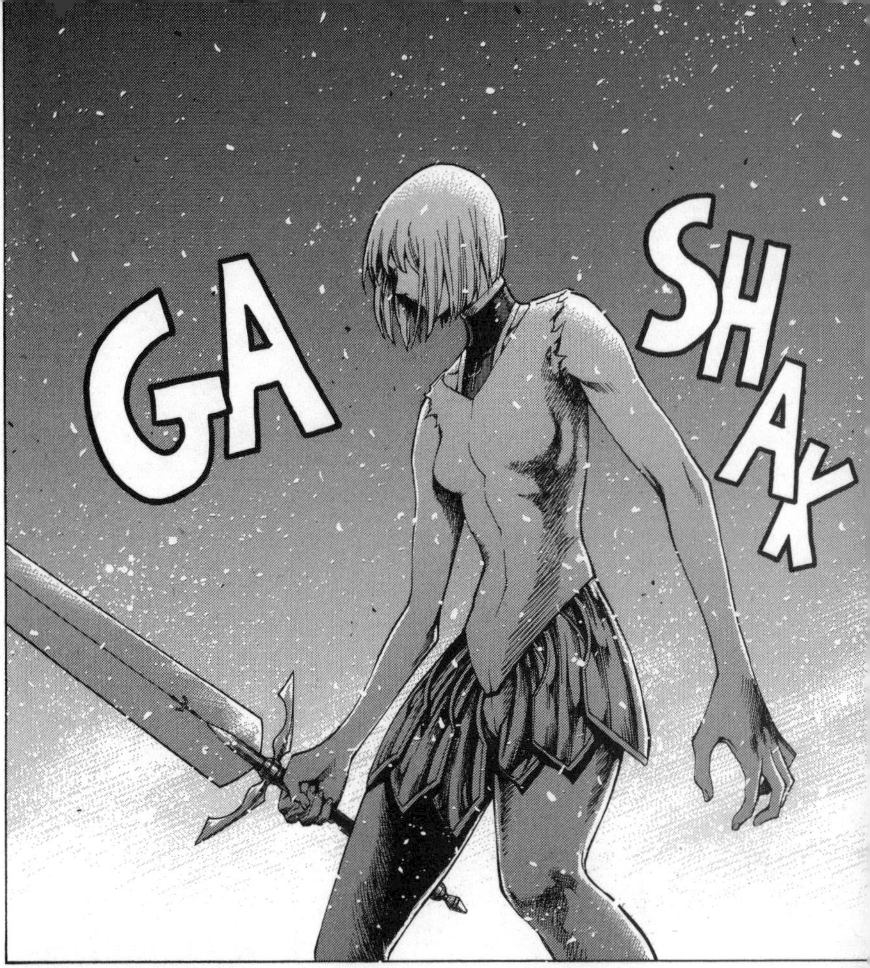
GA
SHAK

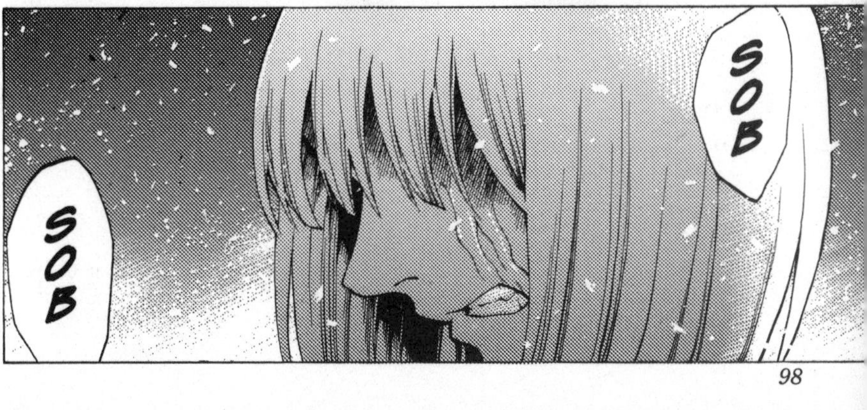
SOB
SOB

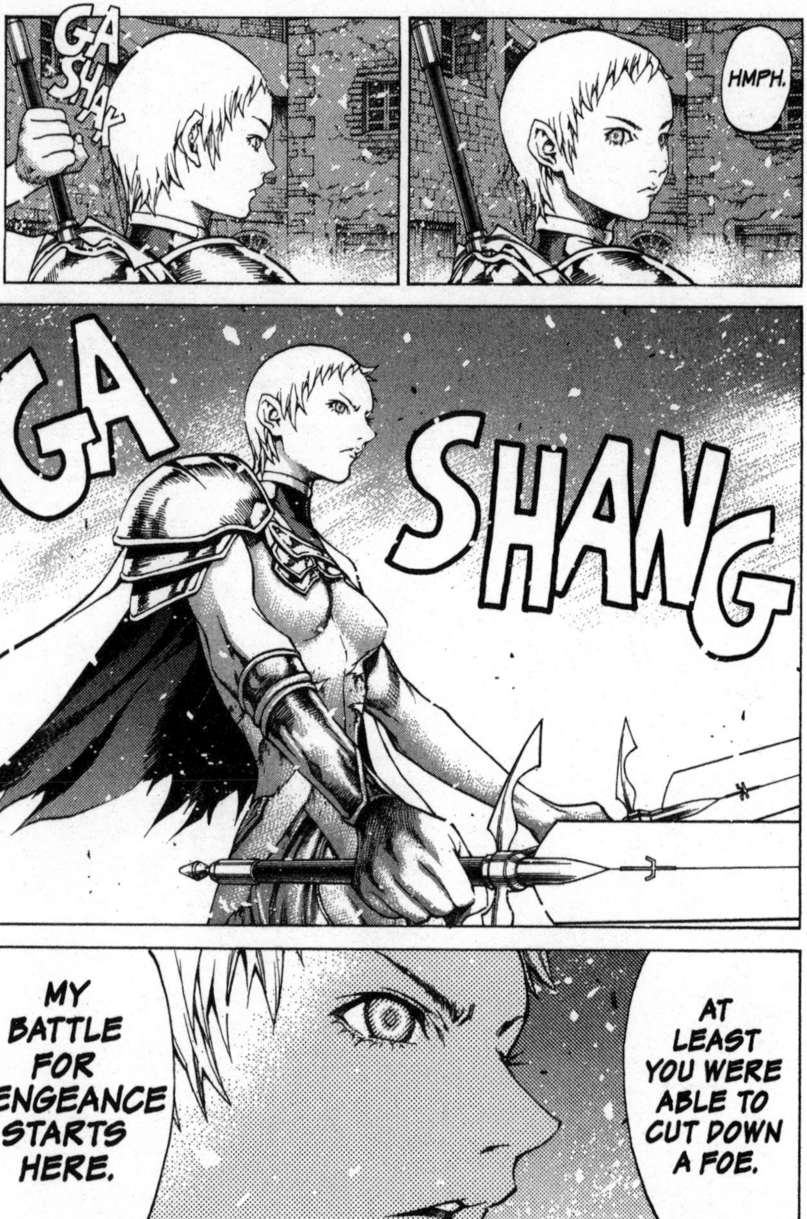
HMPH.
GA SHAK
GA SHANG
AT LEAST YOU WERE ABLE TO CUT DOWN A FOE.
MY BATTLE FOR VENGEANCE STARTS HERE.

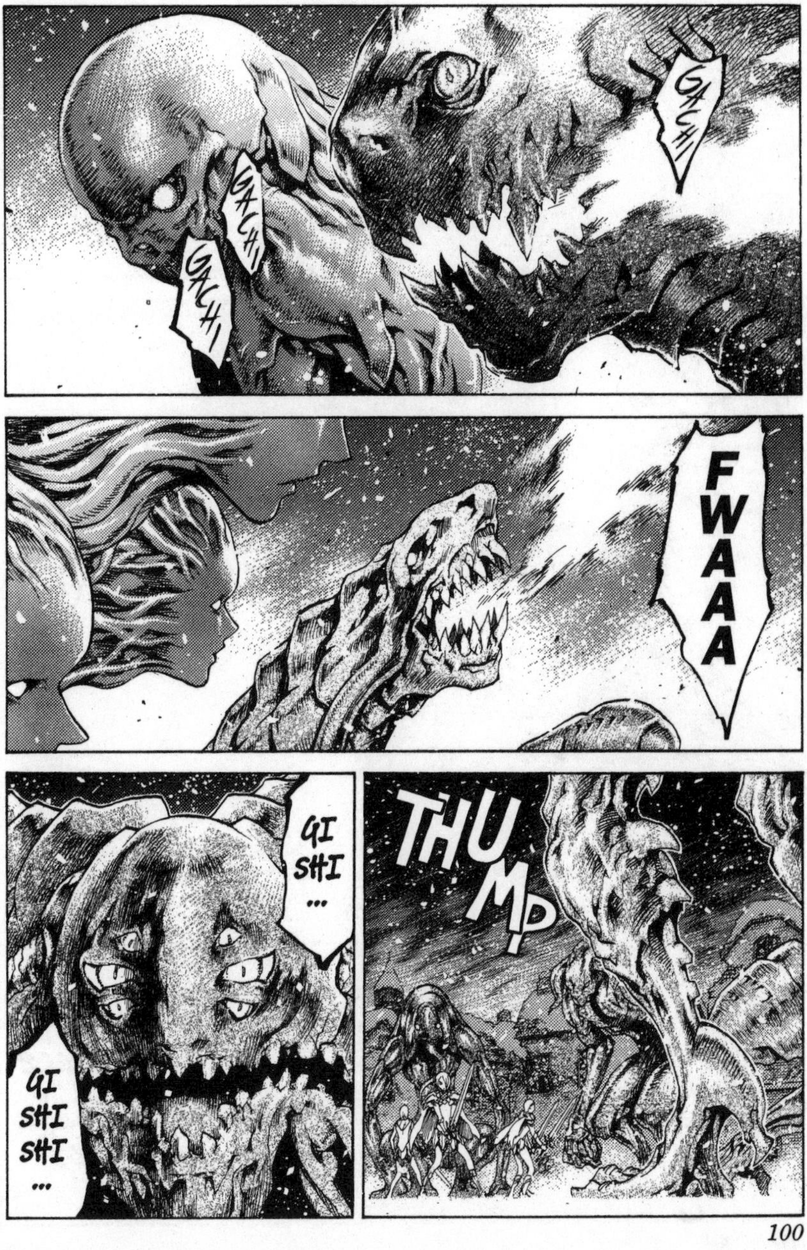
GACHI
GACHI
GACHI
FWAAAA
THUMP
GI SHI ...
GI SHI SHI ...

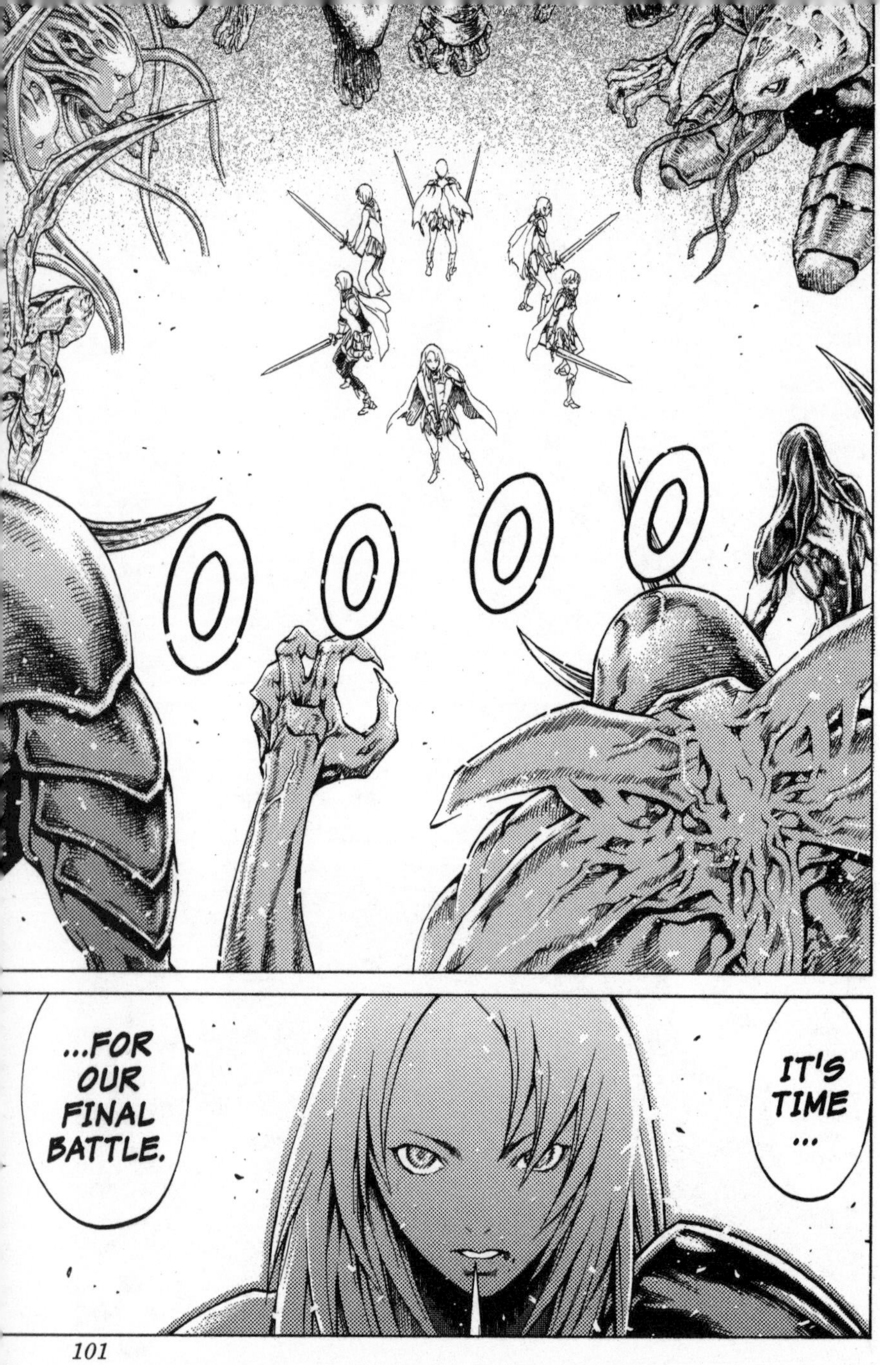
OOOO
IT'S TIME ...
...FOR OUR FINAL BATTLE.

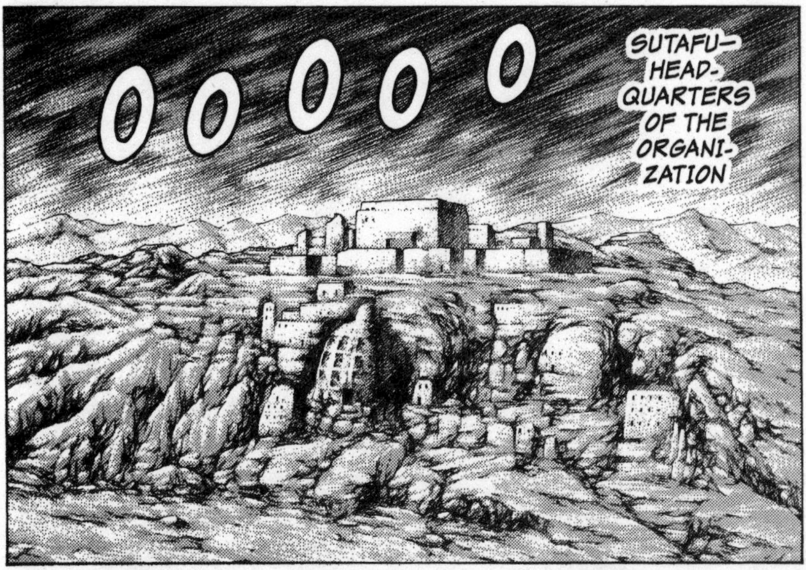
SUTAFU—HEADQUARTERS OF THE ORGANIZATION
OOOOO
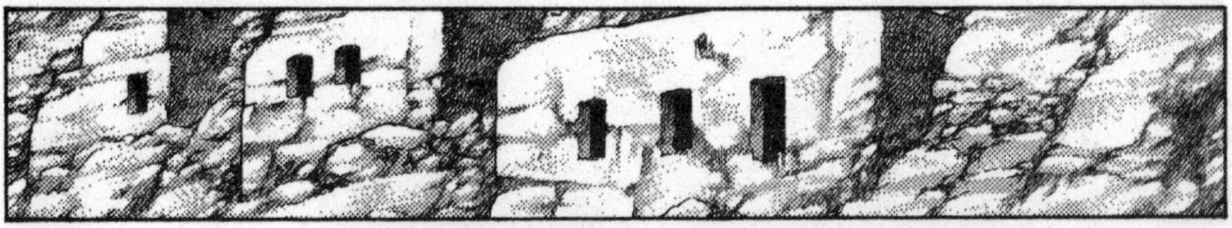
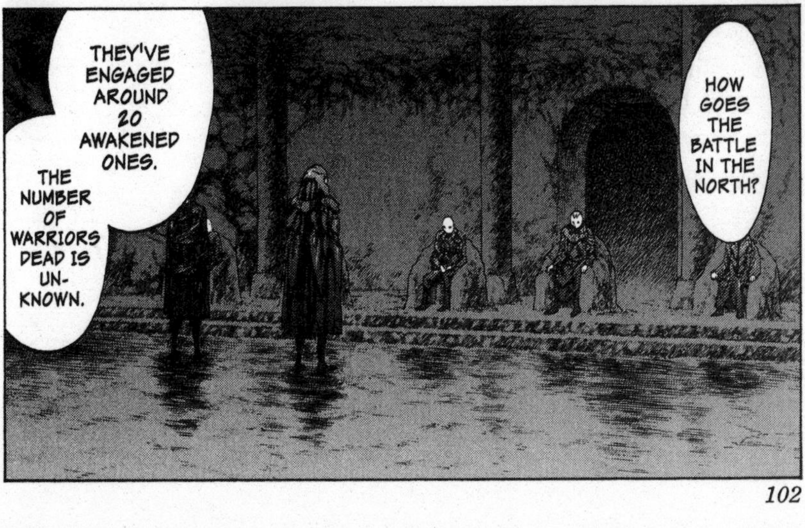
HOW GOES THE BATTLE IN THE NORTH?
THEY'VE ENGAGED AROUND 20 AWAKENED ONES.
THE NUMBER OF WARRIORS DEAD IS UNKNOWN.

READ THIS WAY

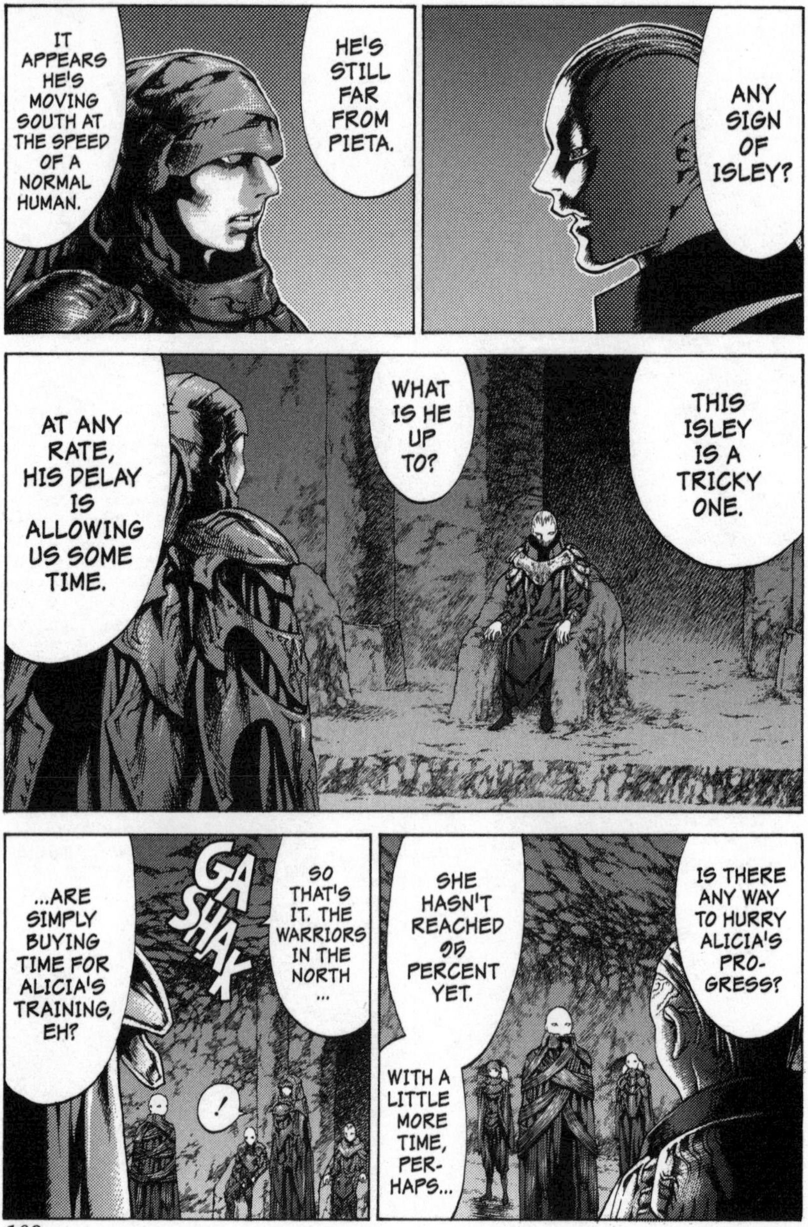
ANY SIGN OF ISLEY?
HE'S STILL FAR FROM PIETA.
IT APPEARS HE'S MOVING SOUTH AT THE SPEED OF A NORMAL HUMAN.
THIS ISLEY IS A TRICKY ONE.
WHAT IS HE UP TO?
AT ANY RATE, HIS DELAY IS ALLOWING US SOME TIME.
IS THERE ANY WAY TO HURRY ALICIA'S PRO-GRESS?
SHE HASN'T REACHED 95 PERCENT YET.
WITH A LITTLE MORE TIME, PER-HAPS...
SO THAT'S IT. THE WARRIORS IN THE NORTH ...
GASHAK
...ARE SIMPLY BUYING TIME FOR ALICIA'S TRAINING, EH?
!

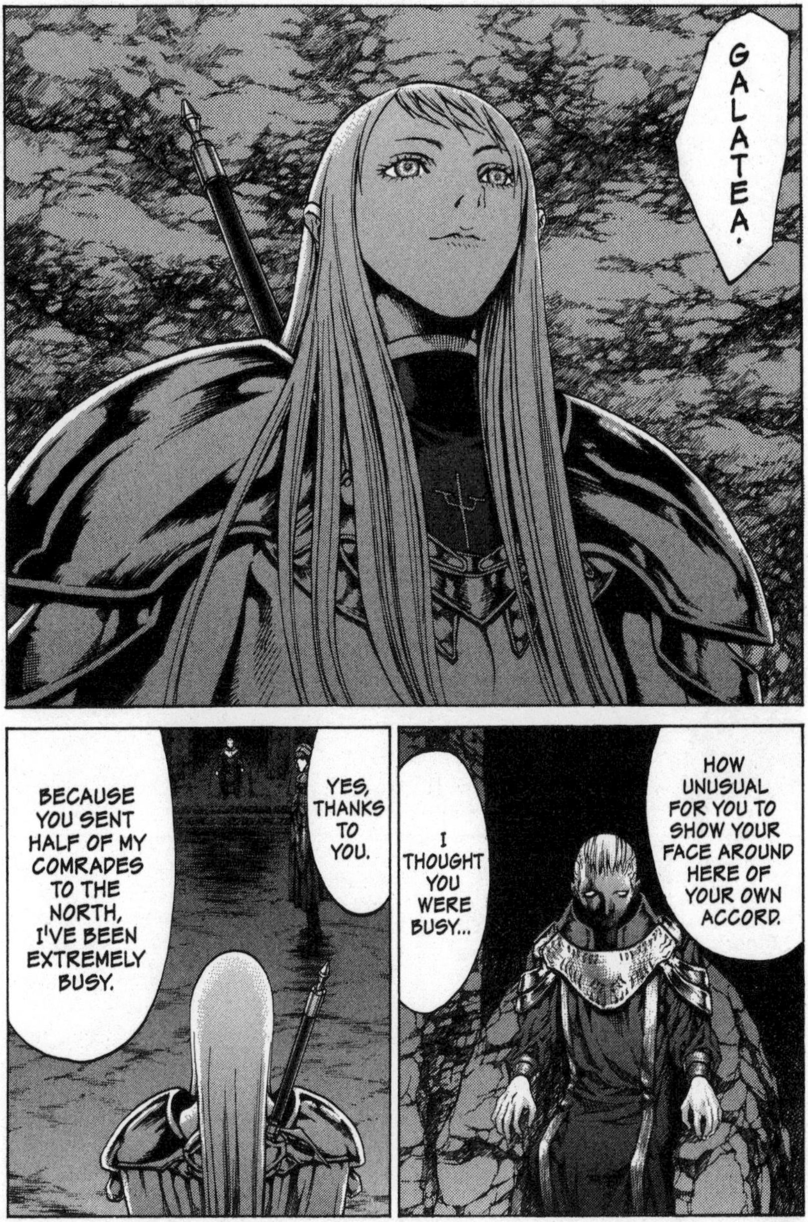
GALATEA.
HOW UNUSUAL FOR YOU TO SHOW YOUR FACE AROUND HERE OF YOUR OWN ACCORD.
I THOUGHT YOU WERE BUSY...
YES, THANKS TO YOU.
BECAUSE YOU SENT HALF OF MY COMRADES TO THE NORTH, I'VE BEEN EXTREMELY BUSY.

READ THIS WAY

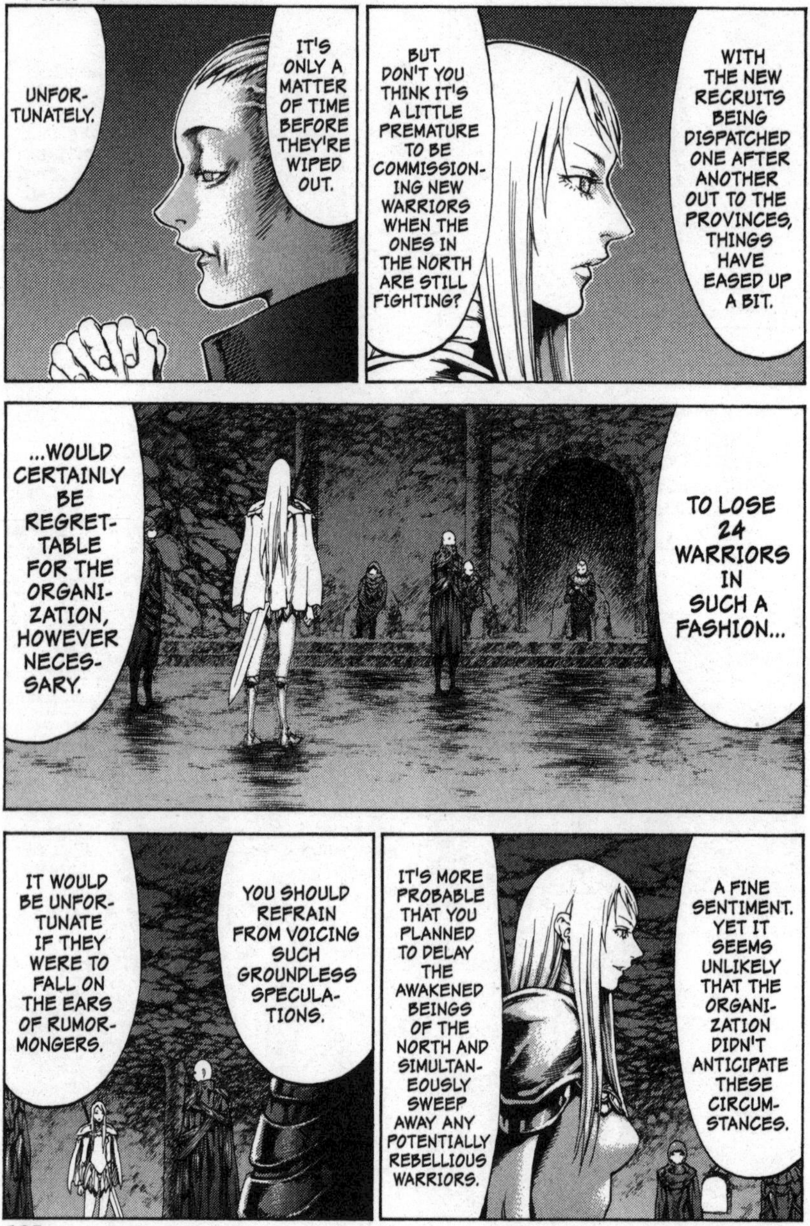
WITH THE NEW RECRUITS BEING DISPATCHED ONE AFTER ANOTHER OUT TO THE PROVINCES, THINGS HAVE EASED UP A BIT.
BUT DON'T YOU THINK IT'S A LITTLE PREMATURE TO BE COMMISSIONING NEW WARRIORS WHEN THE ONES IN THE NORTH ARE STILL FIGHTING?
IT'S ONLY A MATTER OF TIME BEFORE THEY'RE WIPED OUT.
UNFORTUNATELY.
TO LOSE 24 WARRIORS IN SUCH A FASHION...
...WOULD CERTAINLY BE REGRETTABLE FOR THE ORGANIZATION, HOWEVER NECESSARY.
A FINE SENTIMENT. YET IT SEEMS UNLIKELY THAT THE ORGANIZATION DIDN'T ANTICIPATE THESE CIRCUMSTANCES.
IT'S MORE PROBABLE THAT YOU PLANNED TO DELAY THE AWAKENED BEINGS OF THE NORTH AND SIMULTANEOUSLY SWEEP AWAY ANY POTENTIALLY REBELLIOUS WARRIORS.
YOU SHOULD REFRAIN FROM VOICING SUCH GROUNDLESS SPECULATIONS.
IT WOULD BE UNFORTUNATE IF THEY WERE TO FALL ON THE EARS OF RUMORMONGERS.

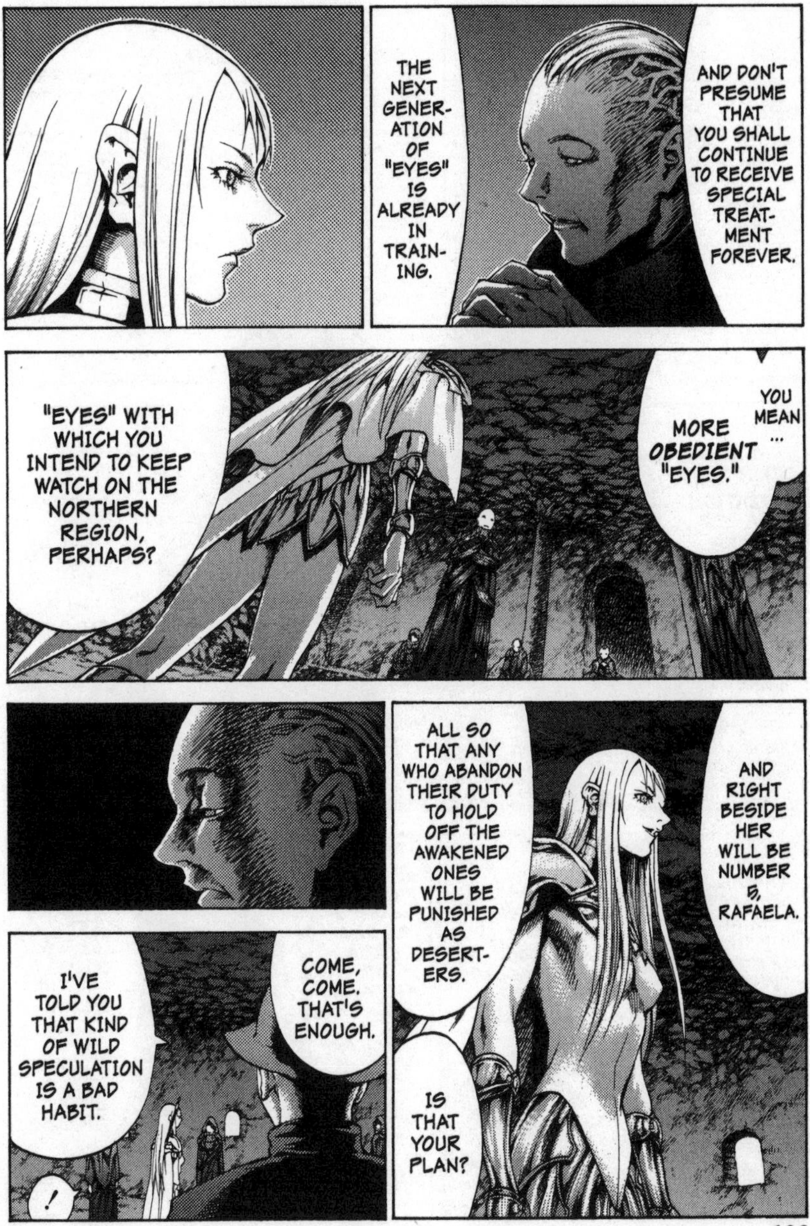
AND DON'T PRESUME THAT YOU SHALL CONTINUE TO RECEIVE SPECIAL TREATMENT FOREVER.
THE NEXT GENERATION OF "EYES" IS ALREADY IN TRAINING.
YOU MEAN ...
MORE *OBEDIENT* "EYES."
"EYES" WITH WHICH YOU INTEND TO KEEP WATCH ON THE NORTHERN REGION, PERHAPS?
AND RIGHT BESIDE HER WILL BE NUMBER 5, RAFAELA.
ALL SO THAT ANY WHO ABANDON THEIR DUTY TO HOLD OFF THE AWAKENED ONES WILL BE PUNISHED AS DESERTERS.
IS THAT YOUR PLAN?
COME, COME. THAT'S ENOUGH.
I'VE TOLD YOU THAT KIND OF WILD SPECULATION IS A BAD HABIT.
!

READ THIS WAY

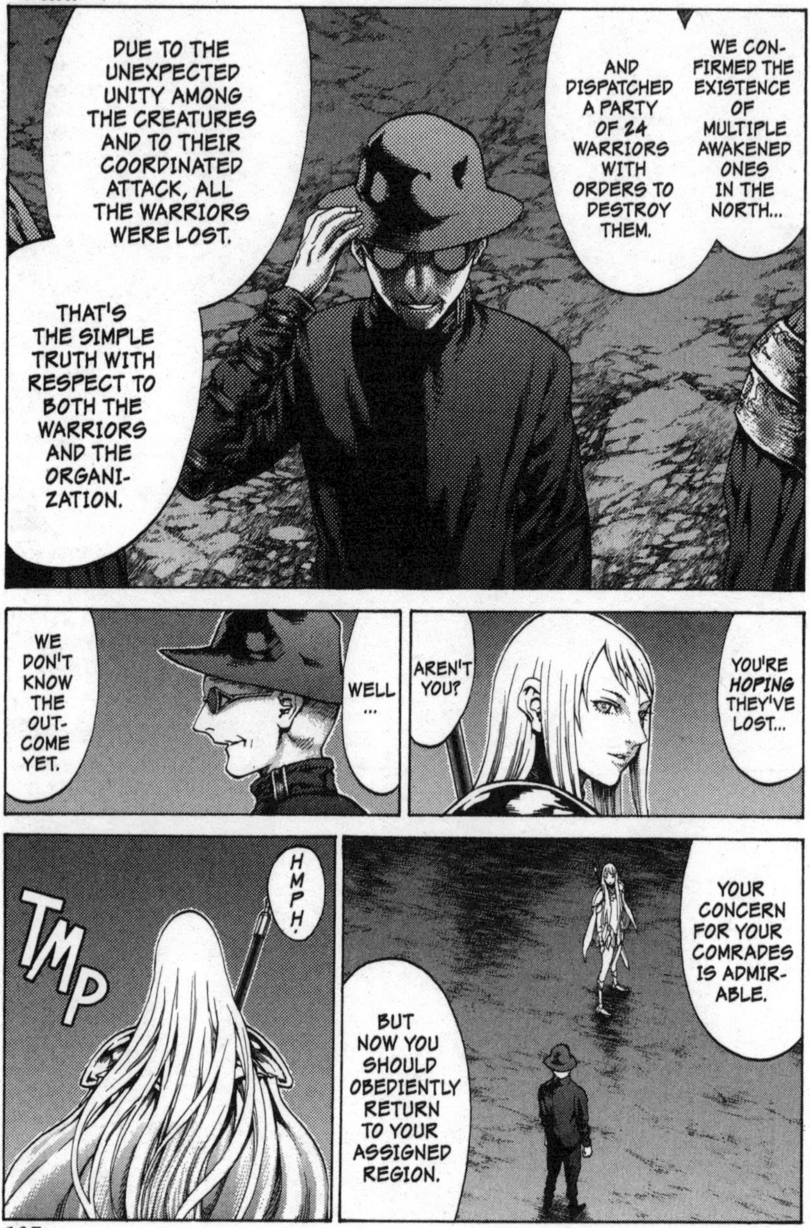
WE CON-FIRMED THE EXISTENCE OF MULTIPLE AWAKENED ONES IN THE NORTH...
AND DISPATCHED A PARTY OF 24 WARRIORS WITH ORDERS TO DESTROY THEM.
DUE TO THE UNEXPECTED UNITY AMONG THE CREATURES AND TO THEIR COORDINATED ATTACK, ALL THE WARRIORS WERE LOST.
THAT'S THE SIMPLE TRUTH WITH RESPECT TO BOTH THE WARRIORS AND THE ORGANI-ZATION.
YOU'RE *HOPING* THEY'VE LOST...
AREN'T YOU?
WELL ...
WE DON'T KNOW THE OUT-COME YET.
YOUR CONCERN FOR YOUR COMRADES IS ADMIR-ABLE.
BUT NOW YOU SHOULD OBEDIENTLY RETURN TO YOUR ASSIGNED REGION.
HMPH.
TMP

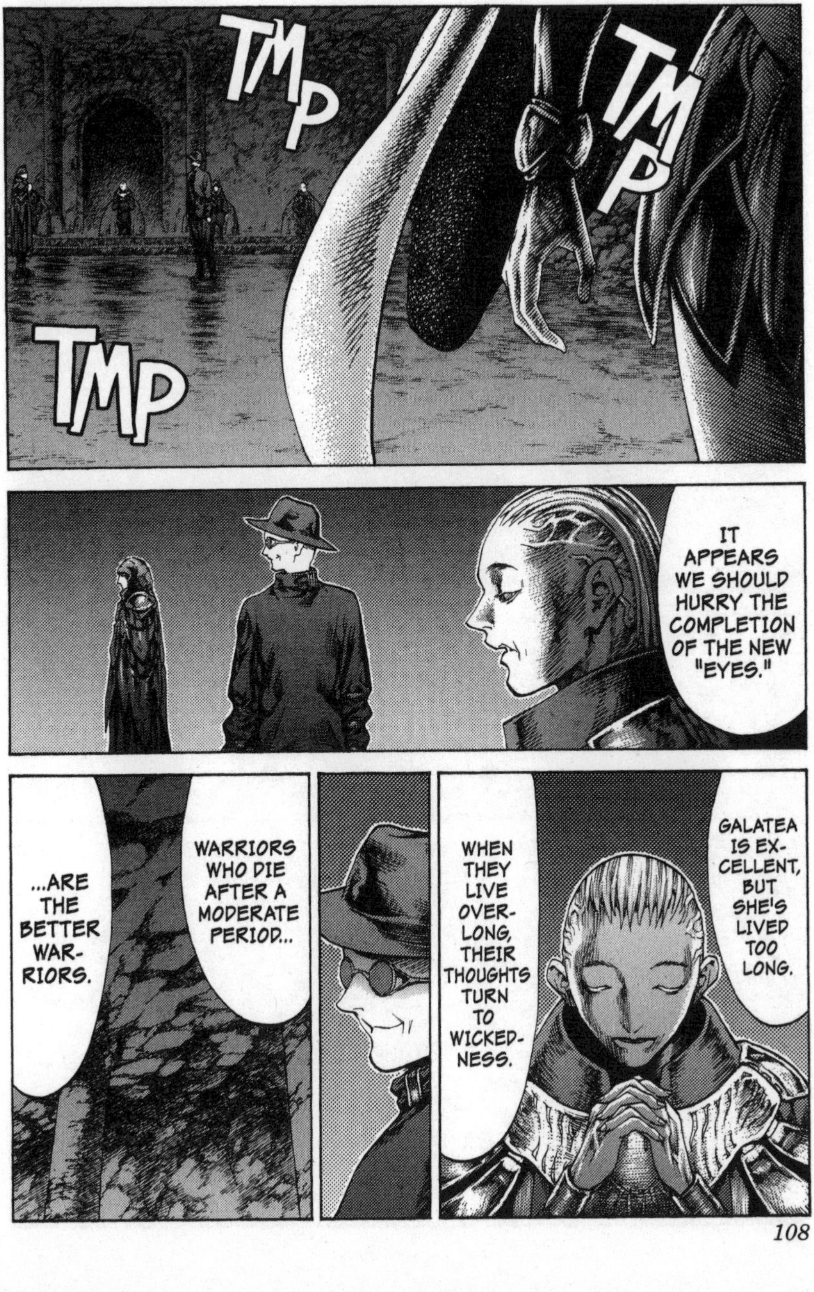
TMP
TMP
TMP
IT APPEARS WE SHOULD HURRY THE COMPLETION OF THE NEW "EYES."
GALATEA IS EXCELLENT, BUT SHE'S LIVED TOO LONG.
WHEN THEY LIVE OVERLONG, THEIR THOUGHTS TURN TO WICKEDNESS.
WARRIORS WHO DIE AFTER A MODERATE PERIOD...
...ARE THE BETTER WARRIORS.

READ THIS WAY

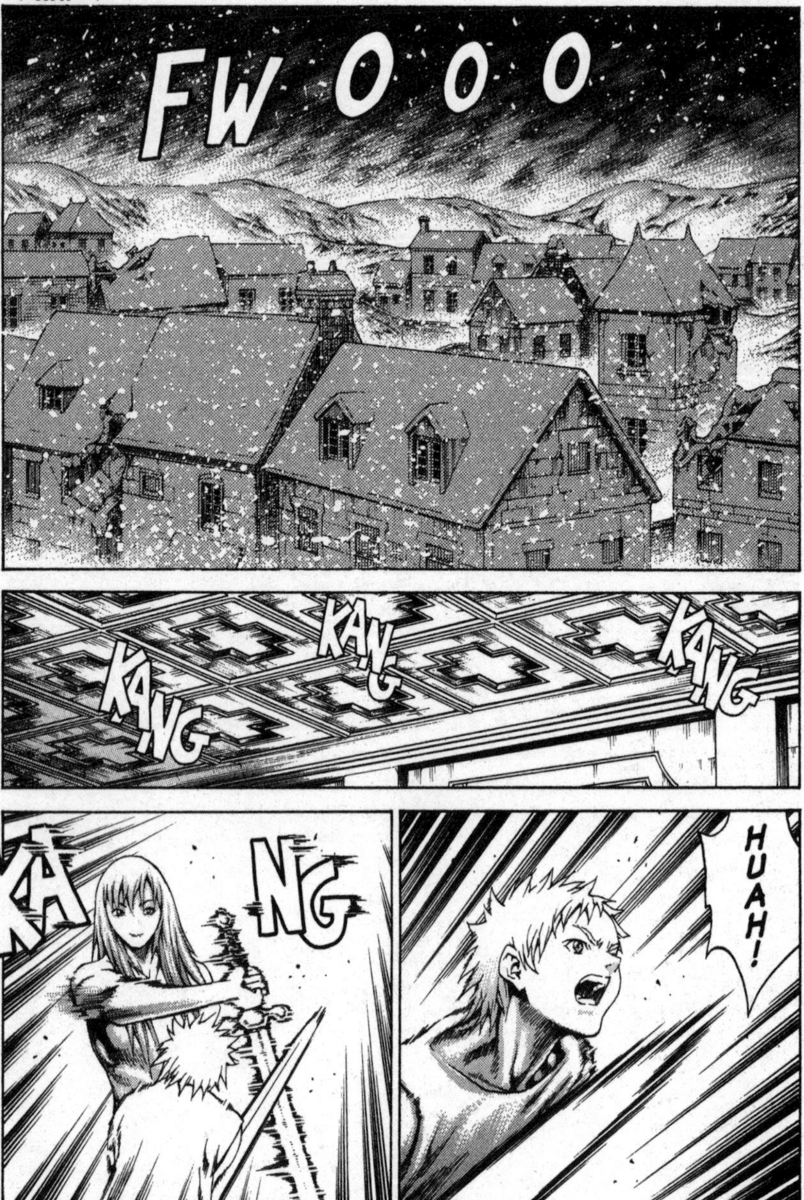
FWOOO
KANG
KANG
KANG
HUAH!
KANG

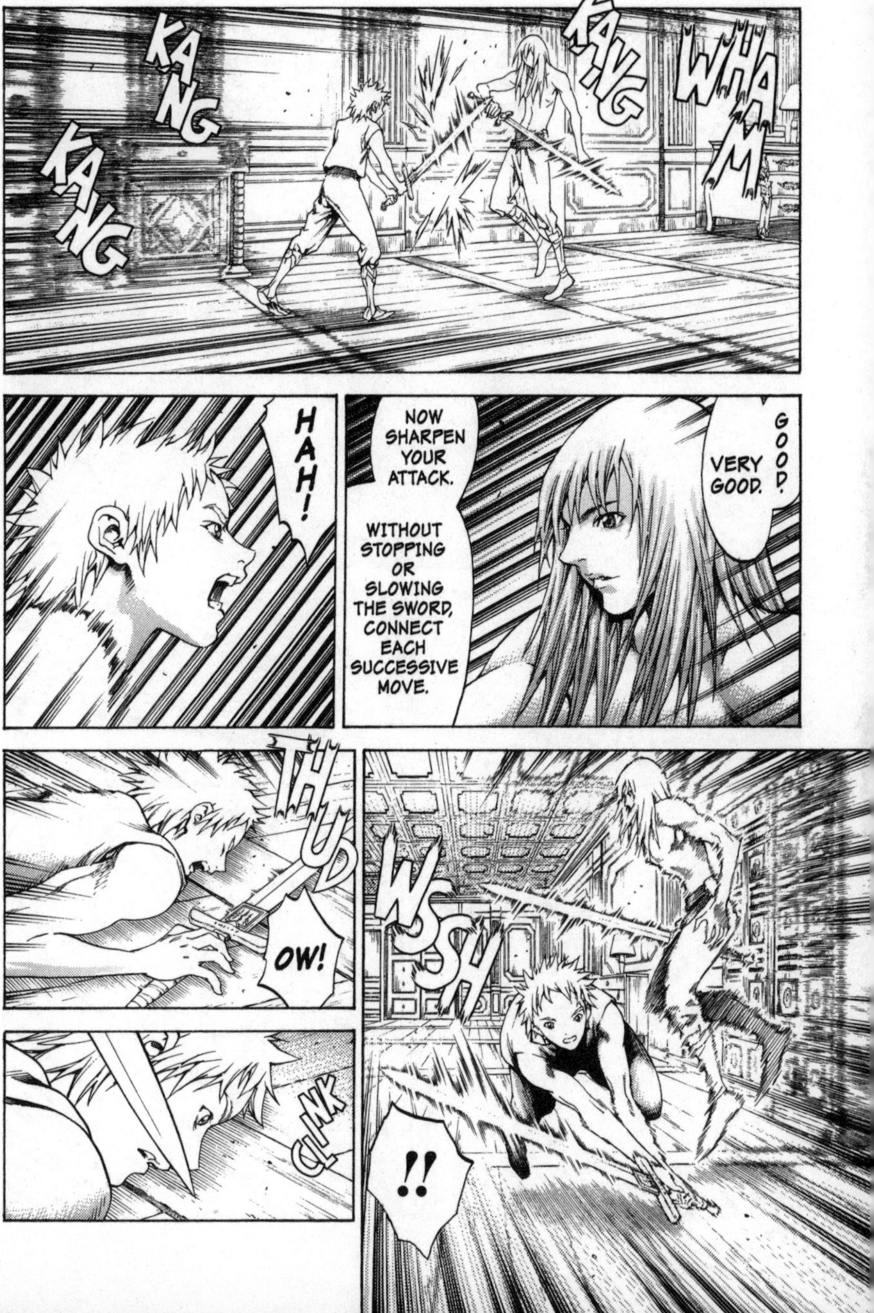
WHAM
KANG
KANG
KANG
GOOD.
VERY GOOD.
NOW SHARPEN YOUR ATTACK.
WITHOUT STOPPING OR SLOWING THE SWORD, CONNECT EACH SUCCESSIVE MOVE.
HAH!
WSSH
!!
THUD
OW!
CLINK

READ THIS WAY

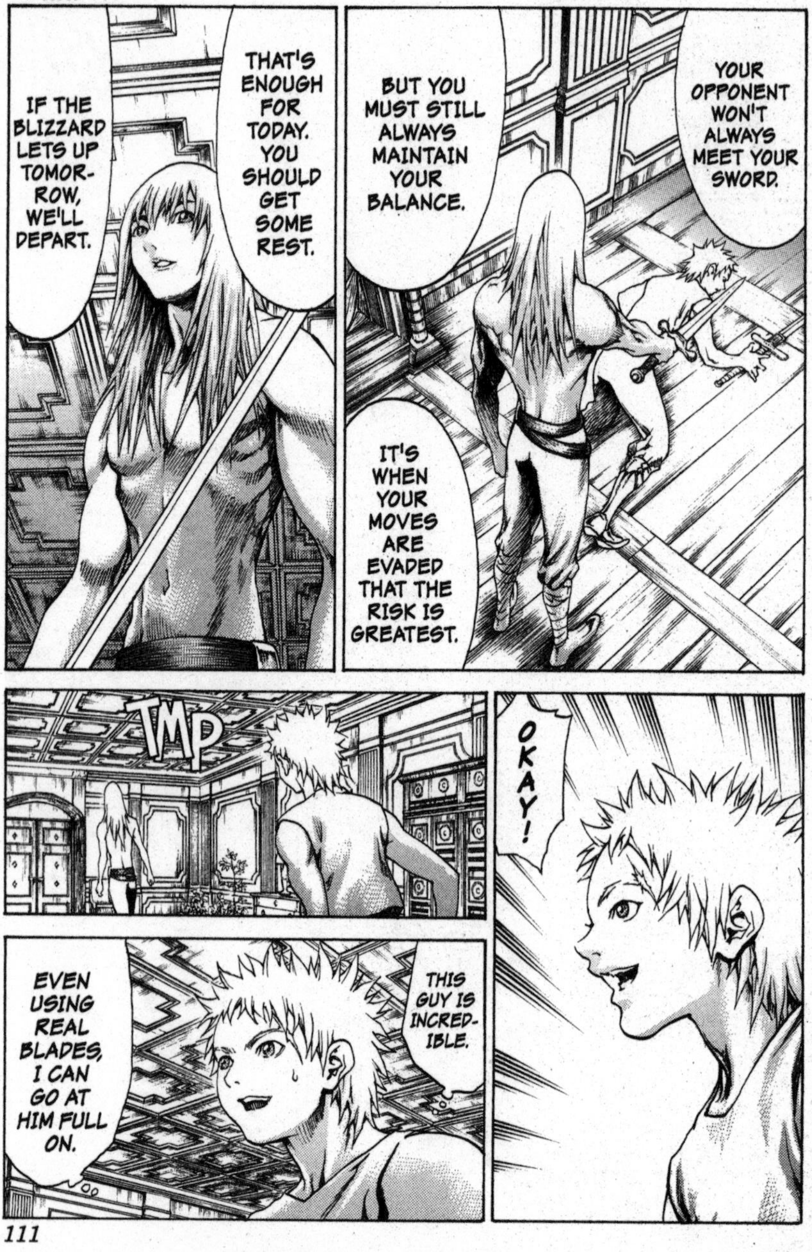
YOUR OPPONENT WON'T ALWAYS MEET YOUR SWORD.
BUT YOU MUST STILL ALWAYS MAINTAIN YOUR BALANCE.
IT'S WHEN YOUR MOVES ARE EVADED THAT THE RISK IS GREATEST.
THAT'S ENOUGH FOR TODAY. YOU SHOULD GET SOME REST.
IF THE BLIZZARD LETS UP TOMORROW, WE'LL DEPART.
OKAY!
TMP
THIS GUY IS INCREDIBLE.
EVEN USING REAL BLADES, I CAN GO AT HIM FULL ON.

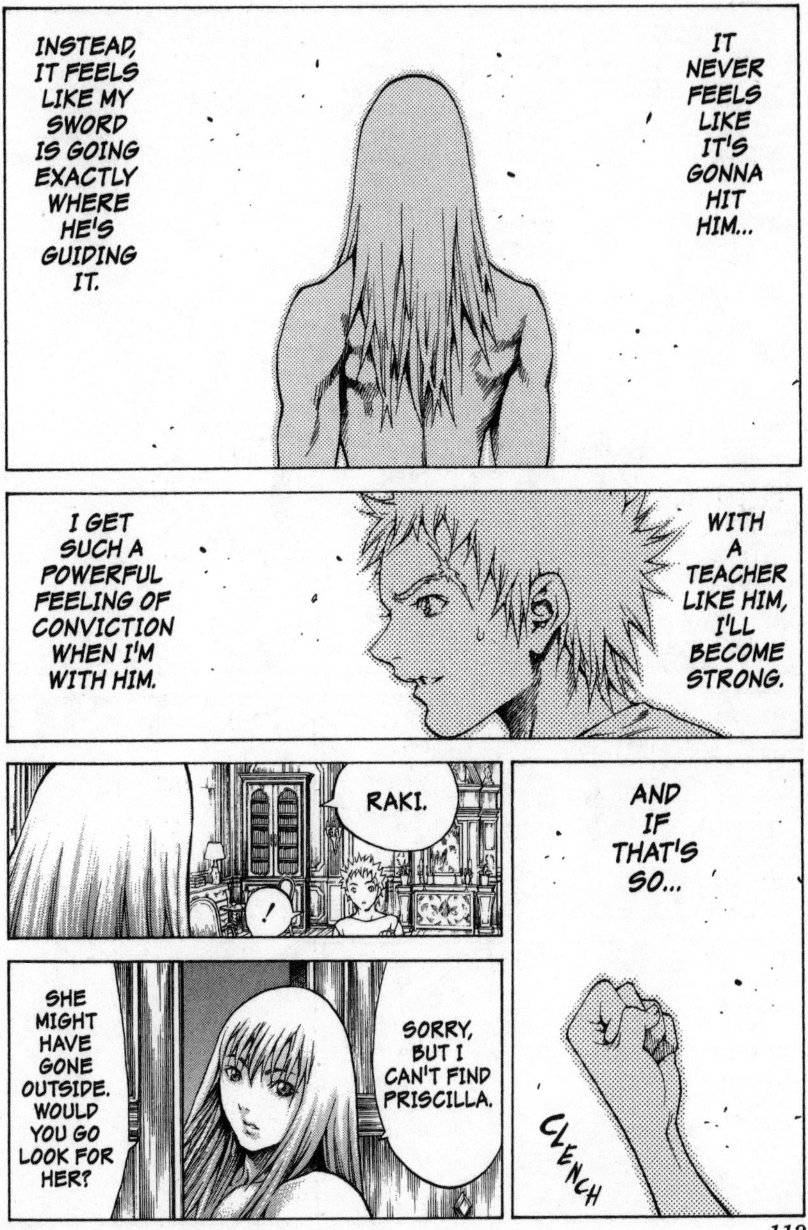
IT NEVER FEELS LIKE IT'S GONNA HIT HIM...
INSTEAD, IT FEELS LIKE MY SWORD IS GOING EXACTLY WHERE HE'S GUIDING IT.
WITH A TEACHER LIKE HIM, I'LL BECOME STRONG.
I GET SUCH A POWERFUL FEELING OF CONVICTION WHEN I'M WITH HIM.
AND IF THAT'S SO...
CLENCH
RAKI.
!
SORRY, BUT I CAN'T FIND PRISCILLA.
SHE MIGHT HAVE GONE OUTSIDE. WOULD YOU GO LOOK FOR HER?

READ THIS WAY

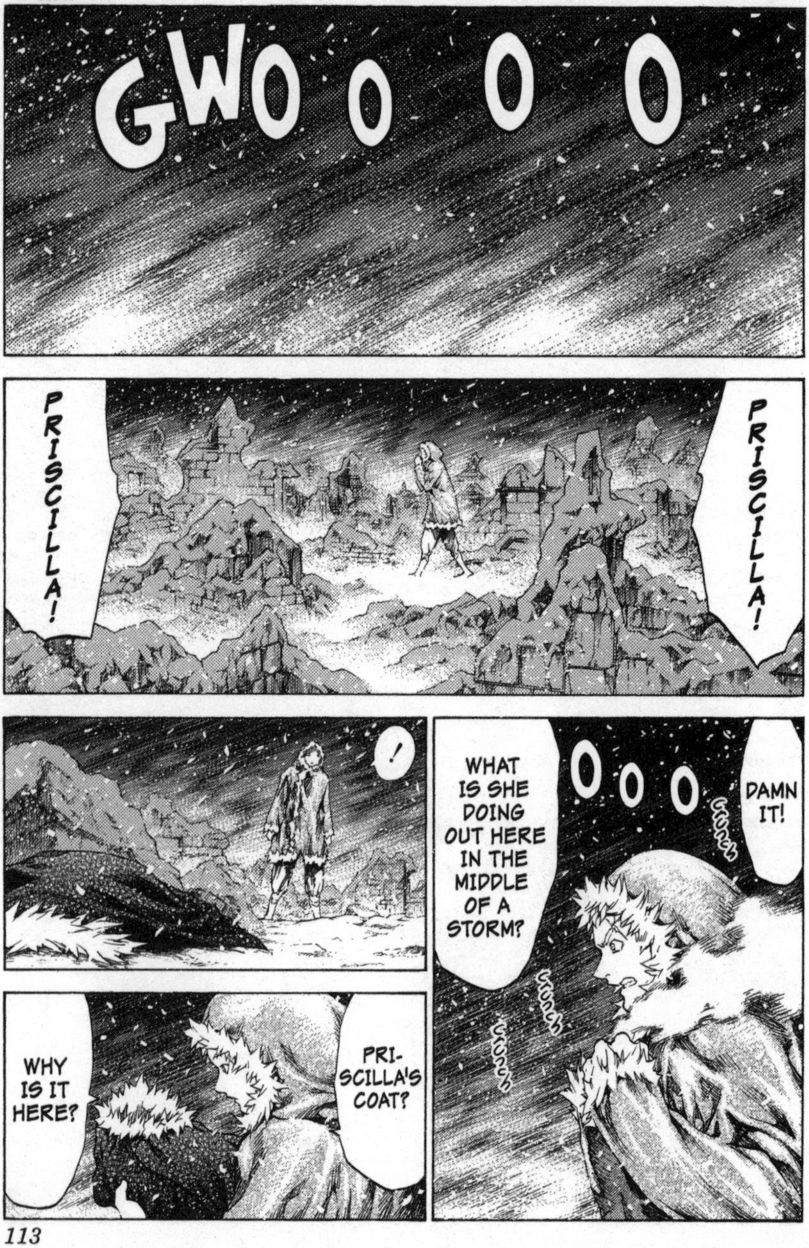
GWOOOO
PRISCILLA!
PRISCILLA!
DAMN IT!
OOO
WHAT IS SHE DOING OUT HERE IN THE MIDDLE OF A STORM?
crunch
crunch
crunch
!
PRI-SCILLA'S COAT?
WHY IS IT HERE?

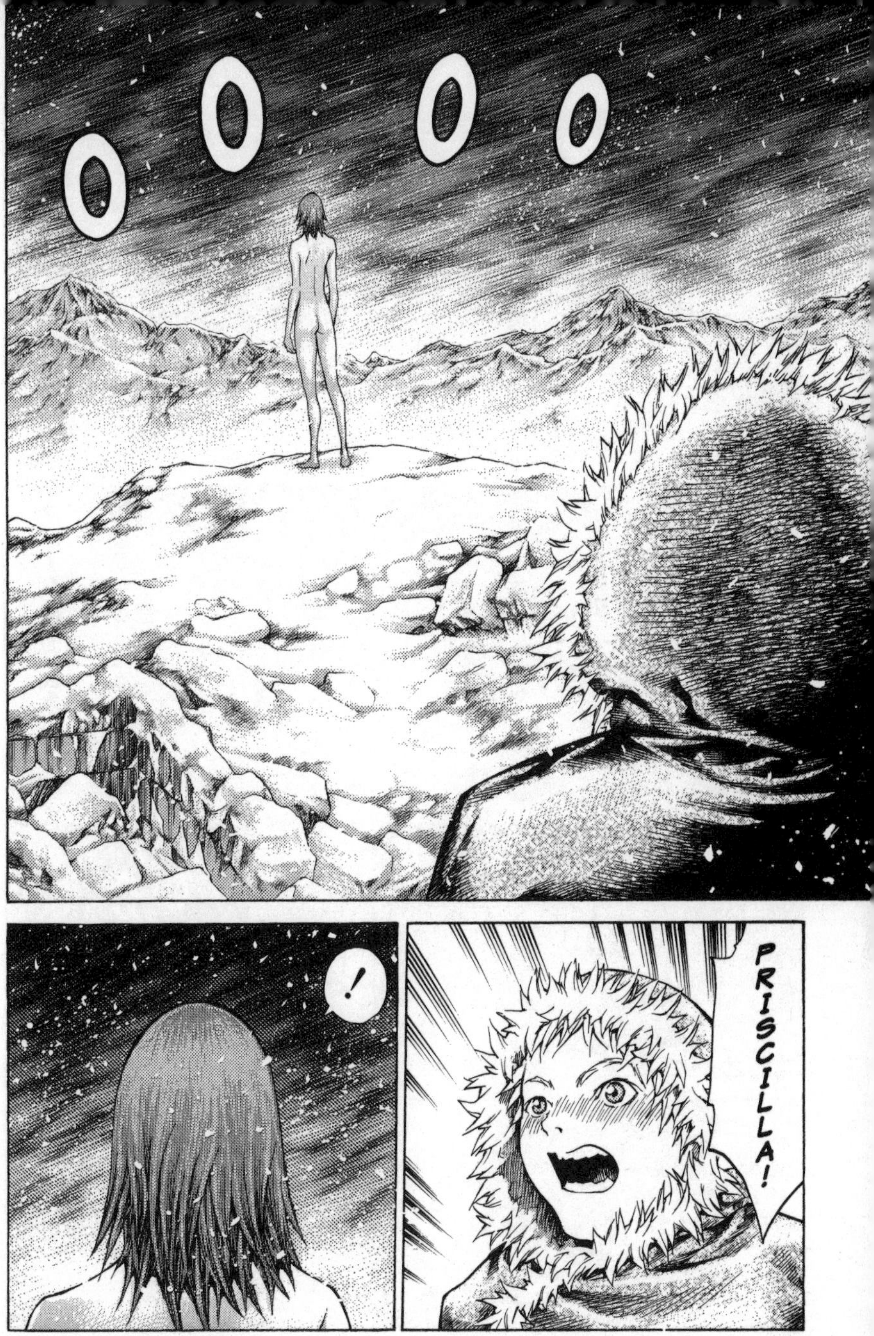
OOOO
PRISCILLA!
!

READ THIS WAY

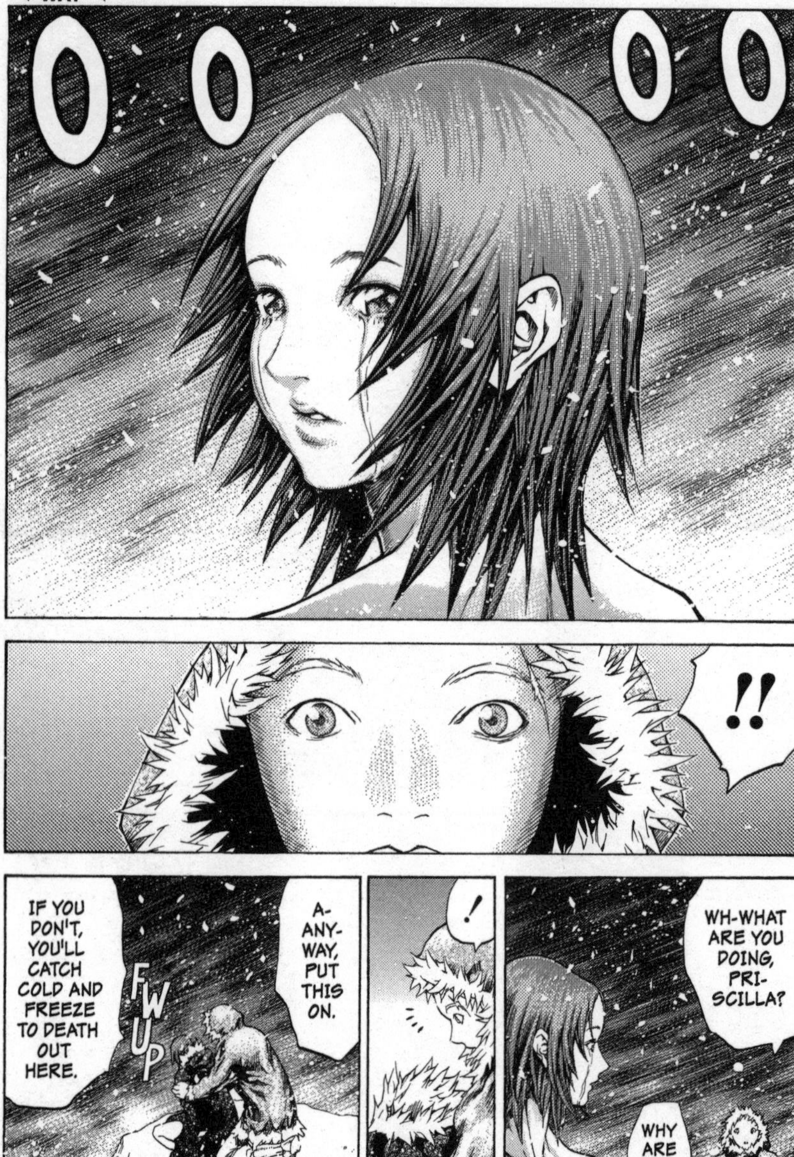
OOOO
!!
WH-WHAT ARE YOU DOING, PRI-SCILLA?
WHY ARE YOU ...?
!
A-ANYWAY, PUT THIS ON.
FWUP
IF YOU DON'T, YOU'LL CATCH COLD AND FREEZE TO DEATH OUT HERE.

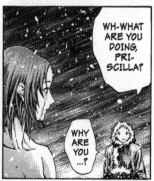

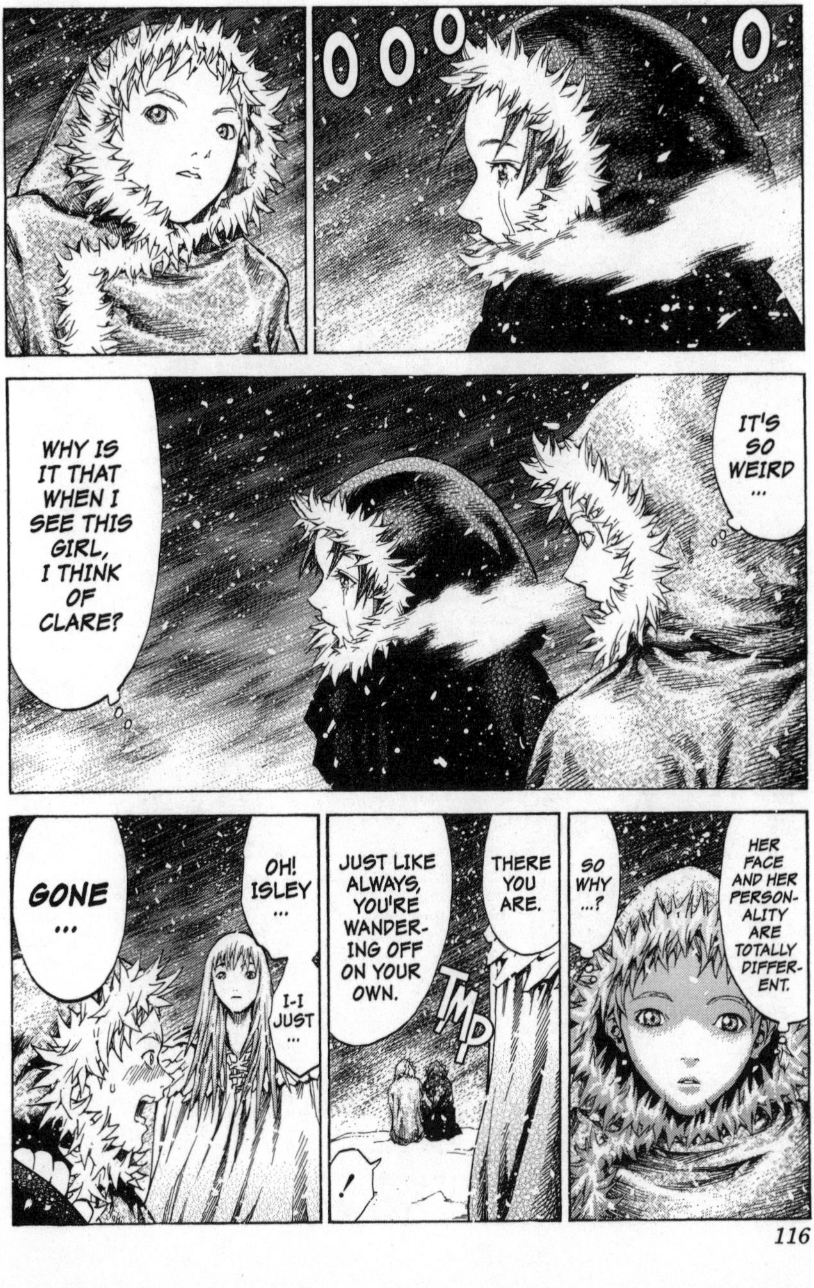
OOOO
IT'S SO WEIRD ...
WHY IS IT THAT WHEN I SEE THIS GIRL, I THINK OF CLARE?
HER FACE AND HER PERSONALITY ARE TOTALLY DIFFERENT.
SO WHY ...?
THERE YOU ARE.
JUST LIKE ALWAYS, YOU'RE WANDERING OFF ON YOUR OWN.
TMP
!
OH! ISLEY ...
I-I JUST ...
GONE ...

READ THIS WAY

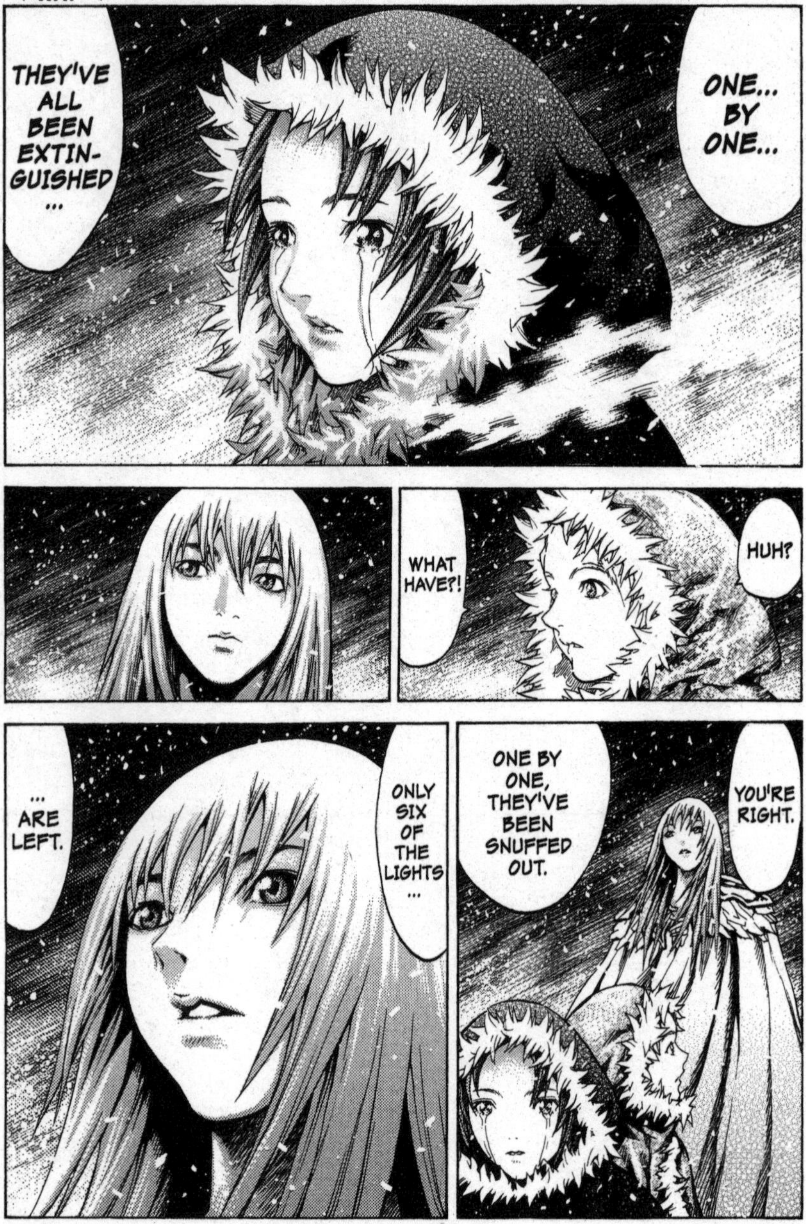
ONE... BY ONE...
THEY'VE ALL BEEN EXTIN-GUISHED...
HUH?
WHAT HAVE?!
YOU'RE RIGHT.
ONE BY ONE, THEY'VE BEEN SNUFFED OUT.
ONLY SIX OF THE LIGHTS...
... ARE LEFT.

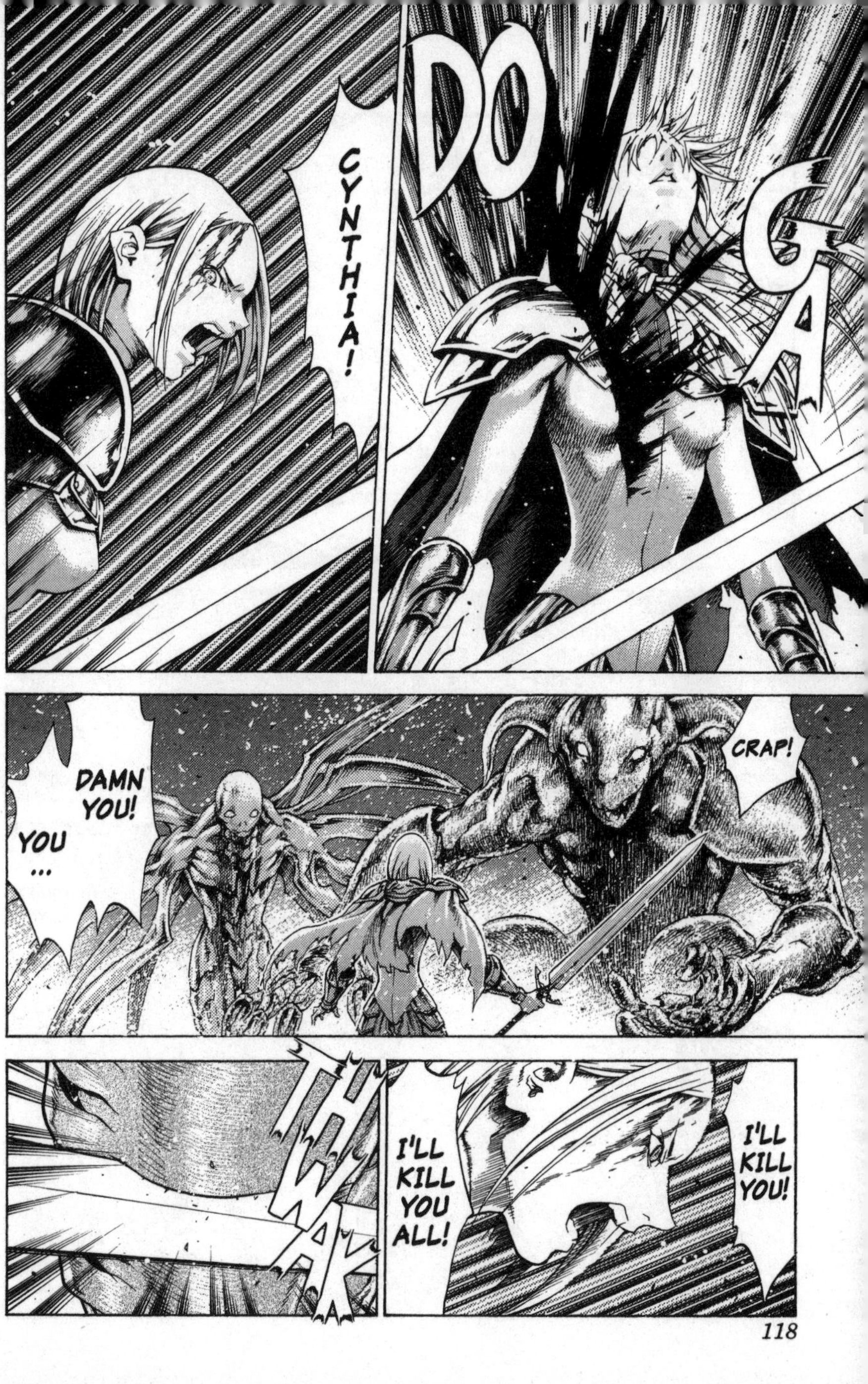
DO GA
CYNTHIA!
CRAP!
DAMN YOU!
YOU ...
I'LL KILL YOU!
I'LL KILL YOU ALL!
THWAK

READ THIS WAY

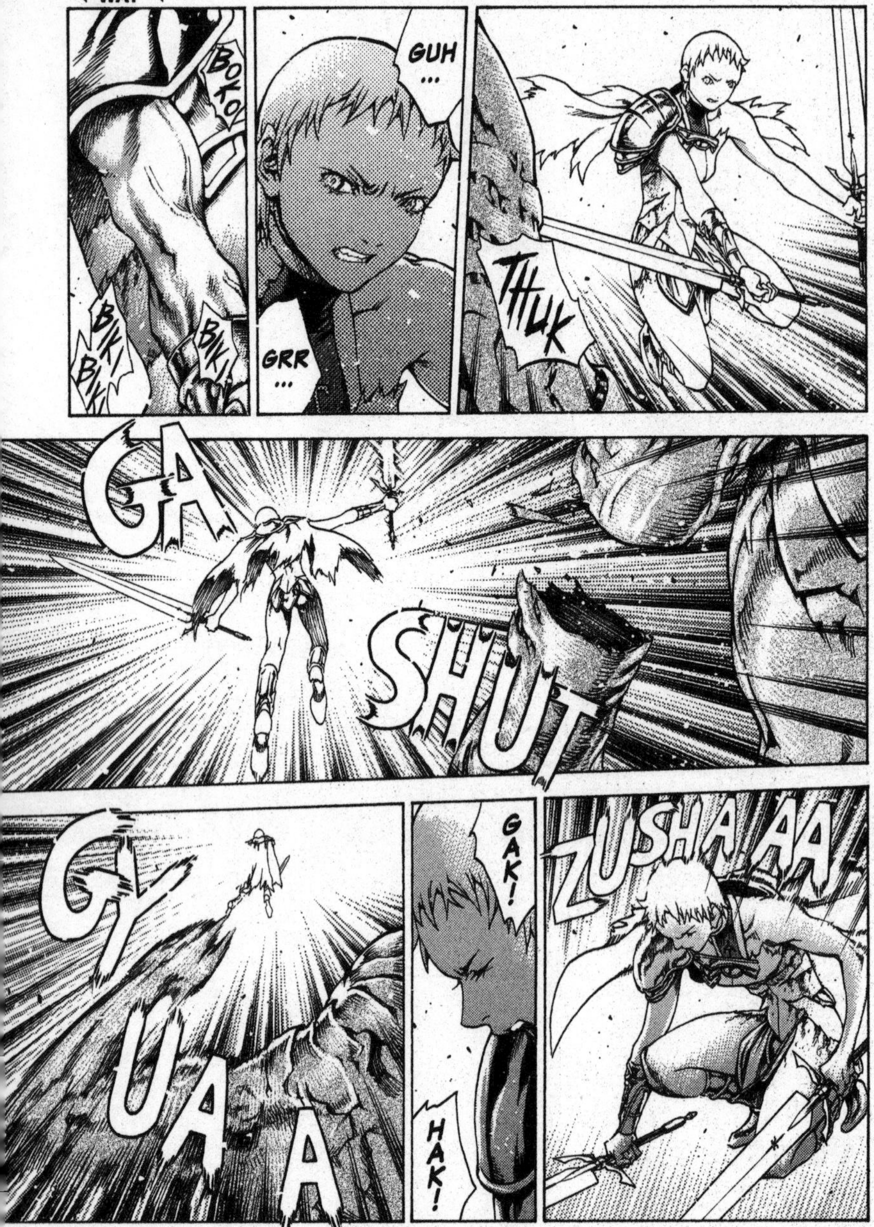
THUK
GUH ...
GRR ...
BOKO
BIKI
BIKI BIKI
GA SHUT
ZUSHAAA
GAK!
HAK!
GYUAA A

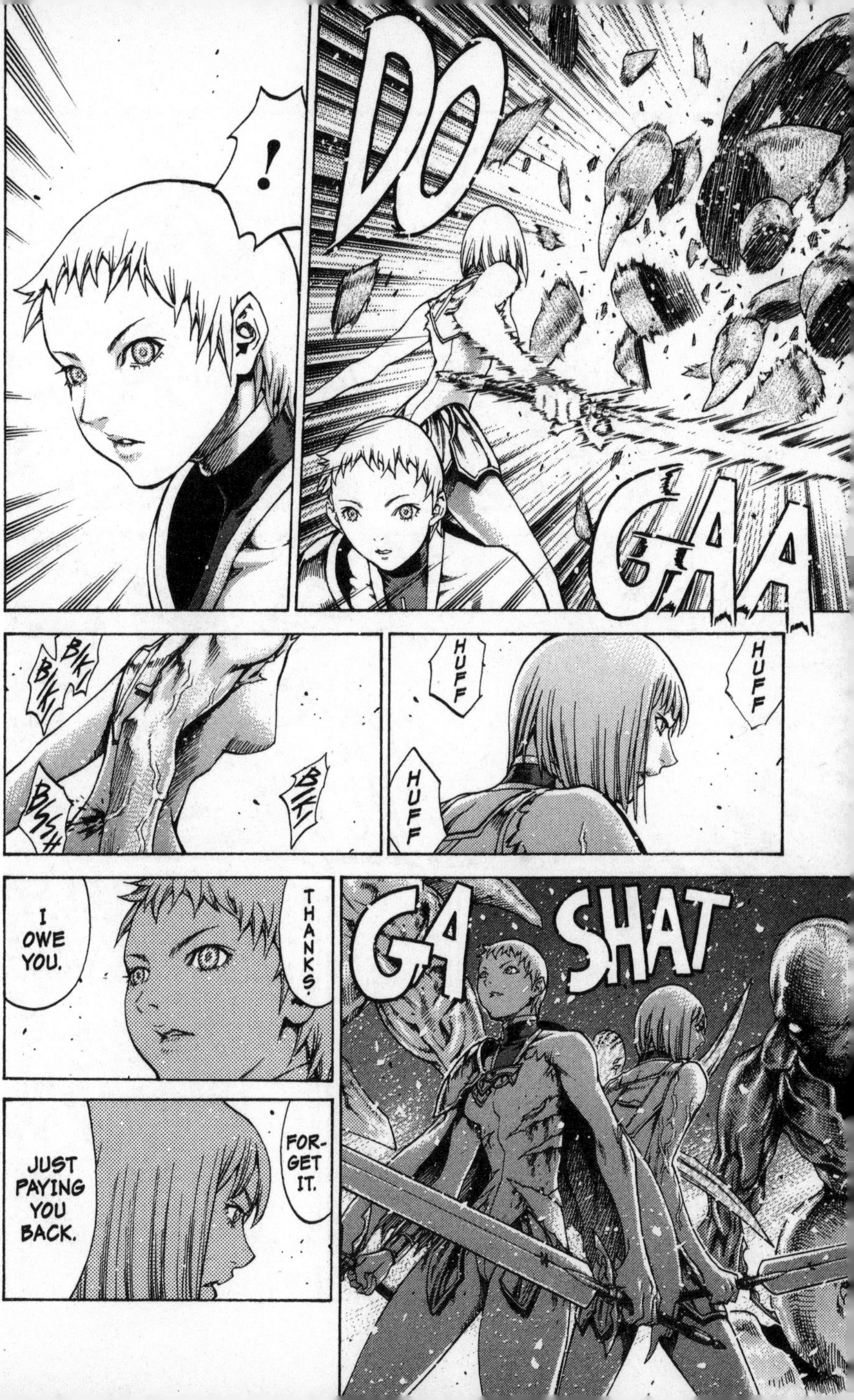
DO
GAA
!
HUFF
HUFF
HUFF
BIKI
BIKI
BSSH
BIKI
GA
SHAT
THANKS.
I OWE YOU.
FORGET IT.
JUST PAYING YOU BACK.

READ THIS WAY

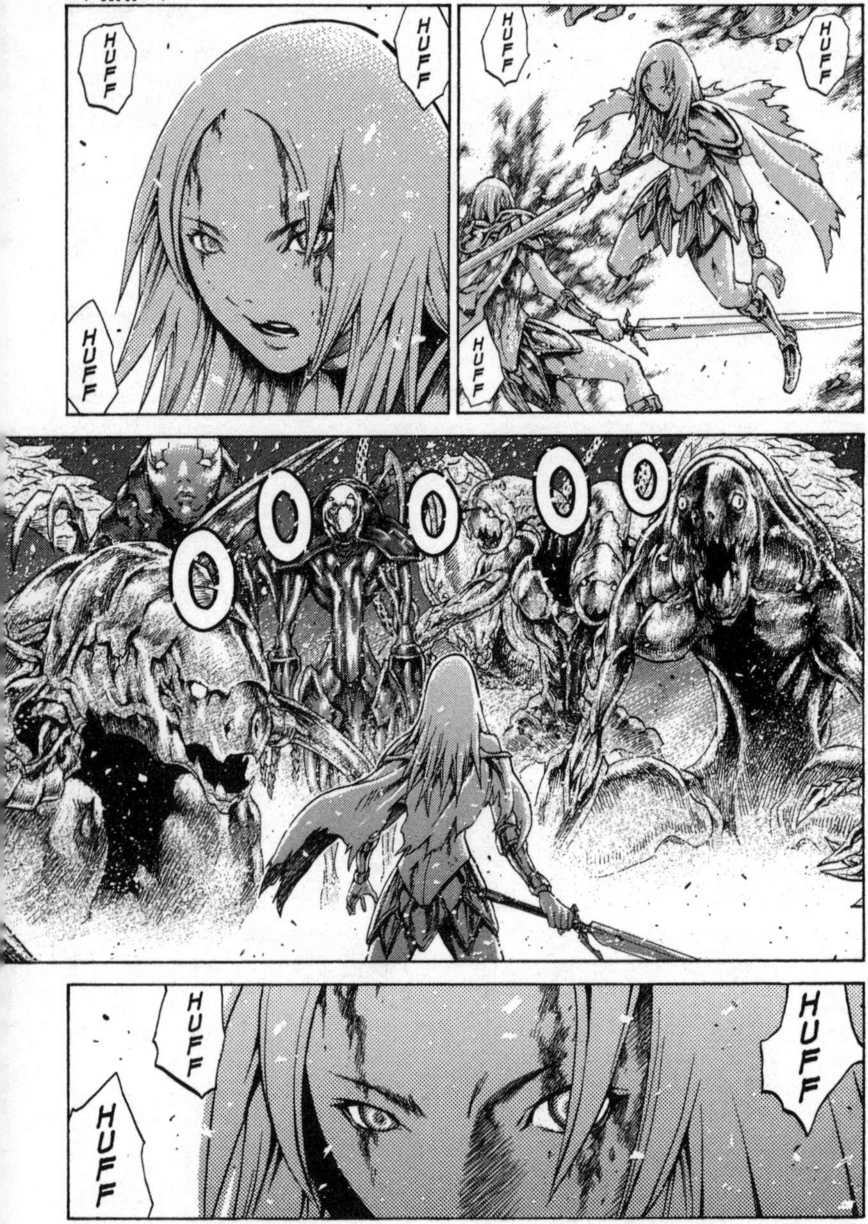
HUFF
HUFF
HUFF
HUFF
HUFF
O
O
O
O
O
O
HUFF
HUFF
HUFF

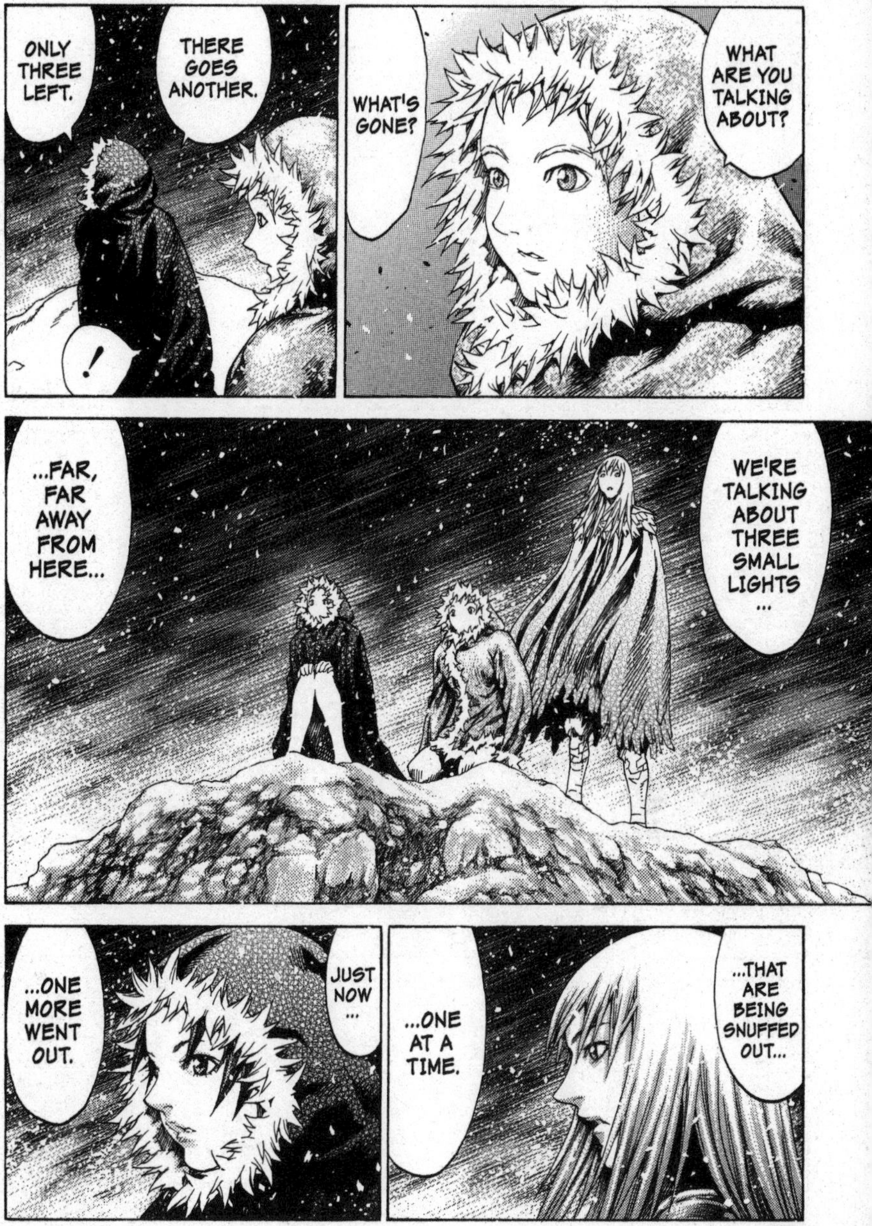
WHAT ARE YOU TALKING ABOUT?
WHAT'S GONE?
THERE GOES ANOTHER.
ONLY THREE LEFT.
!
WE'RE TALKING ABOUT THREE SMALL LIGHTS ...
...FAR, FAR AWAY FROM HERE...
...THAT ARE BEING SNUFFED OUT...
...ONE AT A TIME.
JUST NOW ...
...ONE MORE WENT OUT.

READ THIS WAY

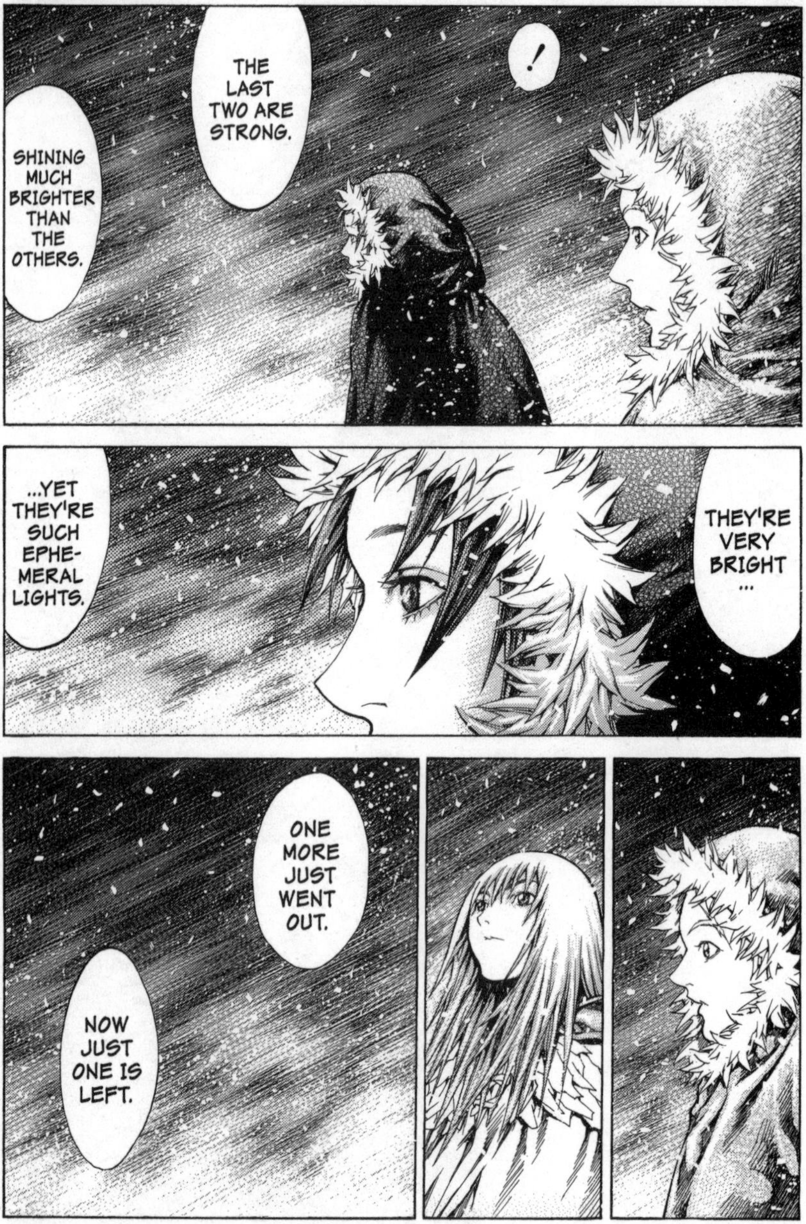
!
THE LAST TWO ARE STRONG.
SHINING MUCH BRIGHTER THAN THE OTHERS.
THEY'RE VERY BRIGHT ...
...YET THEY'RE SUCH EPHEMERAL LIGHTS.
ONE MORE JUST WENT OUT.
NOW JUST ONE IS LEFT.

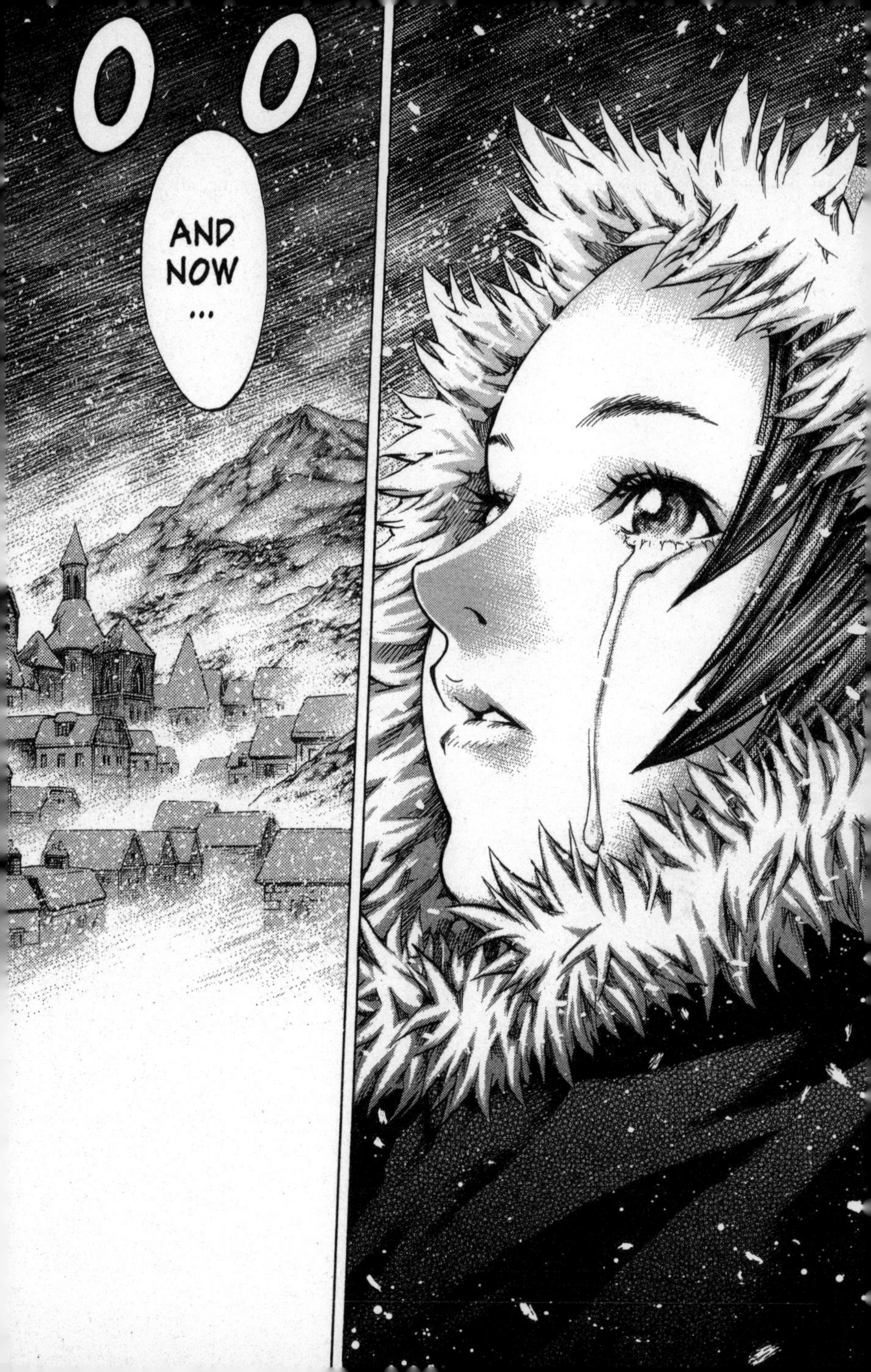
AND NOW ...

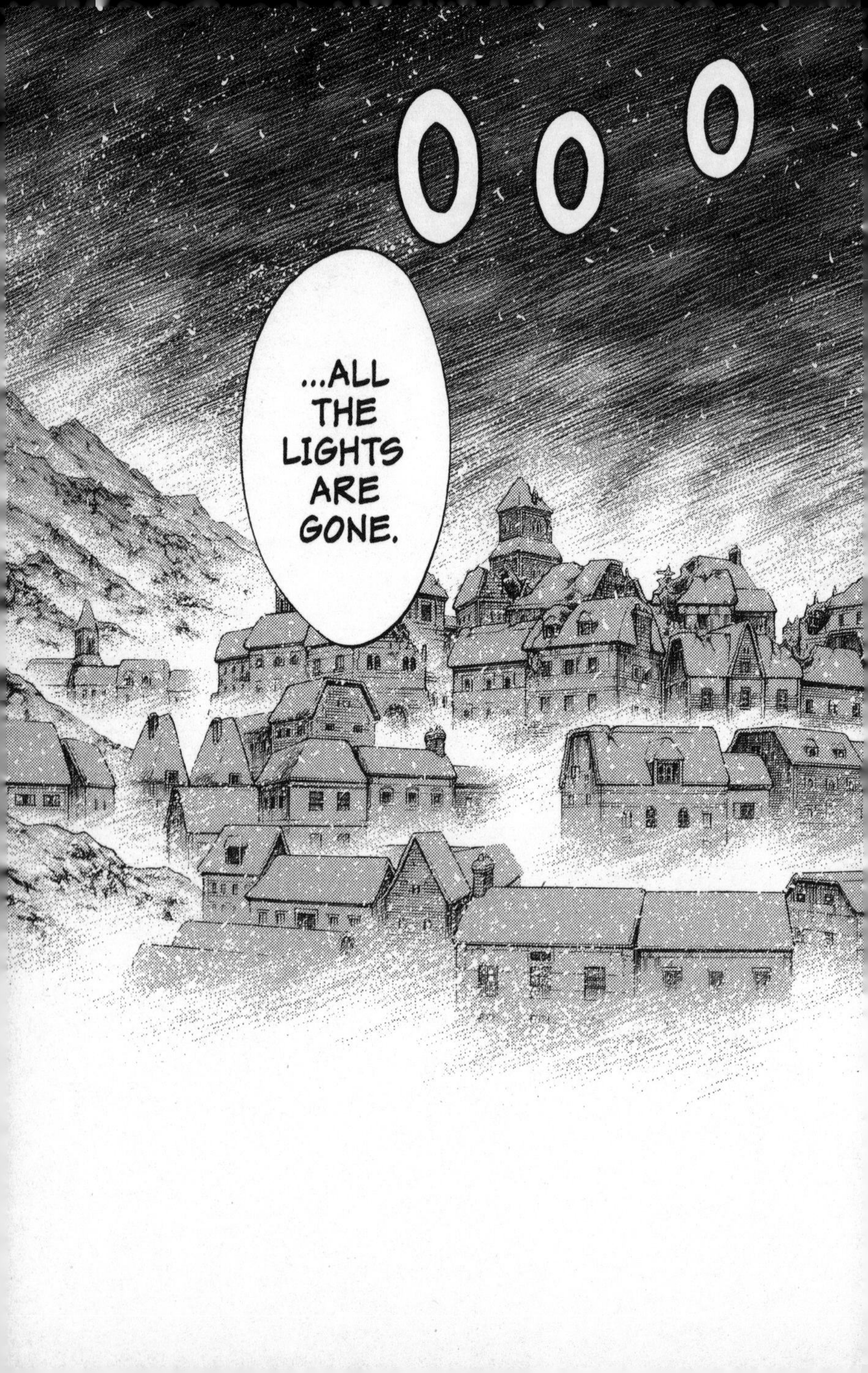
...ALL THE LIGHTS ARE GONE.

Scene 62: Kindred of Paradise, Part 1

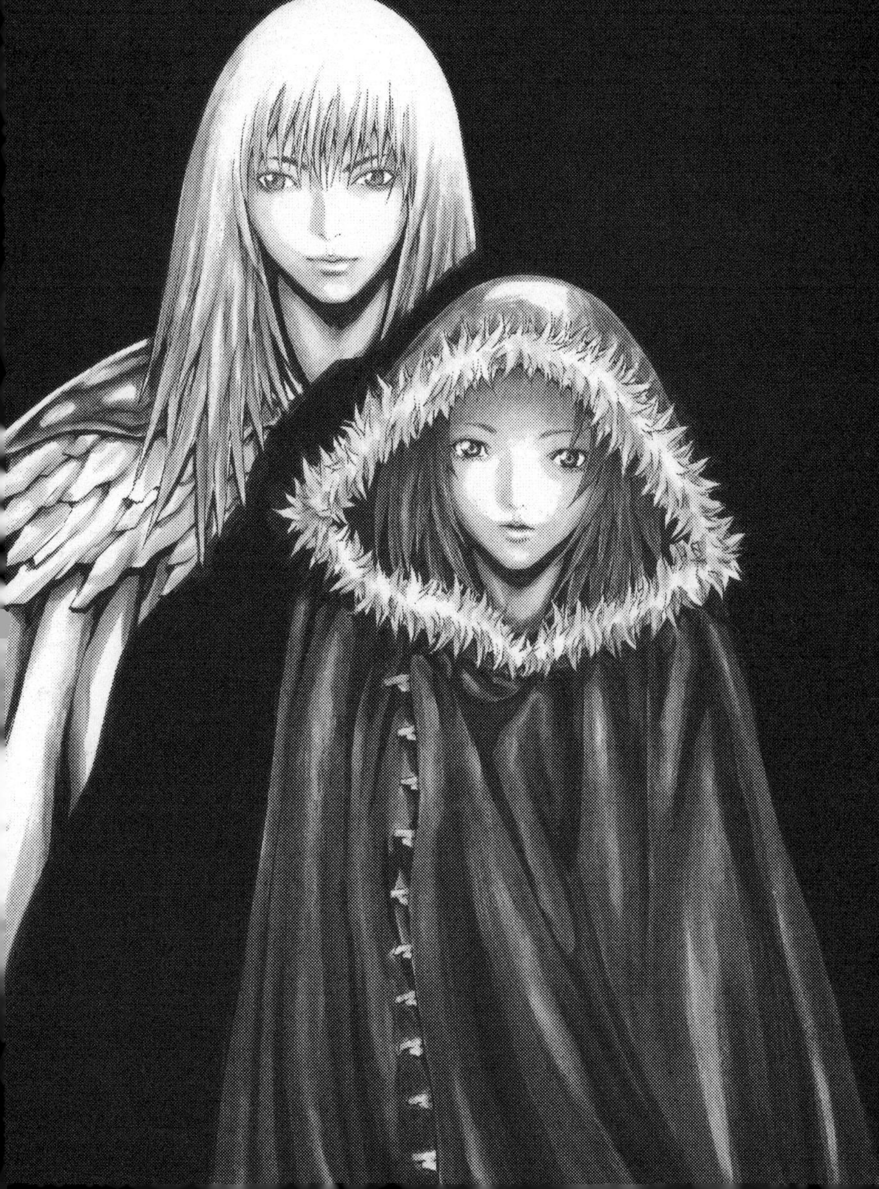

READ THIS WAY

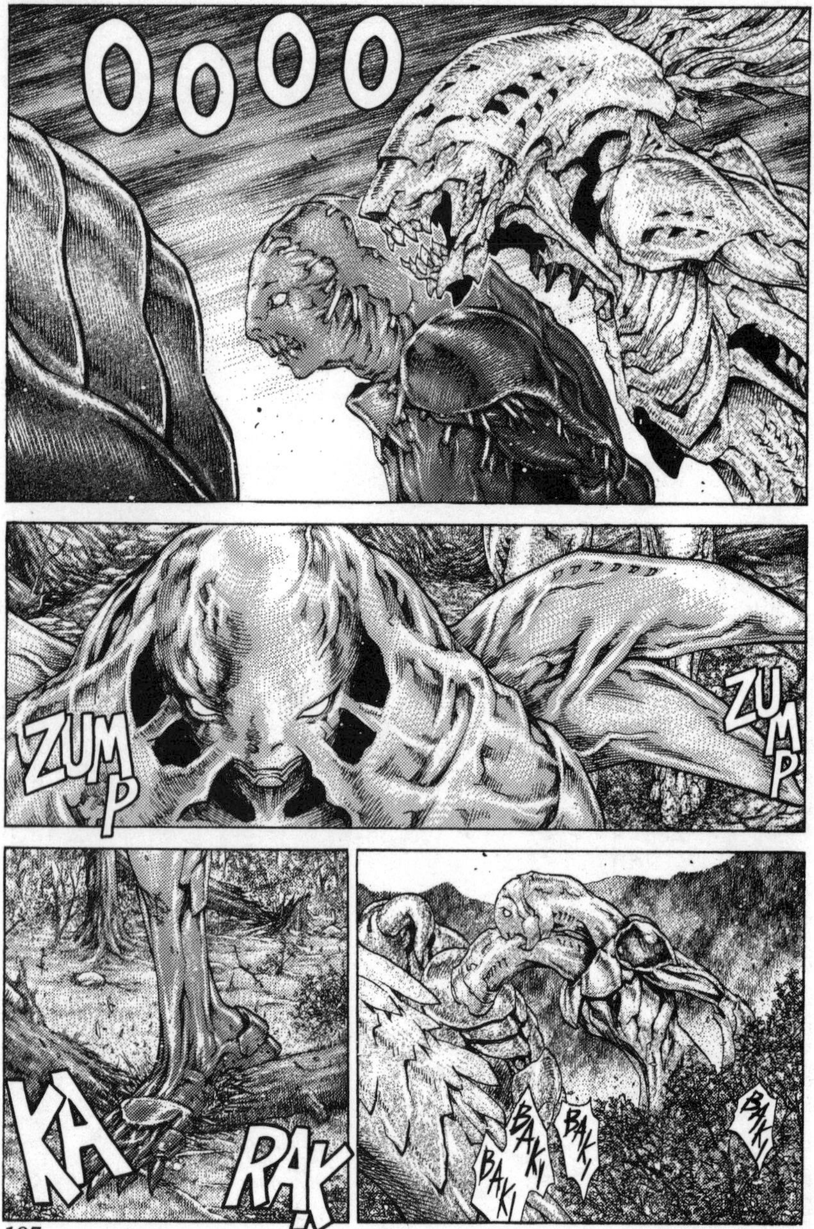
OOOO
ZUMP
ZUMP
BAKI
BAKI
BAKI
BAKI
BAKI
KA
RAK

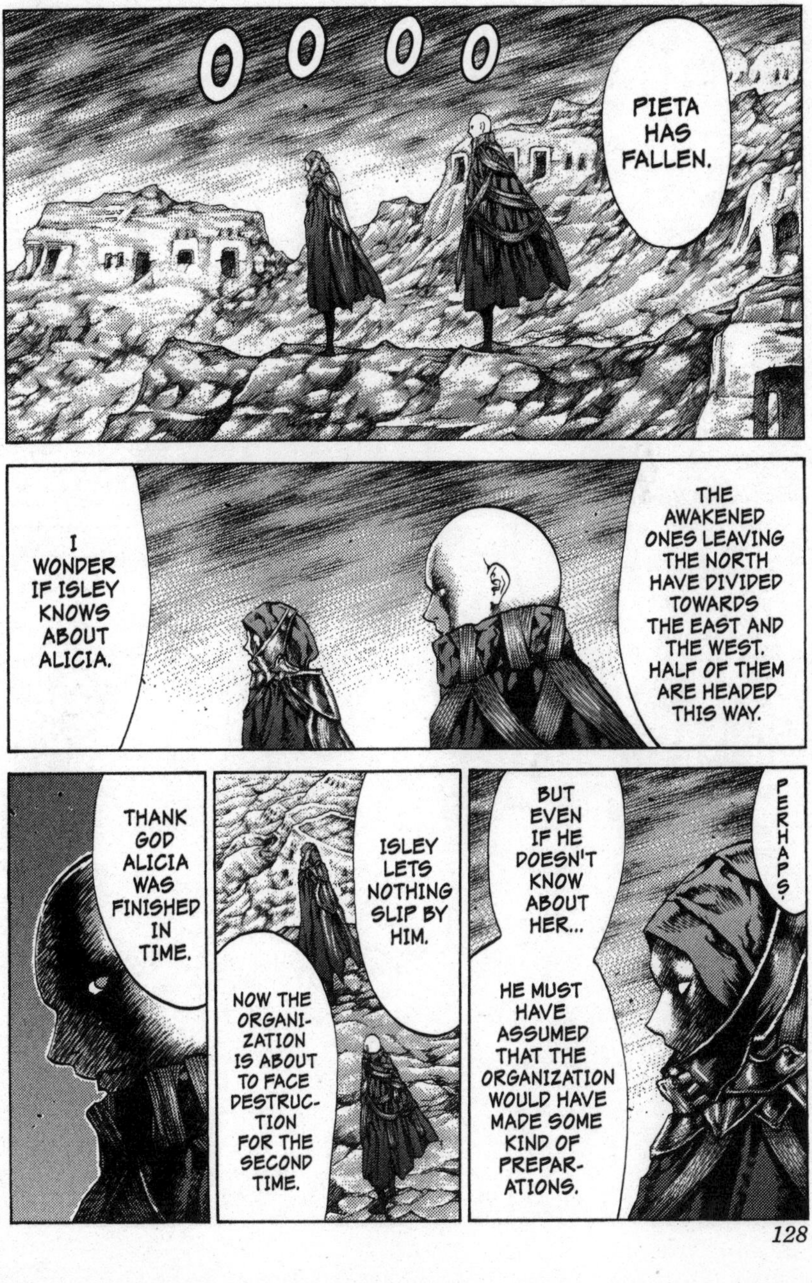
OOOO
PIETA HAS FALLEN.
THE AWAKENED ONES LEAVING THE NORTH HAVE DIVIDED TOWARDS THE EAST AND THE WEST. HALF OF THEM ARE HEADED THIS WAY.
I WONDER IF ISLEY KNOWS ABOUT ALICIA.
PERHAPS.
BUT EVEN IF HE DOESN'T KNOW ABOUT HER...
HE MUST HAVE ASSUMED THAT THE ORGANIZATION WOULD HAVE MADE SOME KIND OF PREPAR-ATIONS.
ISLEY LETS NOTHING SLIP BY HIM.
NOW THE ORGANI-ZATION IS ABOUT TO FACE DESTRUC-TION FOR THE SECOND TIME.
THANK GOD ALICIA WAS FINISHED IN TIME.

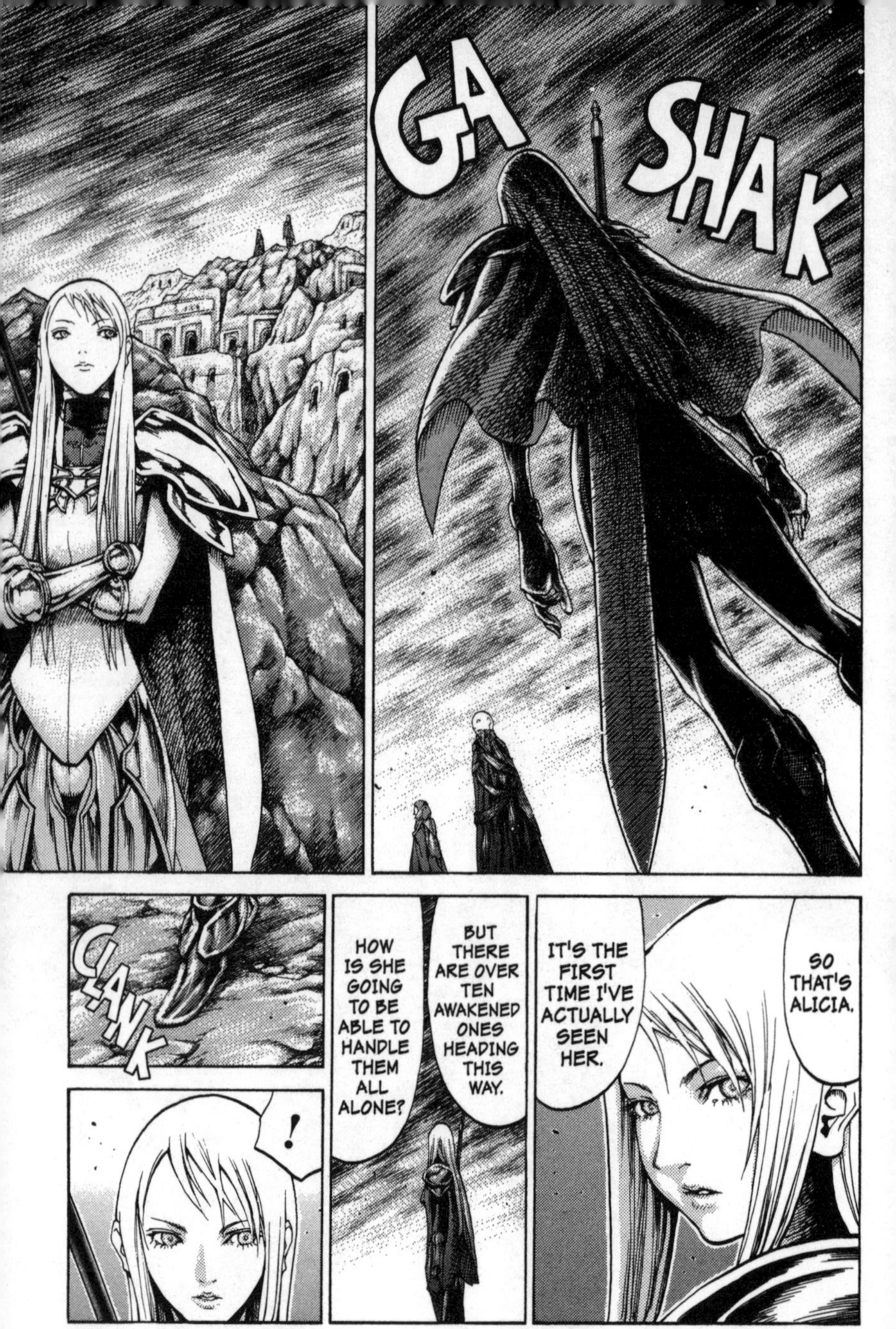
GA
SHAK
SO THAT'S ALICIA.
IT'S THE FIRST TIME I'VE ACTUALLY SEEN HER.
BUT THERE ARE OVER TEN AWAKENED ONES HEADING THIS WAY.
HOW IS SHE GOING TO BE ABLE TO HANDLE THEM ALL ALONE?
CLANK
!

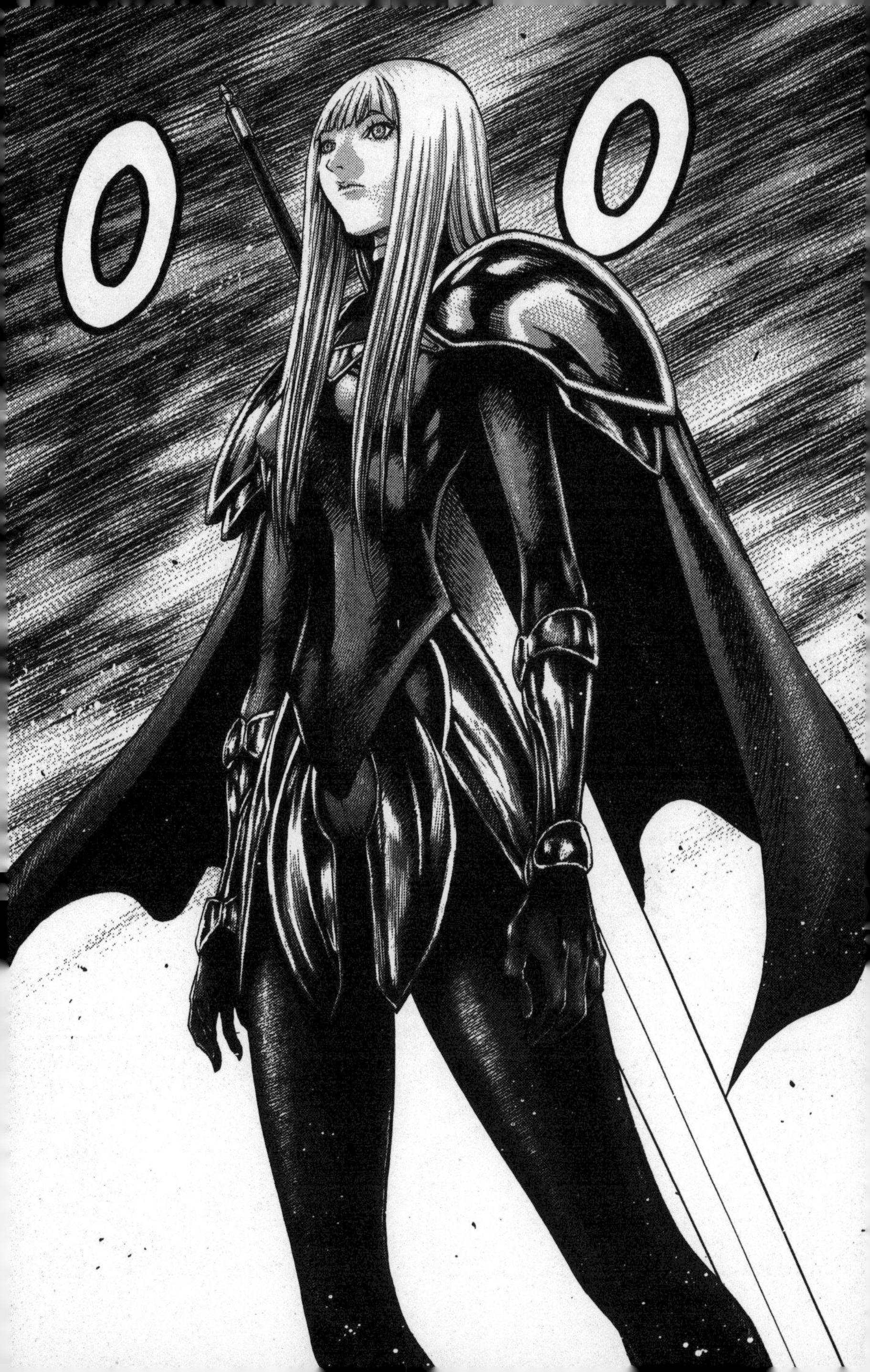
OO

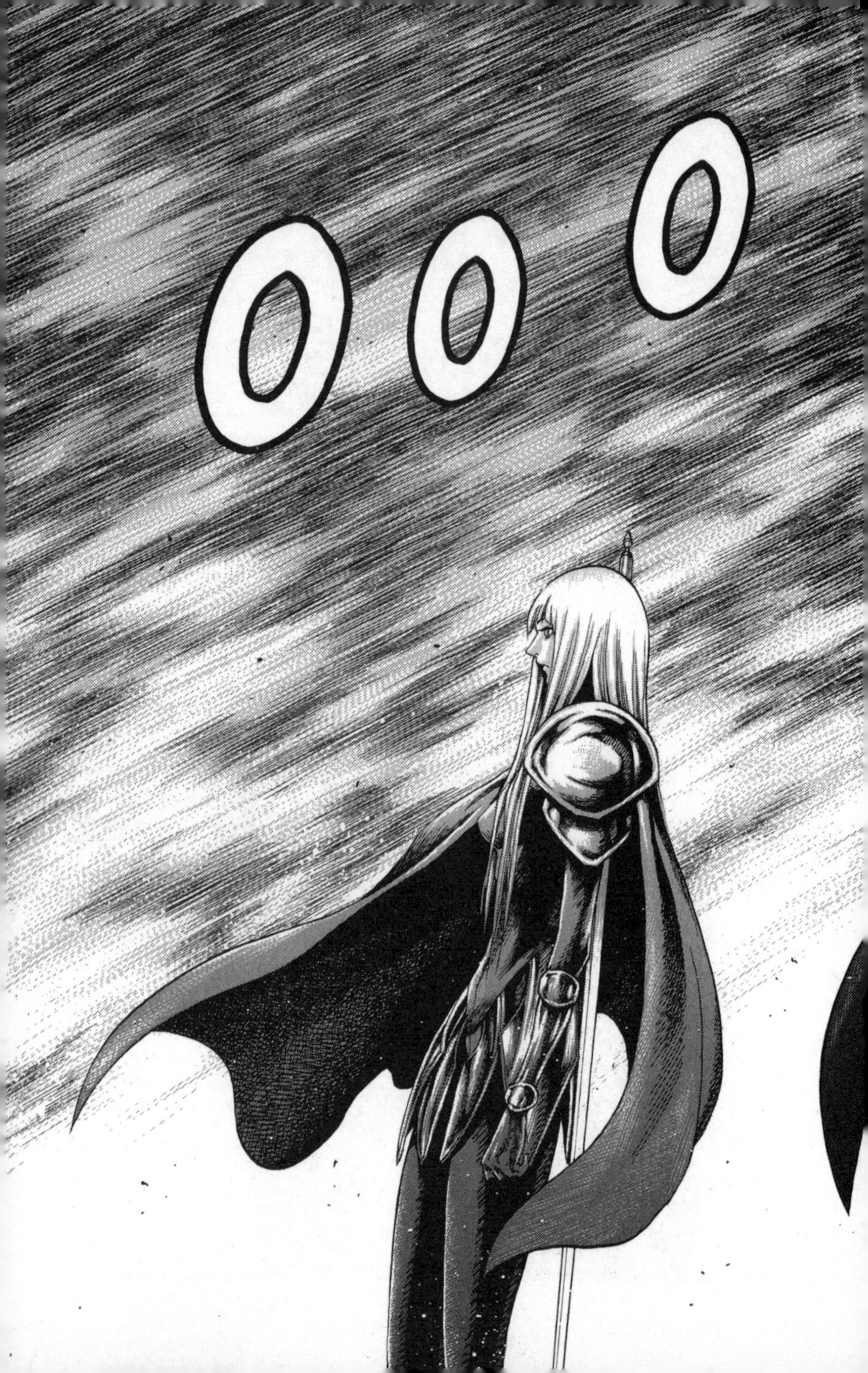
OOO

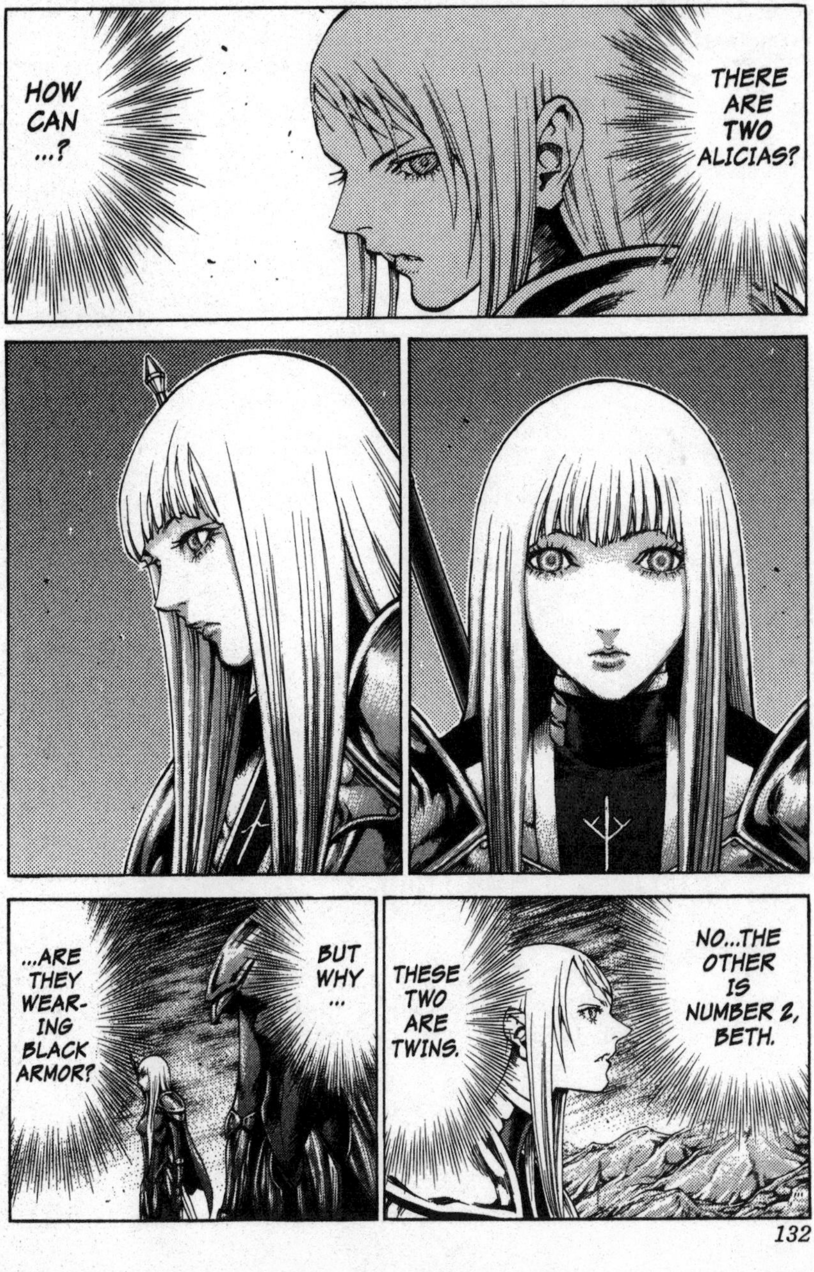
THERE ARE TWO ALICIAS?
HOW CAN ...?
NO...THE OTHER IS NUMBER 2, BETH.
THESE TWO ARE TWINS.
BUT WHY ...
...ARE THEY WEAR-ING BLACK ARMOR?

READ THIS WAY

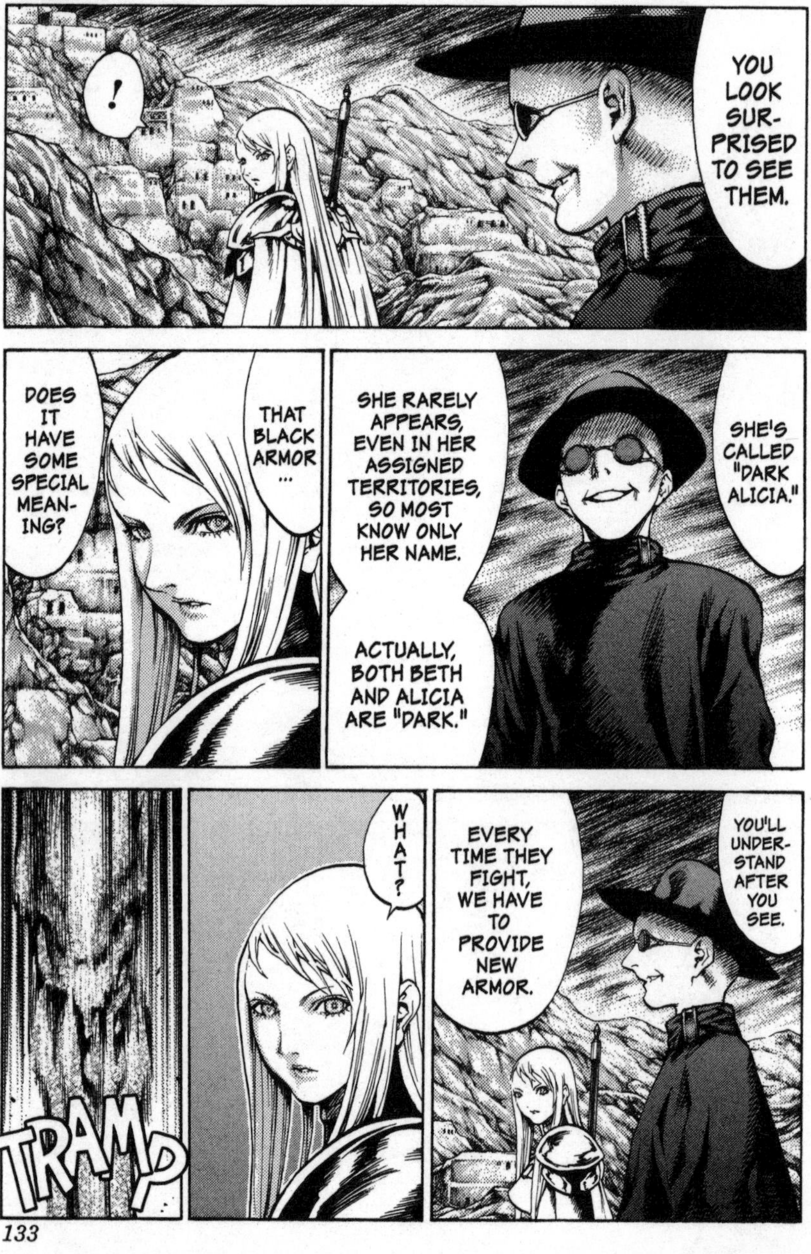
YOU LOOK SURPRISED TO SEE THEM.
!
SHE'S CALLED "DARK ALICIA."
SHE RARELY APPEARS, EVEN IN HER ASSIGNED TERRITORIES, SO MOST KNOW ONLY HER NAME.
ACTUALLY, BOTH BETH AND ALICIA ARE "DARK."
THAT BLACK ARMOR...
DOES IT HAVE SOME SPECIAL MEANING?
YOU'LL UNDERSTAND AFTER YOU SEE.
EVERY TIME THEY FIGHT, WE HAVE TO PROVIDE NEW ARMOR.
WHAT?
TRAMP

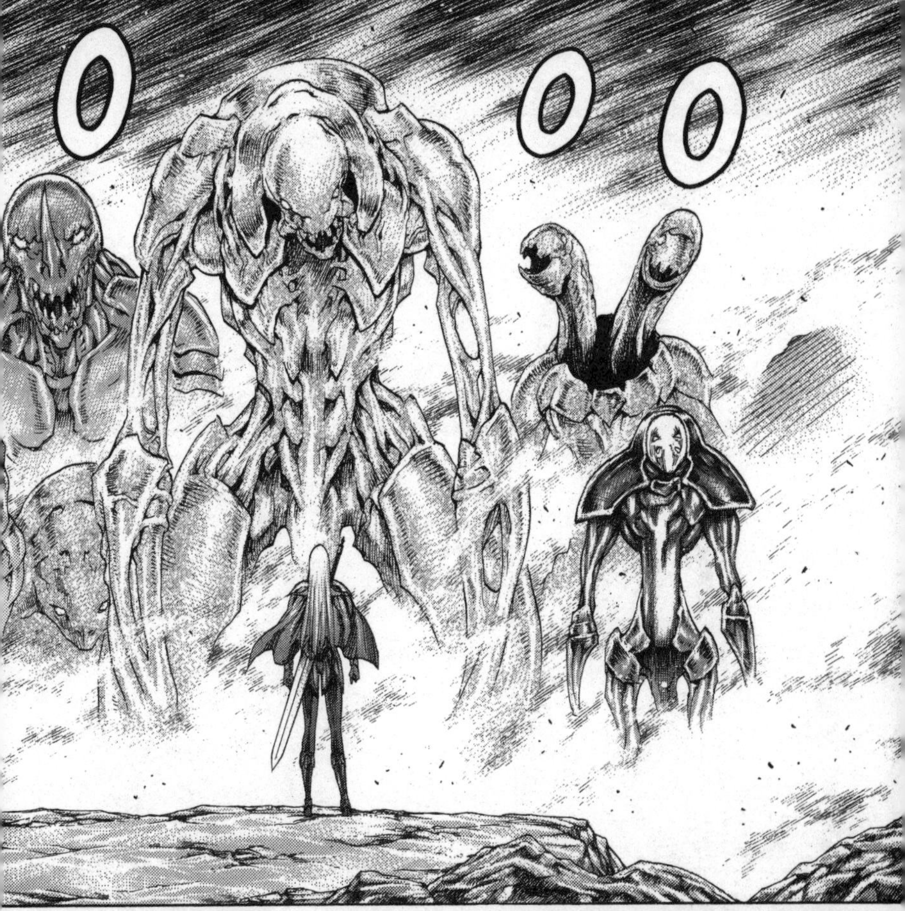
OOO
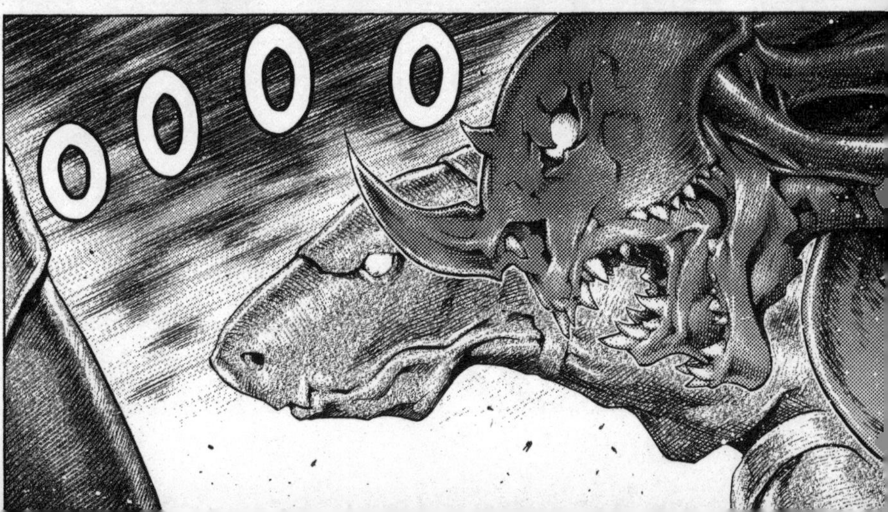
OOOO

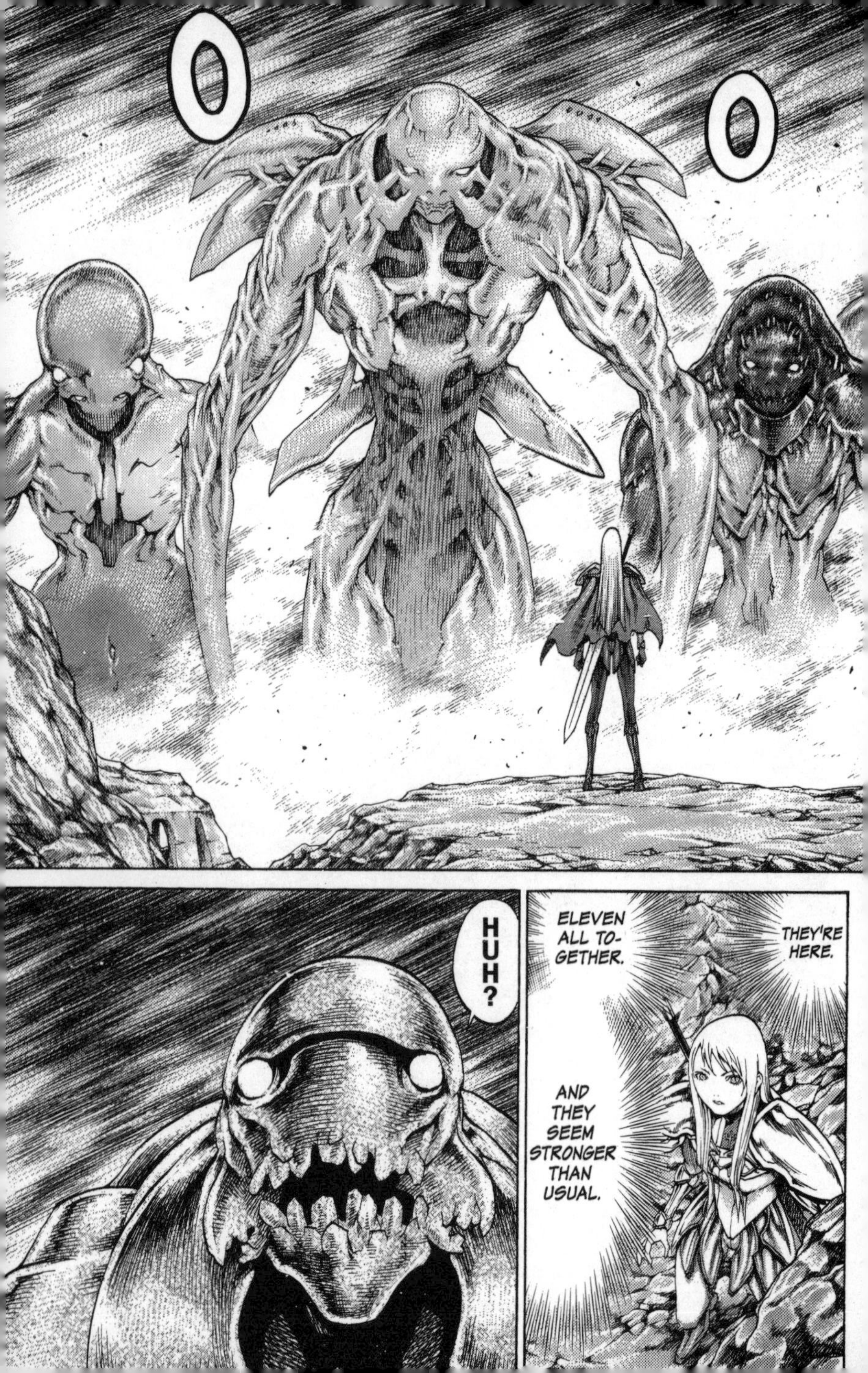
O
O
THEY'RE HERE.
ELEVEN ALL TO-GETHER.
AND THEY SEEM STRONGER THAN USUAL.
HUH?

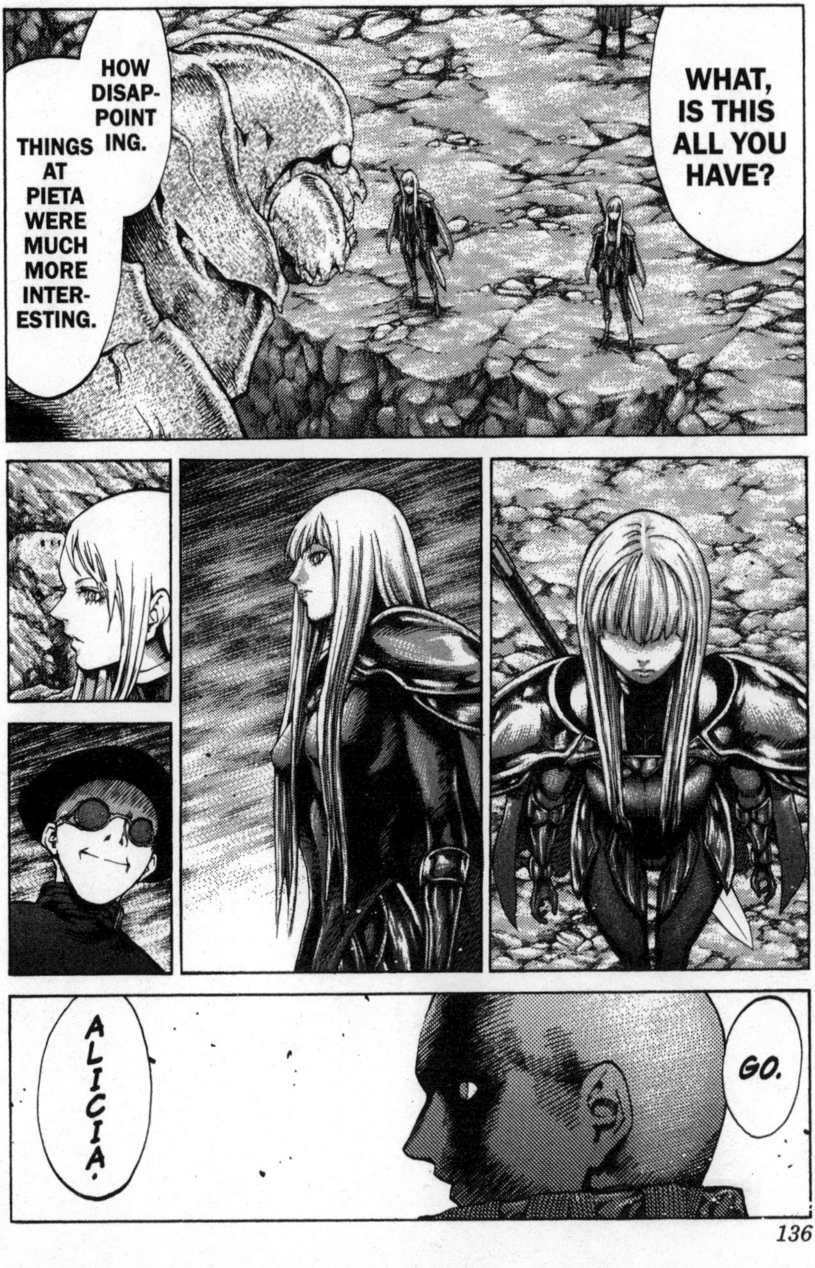
WHAT, IS THIS ALL YOU HAVE?
HOW DISAP- POINT ING.
THINGS AT PIETA WERE MUCH MORE INTER- ESTING.
GO.
ALICIA.

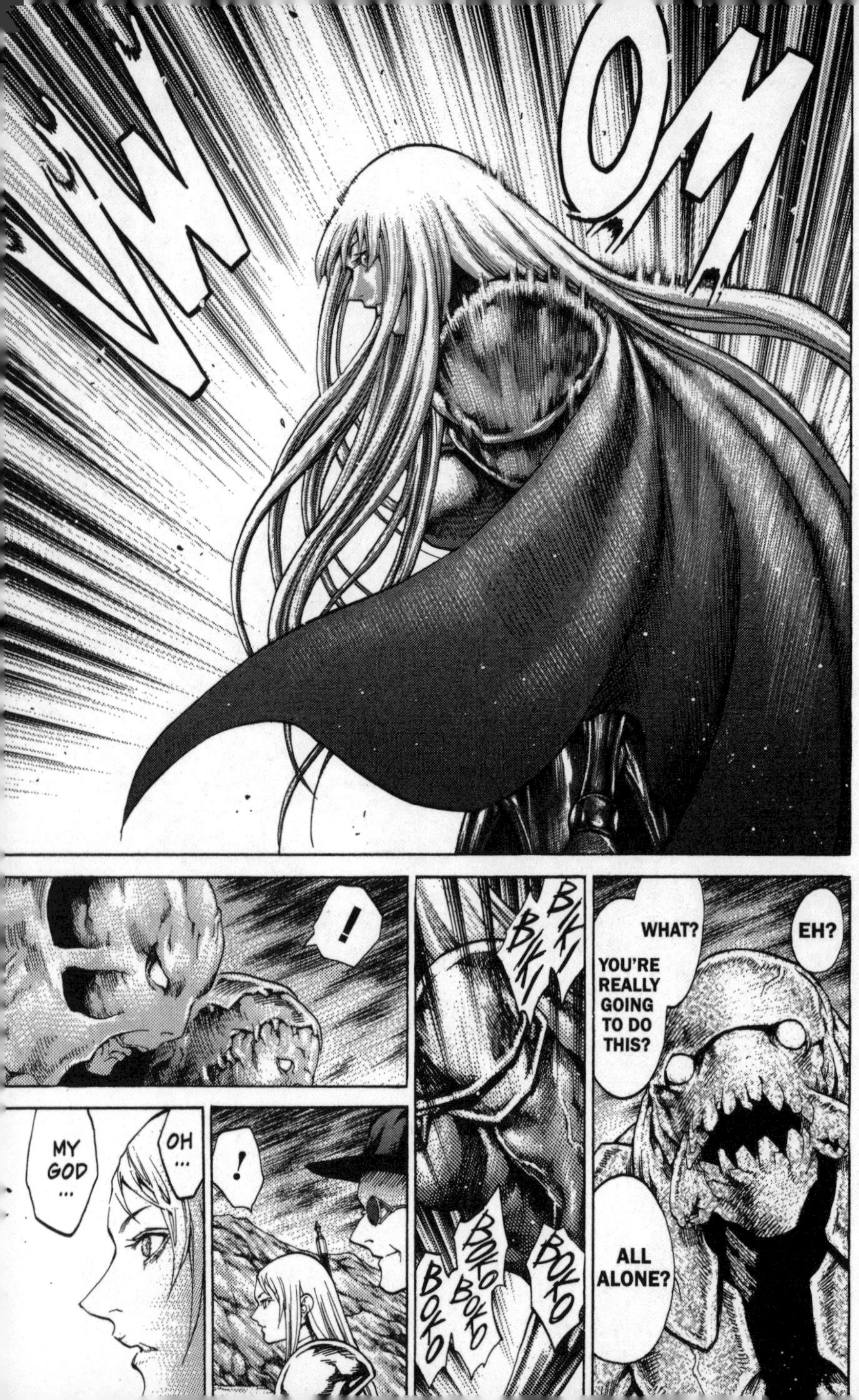
EH?
WHAT?
YOU'RE REALLY GOING TO DO THIS?
ALL ALONE?
BIKI BIKI
BOKO BOKO BOKO BOKO
!
!
OH ...
MY GOD ...

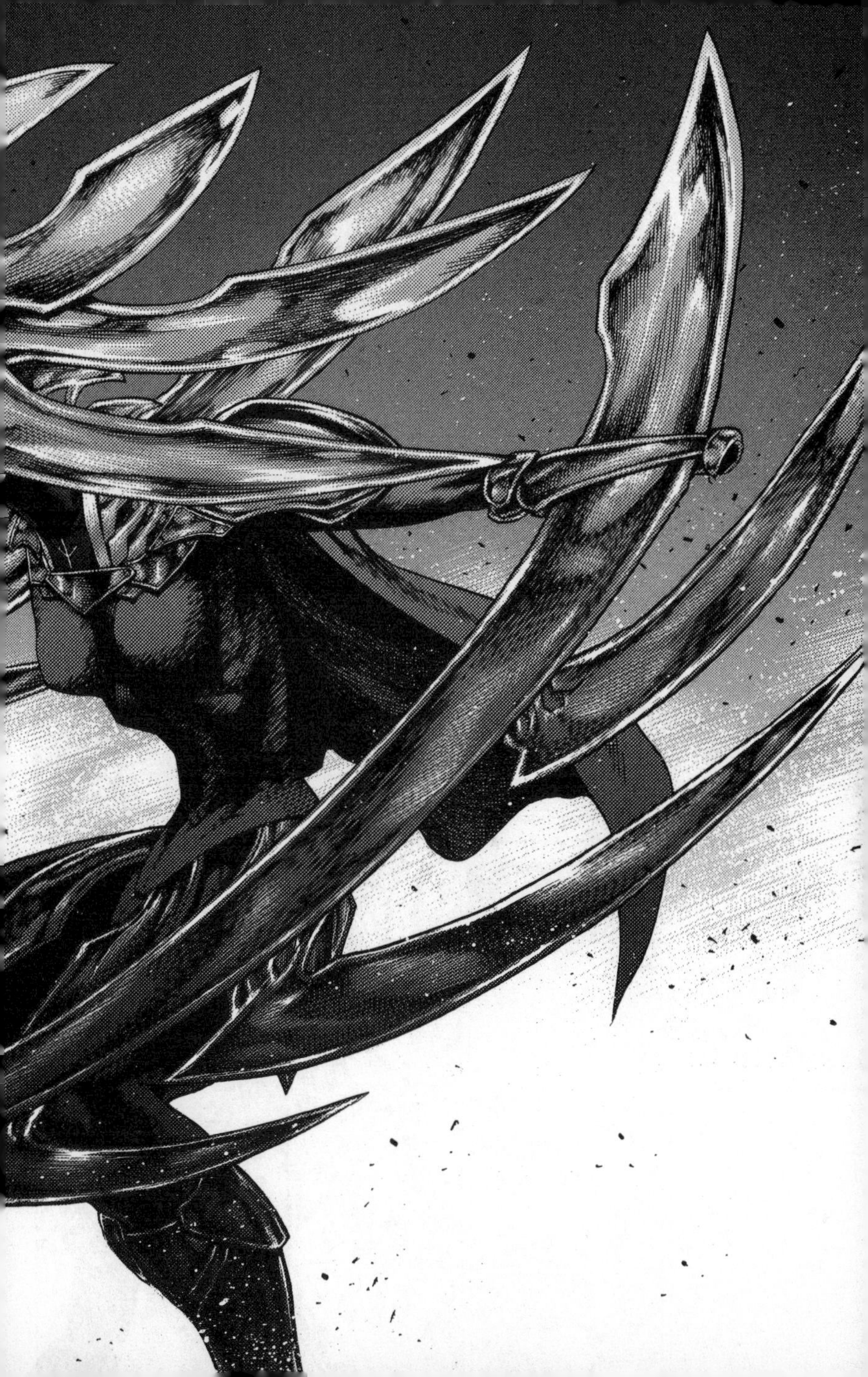

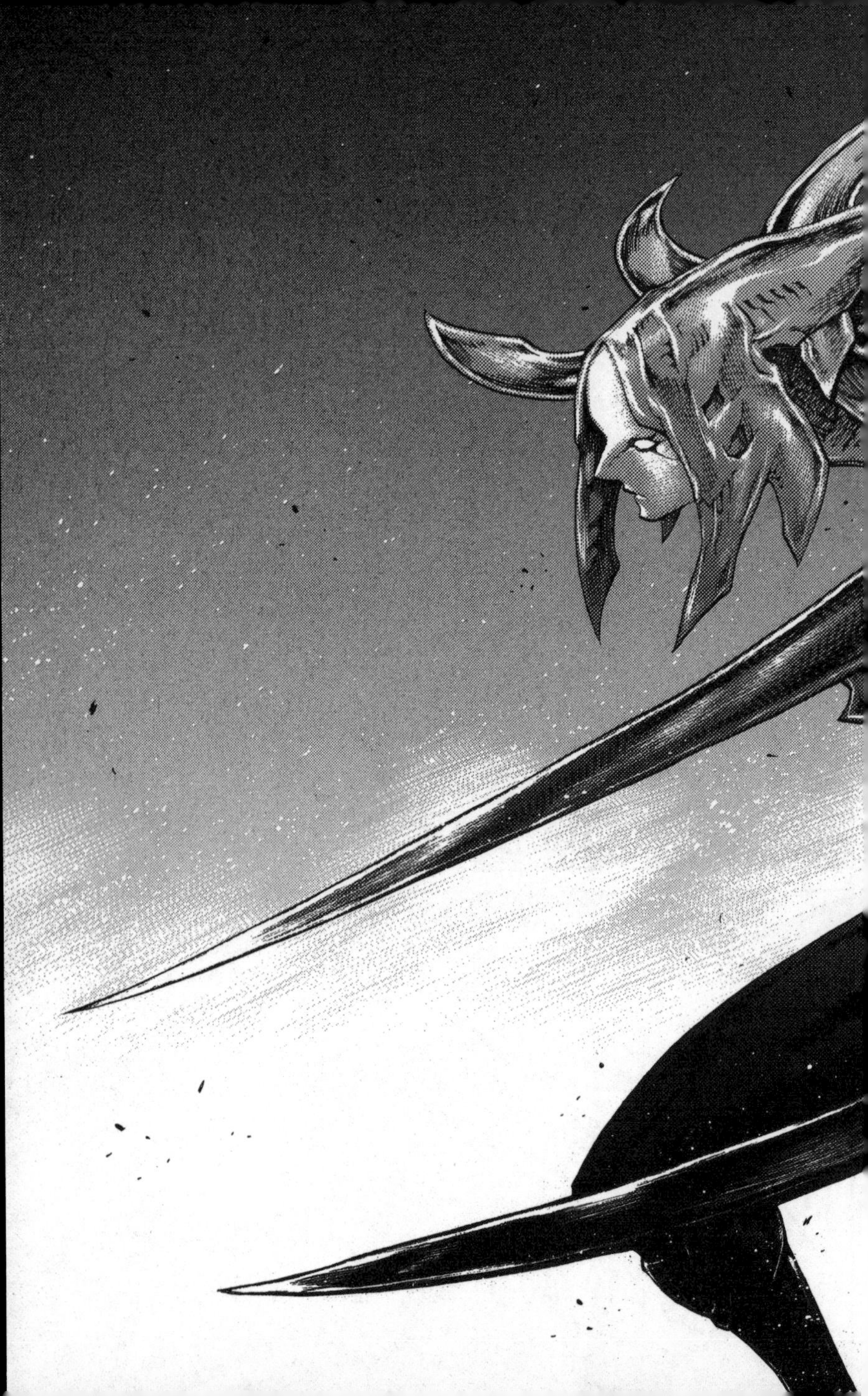

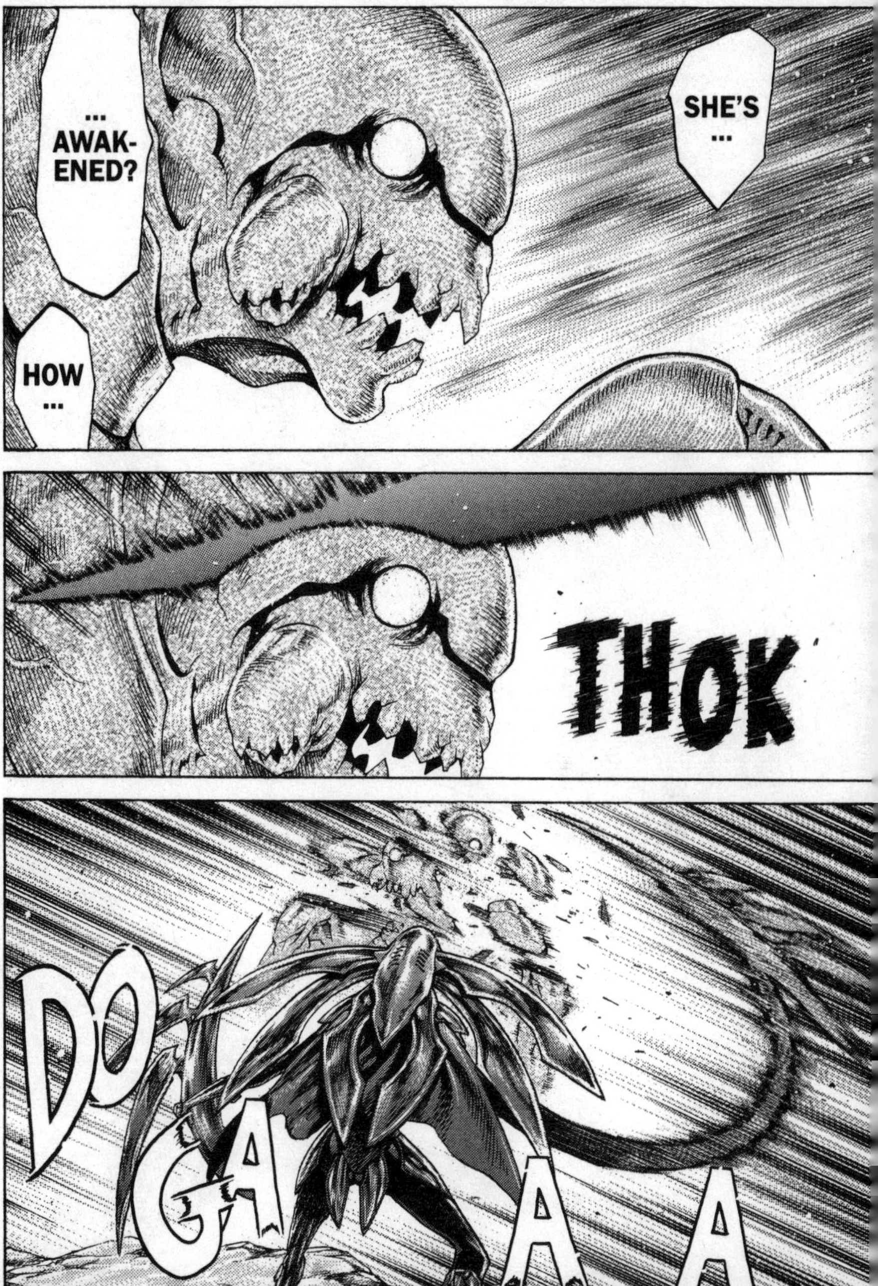
SHE'S ...
... AWAK-
ENED?
HOW ...
THOK
DOGAAA

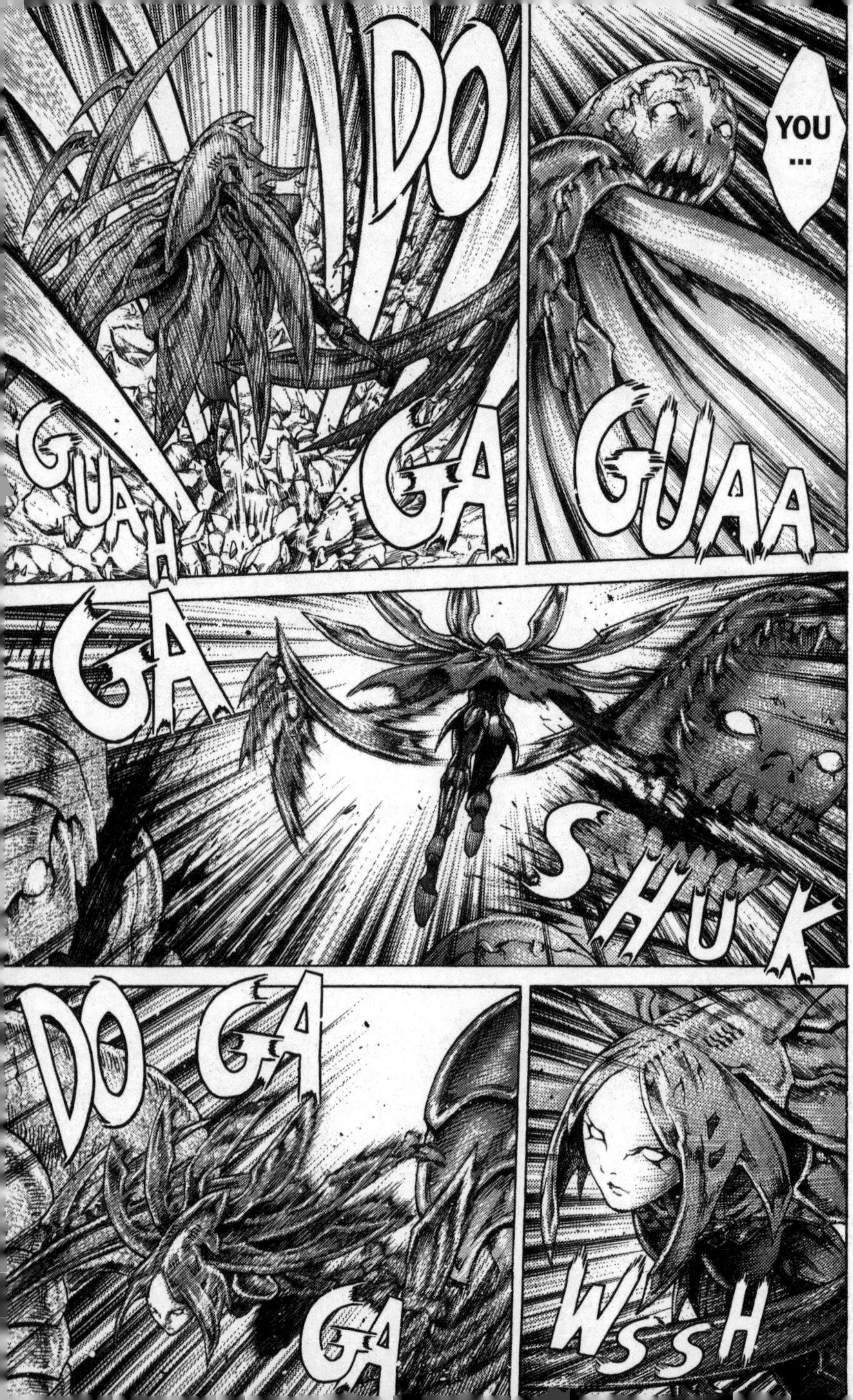
YOU ...
GUAA
DO
GA
GUAH
GA
SHUK
WSSH
DO GA
GA

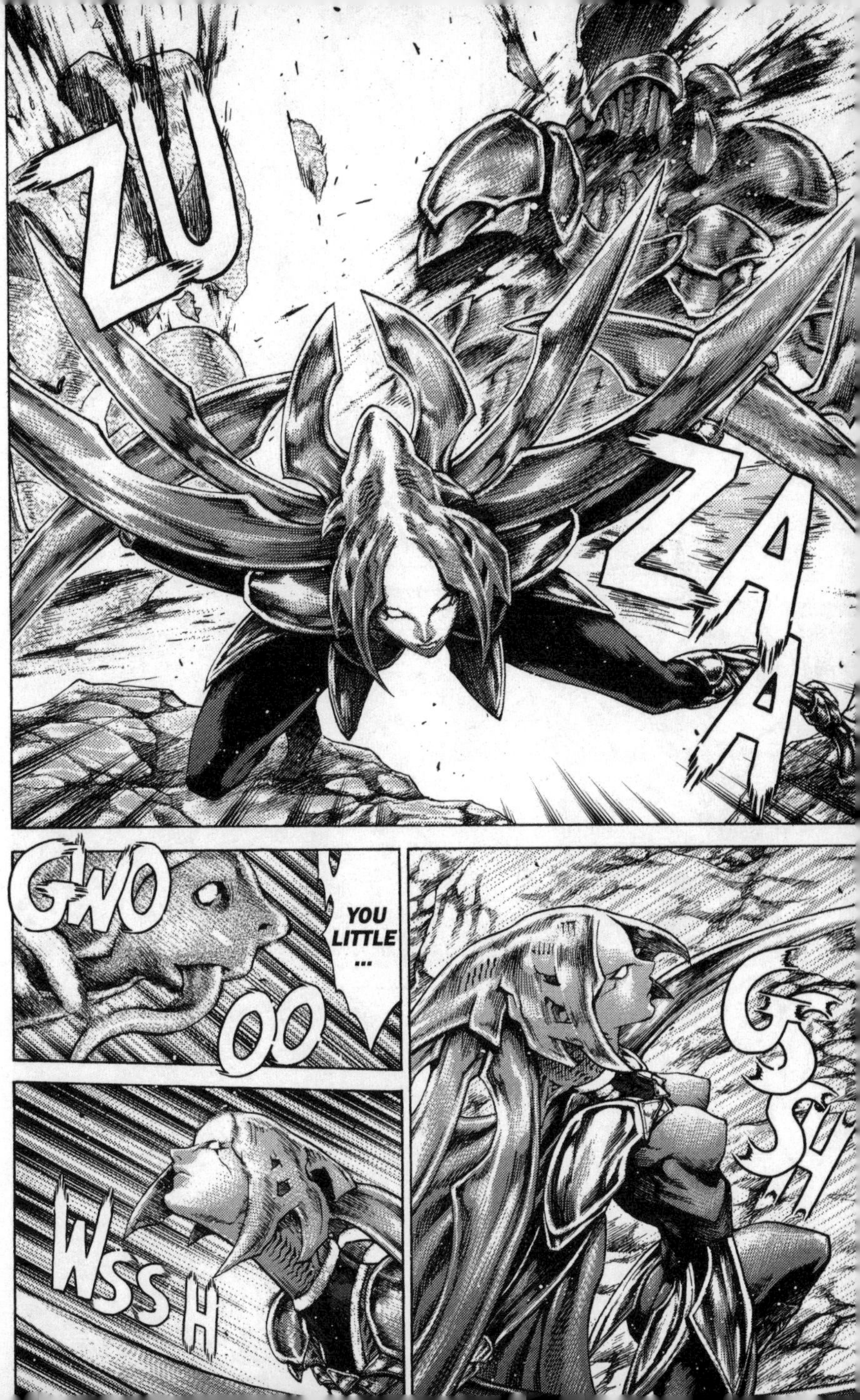
ZU
ZAA
GASH
GNOOO
YOU LITTLE ...
WSSH

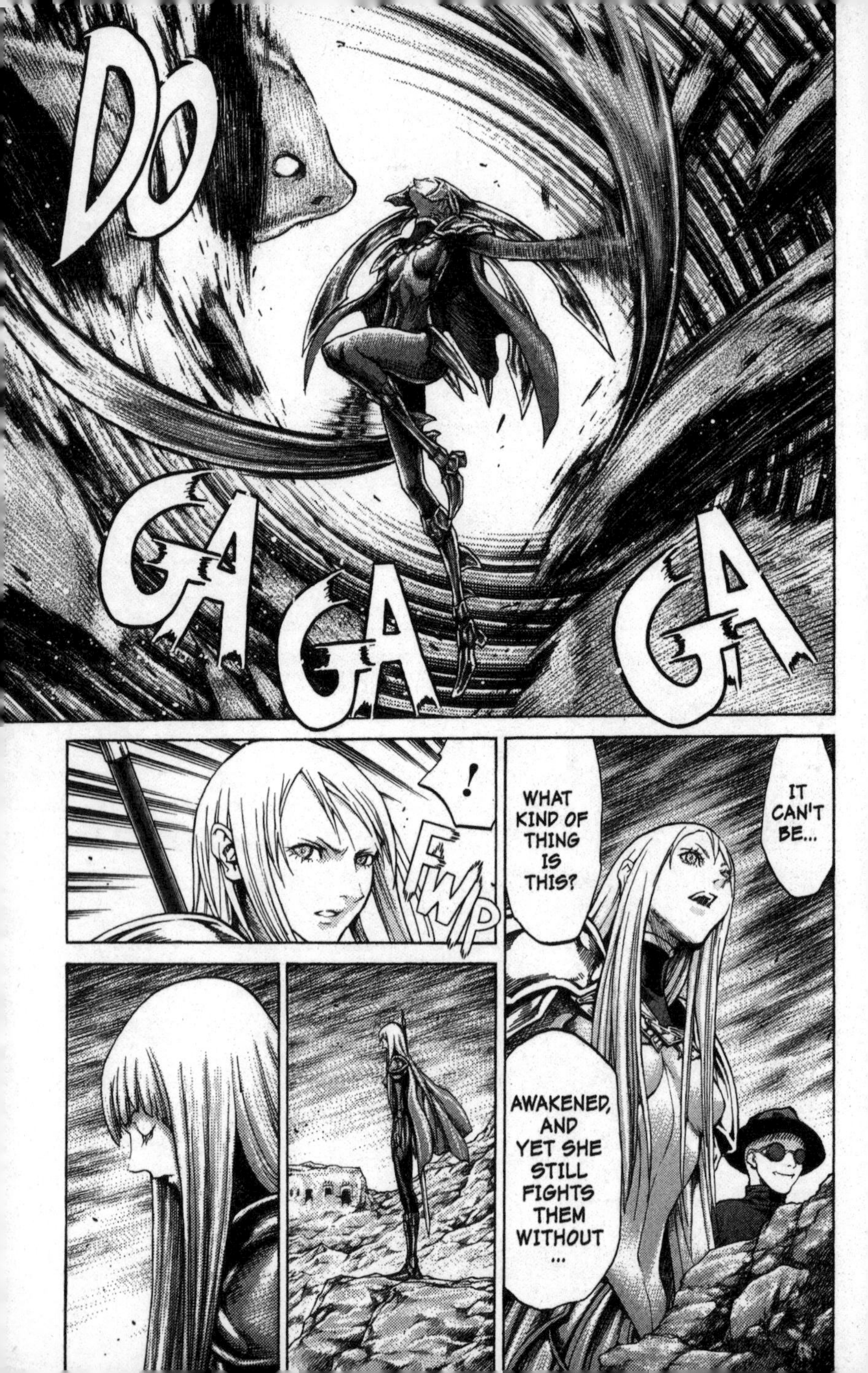
DO
GA GA GA
IT CAN'T BE...
WHAT KIND OF THING IS THIS?
AWAKENED, AND YET SHE STILL FIGHTS THEM WITHOUT ...
!
FWIP

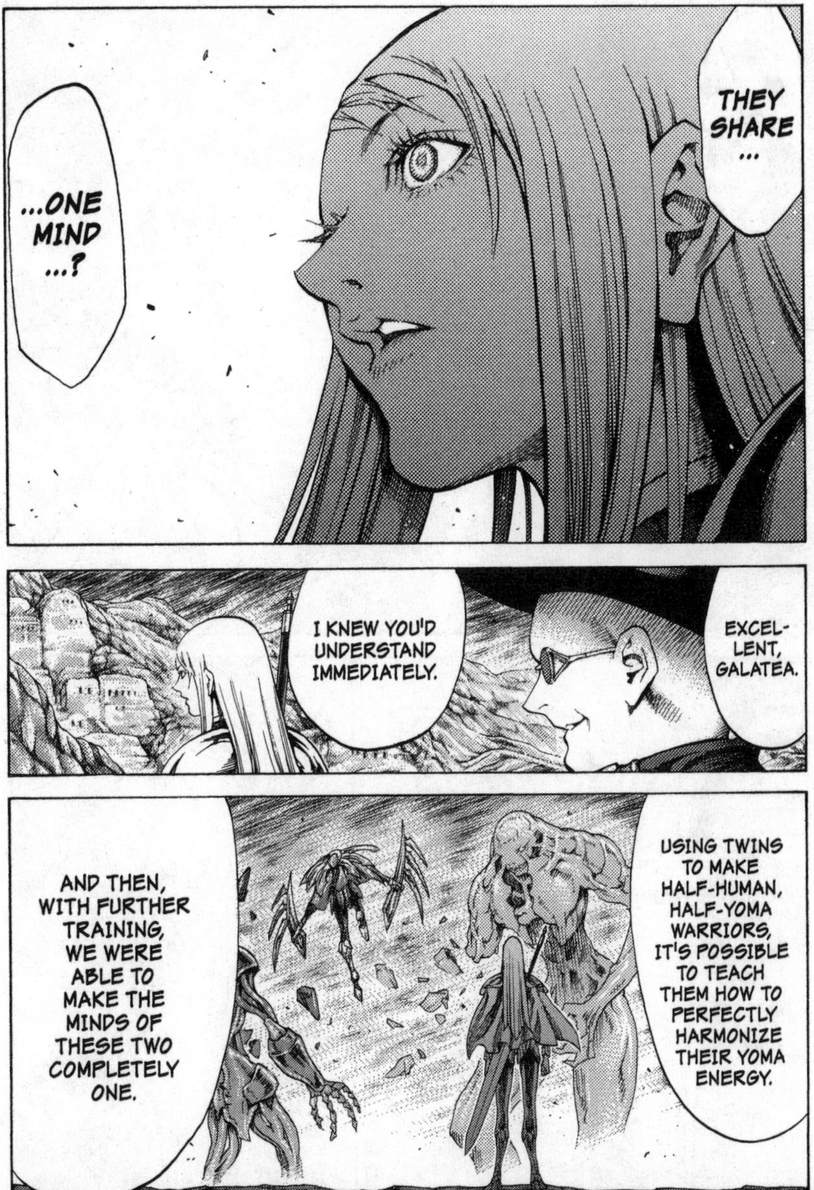
THEY SHARE ...
...ONE MIND ...?
EXCEL- LENT, GALATEA.
I KNEW YOU'D UNDERSTAND IMMEDIATELY.
USING TWINS TO MAKE HALF-HUMAN, HALF-YOMA WARRIORS, IT'S POSSIBLE TO TEACH THEM HOW TO PERFECTLY HARMONIZE THEIR YOMA ENERGY.
AND THEN, WITH FURTHER TRAINING, WE WERE ABLE TO MAKE THE MINDS OF THESE TWO COMPLETELY ONE.

READ THIS WAY

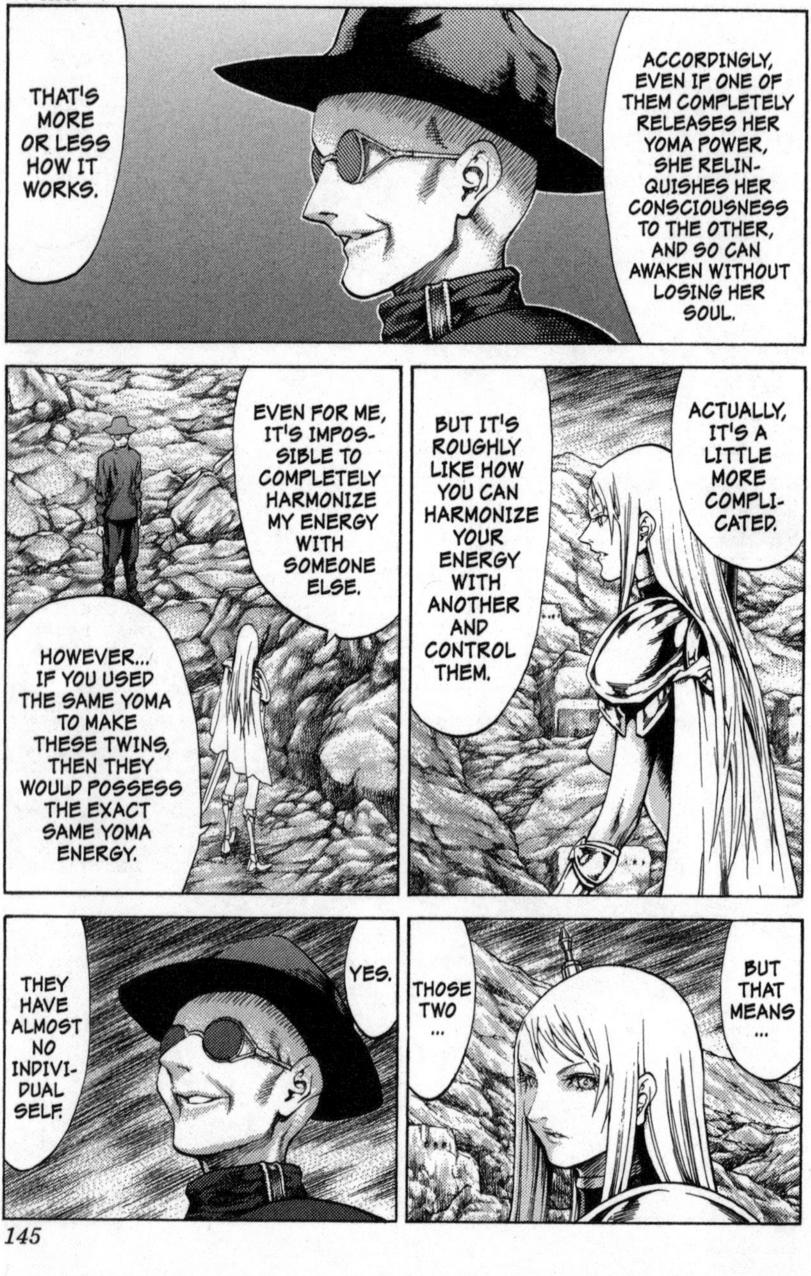
ACCORDINGLY, EVEN IF ONE OF THEM COMPLETELY RELEASES HER YOMA POWER, SHE RELINQUISHES HER CONSCIOUSNESS TO THE OTHER, AND SO CAN AWAKEN WITHOUT LOSING HER SOUL.
THAT'S MORE OR LESS HOW IT WORKS.
ACTUALLY, IT'S A LITTLE MORE COMPLICATED.
BUT IT'S ROUGHLY LIKE HOW YOU CAN HARMONIZE YOUR ENERGY WITH ANOTHER AND CONTROL THEM.
EVEN FOR ME, IT'S IMPOSSIBLE TO COMPLETELY HARMONIZE MY ENERGY WITH SOMEONE ELSE.
HOWEVER... IF YOU USED THE SAME YOMA TO MAKE THESE TWINS, THEN THEY WOULD POSSESS THE EXACT SAME YOMA ENERGY.
BUT THAT MEANS...
THOSE TWO...
YES.
THEY HAVE ALMOST NO INDIVIDUAL SELF.

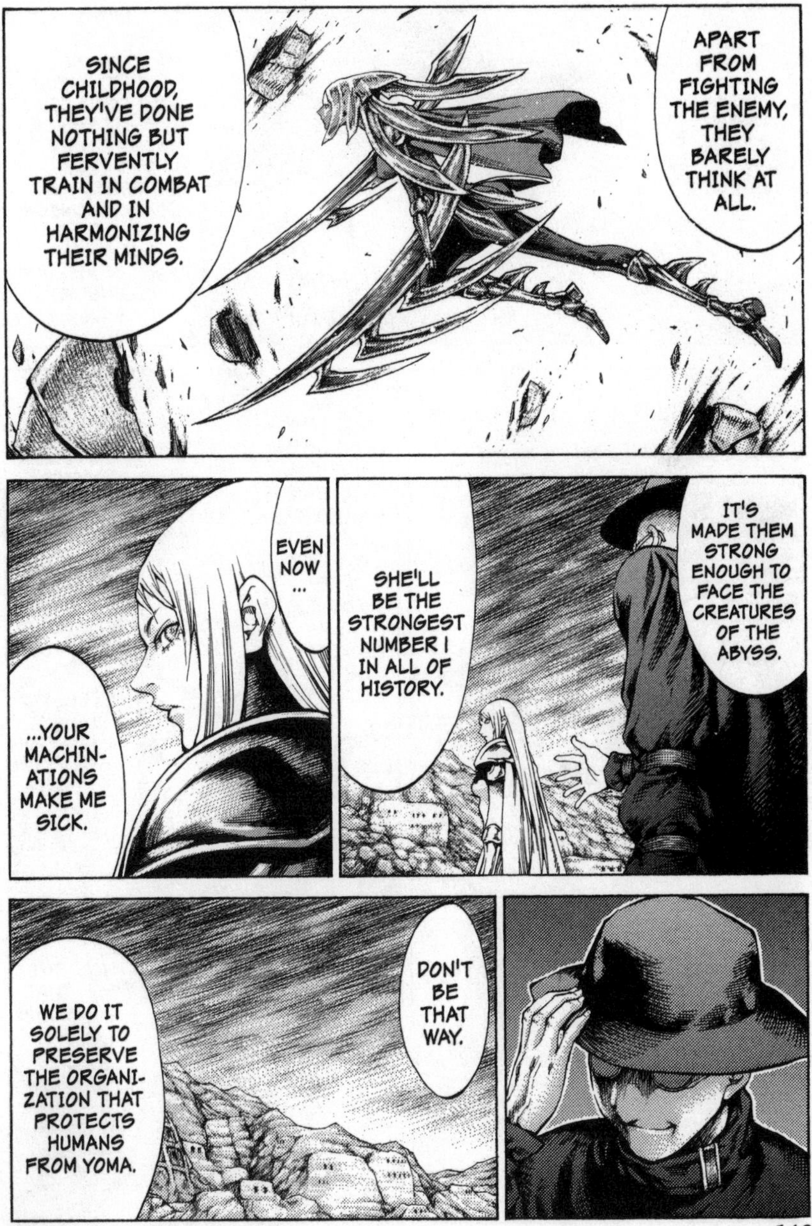
APART FROM FIGHTING THE ENEMY, THEY BARELY THINK AT ALL.
SINCE CHILDHOOD, THEY'VE DONE NOTHING BUT FERVENTLY TRAIN IN COMBAT AND IN HARMONIZING THEIR MINDS.
IT'S MADE THEM STRONG ENOUGH TO FACE THE CREATURES OF THE ABYSS.
SHE'LL BE THE STRONGEST NUMBER 1 IN ALL OF HISTORY.
EVEN NOW ...
...YOUR MACHIN-ATIONS MAKE ME SICK.
DON'T BE THAT WAY.
WE DO IT SOLELY TO PRESERVE THE ORGANI-ZATION THAT PROTECTS HUMANS FROM YOMA.

READ THIS WAY

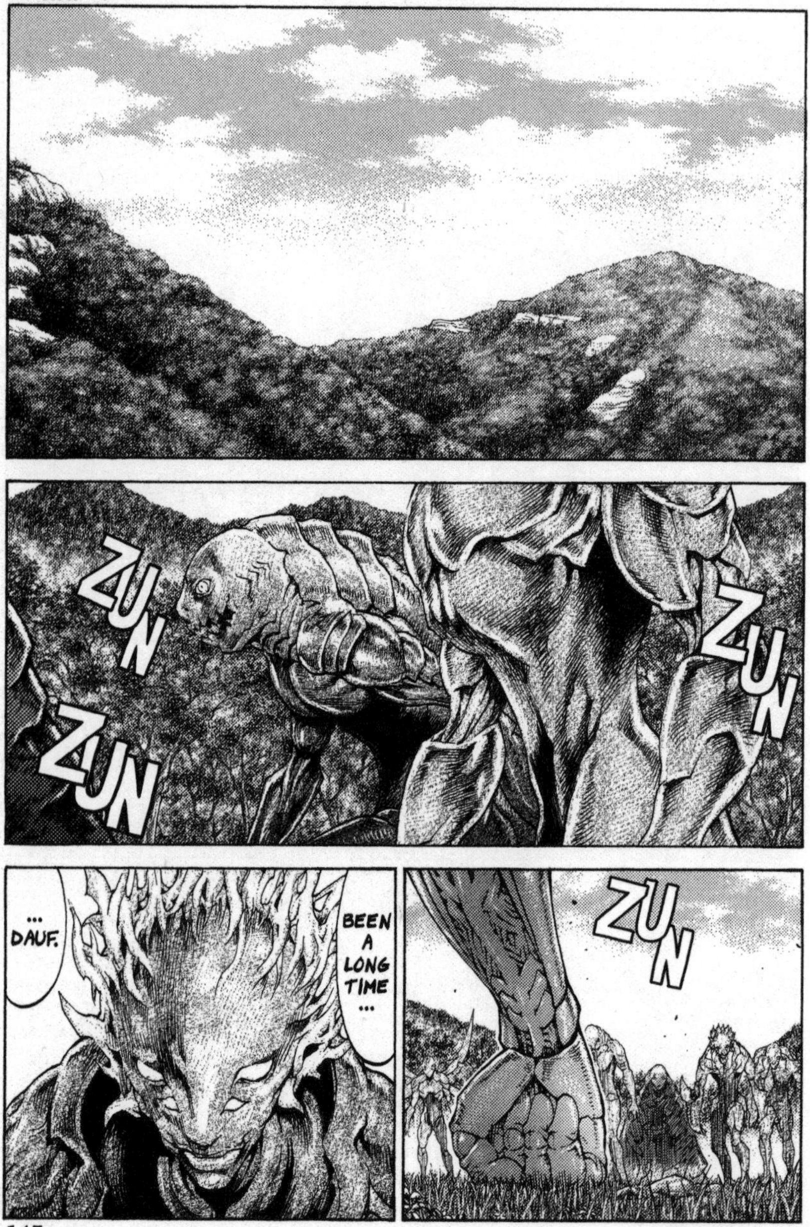
ZUN
ZUN
ZUN
ZUN
BEEN A LONG TIME...
...DAUF.

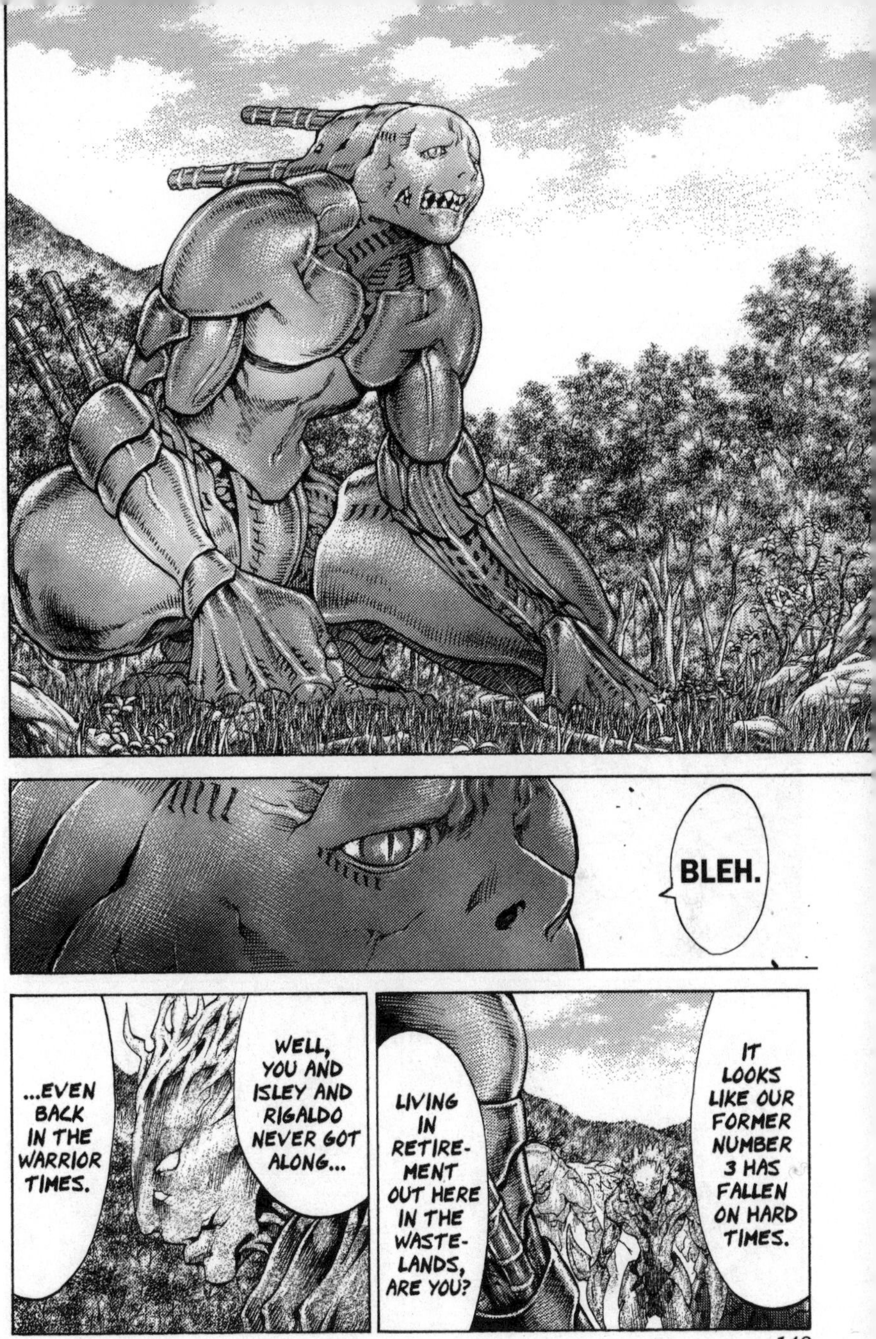
BLEH.
IT LOOKS LIKE OUR FORMER NUMBER 3 HAS FALLEN ON HARD TIMES.
LIVING IN RETIRE-MENT OUT HERE IN THE WASTE-LANDS, ARE YOU?
WELL, YOU AND ISLEY AND RIGALDO NEVER GOT ALONG...
...EVEN BACK IN THE WARRIOR TIMES.

READ THIS WAY

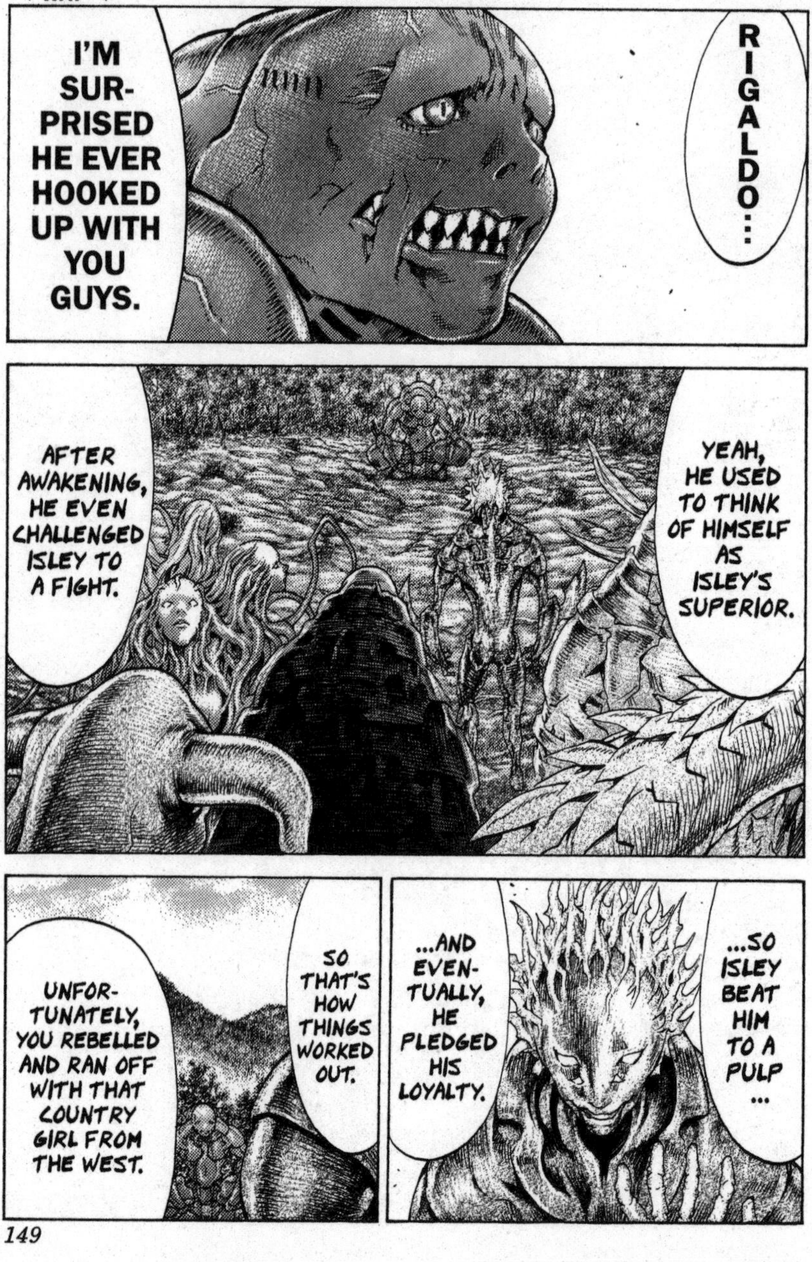
RIGALDO...
I'M SURPRISED HE EVER HOOKED UP WITH YOU GUYS.
YEAH, HE USED TO THINK OF HIMSELF AS ISLEY'S SUPERIOR.
AFTER AWAKENING, HE EVEN CHALLENGED ISLEY TO A FIGHT.
...SO ISLEY BEAT HIM TO A PULP...
...AND EVENTUALLY, HE PLEDGED HIS LOYALTY.
SO THAT'S HOW THINGS WORKED OUT.
UNFORTUNATELY, YOU REBELLED AND RAN OFF WITH THAT COUNTRY GIRL FROM THE WEST.

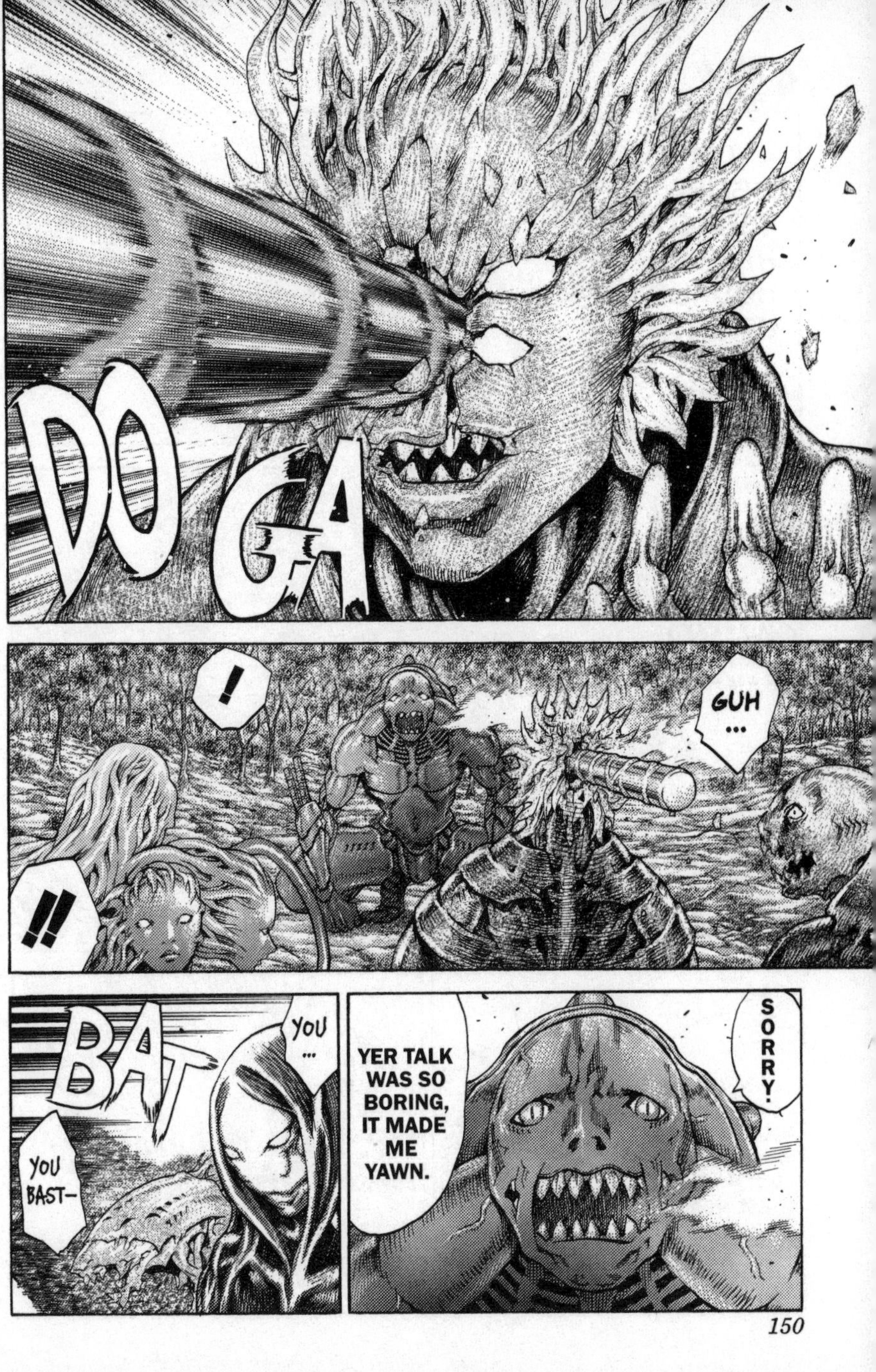
DO GA
GUH ...
!
!!
SORRY!
YER TALK WAS SO BORING, IT MADE ME YAWN.
BAT
YOU ...
YOU BAST-

READ THIS WAY

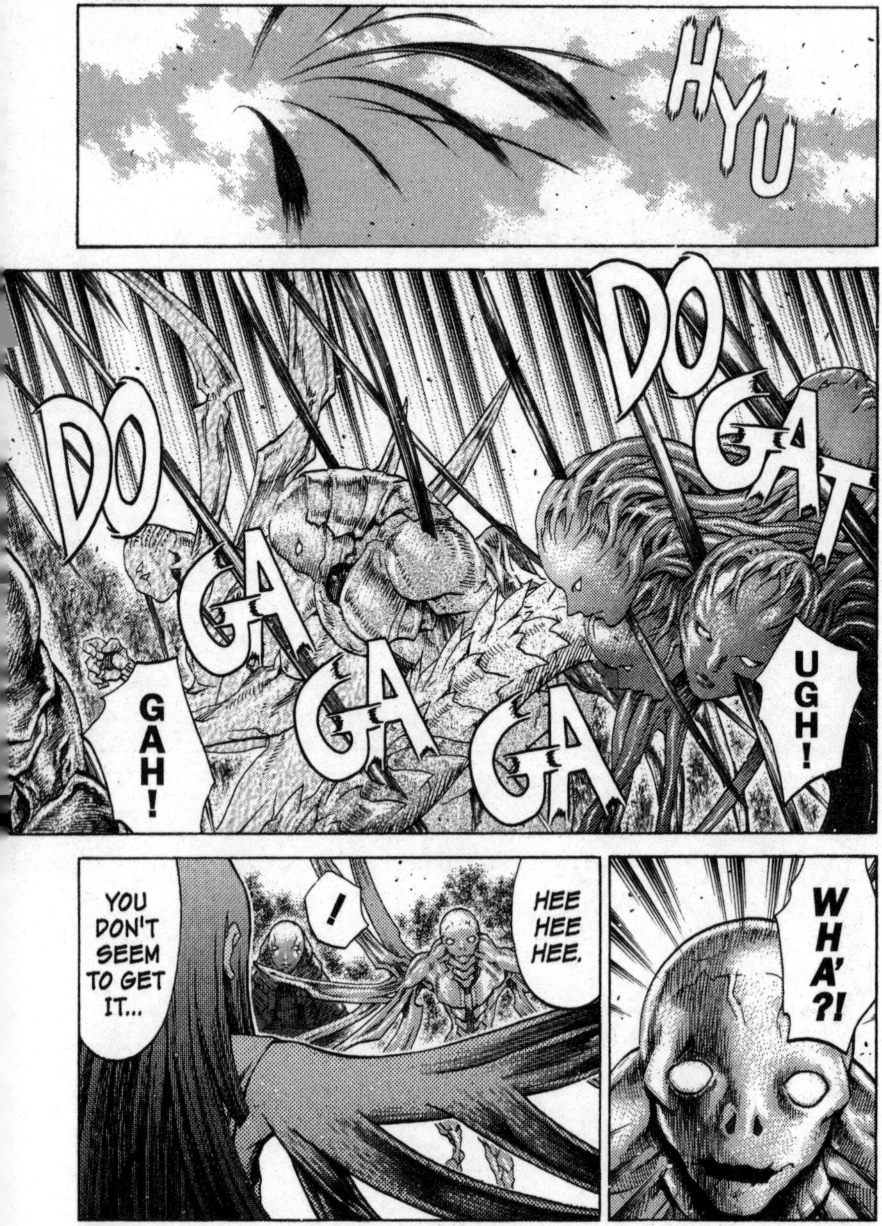
HYU
DOGAT
UGH!
DOGAGAGA
GAH!
WHA'?!
HEE HEE HEE.
!
YOU DON'T SEEM TO GET IT...

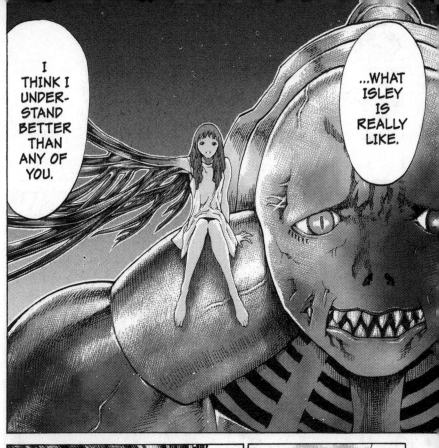

I THINK I UNDER-STAND BETTER THAN ANY OF YOU.

...WHAT ISLEY IS REALLY LIKE.

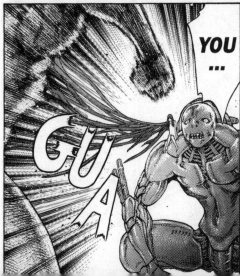

YOU...

GUA

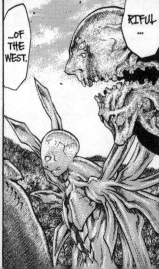

...OF THE WEST.

RIFUL...

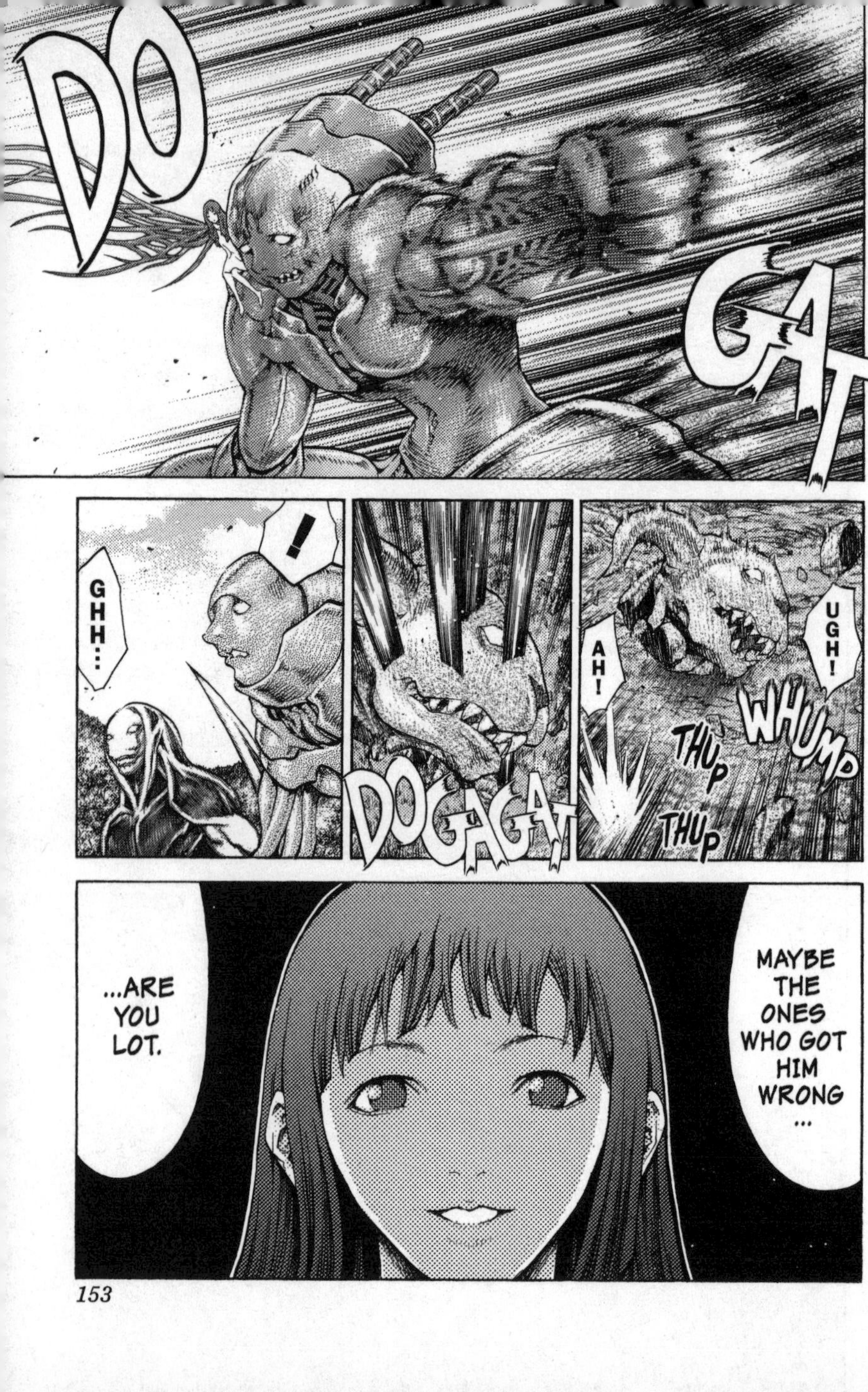
DO
GAT
UGH!
AH!
WHUMP
THUP
THUP
DOGAGAT
!
GHH...
MAYBE THE ONES WHO GOT HIM WRONG...
...ARE YOU LOT.

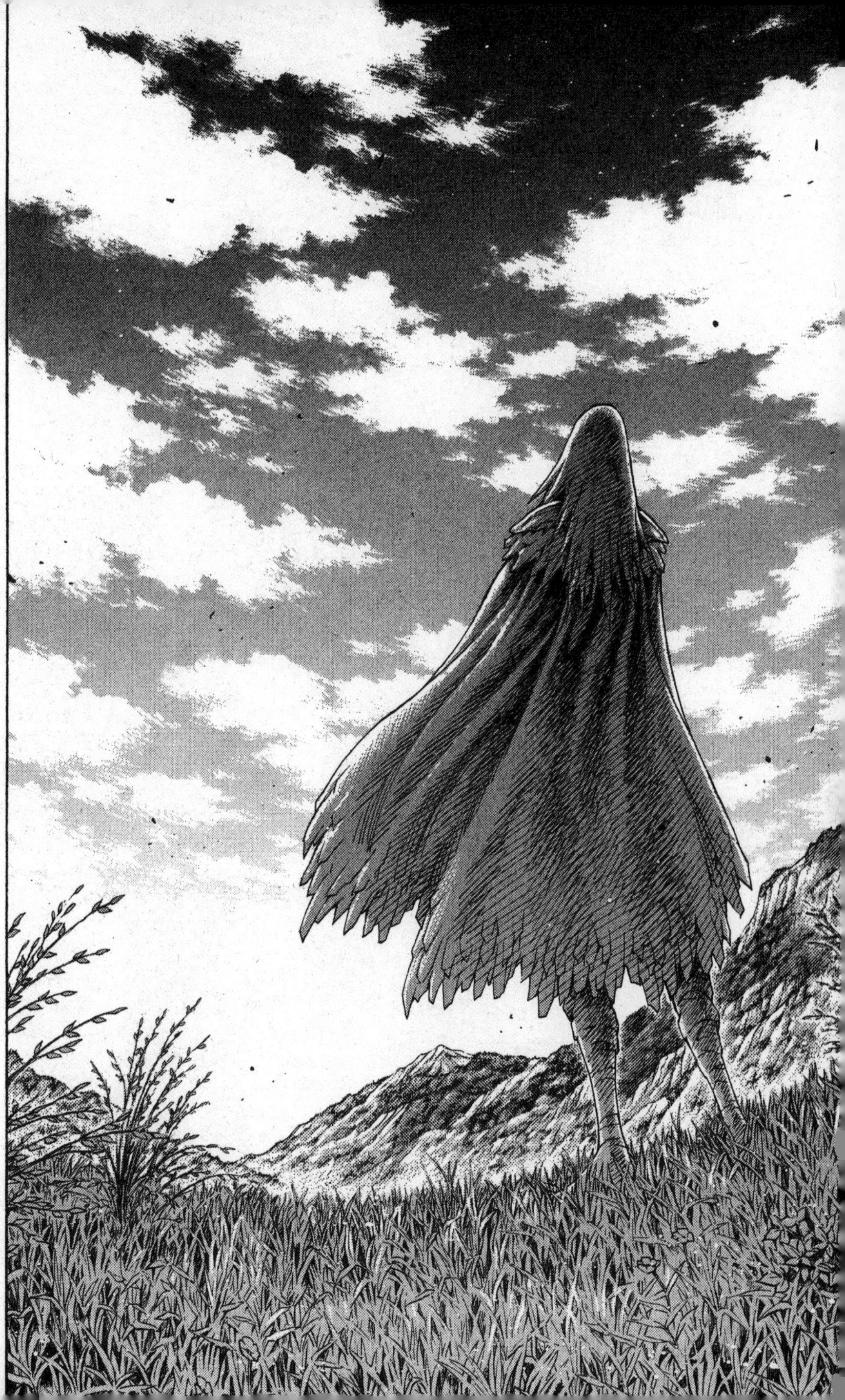

READ THIS WAY

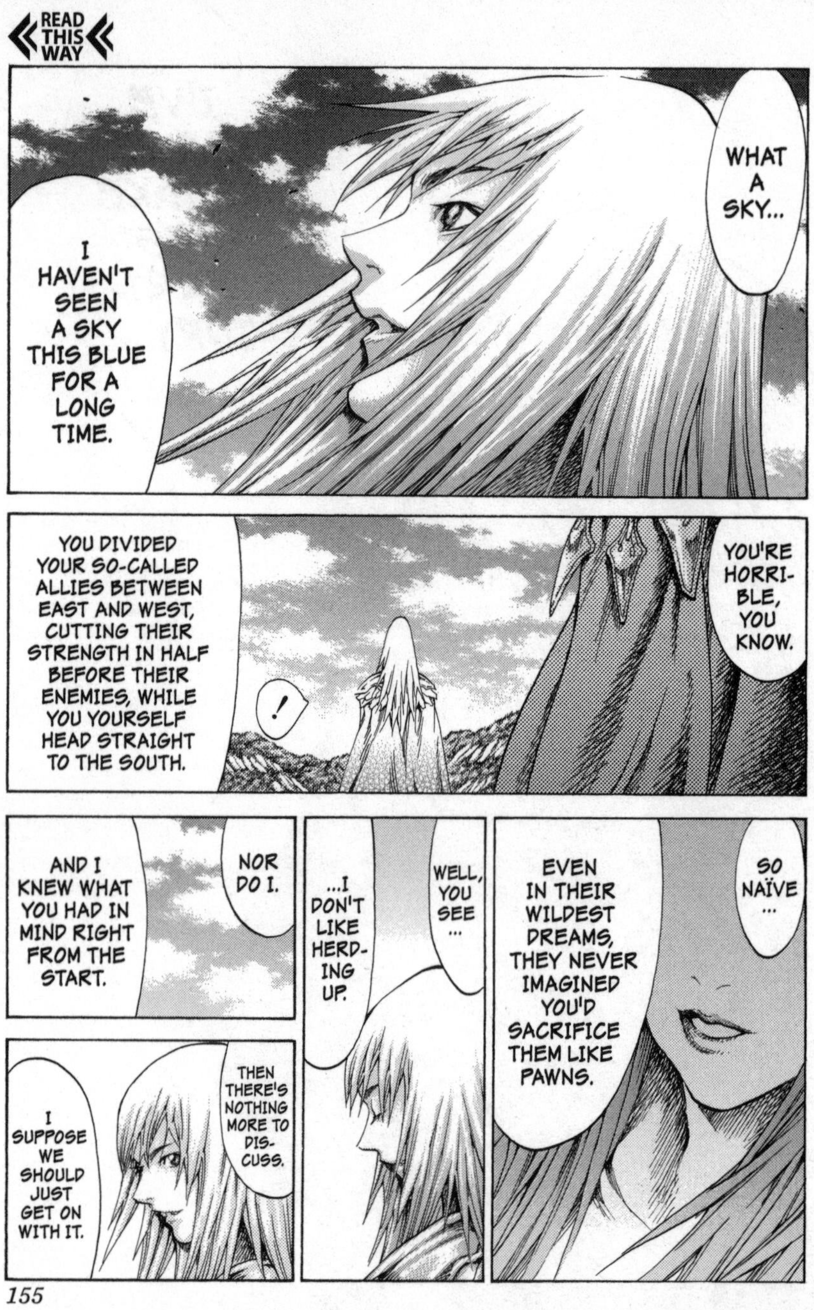
WHAT A SKY...
I HAVEN'T SEEN A SKY THIS BLUE FOR A LONG TIME.
YOU'RE HORRIBLE, YOU KNOW.
YOU DIVIDED YOUR SO-CALLED ALLIES BETWEEN EAST AND WEST, CUTTING THEIR STRENGTH IN HALF BEFORE THEIR ENEMIES, WHILE YOU YOURSELF HEAD STRAIGHT TO THE SOUTH.
!
SO NAÏVE...
EVEN IN THEIR WILDEST DREAMS, THEY NEVER IMAGINED YOU'D SACRIFICE THEM LIKE PAWNS.
WELL, YOU SEE...
...I DON'T LIKE HERDING UP.
NOR DO I.
AND I KNEW WHAT YOU HAD IN MIND RIGHT FROM THE START.
THEN THERE'S NOTHING MORE TO DISCUSS.
I SUPPOSE WE SHOULD JUST GET ON WITH IT.

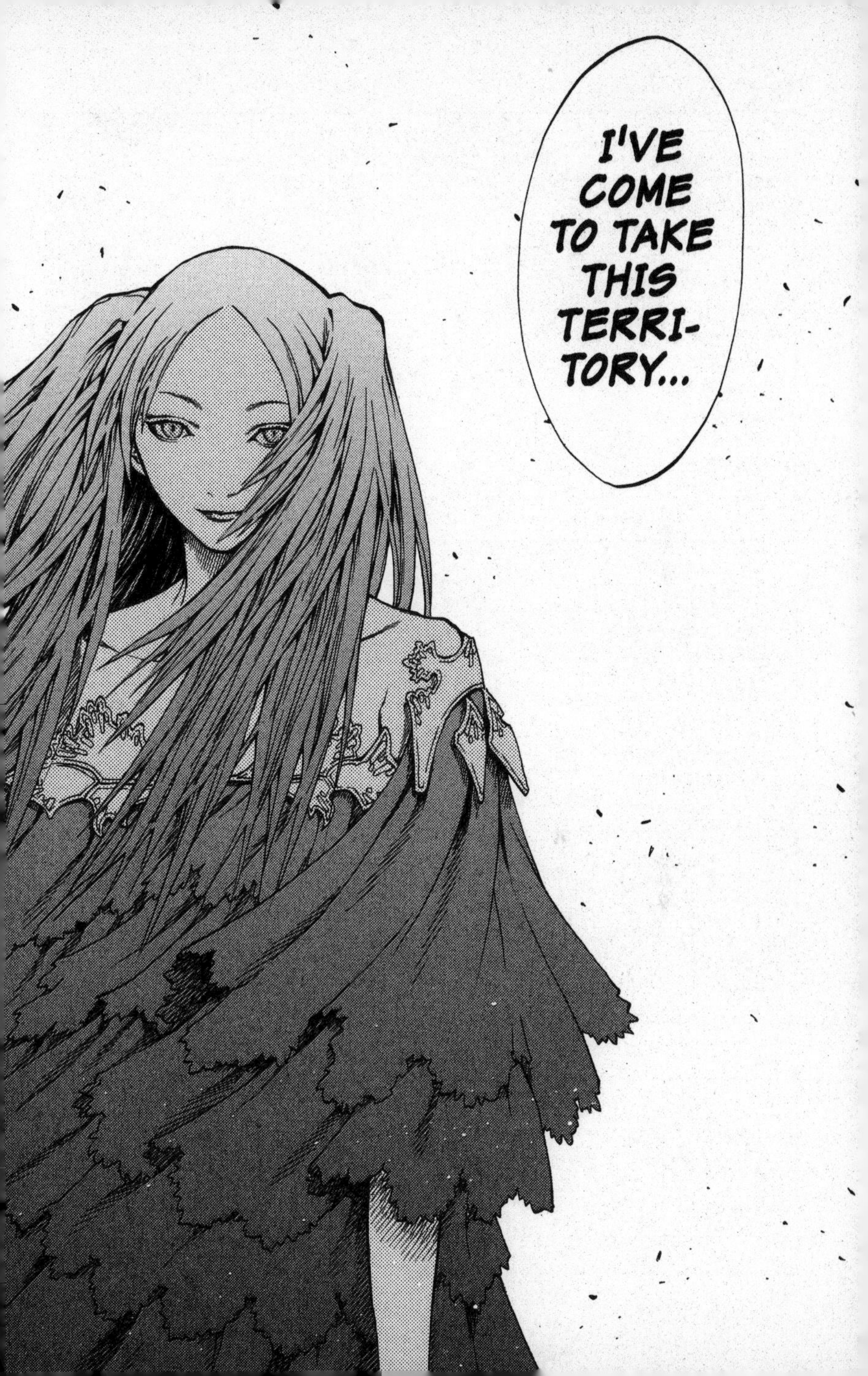
I'VE COME TO TAKE THIS TERRI-TORY...

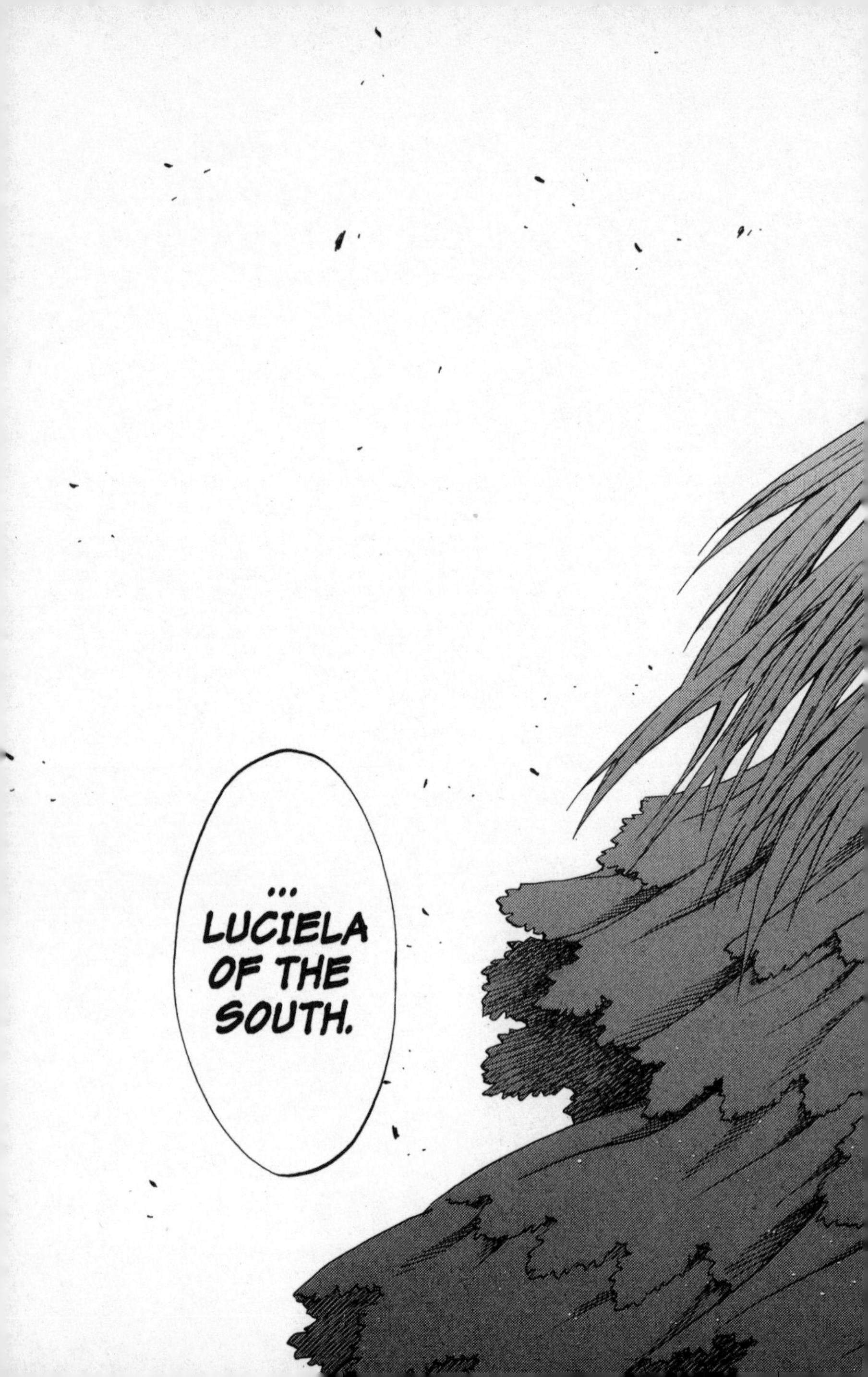
...
LUCIELA
OF THE
SOUTH.

クレイモア
Claymore

Scene 63: Kindred of Paradise, Part 2

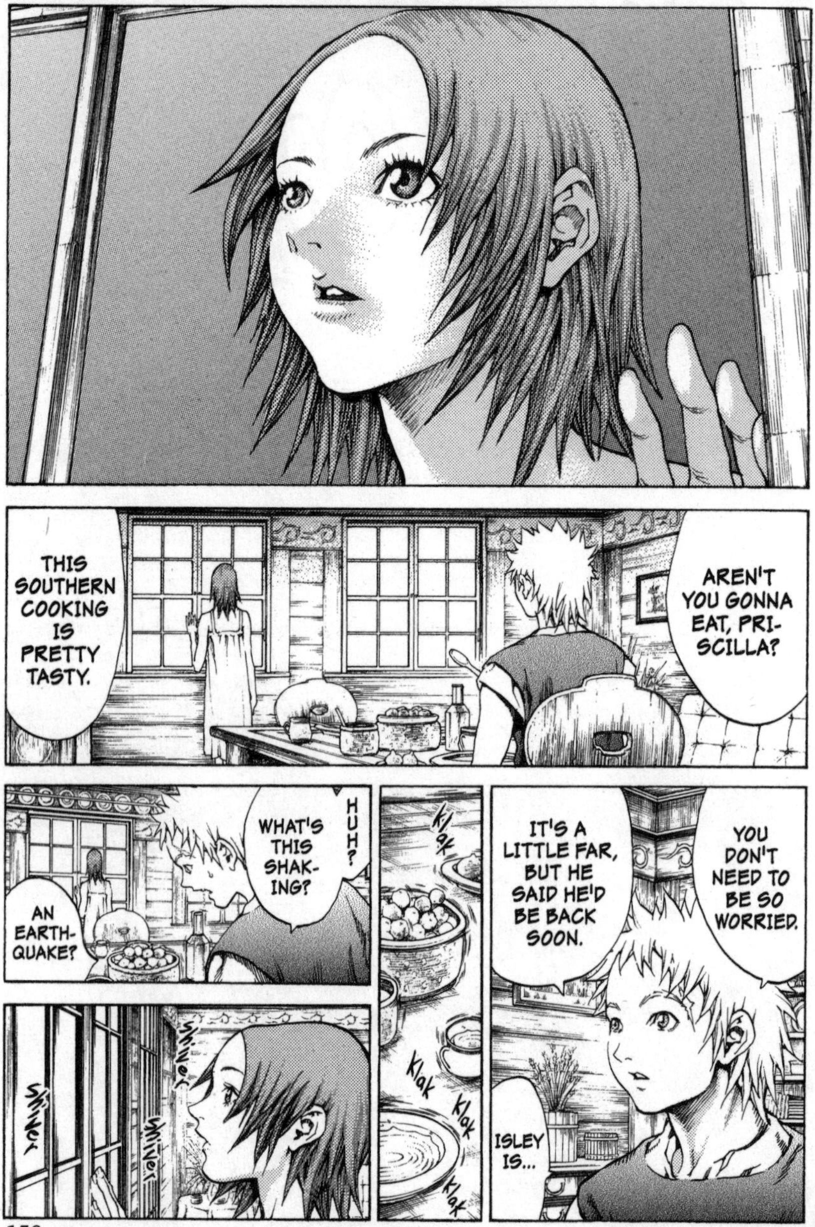
AREN'T YOU GONNA EAT, PRI-SCILLA?
THIS SOUTHERN COOKING IS PRETTY TASTY.
YOU DON'T NEED TO BE SO WORRIED.
IT'S A LITTLE FAR, BUT HE SAID HE'D BE BACK SOON.
ISLEY IS...
klak
klak
klak
klak
HUH?
WHAT'S THIS SHAK-ING?
AN EARTH-QUAKE?
shiver
shiver
shiver

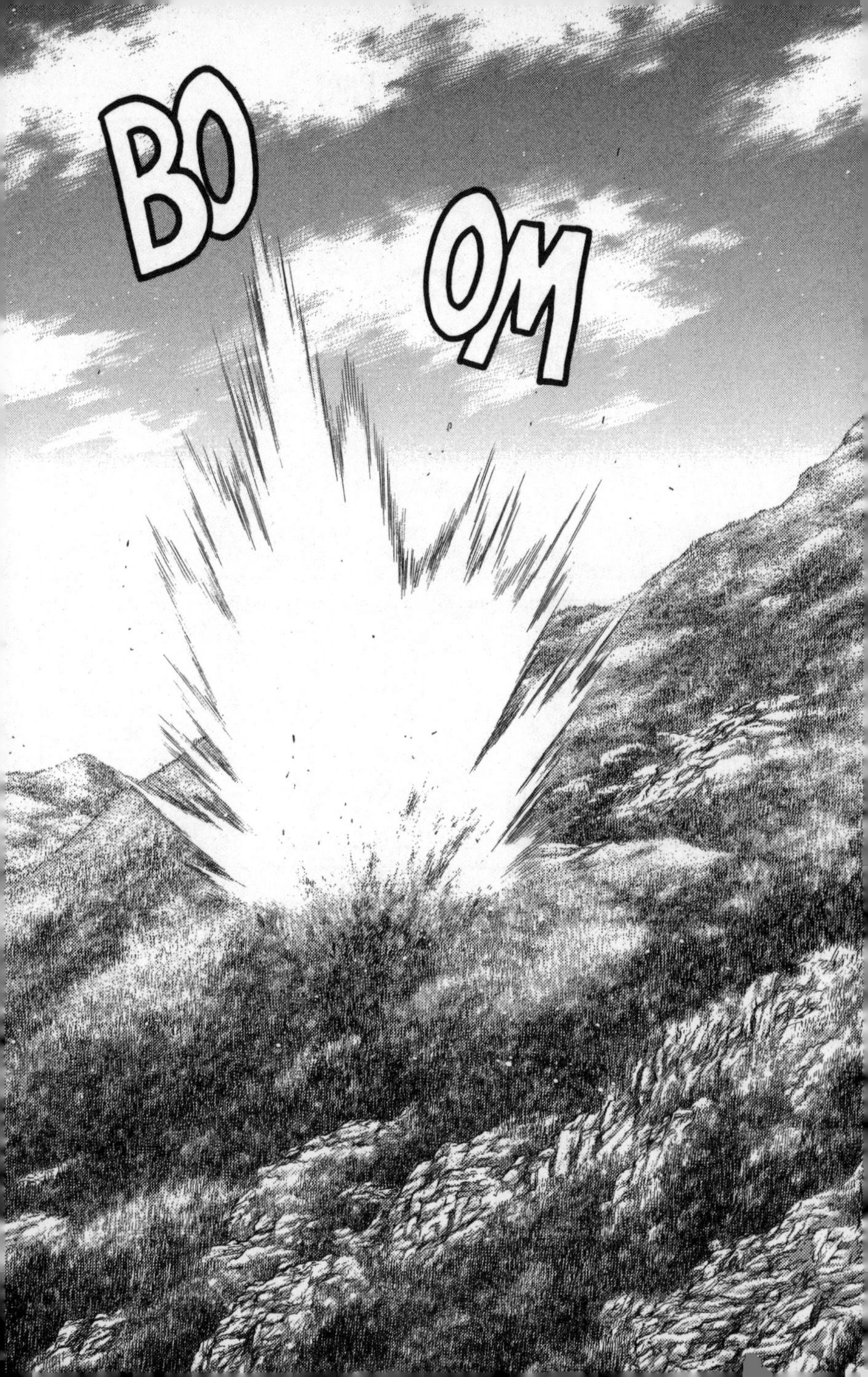
BOOM

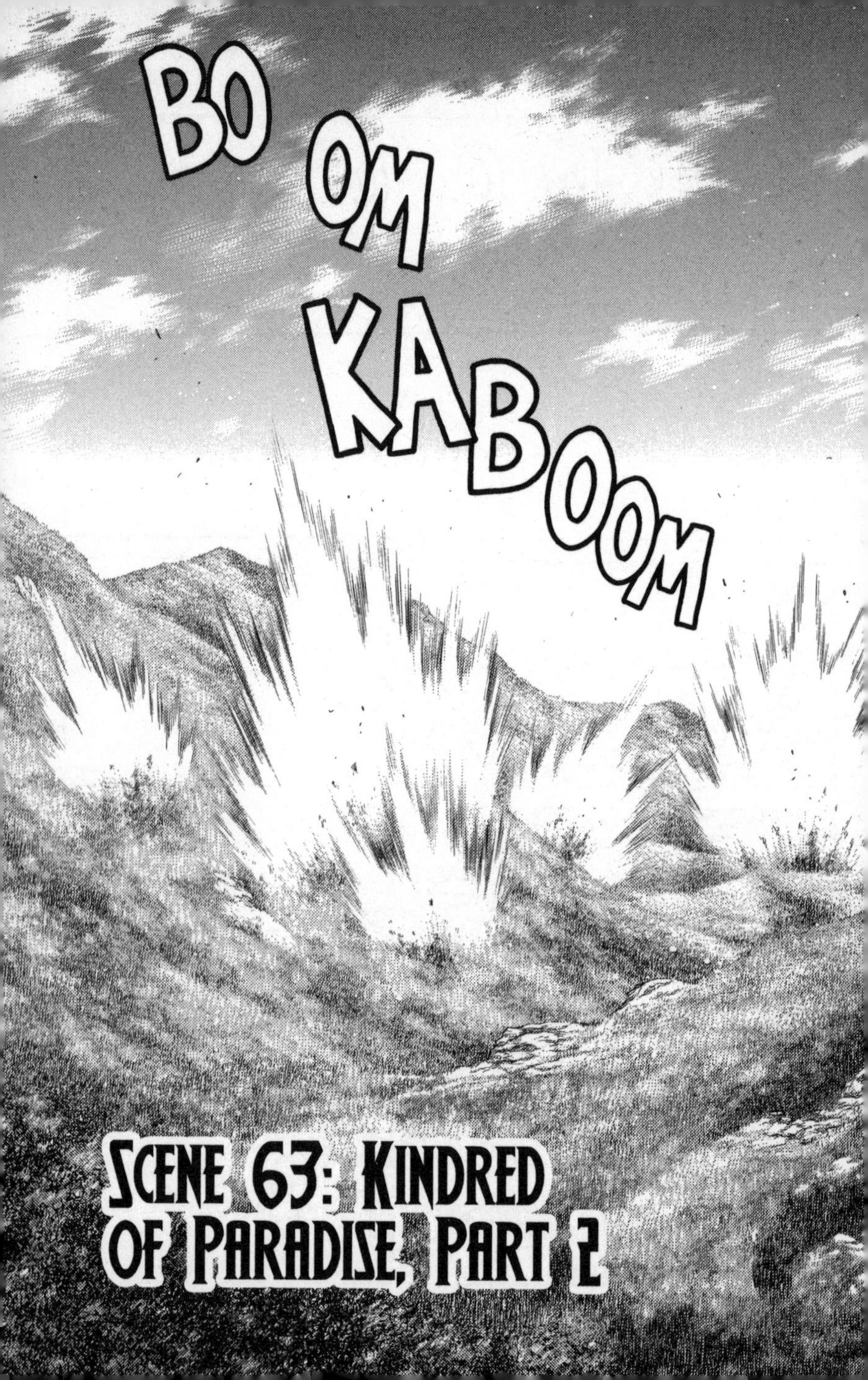
BO OM KABOOM
SCENE 63: KINDRED OF PARADISE, PART 2

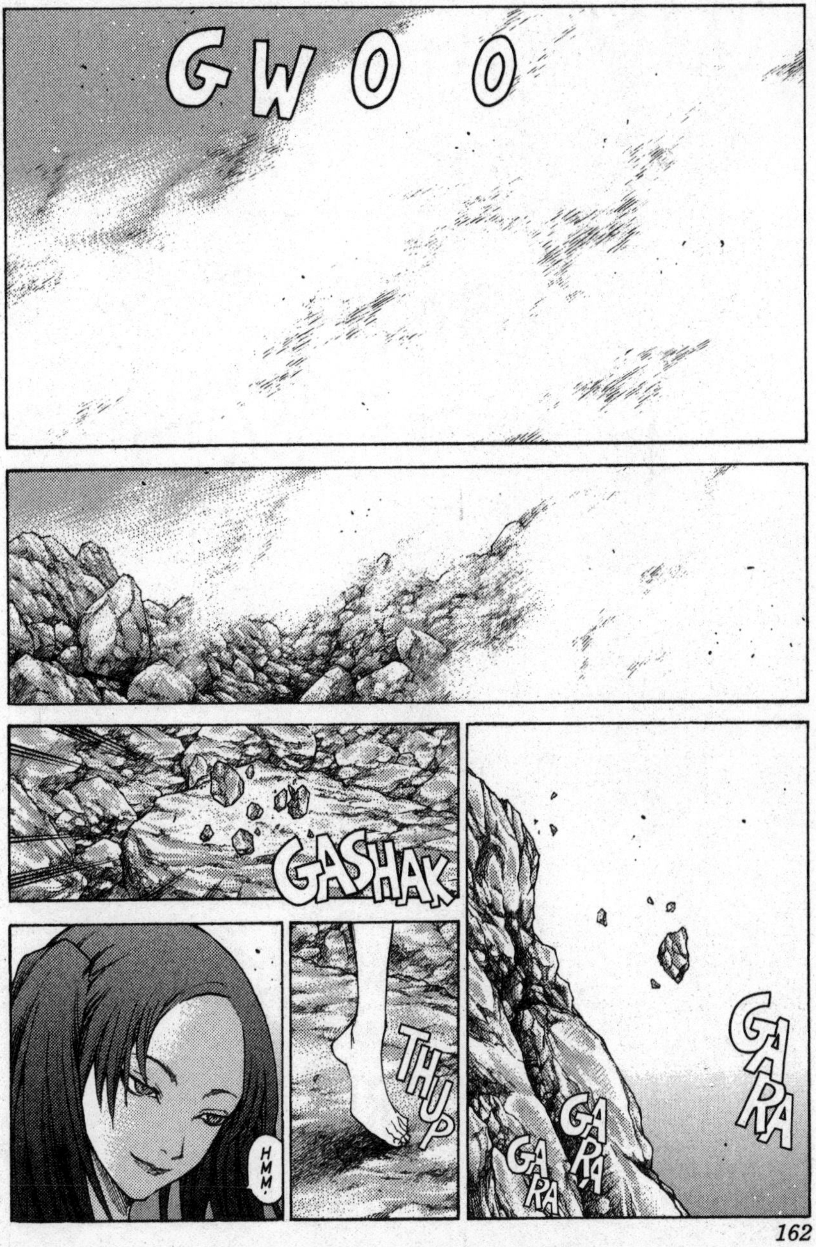
GWOO
GARA
GARA
GARA
GASHAK
THUP
HMM.

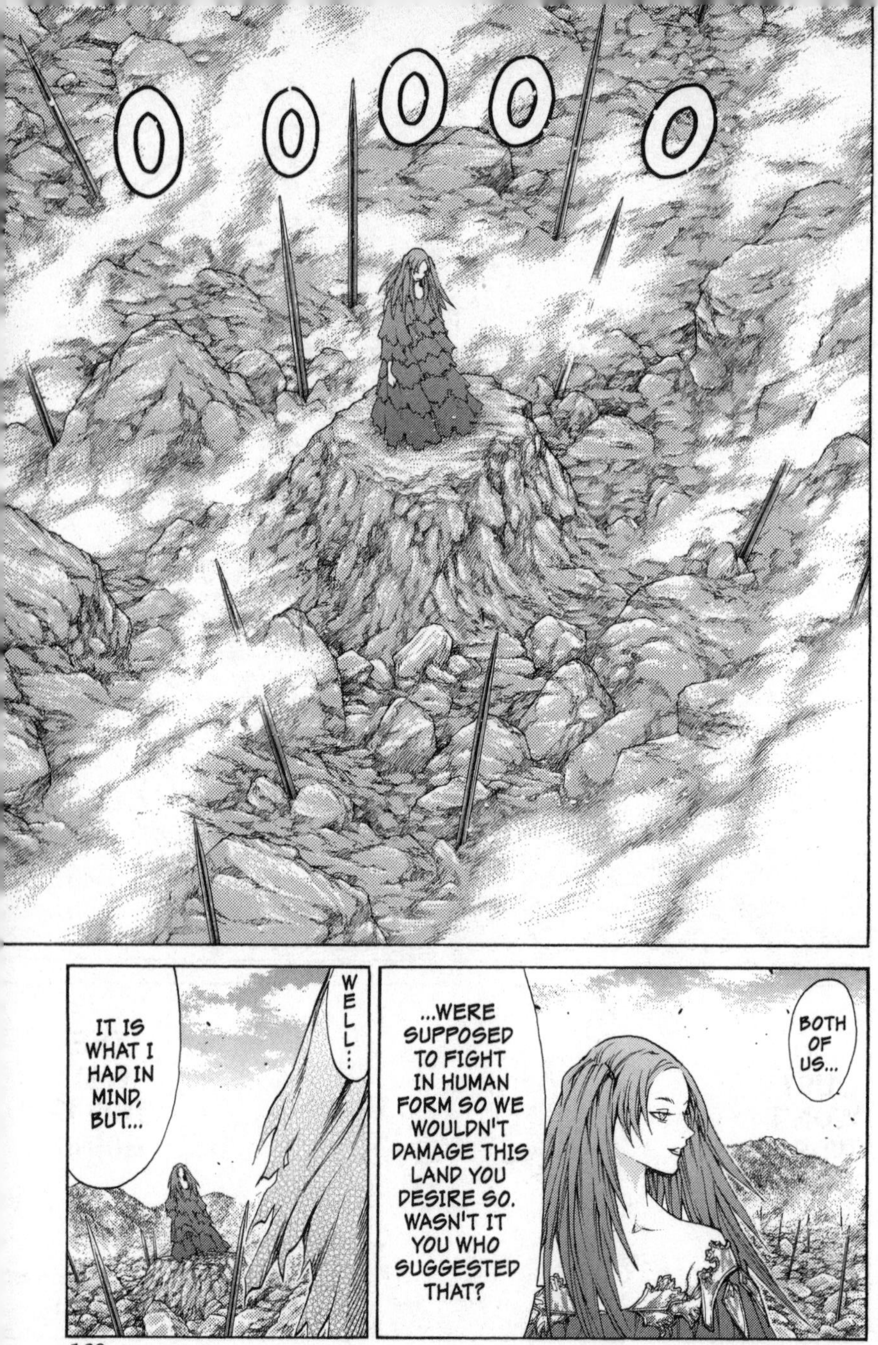

OOOOO
BOTH OF US...
...WERE SUPPOSED TO FIGHT IN HUMAN FORM SO WE WOULDN'T DAMAGE THIS LAND YOU DESIRE SO. WASN'T IT YOU WHO SUGGESTED THAT?
WELL...
IT IS WHAT I HAD IN MIND, BUT...

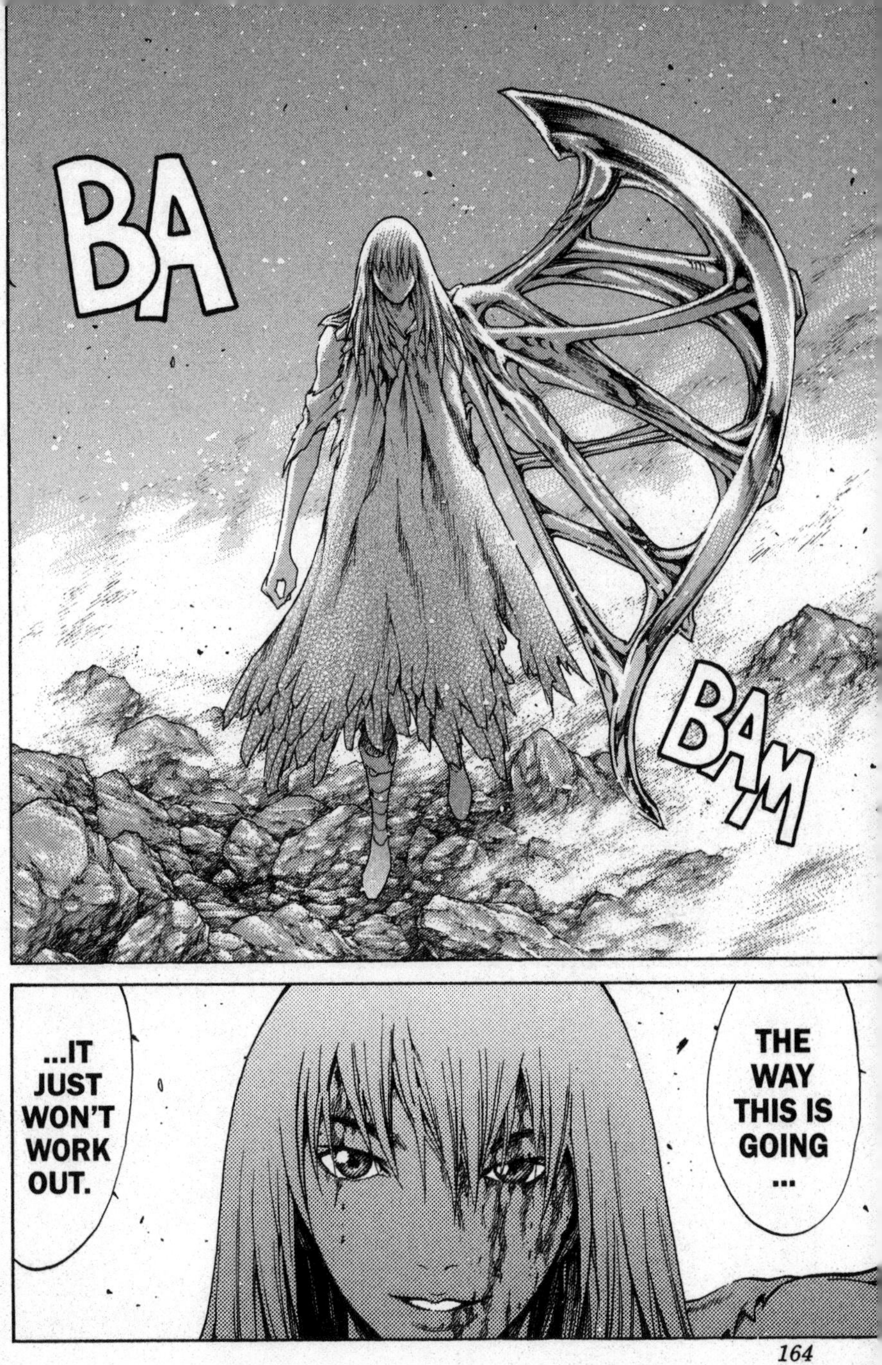
BA
BAM
THE WAY THIS IS GOING ...
...IT JUST WON'T WORK OUT.

READ THIS WAY

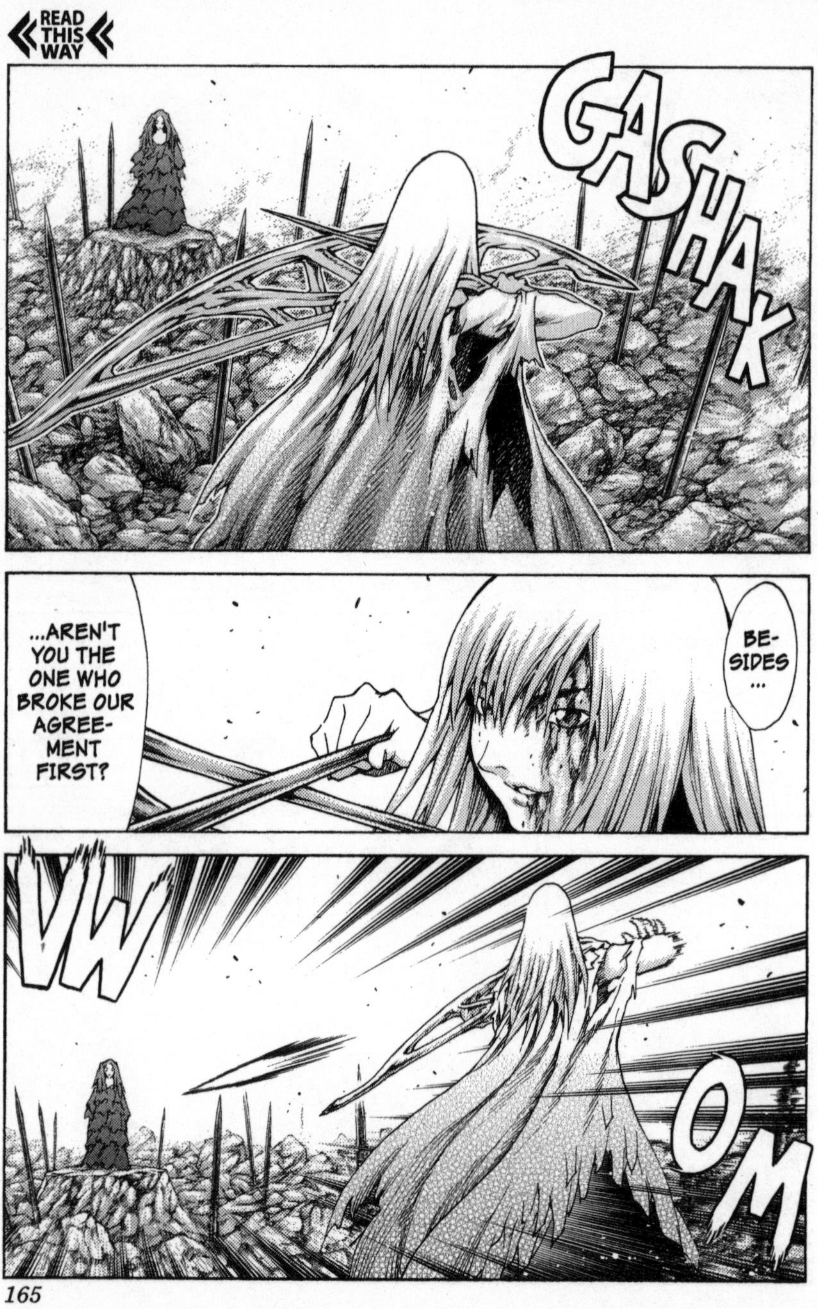
GASHAK
BE-SIDES...
...AREN'T YOU THE ONE WHO BROKE OUR AGREE-MENT FIRST?
VWOOM

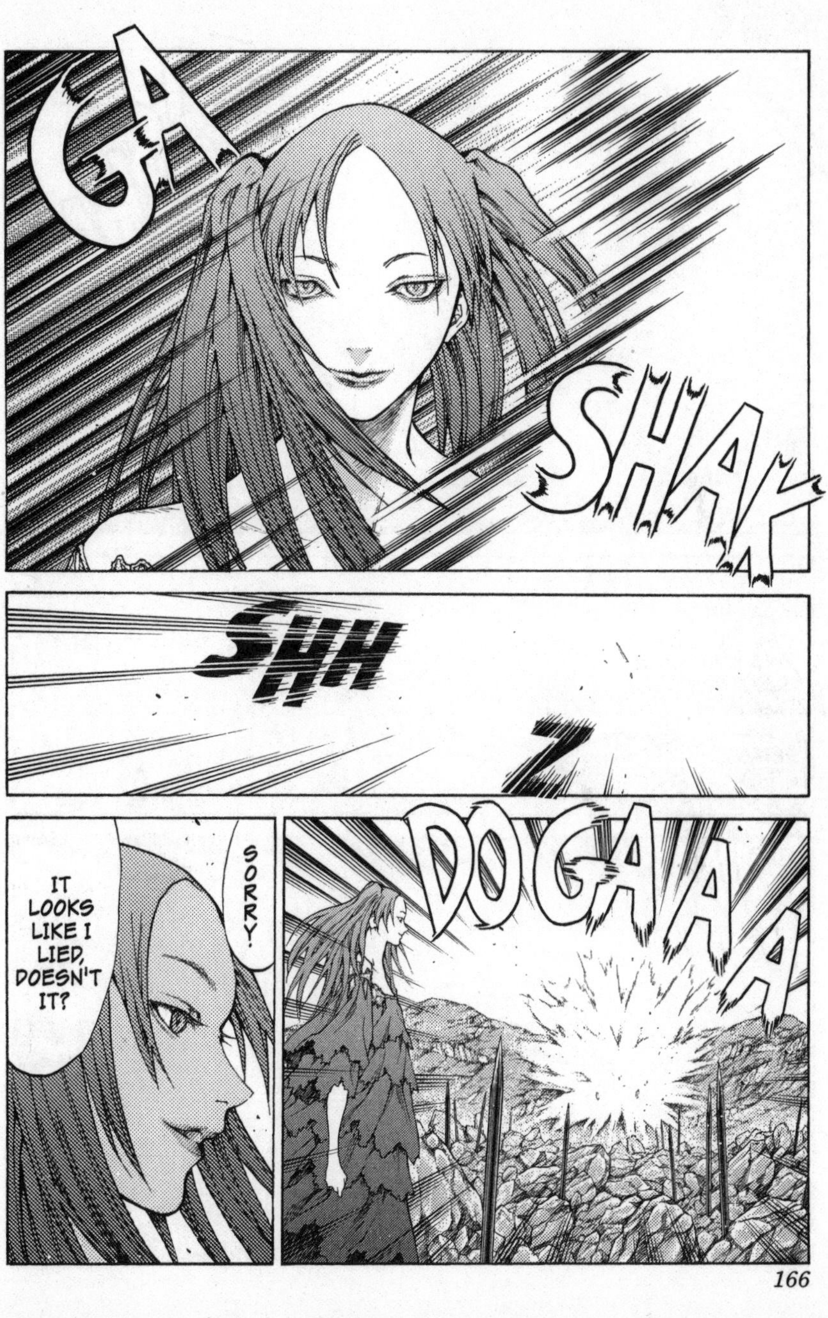
GA
SHAK
SHHZ
DOGAAA
SORRY!
IT LOOKS LIKE I LIED, DOESN'T IT?

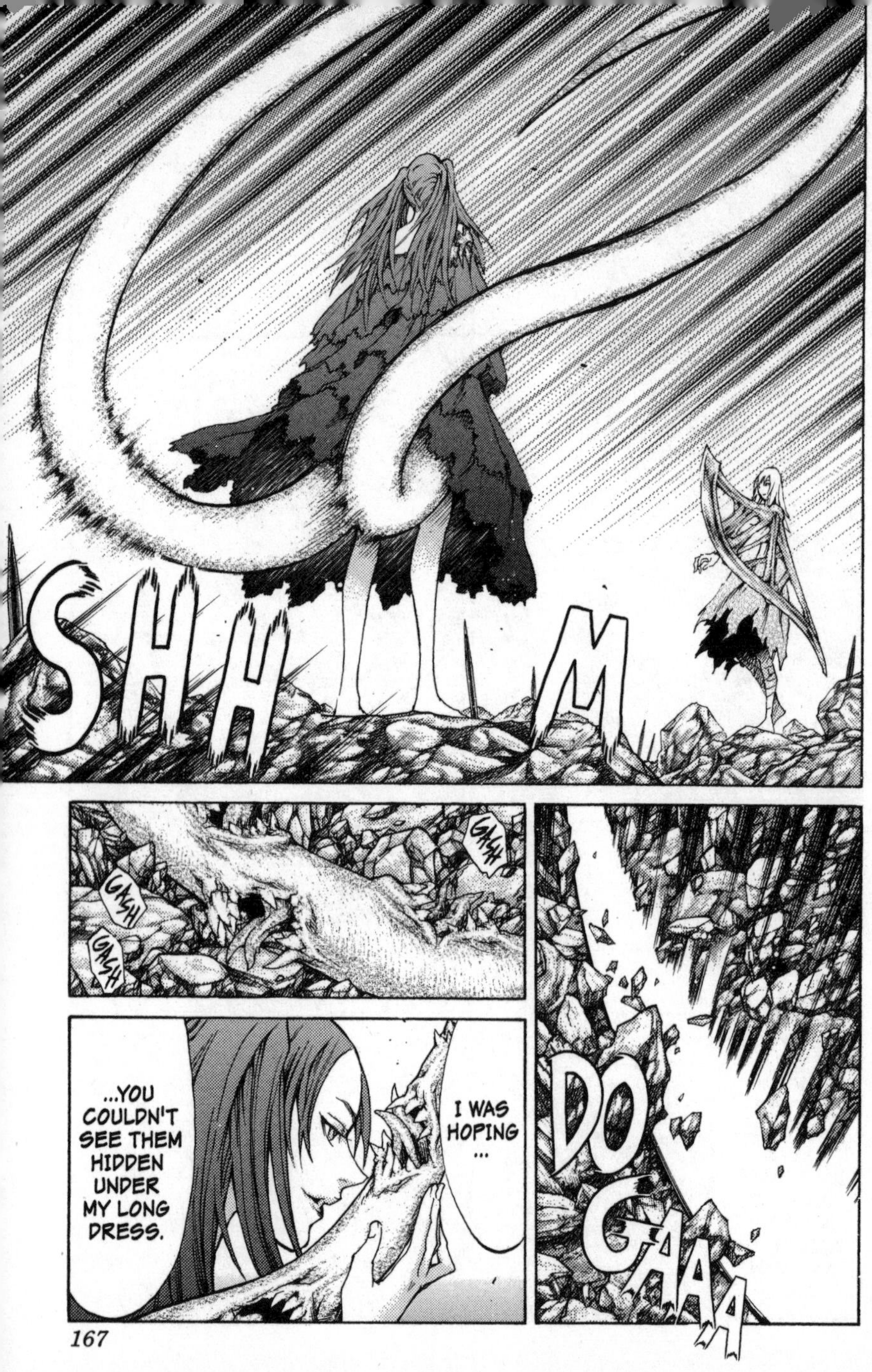
SHHM
DOGAAA
GASH
GASH
GASH
I WAS HOPING ...
...YOU COULDN'T SEE THEM HIDDEN UNDER MY LONG DRESS.

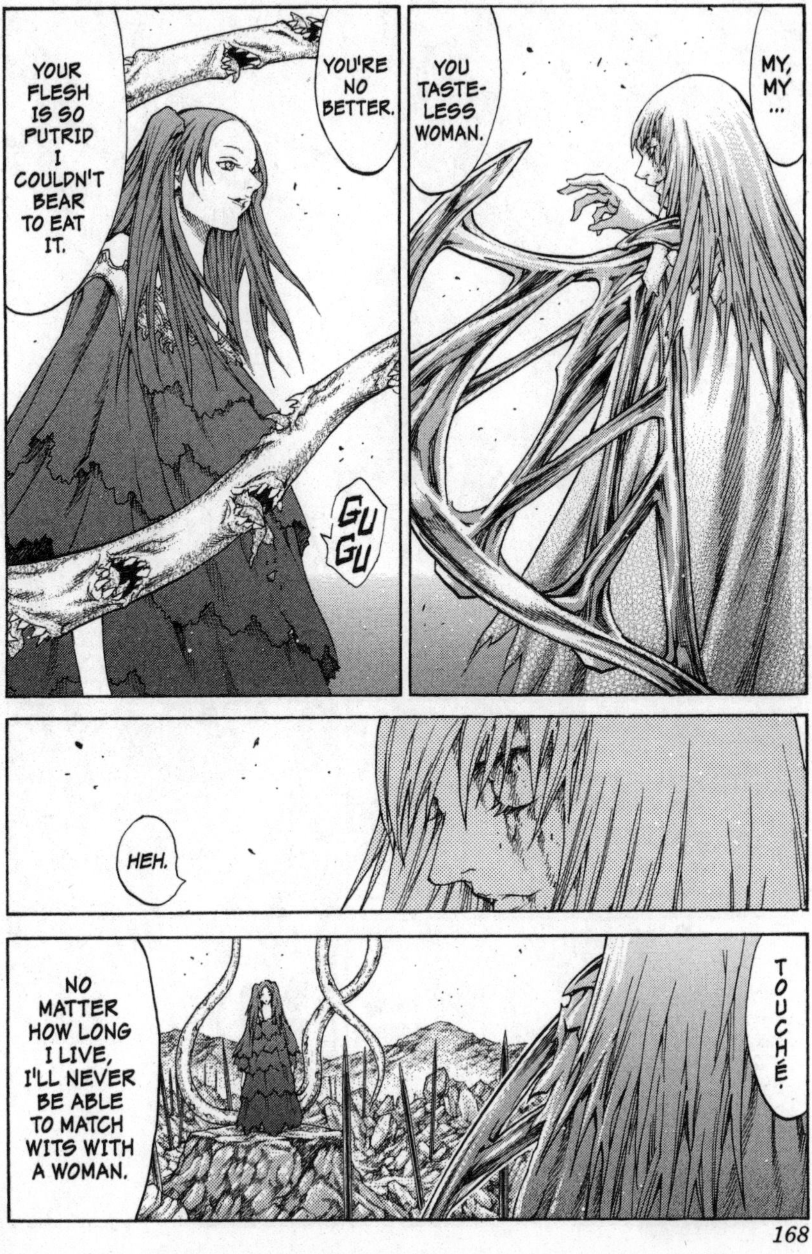
MY, MY ...
YOU TASTELESS WOMAN.
YOU'RE NO BETTER.
YOUR FLESH IS SO PUTRID I COULDN'T BEAR TO EAT IT.
GU GU
HEH.
TOUCHÉ.
NO MATTER HOW LONG I LIVE, I'LL NEVER BE ABLE TO MATCH WITS WITH A WOMAN.

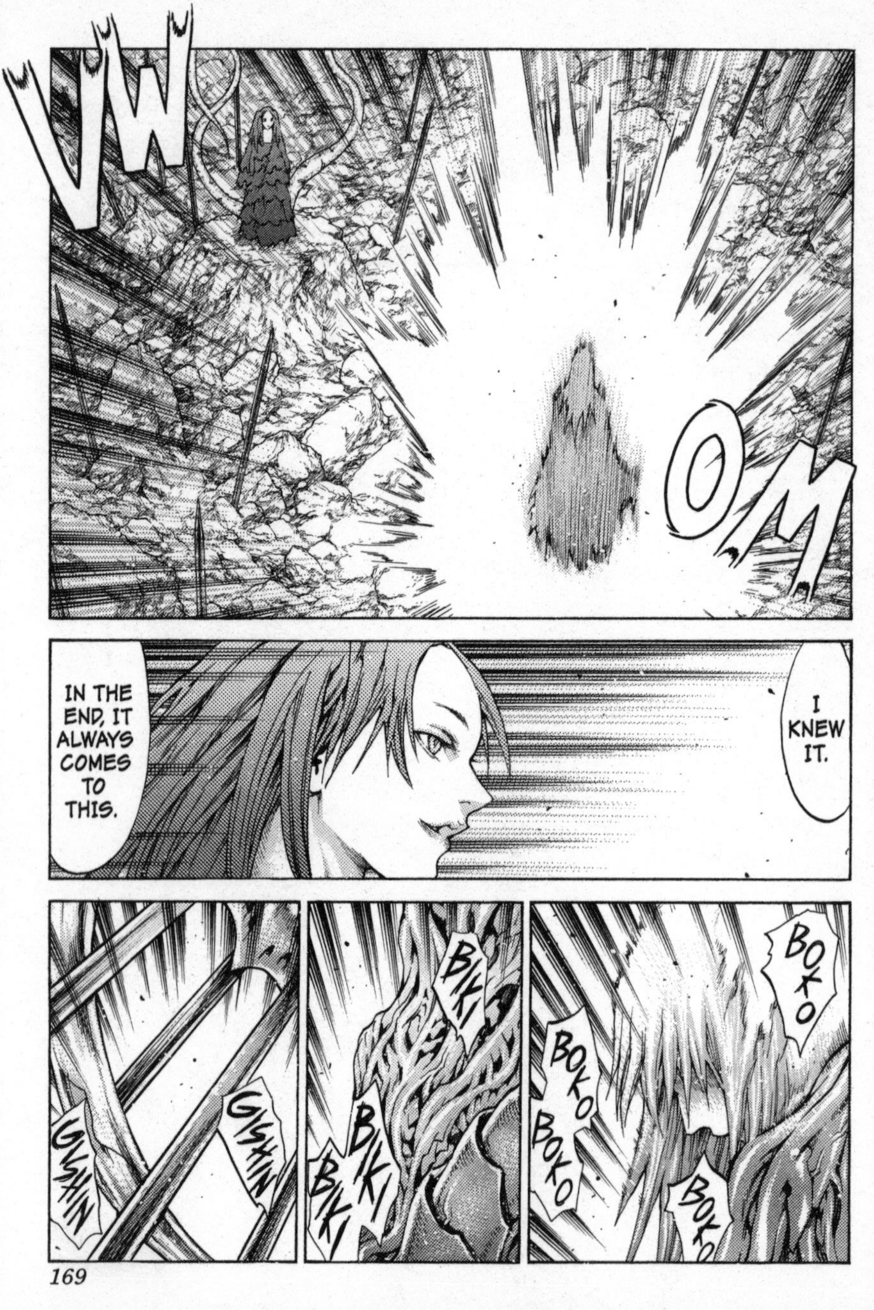
VWOOM
I KNEW IT.
IN THE END, IT ALWAYS COMES TO THIS.
BOKO
BOKO BOKO BOKO
BOKO
BIKI
BIKI
BIKI
GISHIN
GISHIN

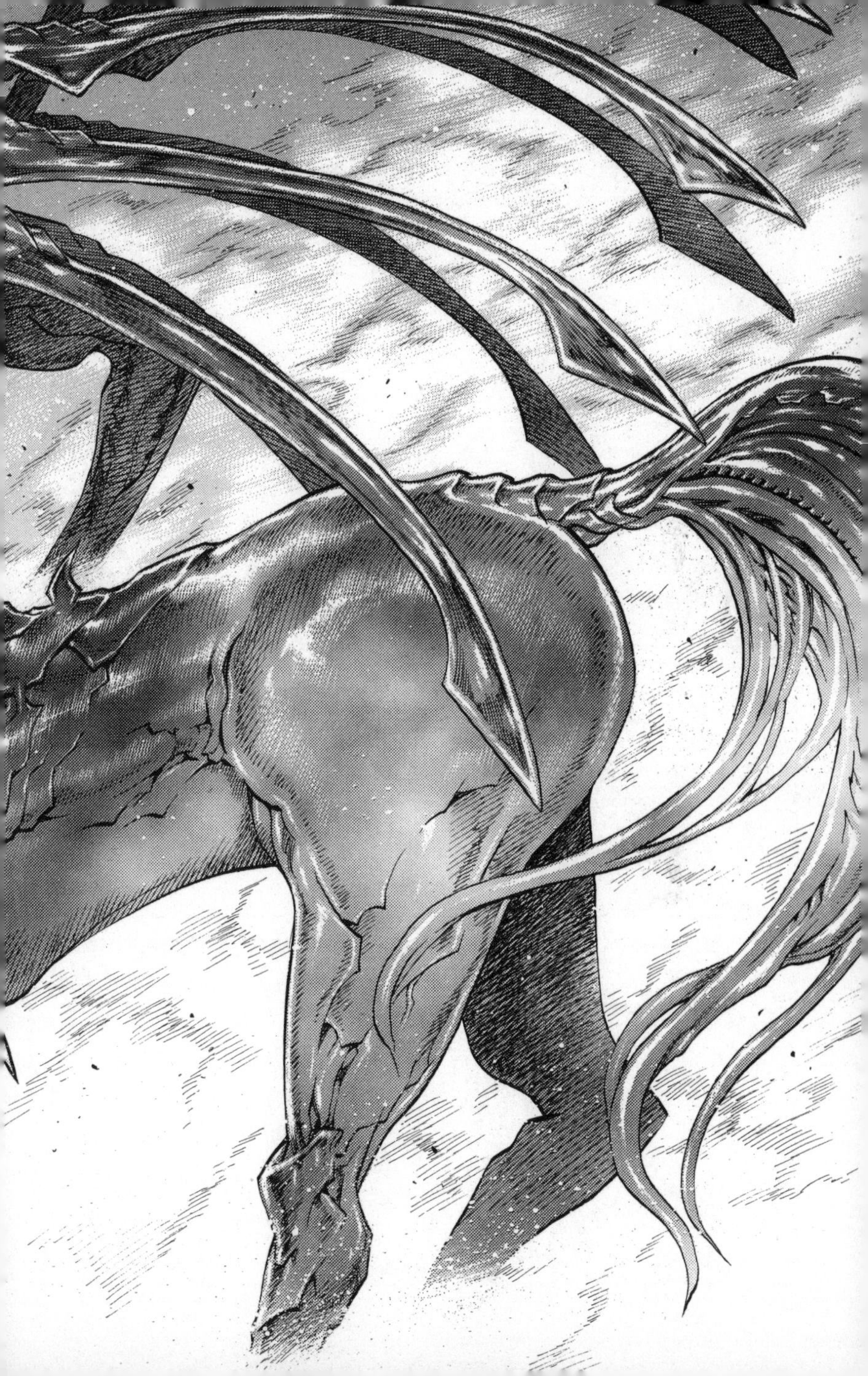

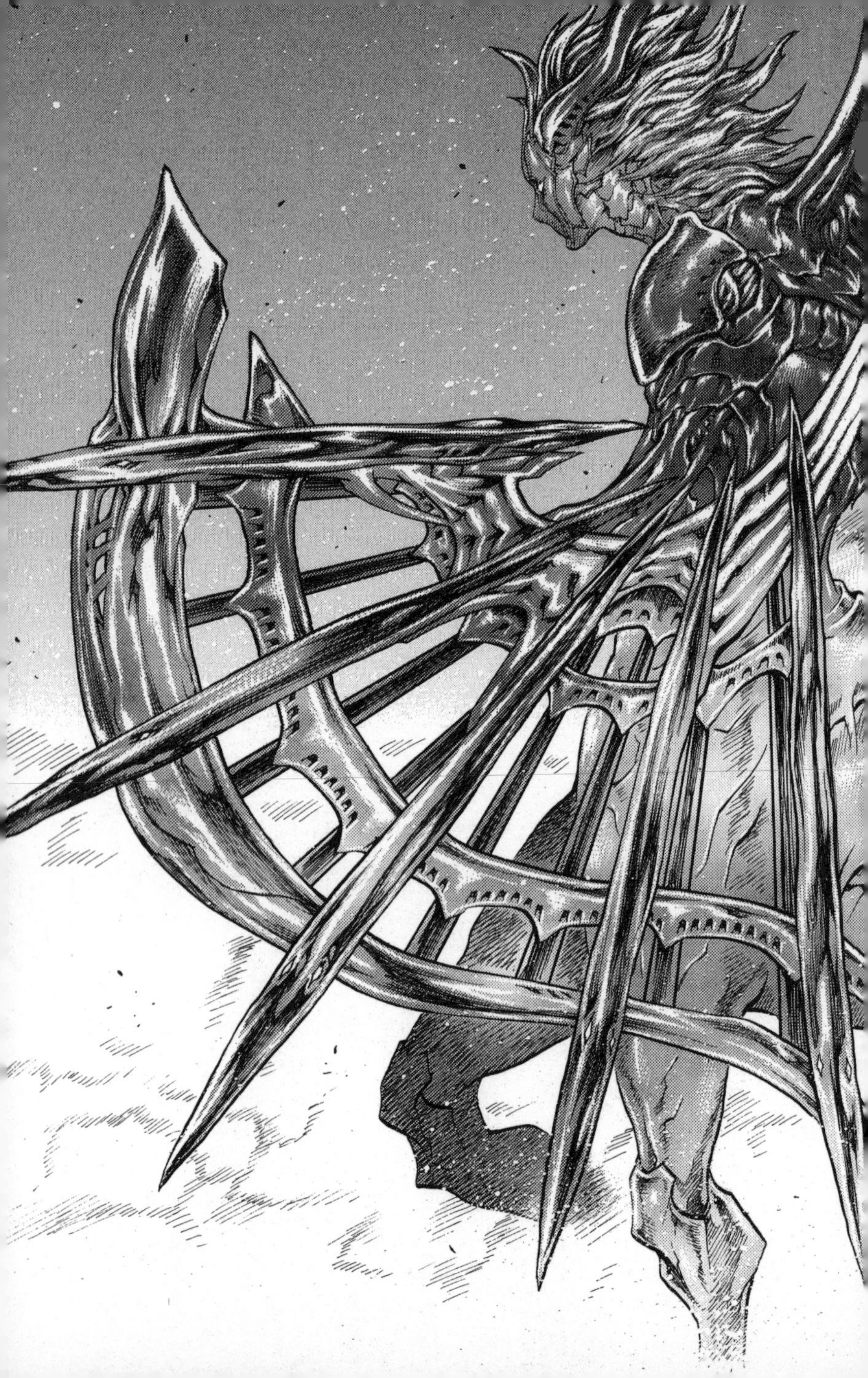

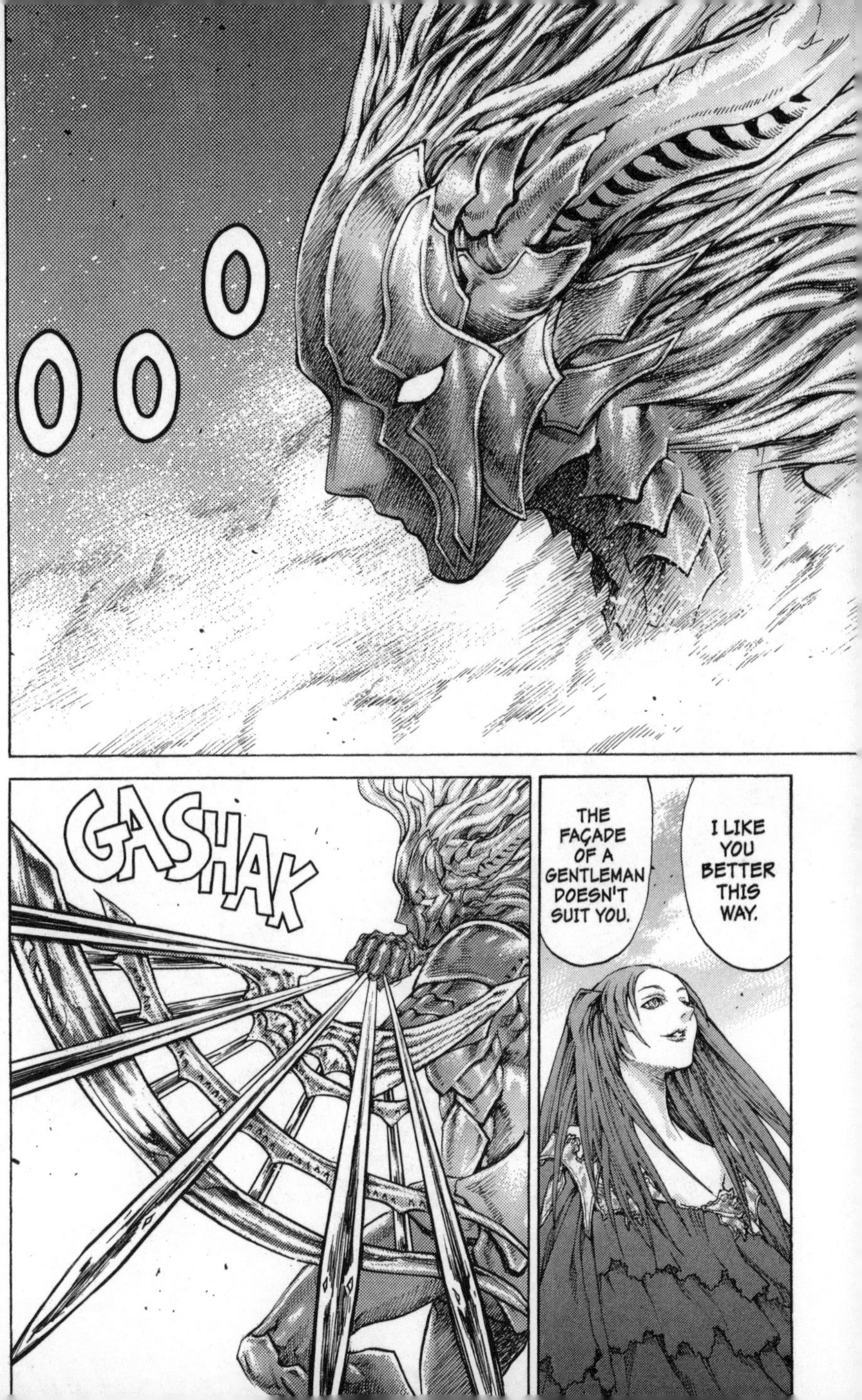
OOOO
I LIKE YOU BETTER THIS WAY.
THE FAÇADE OF A GENTLEMAN DOESN'T SUIT YOU.
GASHAK

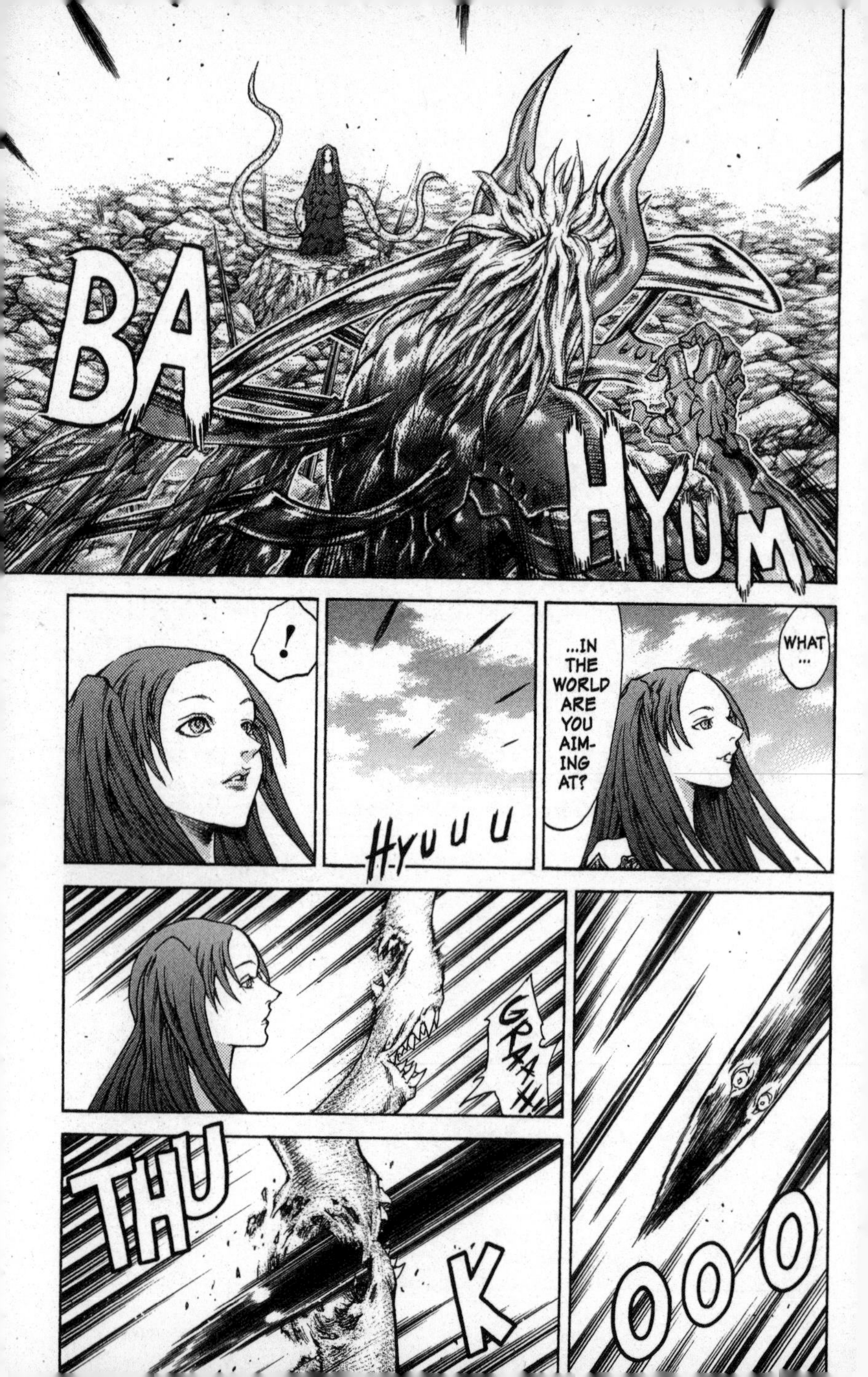
BA HYUM
WHAT...
...IN THE WORLD ARE YOU AIMING AT?
HYUUU
!
GRAAHH
THUKOOO

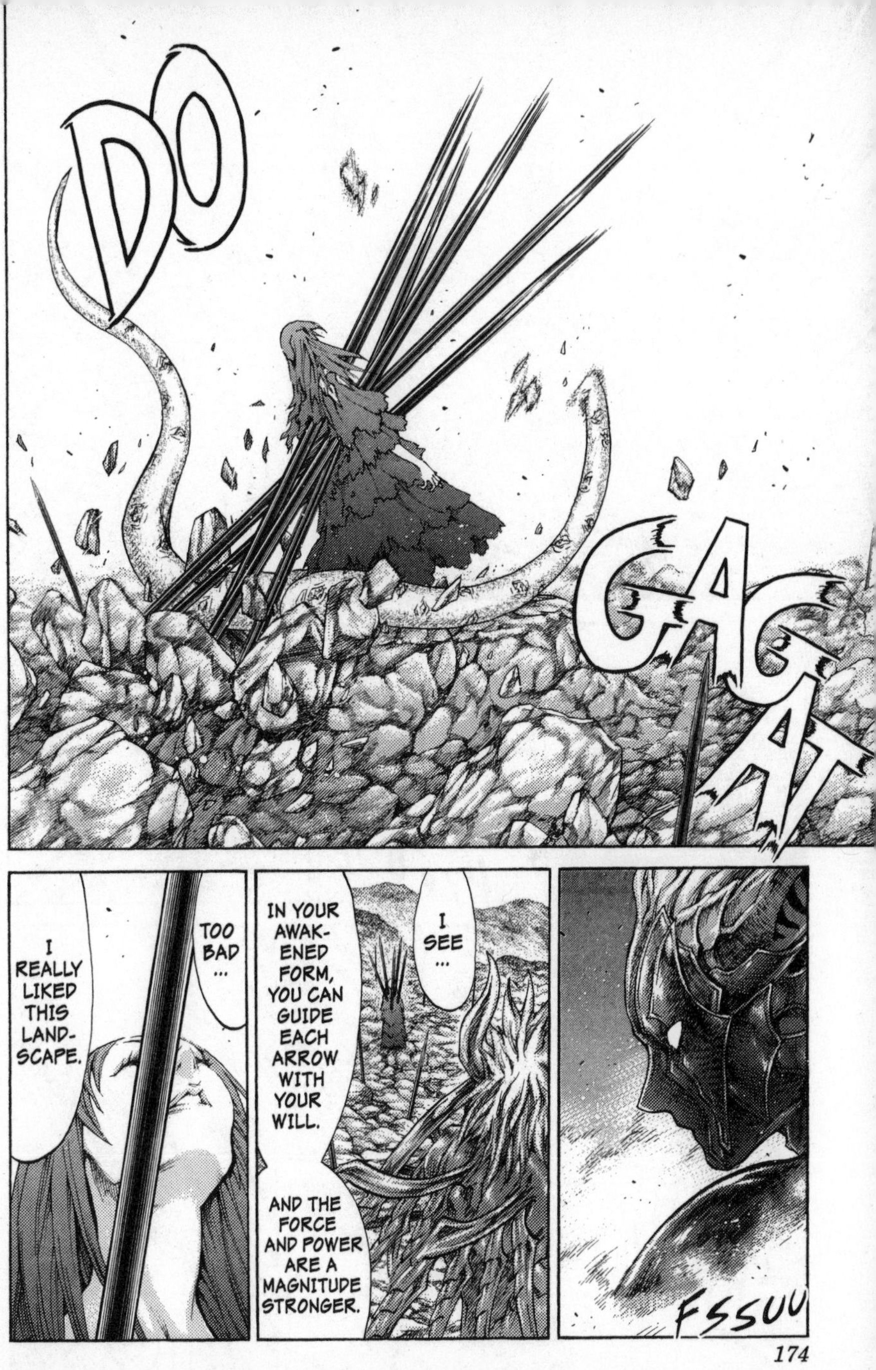
DO
GAGAT
FSSUU
I SEE ...
IN YOUR AWAKENED FORM, YOU CAN GUIDE EACH ARROW WITH YOUR WILL.
AND THE FORCE AND POWER ARE A MAGNITUDE STRONGER.
TOO BAD ...
I REALLY LIKED THIS LANDSCAPE.

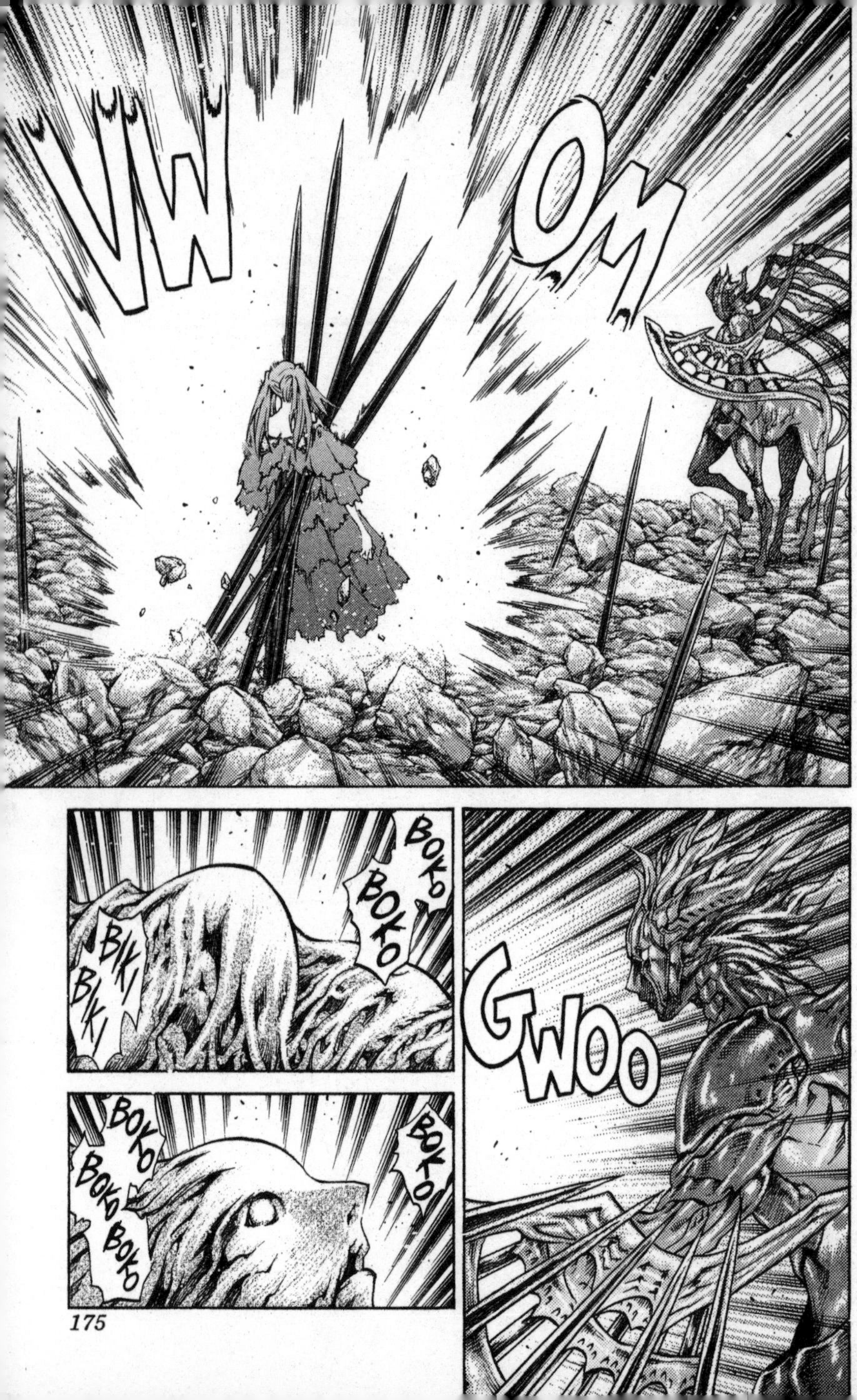
VWOOM
GWOO
BOKO BOKO
BIKI BIKI
BOKO
BOKO BOKO BOKO BOKO

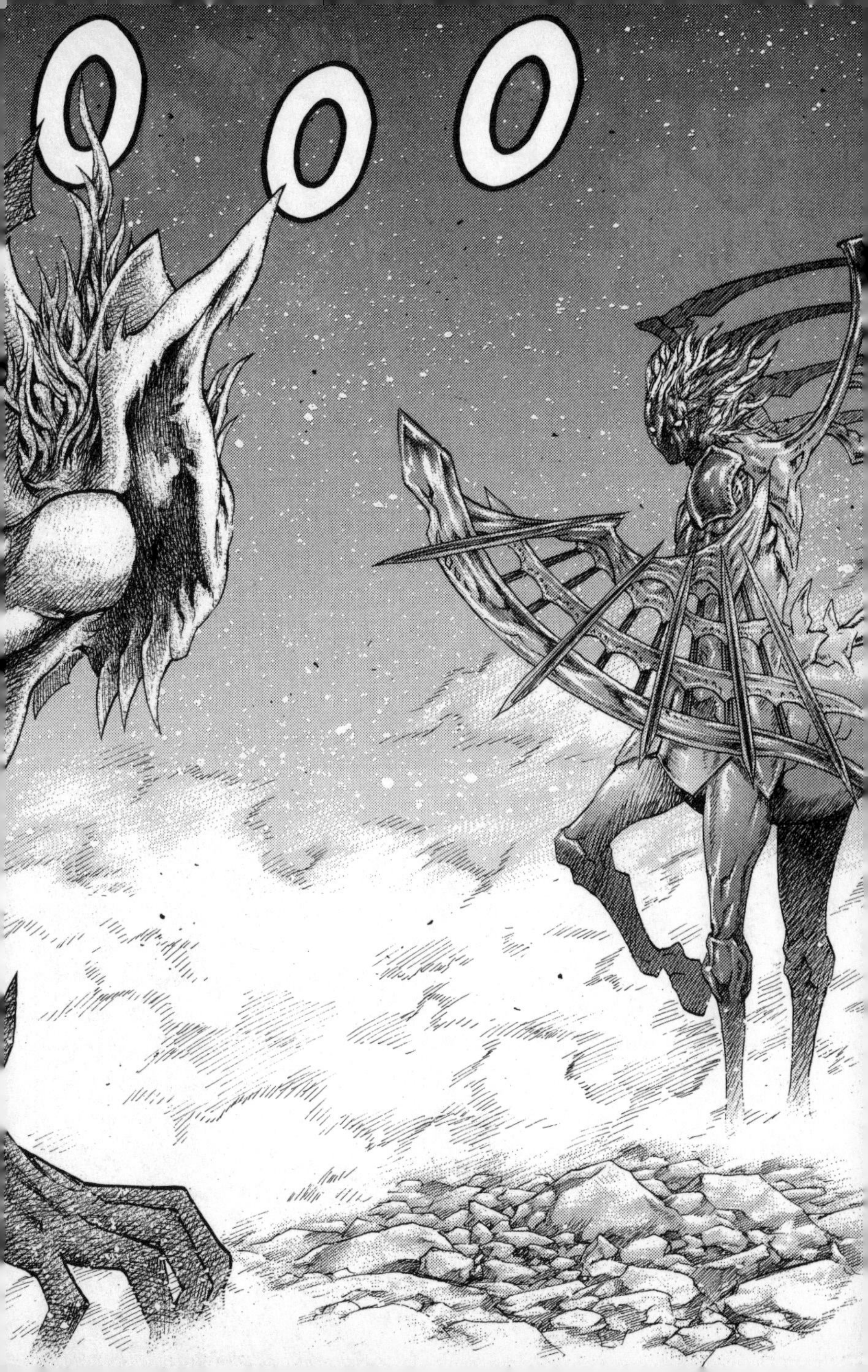
OOO

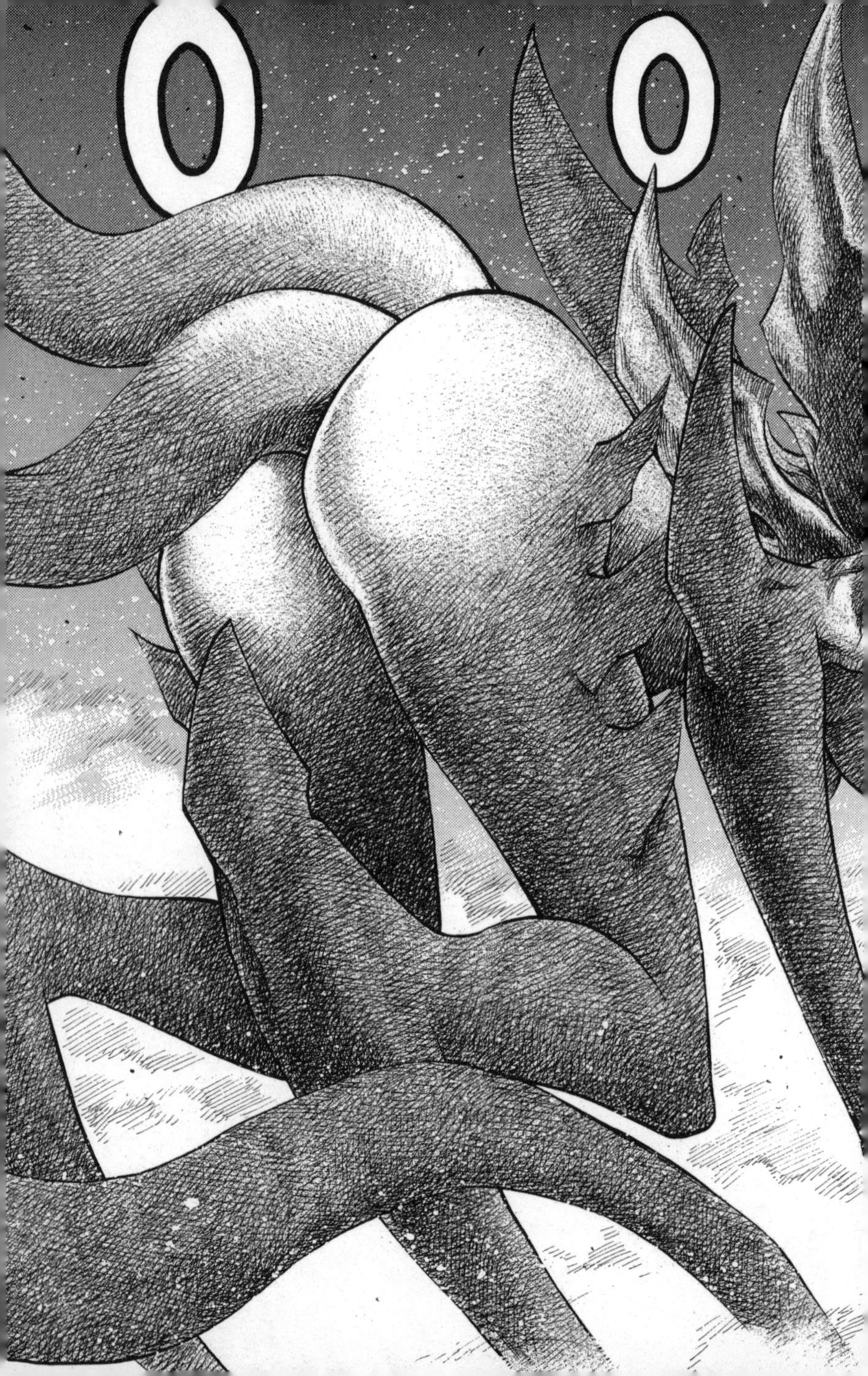

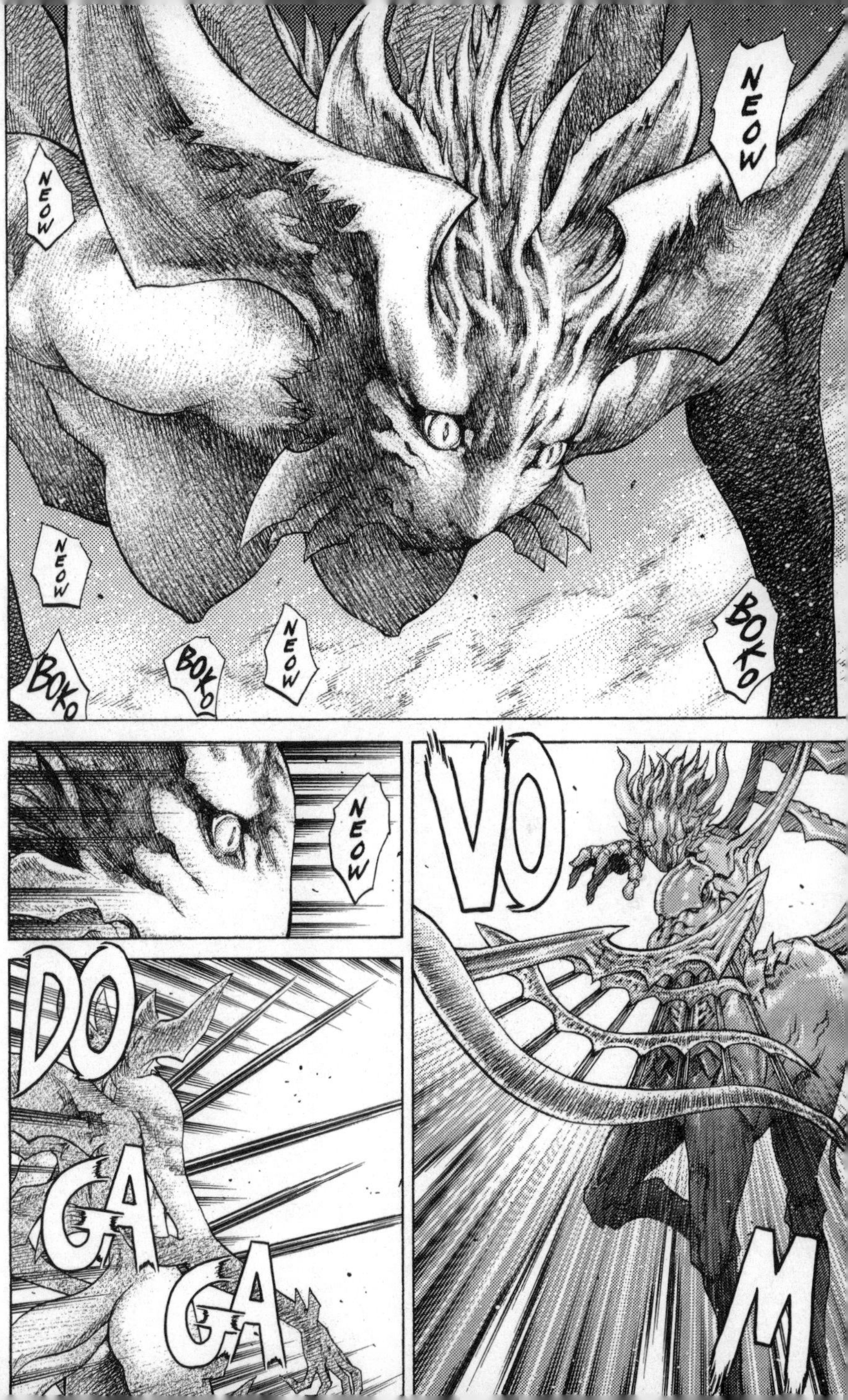
NEOW
NEOW
BOKO
NEOW
NEOW
BOKO
BOKO
VOM
NEOW
DOGAGA

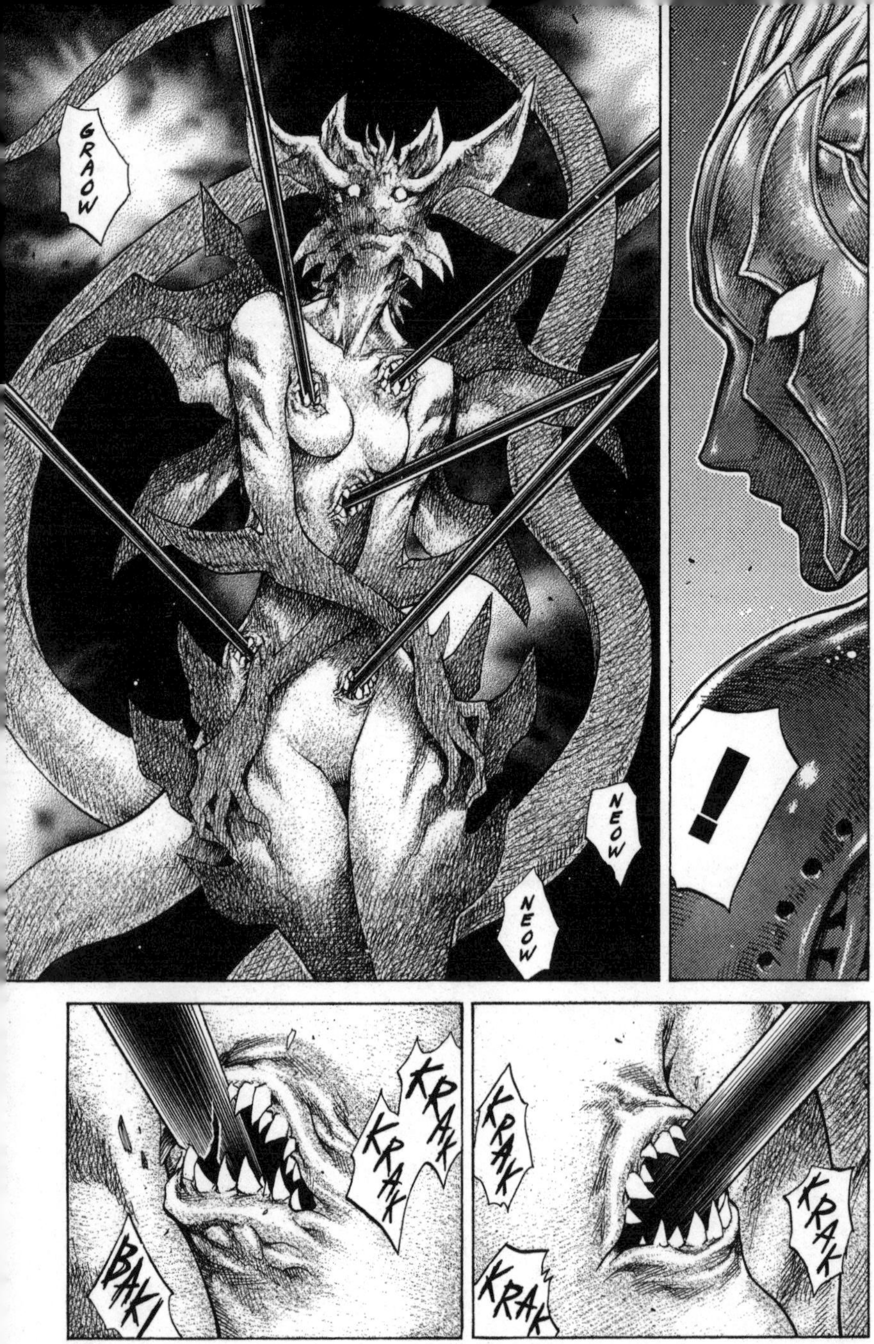
!
GRAOW
NEOW
NEOW
KRAK
KRAK
KRAK
KRAK
KRAK
BAKI

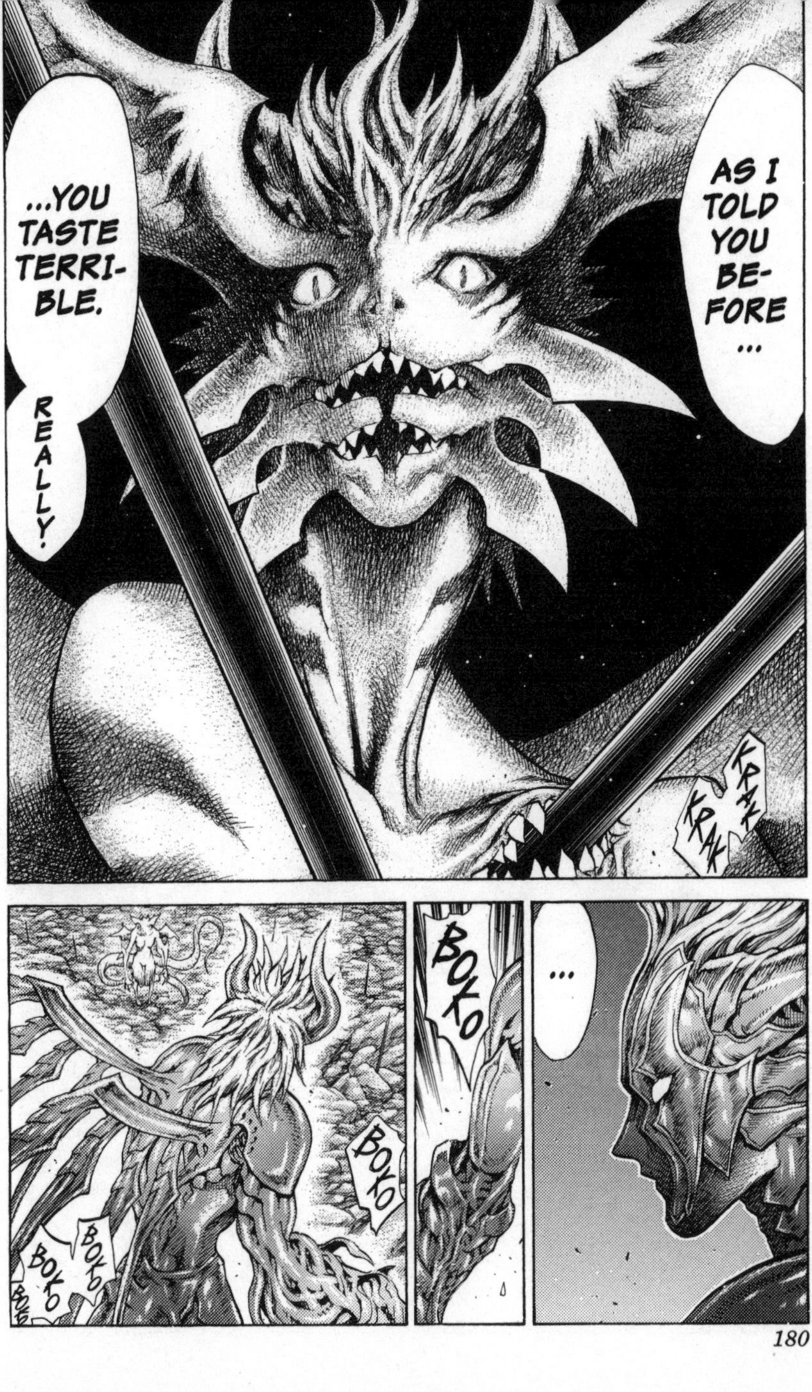
AS I TOLD YOU BEFORE...
...YOU TASTE TERRIBLE.
REALLY.
KRAK KRAK
...
BOKO
BOKO
BOKO BOKO BOKO

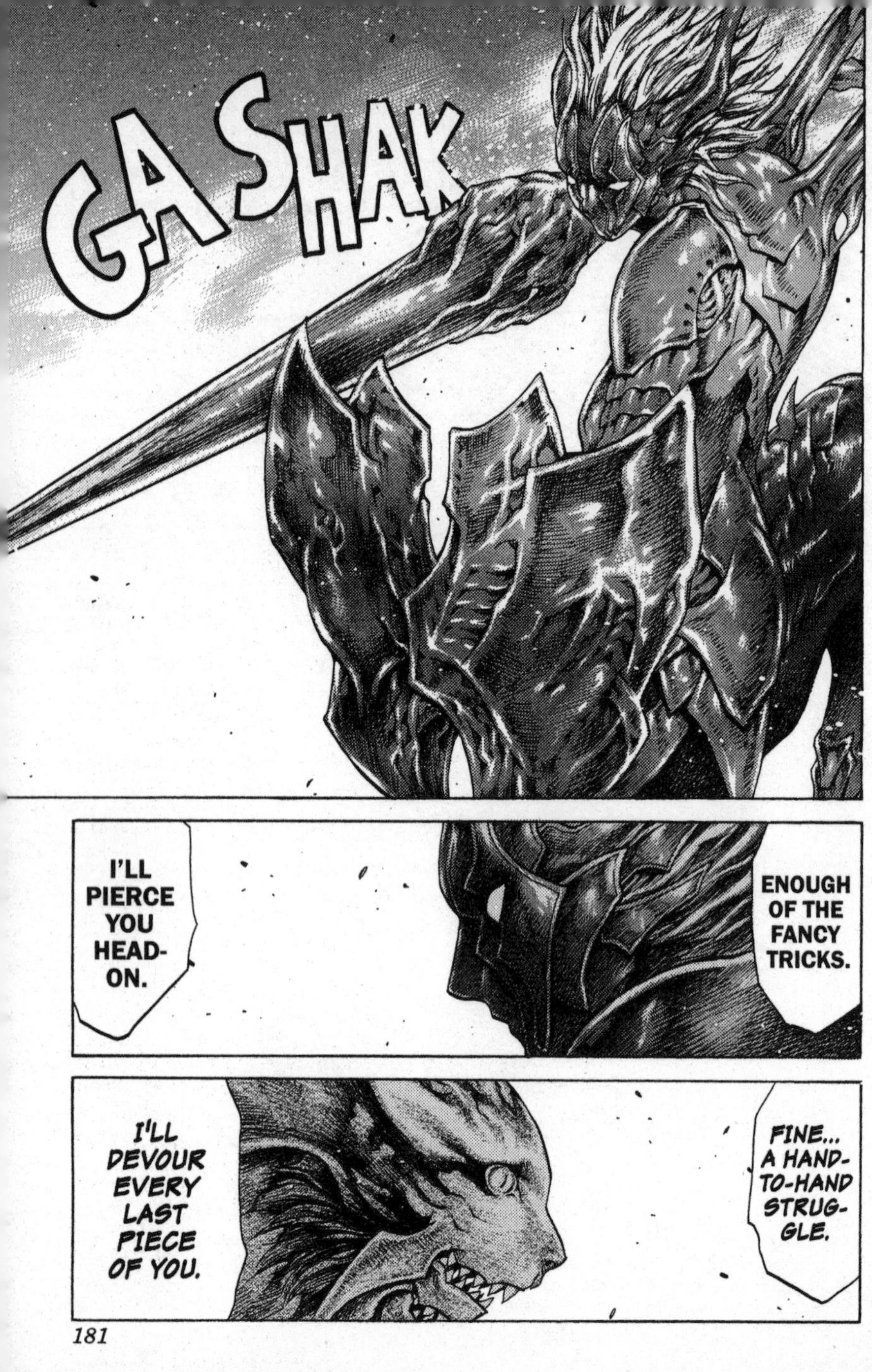
GASHAK
ENOUGH OF THE FANCY TRICKS.
I'LL PIERCE YOU HEAD-ON.
FINE... A HAND-TO-HAND STRUG-GLE.
I'LL DEVOUR EVERY LAST PIECE OF YOU.

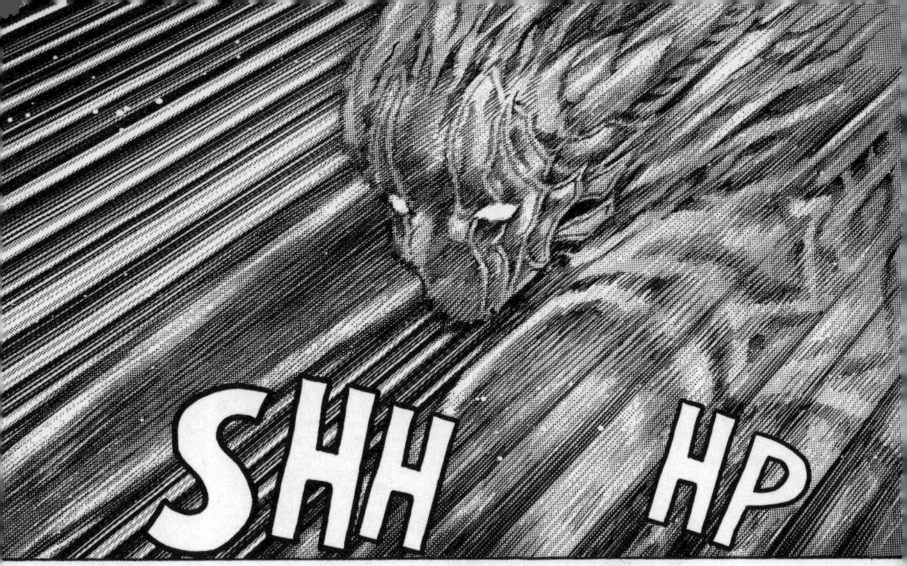
SHH HP
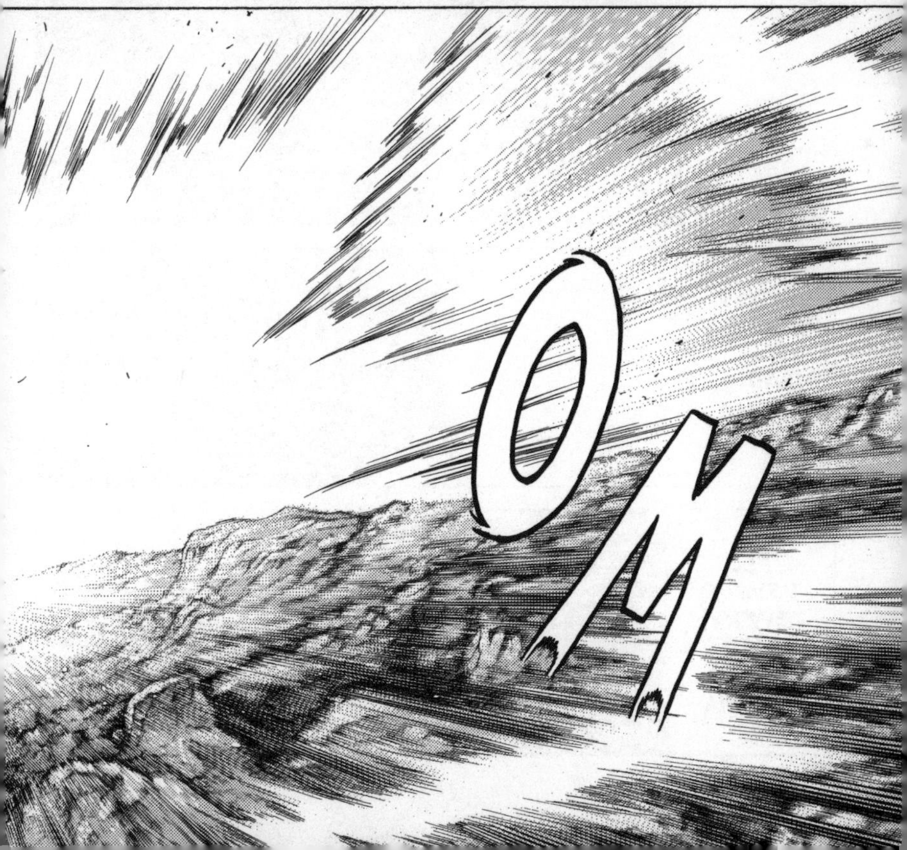
OM

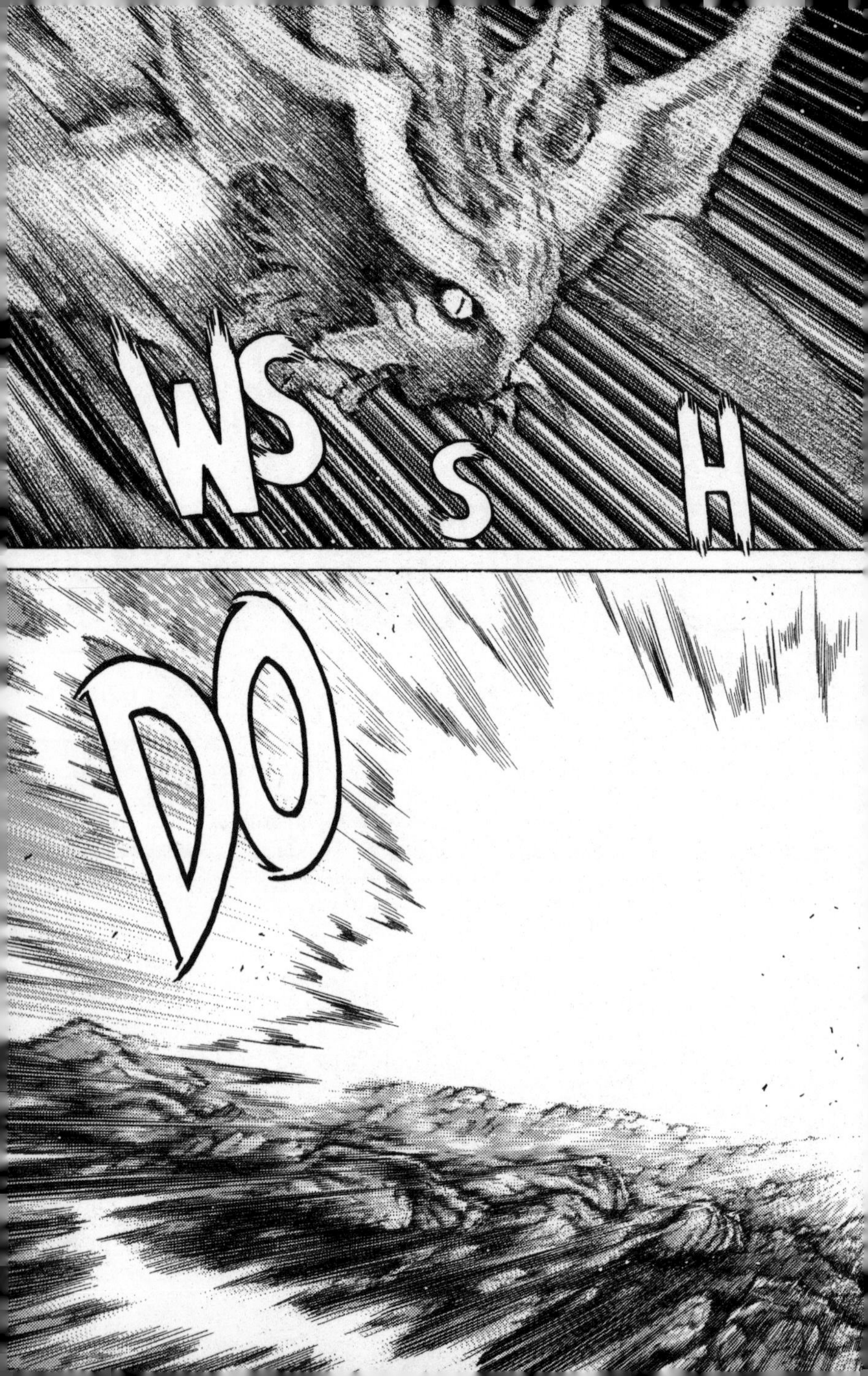
WSSH
DO

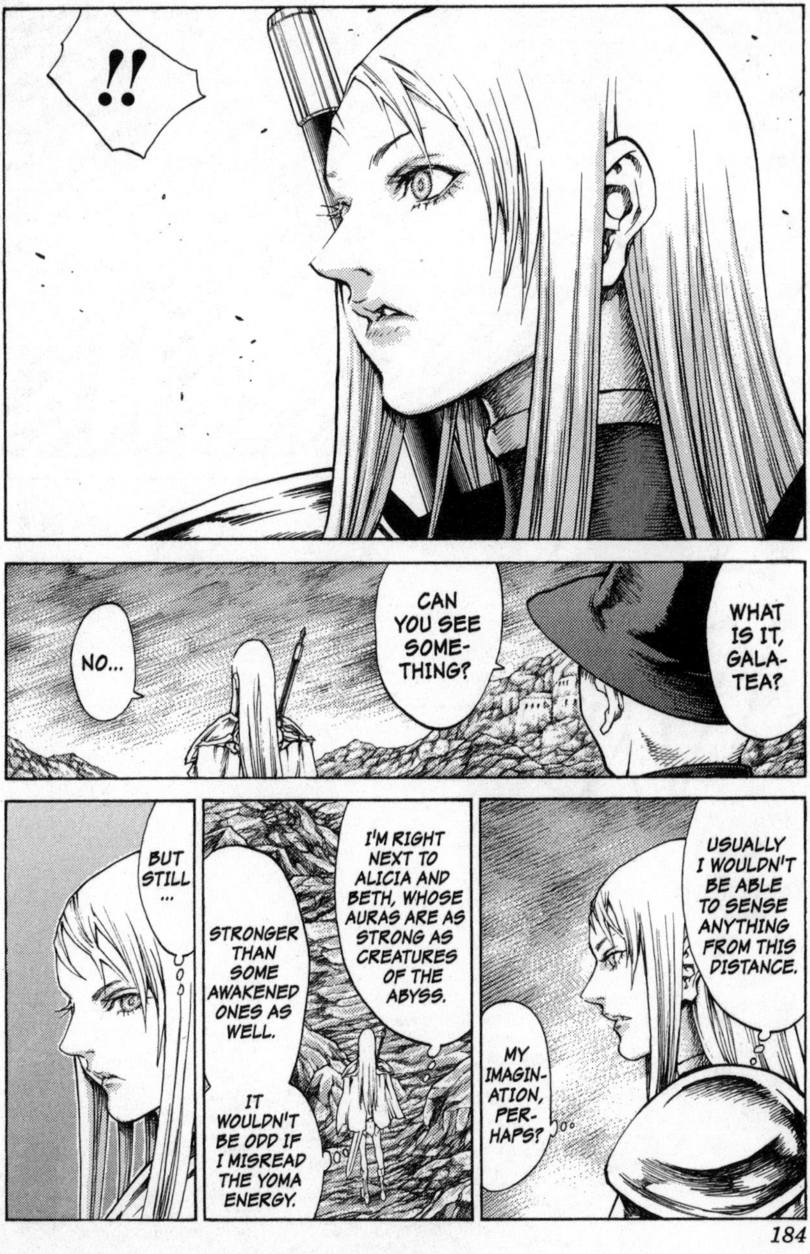
!!
WHAT IS IT, GALA-TEA?
CAN YOU SEE SOME-THING?
NO...
USUALLY I WOULDN'T BE ABLE TO SENSE ANYTHING FROM THIS DISTANCE.
MY IMAGIN-ATION, PER-HAPS?
I'M RIGHT NEXT TO ALICIA AND BETH, WHOSE AURAS ARE AS STRONG AS CREATURES OF THE ABYSS.
STRONGER THAN SOME AWAKENED ONES AS WELL.
IT WOULDN'T BE ODD IF I MISREAD THE YOMA ENERGY.
BUT STILL ...

READ THIS WAY

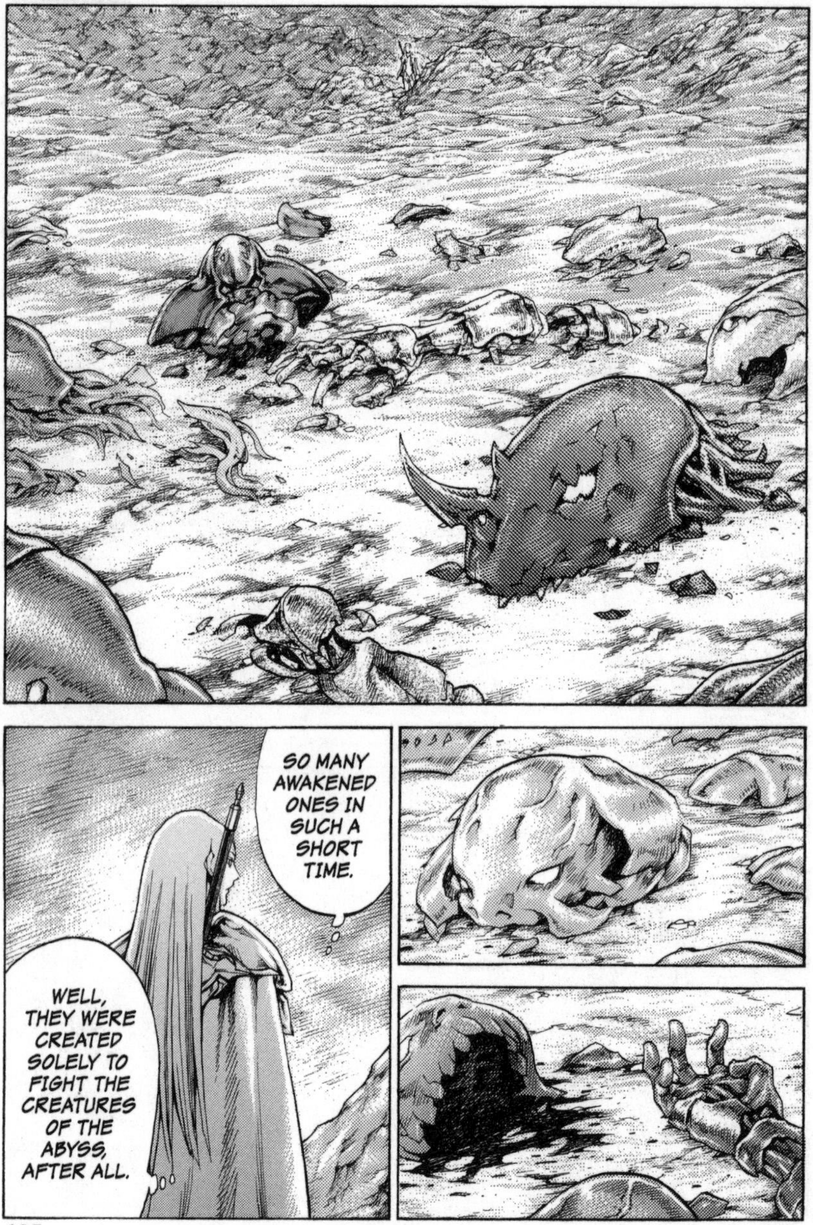
SO MANY AWAKENED ONES IN SUCH A SHORT TIME.
WELL, THEY WERE CREATED SOLELY TO FIGHT THE CREATURES OF THE ABYSS, AFTER ALL.

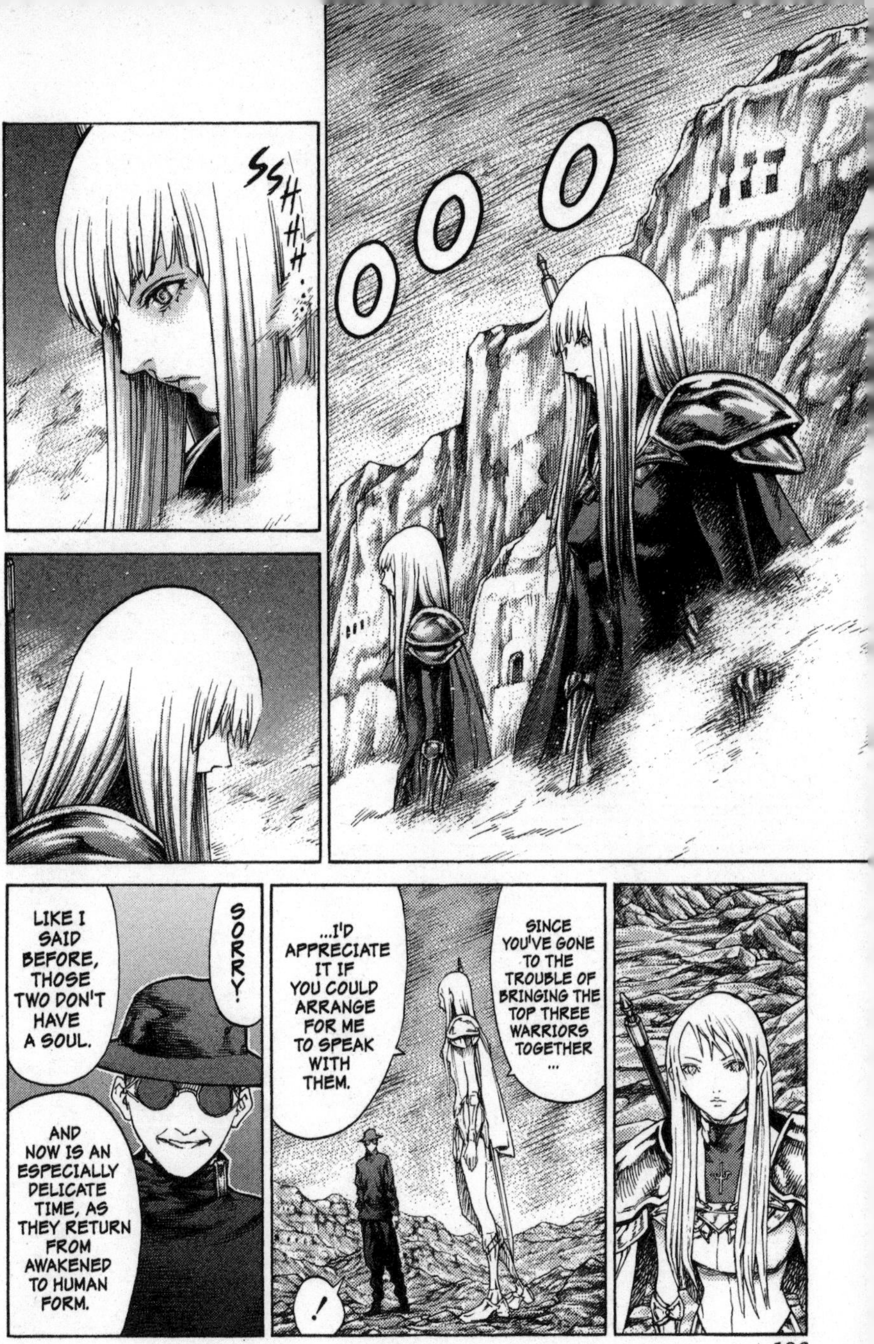
OOOO
SSHHH...
SINCE YOU'VE GONE TO THE TROUBLE OF BRINGING THE TOP THREE WARRIORS TOGETHER ...
...I'D APPRECIATE IT IF YOU COULD ARRANGE FOR ME TO SPEAK WITH THEM.
!
SORRY!
LIKE I SAID BEFORE, THOSE TWO DON'T HAVE A SOUL.
AND NOW IS AN ESPECIALLY DELICATE TIME, AS THEY RETURN FROM AWAKENED TO HUMAN FORM.

READ THIS WAY

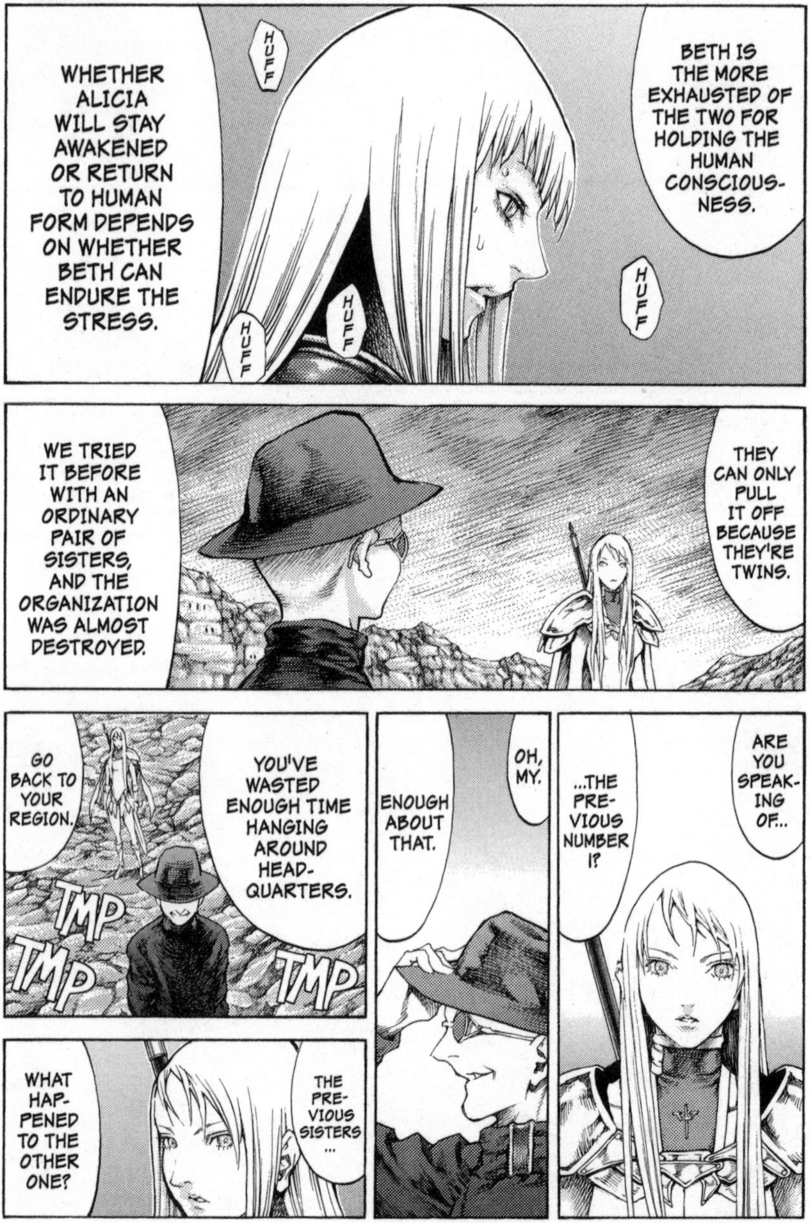
BETH IS THE MORE EXHAUSTED OF THE TWO FOR HOLDING THE HUMAN CONSCIOUS-NESS.
HUFF
HUFF
WHETHER ALICIA WILL STAY AWAKENED OR RETURN TO HUMAN FORM DEPENDS ON WHETHER BETH CAN ENDURE THE STRESS.
HUFF
HUFF
THEY CAN ONLY PULL IT OFF BECAUSE THEY'RE TWINS.
WE TRIED IT BEFORE WITH AN ORDINARY PAIR OF SISTERS, AND THE ORGANIZATION WAS ALMOST DESTROYED.
ARE YOU SPEAK-ING OF...
...THE PRE-VIOUS NUMBER I?
OH, MY.
ENOUGH ABOUT THAT.
YOU'VE WASTED ENOUGH TIME HANGING AROUND HEAD-QUARTERS.
GO BACK TO YOUR REGION.
TMP
TMP
TMP
THE PRE-VIOUS SISTERS ...
WHAT HAP-PENED TO THE OTHER ONE?

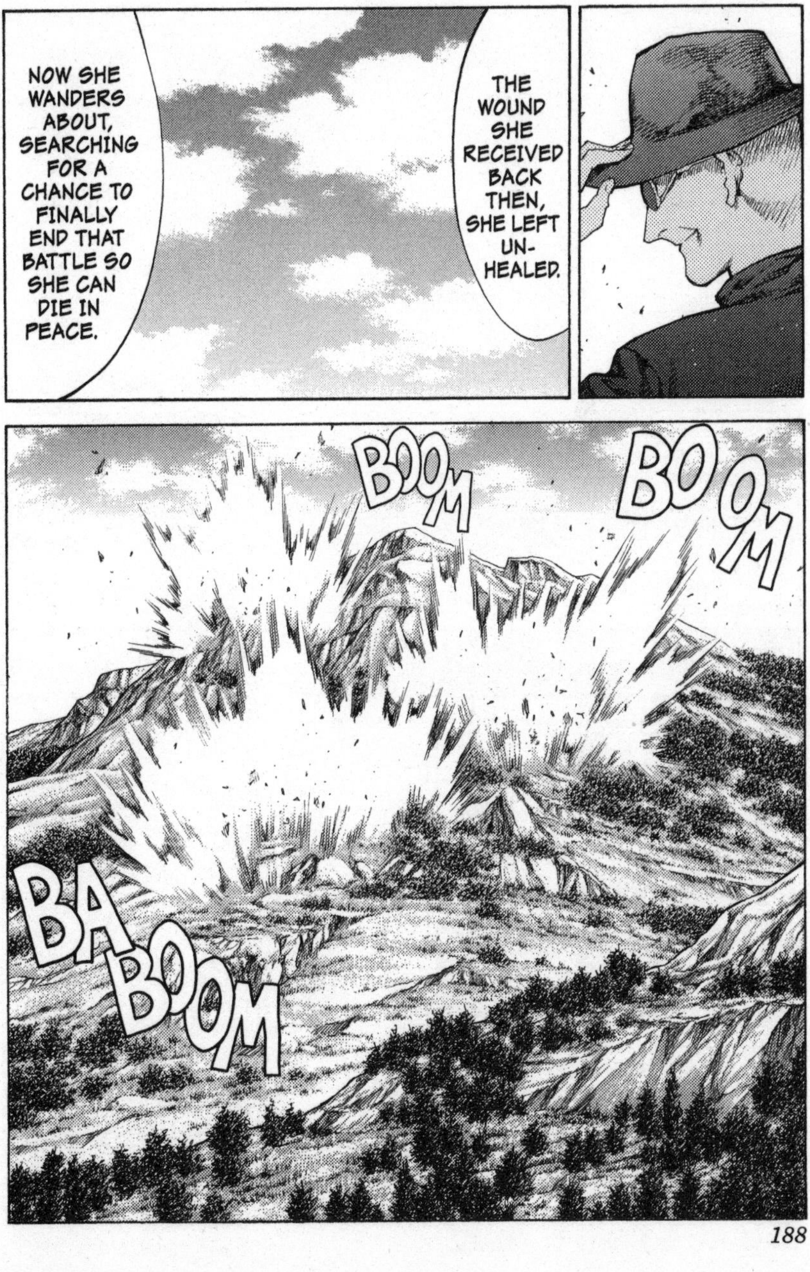
THE WOUND SHE RECEIVED BACK THEN, SHE LEFT UN-HEALED.
NOW SHE WANDERS ABOUT, SEARCHING FOR A CHANCE TO FINALLY END THAT BATTLE SO SHE CAN DIE IN PEACE.
BOOOM
BOOM
BABOOM

READ THIS WAY

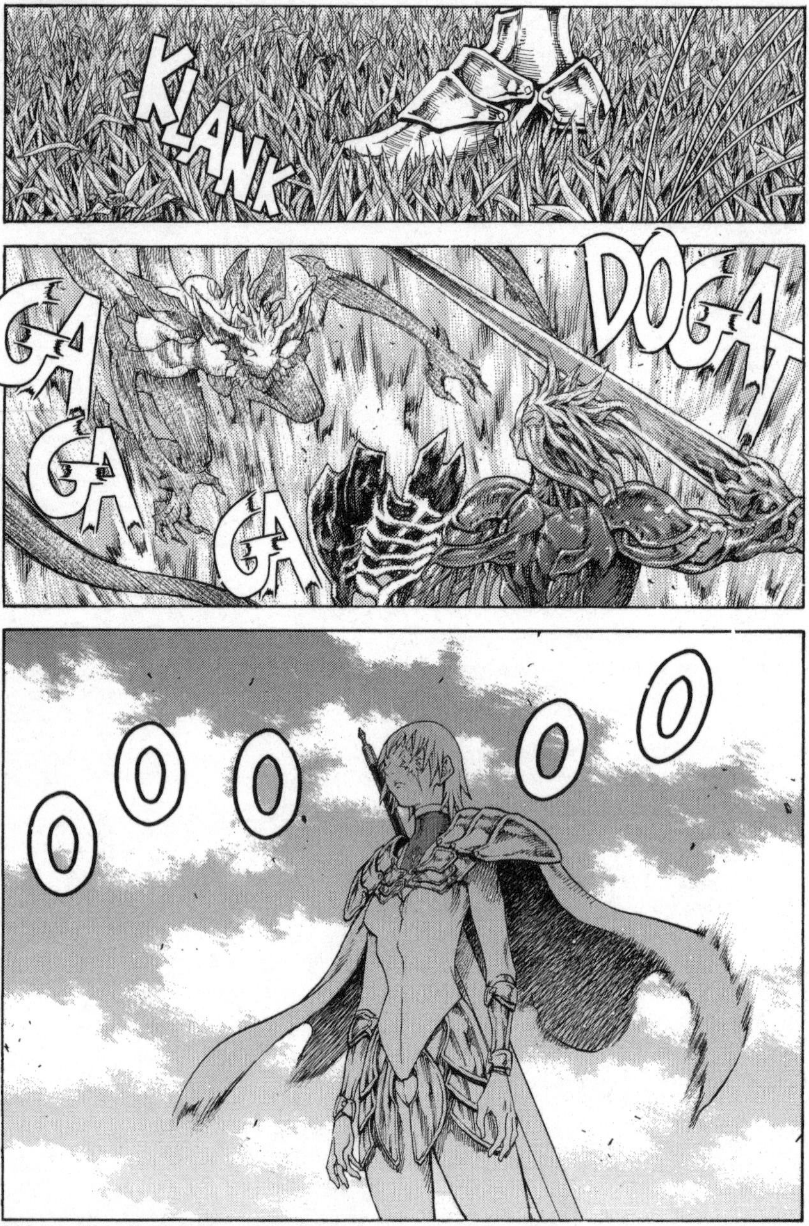
KLANK
DOGAT
GA
GA
GA
OOOOOO

END OF VOL. 11: KINDRED OF PARADISE

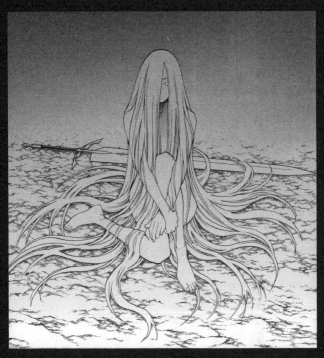

IN THE NEXT VOLUME

Seven years have passed since the devastating battle in Pieta, and now a new generation of Claymores carries on the fight against the Awakened Ones. However, the mystery of Clare's fate, and that of her comrades, resurfaces after a surprising discovery made by a young Claymore.

Available in July 2008

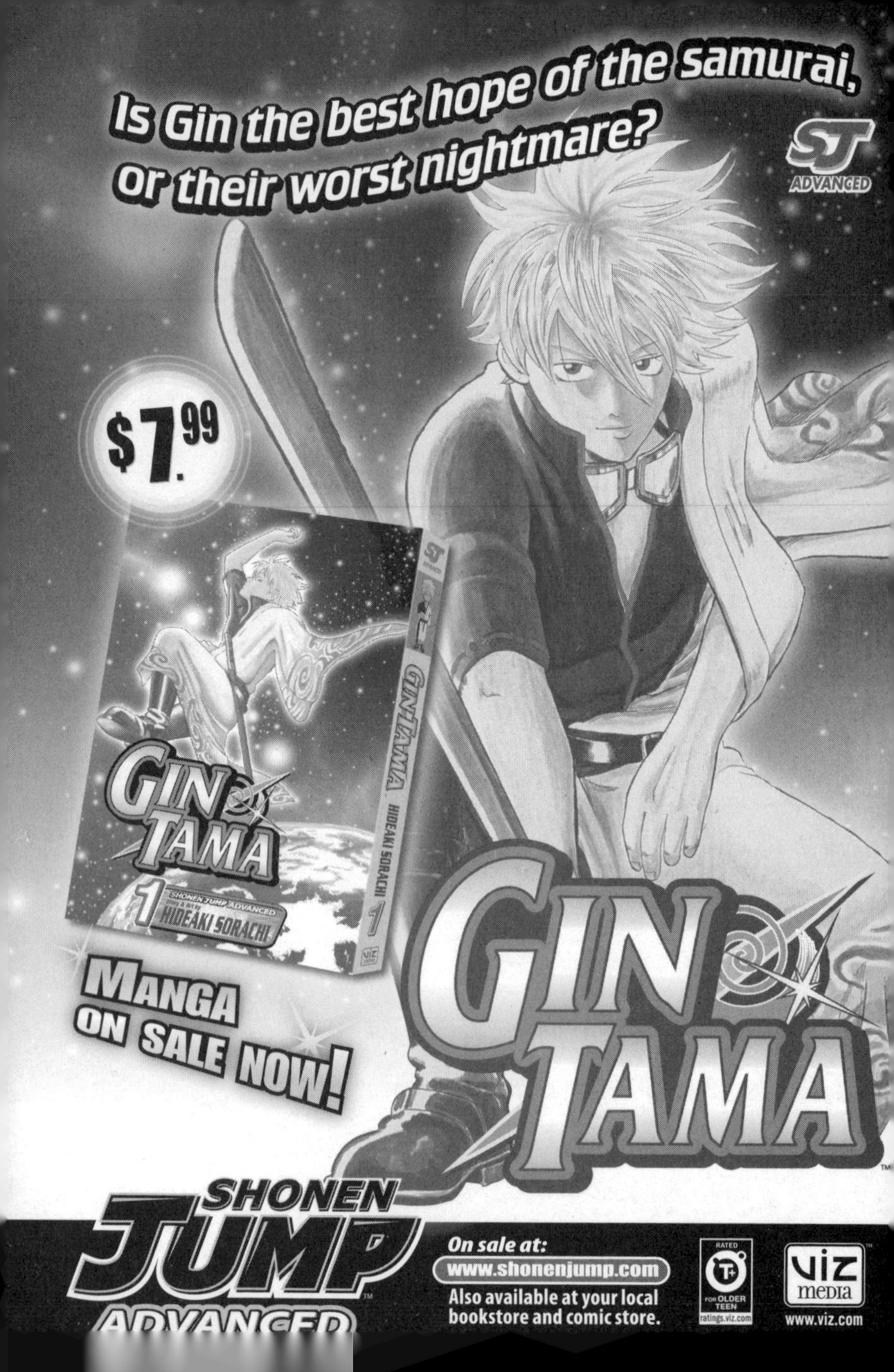
Is Gin the best hope of the samurai, or their worst nightmare?
SJ ADVANCED
$7.99
GIN TAMA
1 SHONEN JUMP ADVANCED HIDEAKI SORACHI
GIN TAMA HIDEAKI SORACHI 1
MANGA ON SALE NOW!
GIN TAMA™
SHONEN JUMP ADVANCED™
On sale at:
www.shonenjump.com
Also available at your local bookstore and comic store.
RATED T+ FOR OLDER TEEN ratings.viz.com
viz media™
www.viz.com

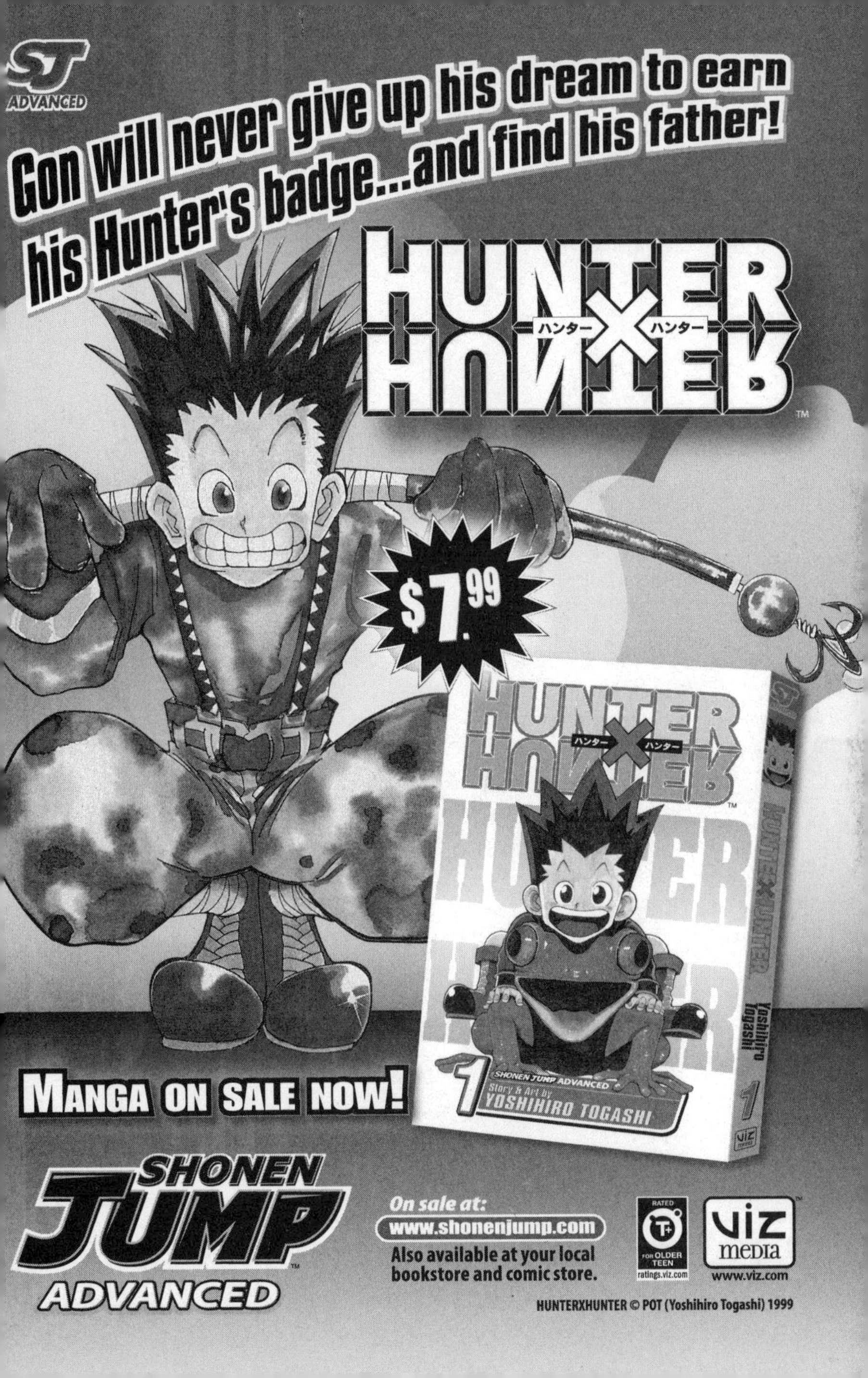
SJ
ADVANCED
Gon will never give up his dream to earn his Hunter's badge...and find his father!
HUNTER ハンター × ハンター HUNTER™
$7.99
HUNTER ハンター × ハンター HUNTER™
SHONEN JUMP ADVANCED
1
Story & Art by
YOSHIHIRO TOGASHI
Yoshihiro Togashi
MANGA ON SALE NOW!
SHONEN JUMP™ ADVANCED
On sale at:
www.shonenjump.com
Also available at your local bookstore and comic store.
RATED T+ FOR OLDER TEEN
ratings.viz.com
viz media™
www.viz.com
HUNTERXHUNTER © POT (Yoshihiro Togashi) 1999

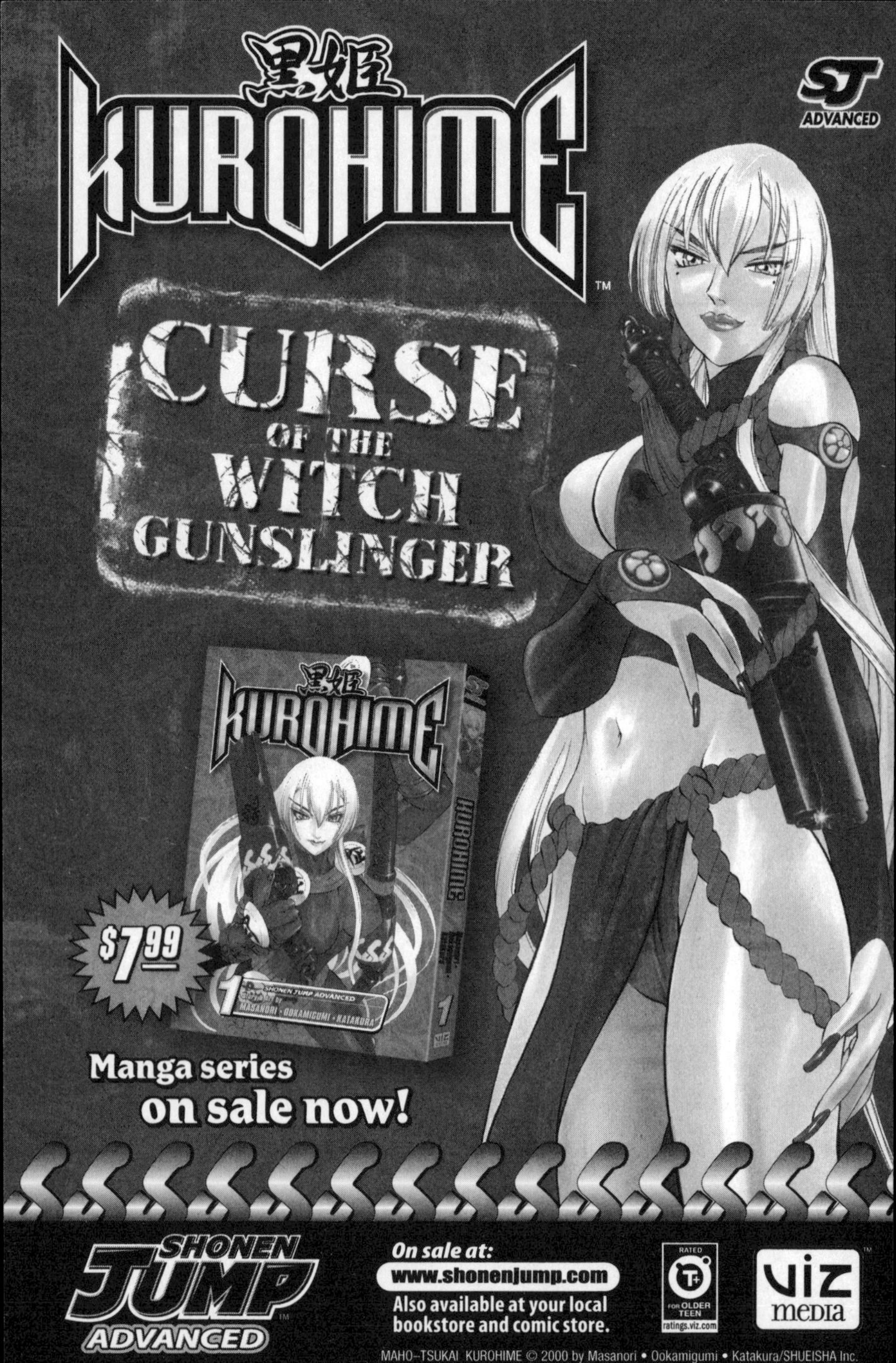

黒姫
KUROHIME™
SJ ADVANCED
CURSE OF THE WITCH GUNSLINGER
KUROHIME
$7.99
Manga series
on sale now!
SHONEN JUMP ADVANCED
On sale at:
www.shonenjump.com
Also available at your local bookstore and comic store.
RATED T+ FOR OLDER TEEN ratings.viz.com
viz media
MAHO-TSUKAI KUROHIME © 2000 by Masanori • Ookamigumi • Katakura/SHUEISHA Inc.

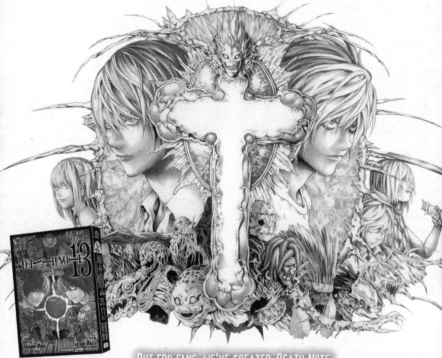

DEATH NOTE 13
デスノート
HOW TO READ

"A god of death has no obligation to completely explain how to use the note or rules which will apply to the human who owns it"

BUT FOR FANS, WE'VE CREATED *DEATH NOTE HOW TO READ 13*—AN ULTIMATE ENCYCLOPEDIA THAT EXPLAINS IT ALL WITH:

PLUS, A BONUS MANGA CHAPTER OF NEVER-BEFORE-TRANSLATED MATERIAL!
•COMPLETE CHARACTER BIOGRAPHIES •DETAILED STORYLINE SUMMARIES •PRODUCTION NOTES •BEHIND-THE-SCENES COMMENTARIES •EXCLUSIVE INTERVIEWS WITH CREATORS TSUGUMI OHBA AND TAKESHI OBATA

GET THE COMPLETE *DEATH NOTE* COLLECTION—BUY THE MANGA, FICTION AND ANIME TODAY!

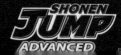

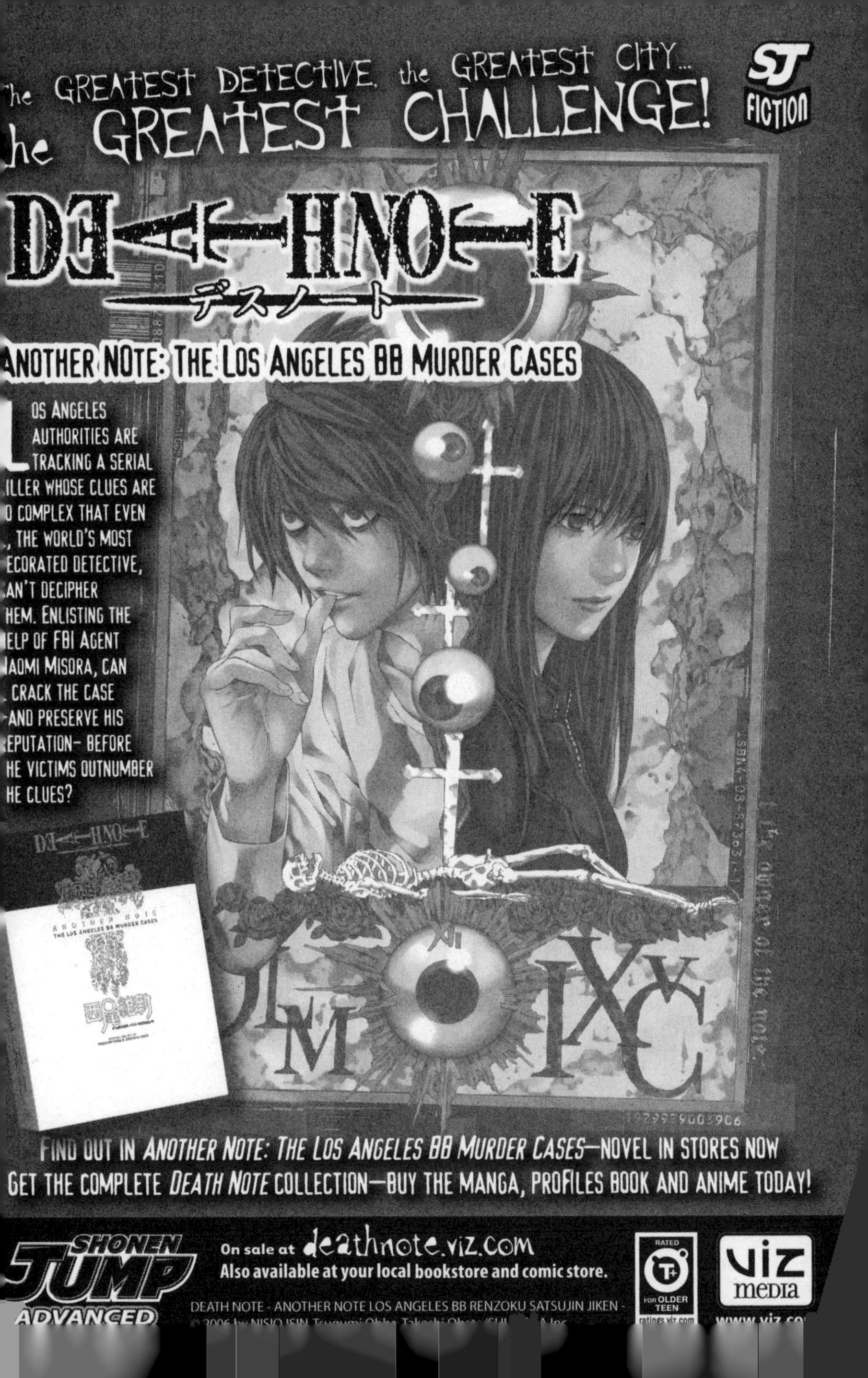

he GREATEST DETECTIVE, the GREATEST CITY...
he GREATEST CHALLENGE!
SJ FICTION
DEATH NOTE
デスノート
ANOTHER NOTE: THE LOS ANGELES BB MURDER CASES
LOS ANGELES AUTHORITIES ARE TRACKING A SERIAL
ILLER WHOSE CLUES ARE
O COMPLEX THAT EVEN
, THE WORLD'S MOST
ECORATED DETECTIVE,
AN'T DECIPHER
HEM. ENLISTING THE
ELP OF FBI AGENT
AOMI MISORA, CAN
CRACK THE CASE
AND PRESERVE HIS
EPUTATION– BEFORE
HE VICTIMS OUTNUMBER
HE CLUES?
FIND OUT IN ANOTHER NOTE: THE LOS ANGELES BB MURDER CASES—NOVEL IN STORES NOW
GET THE COMPLETE DEATH NOTE COLLECTION—BUY THE MANGA, PROFILES BOOK AND ANIME TODAY!
SHONEN JUMP ADVANCED
On sale at deathnote.viz.com
Also available at your local bookstore and comic store.
RATED T+ FOR OLDER TEEN
VIZ media
DEATH NOTE - ANOTHER NOTE LOS ANGELES BB RENZOKU SATSUJIN JIKEN -

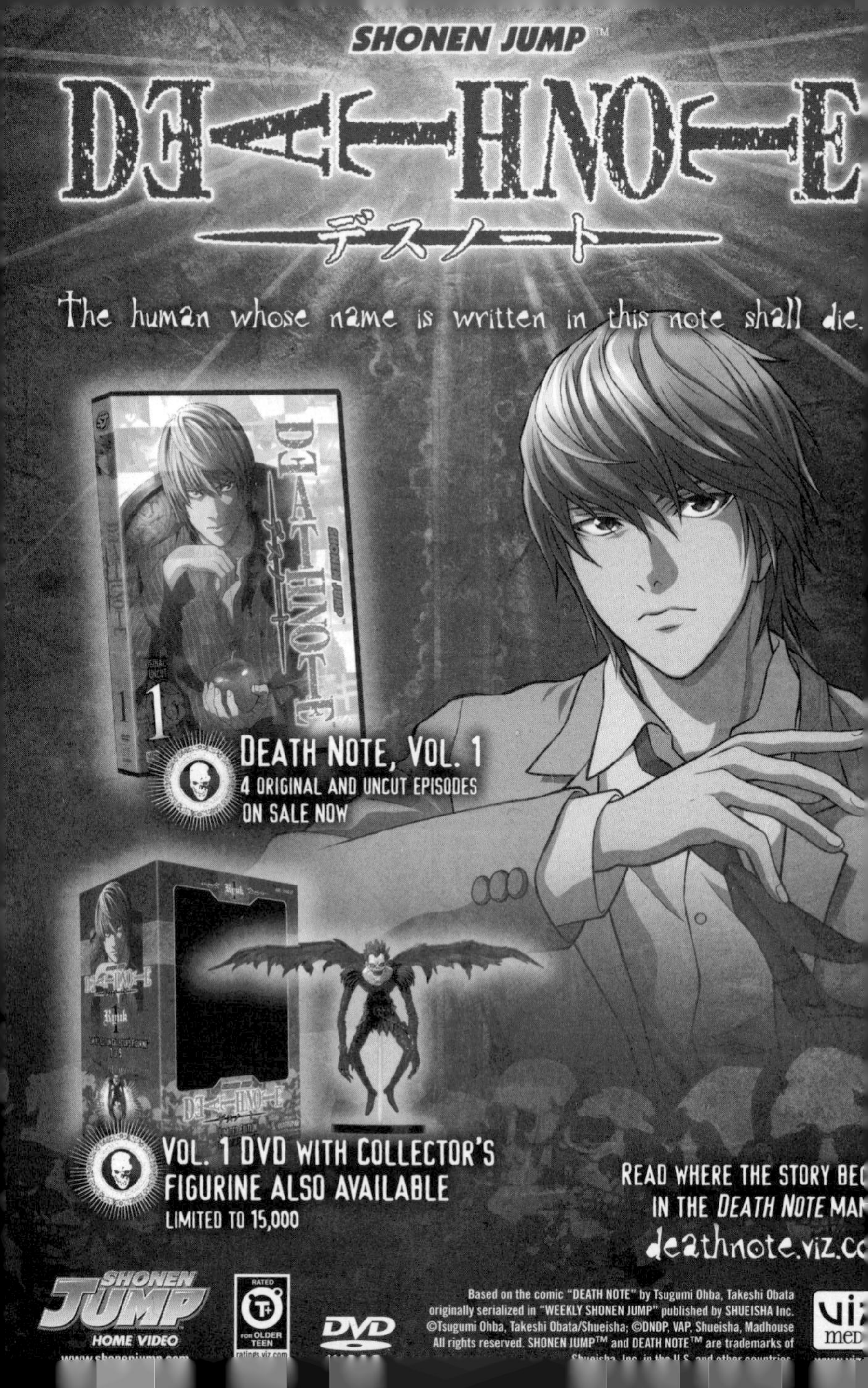
SHONEN JUMP™
DEATH NOTE
デスノート
The human whose name is written in this note shall die.
DEATH NOTE, VOL. 1
4 ORIGINAL AND UNCUT EPISODES
ON SALE NOW
VOL. 1 DVD WITH COLLECTOR'S
FIGURINE ALSO AVAILABLE
LIMITED TO 15,000
READ WHERE THE STORY BEG
IN THE DEATH NOTE MAN
deathnote.viz.co
SHONEN JUMP
HOME VIDEO
RATED
T+
FOR OLDER TEEN
ratings.viz.com
DVD
Based on the comic "DEATH NOTE" by Tsugumi Ohba, Takeshi Obata
originally serialized in "WEEKLY SHONEN JUMP" published by SHUEISHA Inc.
©Tsugumi Ohba, Takeshi Obata/Shueisha; ©DNDP, VAP, Shueisha, Madhouse
All rights reserved. SHONEN JUMP™ and DEATH NOTE™ are trademarks of

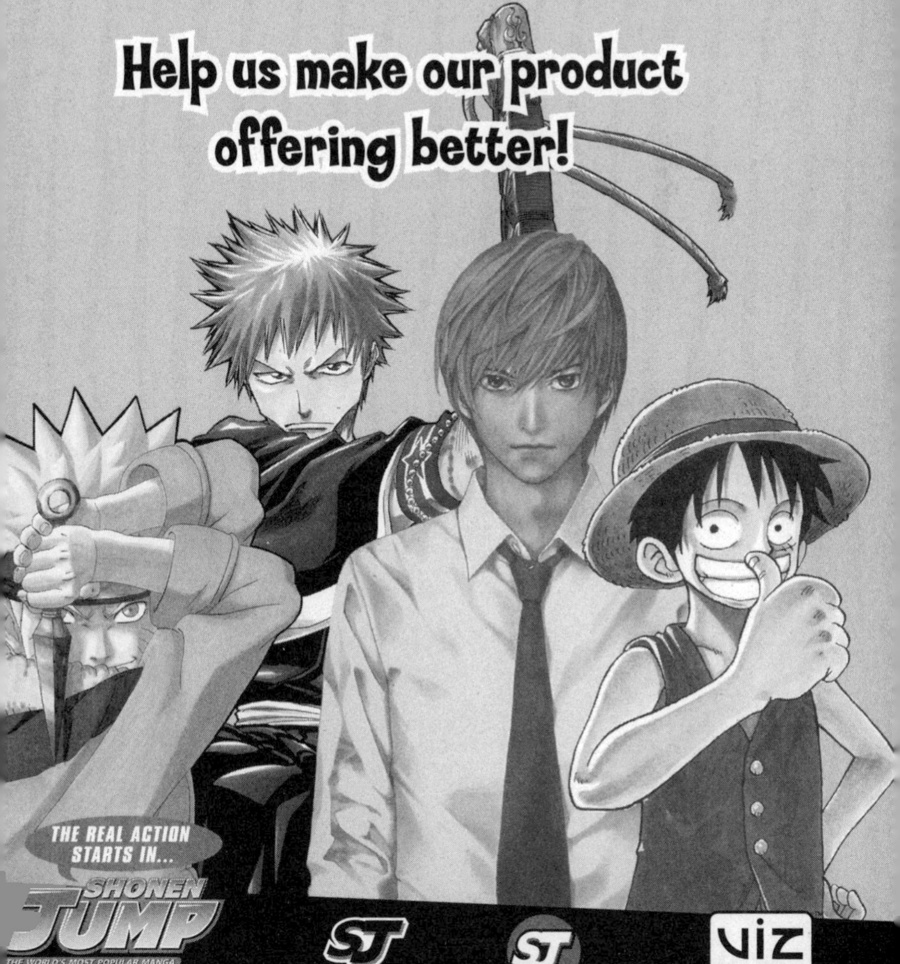

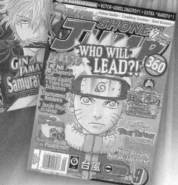
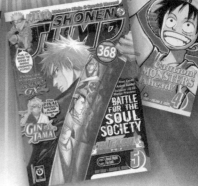

Save **50% OFF**

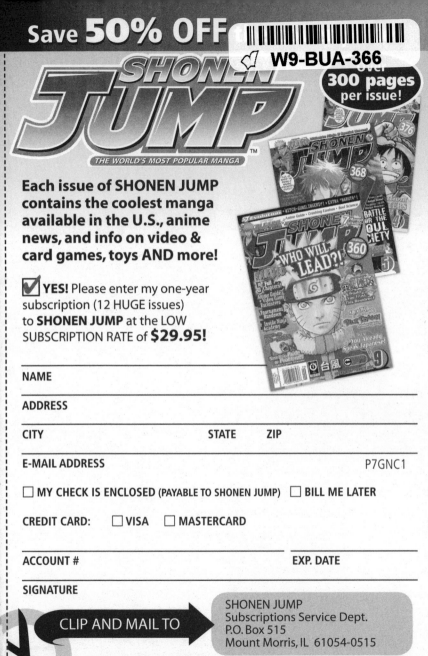